A Motorcycle on Hell Run

Ruth Simms Hamilton
AFRICAN DIASPORA SERIES

The Ruth Simms Hamilton African Diaspora series at Michigan State University Press presents the past and contemporary experiences of African people throughout the world, written by emerging and established scholars in various fields in the social sciences and humanities in pursuit of a reconceptualization of the historical global movements of African peoples. This series pays tribute to the life and legacy of Dr. Ruth Simms Hamilton, a pioneer in African Diaspora Studies, and builds on her seminal work and conceptualization of the African diaspora.

The series editors are particularly interested in innovative book length manuscripts grounded in scholarly research and inquiry that challenge both pre-existing and established notions of the African diaspora by engaging new regions, conceptualizations, and articulations of diaspora that move the field forward. In underscoring new frontiers and frameworks in the study of African descendants' lived experiences, the series presents new approaches to the production of knowledge on African diasporas. In keeping with the tradition of the field, the series is an interdisciplinary undertaking devoted to scholarship on the histories, political movements, institutions, cultures, intellectual discourse, ways of knowing, and identities of African and African descended peoples. Since the diaspora is based largely on movement, the transnational migrations of Africans throughout history and in contemporary times have complicated what it means to be black and or African depending on the political, economic, religious, geographical, and cultural context Africans find themselves. As a result, scholars are forced to confront the evolving realities and constructions of blackness and Africanness in a changing world. While much of the scholarship in the diaspora continues to focus on the Americas due to the enduring legacy of the middle passage and trans-Atlantic slave trade, in addition to these areas the editors encourage manuscript submissions that bring greater visibility to less studied but nonetheless critical areas of the Africana world. This includes internal diasporas within the African continent and African diasporas of the Indian Ocean, Pacific and European regions.

The series highlights the global experiences and dynamic dimensions of peoples of African descent. It maps their historical and contemporary movements, speaks from their radical (unique) narratives and explores their critical relationships with one another. By exploring Afrodescendents within their particular and broader sociocultural, historical, political, and economic contexts, it contemplates similarities, difference, continuity and transformation.

CO-EDITORS
Glenn Chambers, *Michigan State University*
Quito Swan, *Howard University*

EDITORIAL BOARD
Afua Cooper, *Dalhousie University*
Gerald Horne, *University of Houston*
Franklin W. Knight, *Johns Hopkins University*
Besi Muhonja, *James Madison University*
Cheikh Thiam, *The Ohio State University*
Robert Trent Vinson, *The College of William and Mary*

A Motorcycle on Hell Run

TANZANIA, BLACK POWER, AND THE UNCERTAIN FUTURE OF PAN-AFRICANISM, 1964–1974

Seth M. Markle

Michigan State University Press · *East Lansing*

Copyright © 2017 by Seth M. Markle

⊛ The paper used in this publication meets the minimum requirements
of ANSI/NISO Z39.48-1992 (R 1997) (Permanence of Paper).

Michigan State University Press
East Lansing, Michigan 48823-5245

Printed and bound in the United States of America.

26　25　24　23　22　21　20　19　18　17　　1　2　3　4　5　6　7　8　9　10

LIBRARY OF CONGRESS CATALOGING-IN-PUBLICATION DATA IS AVAILABLE
Paper ISBN: 978-1-61186-252-2
PDF ISBN: 978-1-60917-534-4
ePub ISBN: 978-1-62895-303-9
Mobi/prc ISBN: 978-1-62896-303-8

Book design by Charlie Sharp, Sharp Des!gns, East Lansing, MI
Cover design by Shaun Allshouse, www.shaunallshouse.com
Cover image of Queen Mother Audley Moore and President Julius Nyerere (6th Pan
African Congress, Dar es Salaam, 1974) is used courtesy of the *Daily News* Photograph
Archives. Overlay design of photograph by Oroma Elewa.

Michigan State University Press is a member of the Green Press Initiative and is
committed to developing and encouraging ecologically responsible publishing
practices. For more information about the Green Press Initiative and the use of
recycled paper in book publishing, please visit *www.greenpressinitiative.org*.

Visit Michigan State University Press at *www.msupress.org*

In memory of
Gerald R. Gill (1947-2007)
and
George E. Davis (1941-2013)

And psychologically, at least, Africa provides this base for peoples of African origin who are not in Africa. But Africa will not be that base which is a source of strength, if Africa remains weak in the material sense, in the technical sense . . . And I think that you [African Americans] can play that part. I think you people who are in the West (and the West has developed, the West dominates the world) have certain experiences there, which should not be used to intensify the domination of Africa; they should reduce the domination of Africa. I think also you can provide the skills, and attitudes, and an experience, which can help in strengthening that base.

JULIUS NYERERE, *first president of Tanzania (1961-1985)*

Contents

PREFACE xi
INTRODUCTION 1
ABBREVIATIONS 15

PART 1: ENCOUNTERS

CHAPTER 1. Malcolm X, A. M. Babu, and the Seeds of Solidarity 19
CHAPTER 2. Growth and Conflict in SNCC-Tanzania Relations 43

PART 2: DOINGS

CHAPTER 3. Walter Rodney, African Students, and the Struggle
to Define University Education 75
CHAPTER 4. The Drum and Spear Press and the Cultural Politics
of Book Publishing 105

PART 3: UNDOING

CHAPTER 5. Convergence and Rejection at the Sixth Pan-African Congress 141

CONCLUSION 177
NOTES 187
BIBLIOGRAPHY 223
INDEX 255

Preface

In an effort to highlight the importance of Tanzania's national independence to world history, I present a chronological and thematically based narrative that focuses on the parallel and conflicting visions of liberation and solidarity that came out of varied encounters and collaborative projects between black radical activists/organizations and Tanzanian one-party state institutions. What kinds of strategies did diaspora political actors employ in carving out and defining a collective role in Tanzania's nationalist project? What was the nature of the response by the government and its citizens to this desire among people in the diaspora to be active participants in the building of a newly independent African nation? How effective were these collaborations and what were the implications of their successes and failures?

Tanzania's national leaders responded to the diaspora with a mix of enthusiasm and caution. In catering to a palpable diaspora consciousness, I argue that the one-party government actively engaged with the diaspora and sought to utilize its political, cultural, labor, and intellectual capital to further its national building agenda, but on its own terms. This resulted in the incorporation and subsequent marginalization of diaspora political activity in Africa's decolonization movement. Ultimately, this is a book preoccupied with both the character of modern nationhood in Tanzania and the activists in the diaspora who tried to shape it while being intensely affected by it. Like most studies of the African Diaspora, I too am concerned with processes through which diaspora identities are "made and remade" from memories of forced displacement

Preface

and desire to forge a meaningful relationship with the homeland, Africa, both real and imagined. By treating this historical moment as one of connective histories, the story that follows addresses the prospects and challenges black radical activists faced in forming relationships of reciprocity with Tanzanian nationalists and one-party state institutions, in promoting Tanzanian foreign and domestic policies across the globe, and in building a solidarity movement that both celebrated and scrutinized nation-state power in Africa.

I came to this research project by way of a Ghanaian taxicab driver. It was 1998. I was an abroad student enrolled at the University of Legon in Accra looking for a ride to the heart of the city for reasons I now can't remember. Once he realized that I was an African American, the cab driver outright refused to take me where I wanted to go. "Don't worry," he told me. "I'm going to take you to see your people!" In a matter of minutes I had arrived at the former home of W.E.B. and Shirley Graham Du Bois, two African American giants of the pan-Africanism movement who, among many, left the United States for Ghana in the early 1960s to help in building a new nation alongside the country's first president, Kwame Nkrumah. Sometime in the 1990s, when Ghana witnessed another influx of African American repatriates and tourists, the home was converted into the W.E.B. Du Bois Memorial Centre for Pan African Culture, which served as a community center, museum, and library. It was not until I started to volunteer for the African American Reparations and Repatriation Truth Commission (AARTC), a black expatriate-run nonprofit organization that worked out of the center, that my interest in exploring the historical connections and disconnections between African Americans and Africans began to take shape. Though at the time I did not get a chance to thank the Ghanaian taxicab driver for the detour, I feel it necessary to do so here because ever since then I've pursued an academic career studying the rich and complicated history of black diasporan peoples "returning home" to Africa.

Studying abroad in Ghana almost twenty years ago was my first time living in another country and a direct outgrowth of the mentorship I was fortunate enough to receive while an undergraduate student at Tufts University in Medford, Massachusetts. A small contingent of faculty, staff, and grassroots community organizers played a significant role in my intellectual and political development and in sparking an interest in all things Africana. I am especially indebted to the late Gerald Gill, Pearl Robison, Christina Sharpe, the late Nadia Medina, Jeanne Penvenne, and Modhimita Roy for providing exciting courses with demanding workloads and high expectations; for facilitating an appreciation for critical thought and academic rigor; for encouraging self-confidence and self-appreciation; and for issuing tough love when needed. I would like to single out the late George Davis, a West Medford native and former SNCC organizer and Black Panther, whose course on students in the civil rights movement offered at Tufts Experimental College absolutely blew my mind. His lectures were inspirational personal stories on the power of youth agency and collective action. His advice on movement-building strategies for on- and off-campus activism was always coveted and taken to heart.

Pursuing my PhD in history at New York University was eye-opening, exciting, and intellectually stimulating beyond what I could have ever imagined. Thank you to my advisors Robin D. G. Kelley, Michael Gomez, Fred Cooper, Carolyn Brown, and Richard Hull for their guidance and thoughtful and incisive criticism. I also owe a debt of gratitude to graduate students I encountered and built long-lasting relationships with over the years. It was truly a rewarding experience being exposed to the brilliance of Hillina Seife, Sobukwe Odinga, Njoroge Njoroge, Brian Purnell, Marc Goulding, Toja Okoh, Adam Waterman, Chinua Thelwell, Michelle Thompson, Yuko Miki, Katayoun Shaffee, Joaquin Chavez, Gregory Childs, Peter Hudson, Ted Sammons, Khary Polk, Christopher Winks, Erik McDuffie, Ifeona Fulani, Natasha Lightfoot, Aisha Finch, and Tanya Huelett. The Black Marxist Study Group lives on!

Conducting interviews for this project was an experience I will forever cherish. I would like to thank everyone who agreed to be interviewed and shared stories with me about their involvement in the pan-Africanism movement: Charlie Cobb, Courtland Cox, Judy Richardson, Jennifer Lawson, Dera Tompkins, Sylvia Hill, Gerri Augusto, Walter Bgoya, Paul Bomani, P. Bai Akridge, Neville Parker, Anne Forester, Edie Wilson, Pete O'Neal, Karim Hirji, Loretta Hobbs, Kathy Hughes, Flora Kambona, Joseph Kanywanyi, Henry Mopolu, George Liundi, Jacques Wilmore, Hashim Mbita, Ernest Wilson, and Ron Walters.

In piecing together a story about pan-Africanism, I traveled throughout the United States, the Caribbean, and Africa and am deeply grateful for the aid I received from the archivists, librarians, and staffs of the Robert W. Woodruff Library at Atlanta University Center and Emory University; Northeastern University Archives at Northeastern University; Schlesinger Library at Radcliffe College; Schomburg Center for Research in Black Culture; Tamiment Institute Archives at New York University; United Nations Library at New York University; C.L.R. James Institute; the Alma Jordan Library at the University of the West Indies at St. Augustine, Trinidad and Tobago; the East African Archives, University of Dar es Salaam; Tanzania National Archives; the *Daily News* Archives; the Science and Technology Center (COSTECH); and the South African Development Community Research Secretariat's Hashim Mbita Project.

I spent considerable time conducting research in Tanzania. I would like to thank the faculty at the University of Dar es Salaam for their enormous help, most notably Fred Kaijage of the History Department. For a brief stint I was part of a study group comprised of Tanzanian scholars and activists interested in revisiting the political

Preface

history of African Socialism in Tanzania. Mimi napenda kuwaambia asanteni sana Ng'wanza Kamata, Issa Shivji, Ngesa Ngesa, Bernard Baha, Fatima Bapumia, Raphael Ogangi, Emmanuel Mvula, and Shen Narayanasamy for invigorating discussion and debate. Clark Arrington and Rahma Selassie and their three beautiful daughters Leila, Menali, and Ayne were gracious hosts who let me experience firsthand Tanzanian hospitality. A very special thank-you is owed to Mejah Mbuya. Without his contacts in and around Dar es Salaam, his acute knowledge of Tanzanian history and, most importantly, his friendship, I do not think this book could have happened.

I would also like to thank the following scholars who expressed an interest in my research, whether through providing contacts, or dropping pearls of wisdom about research fellowships and publishers, or reading over chapter drafts, or creating conference panels: Adam Green, Marcia Wright, Samuel Roberts, Komozi Woodard, Kali Gross, Minkah Makalani, Jonathan Fenderson, Chris Tinson, Anthony Radcliffe, and Nicole Fleetwood. Also critical to the completion of this project was the year I spent in South Bend, Indiana, as an Erskine A. Peters Dissertation Writing Fellow at the University of Notre Dame. Faculty and graduate students associated with this fellowship under the auspices of the Department of Africana Studies offered support at a critical stage in the writing and research process. I would especially like to thank James Ford, Denise Challenger, Jessica Graham, Richard Pierce, Dianne Pinderhughes, Mark Houser, Hugh Pope, and Beverly Holt.

When I arrived at Trinity College in 2009–2010, I did not expect such a high level of support from colleagues and undergraduate students. I want to express my gratitude to Vijay Prashad, Zayde Antrim, Johnny Williams, Garth Myers, Maurice Wade, Jeff Bayliss, Dario Euraque, Luis Figueroa, Mike Amezcua, Samanthi Gunawardana, Kifah Hanna, Linda Tabar, Tanetta Anderson, Gary Reger, Pablo Delano, Katherine Hart, Sean Coco, Scot Gac, Tom Wickman, Leslie Demangles, Jennifer Regan-Lefebrve, Cheryl Greenberg, Susan Pennybacker, Gigi St. Peter, Anida Ali, Isaac Kamola, Karla Spurlock-Evans, Carol Correa, Kathleen Kete, Michael Lestz, Okey Ndibe, Davarian Baldwin, and Donna Marcano. During my sabbatical year in 2013–2014, I was able to return to Dar es Salaam to conduct further research; I thank Trinity College's Faculty Research Committee (FRC) for providing the necessary funds to make this research trip possible, and the President's office and Study Away Program for funding my research excursions to South Africa and Trinidad over the past four years. For technical assistance and support, the college's Center for Teaching and Learning (CTL) was very helpful for an overwhelmed junior faculty member trying to figure out a healthy balance between teaching and service and research and writing. Special thanks are due to undergraduate students who have enrolled in "Black Internationalism," a seminar course I offer loosely based on this book project. Jesse Allen, McKenzie Angelo,

Camryn Clarke, Adolfo Abreu, Nijel Hill, Omolara Abiona, Shanice Hinckson, Shanelle Morris, Schirin Schemkermayr, Collette Grimes, and James Barrett enhanced the research and writing of this book in subtle yet significant ways.

The editorial and production staff at Michigan State University Press, especially Alex Schwartz and Glenn Chambers, were consistently accommodating, open-minded, and easy to communicate with. A special thank-you must go to Quito Swan, whose phone call inquiring about my manuscript at a time when I was still searching for a press could not have come at a better time.

Close friends and comrades scattered across the globe contributed to this project in a manner that kept me grounded and motivated due to their creative spirits, professional drive, passion for life, and sense of humor. Much love and blessings go to Christina Greer, Emery "Lumumba" Wright, Zachariah Mampilly, Najma Naz'yat, Kenny Bailey, Will "DJ Tuttafucco" Tutt, Abdel Rahim Brown, Nitin Puri, Paul Smith, Dustin Ross, Ibrahim Abdul-Matin, Karim Abdul-Matin, Eli Jacobs-Fantauzzi, Khalil "DJ Kaka Khalil" Jacobs-Fantauzzi, Samra Ghermay, Dana Wright, Tyler Askew and the Rude Movement/My Favorite Things family, Jozan Powell, Ndungi Githuku, the late Njuguna Mutahi, Gaidi Faraj, Lauren Arrington, Dana King, Melanie Lawrence, Catherine Hurley, and Miriam Uti.

To my mother Patricia, aunt Julia, and godmother Joyce; and to my brother Josh and cousin Benjamin, words cannot truly express how appreciative I am for all of your love and support.

Introduction

In an article that appeared in his independently published journal, *The Crusader*, Robert F. Williams, an African American political exile, wrote about his unforgettable 1,500-mile motorcycle journey from Dar es Salaam, Tanzania, to the border of Zambia and back in May 1968. Titled "African Safari: Hells Run on a Motorcycle," a reference to the country's most notorious highway, Williams reflects on his "grueling act of daring." Through daylight and darkness he rode past herds of elephants, zebras, and giraffes, and the corpses of over "50 heavy trucks and trailers overturned" along the side of the road. He also visited and chatted with schoolchildren, farmers, villagers, and people at various marketplaces, making known to them the importance of the African diaspora presence in independent Tanzania. He was, in his words, a "new type of tourist," challenging an African people to reclaim a nationalist consciousness he felt had been hijacked by African ruling elites and their "overrated degrees." It is a peculiar piece that reads part black nationalist manifesto on international solidarity and part misplaced indictment of Tanzanian independence.

Williams's adventure on "Hell Run" became the symbol of the search for a new conception of nationhood and belonging that is emblematic of the complexity of the diaspora experience in Africa. With African decolonization came the desire, yet the struggle, to connect to and understand Africa's new historical moment and where they fit in a world profoundly being shaped by the formation of new nation-states. Tanzania emerged as one dynamic force that seized the attention of black political activists, extending, deepening, and complicating their relationship with Africa and their conceptions of pan-Africanism. Between 1964 and 1974, a number of Caribbean and African American nationalists, leftists, and pan-Africanists traveled to and settled in Dar es Salaam to live and work in a nation that many believed was on the forefront of Africa's liberation struggle. As the first historical study of its kind, *A Motorcycle on Hell Run* therefore revisits "Africa" of the diaspora imagination, focusing on the radical politics and culture that came into being in Dar es Salaam in the 1960s and 1970s.

In looking to the African Diaspora, a new and more revealing tale comes into sharper focus about decolonization and the emergence of independent states in Africa. This historical study attempts to reconstruct the political landscape of a crucial period when African American, Caribbean, and Tanzanian histories overlapped. Under the charismatic leadership of its first president, Julius Nyerere, Tanzania would be regarded as a beacon of hope, a model of nation-building, and a leading frontline state in the struggle for African liberation on the continent and beyond. Its foreign policies of pan-Africanism and Third World solidarity and domestic policy of African socialism (Ujamaa na Kujitegemea) left a global imprint that has yet to be fully appreciated in historical scholarship. Thus, this is a story of travel, collaboration, and conflict that critically interrogates pragmatic partnerships and exchanges between the Tanzanian state and its leaders and diaspora political activists, intellectuals, and organizations associated with the Black Power movements in the United States and the Caribbean.

▪ ▪ ▪ ▪

On December 9, 1961, seventy-five thousand spectators filled the seats of the National Stadium in Dar es Salaam to witness the newly elected prime minister Julius K. Nyerere receive the "instruments of independence" from the Duke of Edinburgh, Prince Philip.[1] Approximately a year later, Tanganyikan citizens and foreign dignitaries would reconvene at the stadium to truly celebrate the nation's freedom as a republic. Three days of activities were planned, starting on December 8. Radio broadcasts in English and Kiswahili informed the masses of the events: celebrations at each regional headquarter of the ruling party, the Tanganyika African National Union (TANU), a youth rally, a traditional African dance exhibition, parades, a football match, a presidential reception for all British Commonwealth nations, a state ball, and an opening ceremony for the parliament. All of these activities revolved around the swearing-in ceremony for Julius K. Nyerere as the nation's first president.[2]

The independence festivities blended the traditional with the modern. The sound of traditional drumming and the marching of a contingent of soldiers and police signaled the arrival of Nyerere, which was followed by the singing of the new national anthem. After giving his presidential oath in Kiswahili, Chief Masengo presented Nyerere with a robe, spear, and shield. The robe symbolized his new role as Baba wa Taifa (Father of the Nation), while the spear and shield symbolized courage and defense of the nation. Once this ceremony was completed, another chief anointed Nyerere with water and flour "so that with the power of the Almighty God, your ruling should bring forth blessing, peace, health, success and prosperity all the time."[3]

Forty-two nations were on hand to take part in these independence ceremonies along with representatives of African liberation movements from Northern Rhodesia, Basutoland, Swaziland, South Africa, Namibia, and Mozambique. On December 10, the former schoolteacher who had risen to the position of the country's first president delivered an inaugural address to the Tanganyika Parliament where he addressed the event's significance in the making of a new nationalist identity rooted in collective sacrifice and a postcolonial struggle for socialism:

> We want Tanganyika to become an African socialist country. By this, I mean a country in which the society, including the State, recognizes its responsibility in every individual member whilst calling upon every individual to recognize his responsibility to society. We want to build a country in which no citizen can go hungry while others have food, in which no one is denied the opportunity to develop himself for his maximum capacity for service of others, in which there will be a marriage between the freedom of the individual and the need for unity of action and harmonious relationships between all the members of society. To this end, we shall try to build on the past African tradition in which every family was responsible for all its members, and every member responsible for the family ... We believe that we can build up the attitude of mind, which looks to the needs of the country rather than the desires of the individual.[4]

Julius Kambarage Nyerere was born on April 12, 1922, in the village of Butiama on the eastern shore of Lake Victoria in northwest Tanganyika. His father, Nyerere Burite, was a respected Wazanaki chief who is credited for his son's oft-cited humility. Chief Nyerere had twenty-two wives, the fifth one being Julius's mother, Mugaya, who also bore eight other children, three of whom died in childbirth. At the age of twelve, in 1934, a young Kambarage began his formal education—a journey that would span the next eighteen years. Through Catholic missionary efforts, his primary education occurred twenty-six miles from home in the town of Musoma, where he enrolled at Mwisenge Primary, a Native Administration school. Having passed the territorial examination in 1936, he advanced on to the elitist Catholic Mission Secondary School of St. Mary's in Tabora in central Tanganyika. This is also a time when he began his conversion to Catholicism, which culminated in his baptism in December 1943. In that same year, he again was awarded a scholarship to Makerere University College in Uganda, the most prestigious institution of higher learning in East Africa, where he earned a Teaching Training diploma with a specialization in biology and English. At Makerere, Nyerere got his first taste of the kind of African anticolonial nationalist politics gaining ground across the continent by cofounding both the Tanganyika African Welfare Association (TAWA) and the university branch of the Tanganyika African Association (TAA), the latter of which was a social group founded in 1929 absent an explicit political orientation. In one of his last interviews before his death in 1999, Nyerere recalled: "I wrote an essay in 1944 called 'The Freedom of Women.' I must be honest and say I was influenced by John Stuart Mill, who had written about the subjugation of women. My father had 22 wives and I knew how hard they had to work and what they went through as women. Here, in this essay, I was moving towards the idea of freedom theoretically. But I was still in the mindset of improving the lives and welfare of Africans."[5]

In 1946, he returned to colonial Tanganyika to teach biology and English at his alma mater, St. Mary's Secondary School in Tabora. For the next three years, Nyerere would act as both teacher and TAA anticolonial agitator. Despite efforts by a local British colonial officer to prevent Nyerere from studying abroad because of his politics, he went to the United Kingdom to pursue graduate studies at the Edinburgh University in Scotland. The two years spent in Scotland and the one year in London proved to nurture his intellectual growth and harden his anticolonial nationalist convictions. As he would later recall about his time at Edinburgh: "I found that I had ample time to read many things outside my degree . . . I evolved the whole of my political philosophy while I was there."[6] Although Nyerere had briefly settled in the UK, he arrived there four years after the historic Fifth Pan-African Congress held in Manchester, which brought together African anticolonial nationalists to address the end of colonial rule in Africa, with many of the African participants going on to lead independence struggles in their home countries. Nyerere did not directly participate in the congress, but the pan-Africanism movement, as well as other articulations of self-determination in the Third World, left an indelible imprint, especially when seeing firsthand its effect on African students from the Gold Coast: "The significance of India's independence movement was that it shook the British Empire. When Gandhi succeeded I think it made the British lose the will to cling to empire. But it was events in Ghana in 1949 that fundamentally changed my attitude. When Kwame Nkrumah was released from prison this produced a transformation. I was in Britain and oh you could see it in the Ghanaians! They became different human beings, different from all the rest of us! The thing of freedom began growing inside all of us. Under the influence of these events, while at university in Britain, I made up my mind to be a full-time political activist when I went back home."[7]

Edinburgh University provided Nyerere with time and distance to explore a number of topics and ideas that proved valuable to his political and intellectual development. He studied history, economics, and philosophy, and joined Fabian Socialist society. Much later he described his time at Edinburgh as a political education of a "Western liberal type" that also drew his attention to socialism but never to the extent that it trumped the priority placed on dismantling colonial rule in Africa. "As for socialism, my first contact was with European, mainly British, socialism, not with the socialism of Marx and Lenin. When I started the movement towards independence, we talked of independence, not socialism, about which we had some vague ideas."[8] He also began writing political essays on the colonial question in East Africa, focusing his attentions on the race problem in East Africa. He eventually graduated from Edinburgh University with an Ordinary Degree of Master of Arts in July 1952, after which he spent a year in London to research British educational institutions.

Nyerere returned to Tanganyika in 1953 working as a history, English, and Kiswahili teacher at St. Francis College in Pugu, located on the outskirts of Dar es Salaam. Just like during his time before studying abroad in Britain, Nyerere had to balance his teaching duties with his subversive political activism within an increasingly politicized TAA. However, in 1954, he was soon given an ultimatum by the colonial government to choose between teaching and politics. Nyerere, who had just been elected president of the Tanganyika African National Union (TANU), a newly formed political organization, decided to join the movement for African liberation full-time. Within a year of his presidency, TANU's membership had ballooned to well over 250,000, comprising Tanganyikans of African, Asian, Arab, and European descent. TANU pursued a strategy of nonviolent direct action, mass mobilization, and political education, and pressured Britain to institute constitutional reforms over a period of six years. In 1958, Nyerere, who unlike some of his notable contemporaries avoided imprisonment before ascending to the highest post of the colonial government, was elected to the Legislative Council, the colonial governing body. Two years later he was its chief minister, tasked with ushering the country to self-government in December 1961 and to a united republic a year later.[9]

Nyerere's rise to the position of head of state reads a lot like the biographies of his African peers. Formally educated with advanced degrees and a life abroad as a colonial subject and university student in the West; philosophically open to ideas of African unity, socialism, and communism; hated and then reluctantly embraced by colonial powers—these were just some of the similarities Nyerere held with emergent African leaders such as Kwame Nkrumah (Ghana), Jomo Kenyatta (Kenya), Ben Bella (Algeria), Gamal Abdel Nasser (Egypt), Sekou Toure (Guinea), Patrice Lumumba (Congo), Leopold Senghor (Senegal), to name but a few.[10] By the time Nyerere formed TANU, the nationalist situations in the Gold Coast, Kenya, and the Congo were foremost on the minds of African Americans to a much a greater extent than what was taking place in colonial Tanganyika. Kenyatta's Mau Mau heroics became the stuff of revolutionary myth and legend, while Lumumba's sudden yet rapid rise led African Americans to storm the United Nations en masse in protest of his assassination.[11]

But Kwame Nkrumah and the Ghana revolution eclipsed them all. What made Nkrumah more appealing than Nyerere to African Americans? As early as 1958, Nkrumah called on them to return to Ghana with their technical skills for nation-building purposes—a call that African Americans and West Indians took seriously to heart. Nyerere, on the other hand, had operated on the margins of the pan-Africanism movement during his early political career. He had not attended the Fifth Pan-African Congress in 1945 and therefore had not fully tapped into its diaspora network of political friendships and contacts. To most black people in the United States, for instance, he was relatively unknown until Tanganyika independence seemed a foregone conclusion. Interestingly, his anticolonial and pan-Africanist activities went largely under the radar in the African Diaspora.

Between 1955 and 1963, conscious of the intensification of decolonization struggles in Africa, U.S. activists, black and white, set about educating the American public on developments in Tanganyika. In the six years leading up to national independence in December 1961, the American Committee on Africa (ACOA) and African American labor leaders such as A. Philip Randolph, George McCray, and, most important, Maida Springer played critical roles in TANU and the Tanganyika Federation of Labor (TFL), in the words of Springer's biographer, in interpreting "for the West the reasons Africans desired independence and to explain their positions and struggles in relation to the cold war."[12] Founded in 1953, ACOA was a multiracial, anticommunist, and pan-Africanist organization that was an outgrowth of a partnership formed between the Fellowship of Reconciliation (FOR) and Congress of Racial Equality (CORE), two civil rights organizations that initiated desegregation campaigns in the 1940s.[13] For its first two years of existence, ACOA focused its energies on anti-apartheid struggles in South Africa and decolonization developments in the Gold Coast by fundraising for development projects in colonial Africa, holding "discussion series" and lectures, and befriending African leaders at the United Nations and lobbying on their behalf.[14] In 1955, one year after TANU was formed, ACOA's journal, *Africa Today*, featured its first profile of Julius Nyerere during his visit to New York City and the United Nations Trusteeship Council's 15th session to advocate for self-government, offering in the space of three pages a biographical sketch that included his cultural and educational background and his role as "part-time politician" and full-time history teacher. "It is clear that, although politics may be his "hobby", it is a hobby to which he cleaves with passion, and out of a deep sense of duty to his country," writes ACOA member George Shepherd. "There are times when one gains the impression that he finds the burden of current history a heavy one to bear, and that he would much prefer to deal with the history of the past—a so much more manageable commodity."[15] Shepherd made sure to note that Nyerere was no communist and any questioning of his leftist leanings was a debate left for the academics of the world—for Nyerere was a man open to socialist ideas but too preoccupied with issues of "education, politics, cattle, crops and the lack of any publication giving the view of Tanganyikan nationalists."[16] A year later, ACOA covered Nyerere's visit to the UN in December 1956 by publishing a summary of Nyerere's remarks that highlight the TANU chairman's views on colonial problems such as land dispossession, the lack of access to education, and political disenfranchisement.[17]

ACOA activists were not the only ones drawn to Nyerere's leadership and personality, and the nonviolent character of TANU's anticolonial nationalist struggle. The urgent search for answers to economic empowerment on the part of Tanganyikan nationalists further stoked U.S. activists' interest in the East African colony. Randolph, McCray, and Springer became committed advocates of both Tanganyika independence and the development of an autonomous trade union movement in Tanganyika led by the Tanganyika Federation of Labor (TFL). Springer proved to be TANU and TFL's most important African American contact during the late 1950s and early 1960s. Between 1956 and 1961 she forged political friendships with TANU leaders Nyerere and Rashidi Kawawa; Bibi Titi Mohammed, leader of TANU's women's wing; and Maynard Mpaganla, the assistant general secretary of the TFL. As an affiliated member of AFL-CIO and the International Ladies' Garment Workers' Union (ILGWU), Springer developed an interest in the African labor movement when she attended a three-week seminar in Africa on African labor conditions in 1955. Two years later, in 1957, Springer found herself living in Dar es Salaam working closely with TFL leaders and training and consulting with agricultural and industrial unions in Tanganyika and Kenya. When she returned to the United States in the same year, she opened up her home to the African anticolonial, nationalist, and trade unionist leaders who were consistently lobbying for self-government on the floor of the UN, and morphed into one of their confidants.

African American jazz musicians saw the UN headquarters in New York as space to build connections with Tanganyikan anticolonial nationalists as well. Around the time the United Nations Jazz Society was created in 1959, Randy Weston, a jazz composer and pianist from Brooklyn, was conducting research on African languages and traditional African music at the UN library. This interest in learning about his African heritage was initially sparked under the tutelage of his father and grew from there. African independence seemed to only fuel his search for more knowledge about African history, arts, and culture to the point that, by the late 1950s, he was poised to compose an album that he hoped not only celebrated African liberation, but also inspired African Americans to think of themselves as part of the African Diaspora whose political fate in the United States was directly tied to the success of African anticolonialism.[18] At the UN, Weston befriended Africans, eagerly holding informal conversations with them that often centered on the question of which African language best represented the continent. "I was anxious to use an African language [in the album] because I was quite upset by the Tarzan movies and how they depicted Africans," he later recalled. "I spent time at the United Nations and met several African ambassadors and asked them what language I should choose." This question brought him in contact with Tuntemeke Sanga, a Tanganyikan nationalist serving as a petitioner at the UN Trusteeship Council. He also happened to be a scholar and staunch advocate of Kiswahili, an African language widely spoken throughout eastern, central, and southern Africa. Weston, therefore, needed little convincing that Kiswahili provided a dynamic example of an African language that, as he later recalled, the people would hear the "beauty" and "depth of." Backed by an orchestra comprised of twenty-four musicians and two vocalists, Weston recorded the album *Uhuru Africa*, which was released on Roulette Records in late 1960. According to historian Robin D. G. Kelley, it was a landmark recording, one that was emblematic of an exploration many African American musicians of the era took in mapping jazz music's "African roots."[19]

For the song "Introduction: Uhuru Kwanza (Part One)" (Kiswahili for "Freedom First"), Weston was joined by Sanga, who in perfect English and Kiswahili recited a poem originally penned in English by the acclaimed African American poet Langston Hughes:

> Africa, where the great Congo flows
> Africa, where the whole jungle knows
> A new dawning breaks! Africa!
> A young nation awakes! Africa!
>
> Freedom!
> Freedom!
>
> Afrika, ambako jua la angaza sana
> Afrika, ambako ulimwengu wote kwanza
> Afrika, kutoka usiku wa jana: Uhuru!

Upepo wa Uhuru!
Upepo wa Uhuru unavuma![20]
The Freedom wind blows!

Out of yesterday's night, Uhuru.
Freedom!
Uhuru! Freedom!
Uhuru! Freedom![21]

Sanga narrates this poem about African self-determination in a slow, melodic voice punctuated by the Conga rhythms in the background drummed by Candindo Camero. Many years later, Weston remembered how wonderful it was to have Sanga's voice and diction on the song (and throughout the album for that matter), revealing how the Tanganyikan nationalist's participation helped spawn an album that, in his words, talked about "freedom of a continent, the continent that has been invaded and had its children taken away, the continent of the creation of humanity."[22]

ACOA activists, African American trade unionists, and jazz musicians managed to bring Nyerere (and Tanganyika) into America's public consciousness. The activists, however, did so in ways that cast Nyerere as a moderate leader, which, in turn, helped assuage U.S. government fears of communism replacing colonialism in Africa. Because of Nyerere's anti-racialist politics, accessible demeanor, and magnetic personality, Tanganyikan statehood could possibly represent a model that challenged radical "racialist" leaders such as Kwame Nkrumah of Ghana and Jomo Kenyatta of Kenya. This image of moderation gained currency by 1960 when it was announced in March that Tanganyika's official independence date was scheduled for December 9 of the following year. Tanganyikan independence marked a clear uptick in U.S. national news coverage of Nyerere, which often depicted the leader in anticommunist terms. In 1959, the *Washington Post* quoted Nyerere saying that he doesn't think in terms of rubles but rather in "pounds and dollars"—a clear indication of his diplomatic acumen more so than his anticommunist leanings.[23] By 1960, the *New York Times* pegged the "slight, mild, boyish and quiet" Nyerere as the "key" to Tanganyika's postcolonial future and a leader "fifty years ahead of anyone else in the African nationalist movement" and one of the "best examples of indigenous leadership a new Africa can produce."[24] Writing for the *New York Times*, the journalists Jay Walz and Leonard Ingalls declared in two separate reports that Nyerere was a "moderate nationalist" and "one of the most outstanding leaders in East Africa," evidenced in his gradualist approach to continental unification through regional federations.[25]

The *Washington Post* provided similar reports of Nyerere as a representation of alternative African nationalist leadership, claiming that his vision and efforts to build a harmonious multiracial society won him a "reputation for sound and balanced political leadership."[26] Mainstream media praise for Nyerere carried over into 1961, the year of Tanganyikan independence, when the *Washington Post* interviewed Assistant Secretary of State G. Mennen Williams, who naively proclaimed that the country had no racial problems, no interethnic rivalries, and no "intense political party factionalism." "Julius Nyerere," remarked Williams, "is a sort of George Washington, Abraham Lincoln and Franklin D. Roosevelt rolled into one."[27] Even when Nyerere increasingly vocalized his opposition to apartheid in South Africa and called out Western nations like the United States and Britain for supporting the apartheid regime, the Western press still found little to criticize concerning his "non-racialist" beliefs. In the months leading up to independence, the U.S. national news found more plaudits to bestow on the newly minted chief minister of the Legislative Council. The granting of land titles to expatriates, the appointment of two Europeans and one Asian to his cabinet, and the curbing of a black nationalist faction within TANU fed his image as "Africa's most promising statesman."[28]

U.S. black newspaper coverage of Nyerere did not deviate sharply from such mainstream media depictions. While the *Afro-American* commended Nyerere for his "wise," "calm," and "judicious" leadership, the *Chicago Defender* lauded him for being a "moderate, broad minded—by contemporary African standards—implicitly democratic leader" leading up to and at the time of independence.[29] The *Negro Digest* pegged Nyerere as "the only politician in East Africa to have surmounted the mental obstacle of thinking of independence in terms of black-vs-white."[30] Equally appealing was his pan-Africanist politics, which were mapped in sporadic coverage of his leadership role in the Pan African Freedom Movement of South and Central Africa (PAFMESCA), a regional anticolonial organization Nyerere cofounded that coordinated activities of political parties hailing from Kenya, Uganda, Nyasaland, Northern and Southern Rhodesia, Rwanda-Burundi, Congo, Mozambique, South Africa, and Tanganyika. Under PAFMESCA's auspices, Nyerere's effort to delay Tanganyikan independence in January 1961 so that Uganda, Kenya, and Tanganyika could usher in independence as a single-federated state was not lost on African American pan-Africanists.

Between 1961 and 1963, Nyerere's pan-Africanist politics was viewed in comparison to Nkrumah. When the Organization of African Unity (OAU), a continental institution of independent states that supported complete decolonization and economic and political alliances, was founded in 1963, Nyerere's pan-Africanism was positioned to the right of Nkrumah's, leading him to garner a reputation as a "conciliator" between the radical African and conservative African states. While Nkrumah saw immediate continental unification as the only solution to the threat of colonialism and imperialism in Africa, Nyerere indeed chose the gradualist route by favoring regionalist integration.

Despite this reputation for moderate politics, there was no denying Nyerere's militancy when it came to the issue of apartheid in South Africa. His decisions to not allow Tanganyika to enter the British Commonwealth in 1961 and to boycott trade with South Africa in 1963 over the issue of apartheid started to challenge prevailing assumptions about Nyerere's moderate politics.

What became equally appealing about Nyerere's pan-Africanism was that it was not exclusive to continental affairs, but rather extended to the struggles of black peoples in the United States. Nyerere's support of the civil rights movement was an outgrowth of the contacts and friendships he made with ACOA activists and African American labor leaders during the 1950s. Indeed, Nyerere publicly criticized the "evils of racism" not only in Tanganyikan and South African societies but in U.S. society as well. "When there is a Little Rock in the United States," Nyerere remarked in an article for the *New York Times* when asked about the civil rights campaign to end segregation of public schools in Arkansas, "we on the African continent get annoyed. We say this is nonsense."[31] Nyerere was attracted to the nonviolent, multiracial character of the postwar civil rights movement that sprung up in the U.S. South, finding that it held philosophical commonalities with the anticolonial nationalist movement in Tanganyika. As anti-black violence against civil rights protestors escalated during the early 1960s, Nyerere would continue to speak out in support of the civil rights cause. His most public attempt at solidarity came in July 1963 when Nyerere visited the United States for an official state visit. With Tanzanian representatives, state department officials, Peace Corps executives, and the national press in the audience, Nyerere spoke at the National Press Club luncheon in Washington on July 15. His speech was tailored to stress continual unity, the merits of socialist economic development for newly independent nations, and Tanganyika's opposition to all forms of "racialism." Racism was a global human rights issue, he proclaimed, and it did not dictate his domestic policies nor should it be tolerated in South Africa, the Portuguese colonies, or the United States. However, in calling attention to the U.S. racism, Nyerere made it known that he believed it was being solved and that the U.S. government was "ashamed of racial discrimination" and "feel it is un-American."[32]

In the luncheon's aftermath, Nyerere further elaborated on his views about racism in the United States, urging the Kennedy administration to pursue policies of racial equality out of a moral commitment to advancing the cause of human justice rather than an ideological commitment to cold war politics.[33] "It is for this reason that I dare to speak on color while I am a guest here, knowing that you are currently engaged in finding a solution to your own color problem. By serving a man in a restaurant, or by refusing to educate a man's children, a person may be taking part in this fight about racialism, wherever he does it. For the struggle goes on everywhere, in the United States and in Tanganyika . . . To argue racial privilege is to take the language of Verwoerd [South Africa's prime minister]."[34]

Three days following the luncheon, Nyerere and his delegation were guests at a reception dinner held at the home of a state department official. There, he met civil rights leader Martin Luther King for the second time and discussed the state of the civil rights struggle.[35] The last time they had met was at the 1957 Ghana independence celebrations in Accra. In the six years since, both had emerged as two of the most popular leaders of the 1960s era. Nyerere took this public encounter as an opportunity to express his solidarity with the civil rights movement by endorsing the aims and objectives of the March on Washington planned for August. However, throughout his stay, he tempered his remarks on civil rights activism with comments expressing his confidence in President Kennedy's leadership. He publicly asserted that the struggle for racial equality in the United States was "showing signs of progress." It was an attitude directly shaped by a close diplomatic friendship he had forged with President Kennedy ever since he took office in 1960. A month prior to Nyerere's visit, Kennedy had penned a letter to Nyerere indicating his sincere desire to rid the United States of this "infectious disease."[36]

To African Americans, the leeway accorded to the U.S. government did not seem to overshadow Nyerere's pro-civil rights position. The church bombing in Birmingham, Alabama, that killed four little girls in September, and Kennedy's assassination in November in 1963 raised questions about the rate of "racial progress" in the United States. The U.S. government was so concerned about the implications of the Birmingham bombing for its image abroad that Assistant Secretary of State G. Mennen Williams sent a memo to the U.S. embassy in Dar es Salaam urging the U.S. ambassador to Tanganyika to issue a statement assuring the TANU government and Tanganyikan people that the "tempo for civil rights progress . . . will not abate but increase."[37] Kennedy's assassination, on the other hand, an event that reportedly brought Nyerere to tears, meant the loss of an important ally to the civil rights struggle in the opinion of the Tanganyikan president.[38] Although Nyerere was not widely regarded as a radical militant like some of his African and Third World contemporaries, his pan-Africanism served as a point of attraction for African Americans of different political outlooks. However, it was a series of events that unfolded in East Africa over the first four months of 1964 that drew the attention of black radicals in the African Diaspora to developments in East Africa. Starting with the revolution in Zanzibar, Tanganyika's island neighbor, in January and ending with the formation of the United Republic of Tanzania in April, black radicals processed these events from afar, seeing them as evidence of a major turning point in Tanzania–African Diaspora relations.

Introduction

In the period between 1964 and 1974, Tanzania took on added significance to the Black Power movements in the African Diaspora. African decolonization continued at a steady though increasingly violent pace, coinciding with and playing an influential role in the increasing radicalization of African Americans. The rise of black radical militancy by the mid-1960s was captured in the slogan "Black Power," made popular by the Student Nonviolent Coordinating Committee (SNCC), a student-led civil rights organization working in local black communities in the southern United States. Fed up with the slow pace of racial progress, the intensification of local repression, and U.S. government inaction to protect civil rights protestors, hardened civil rights workers started to question the efficacy of their nonviolent strategies, their reliance on the U.S. government and white liberal funding, and their vision of a multiracial, integrated society. Black Power, however, was a concept that encapsulated so much more. Outside the segregated South, long-held frustrations over racism exploded into uprisings in many cities in the urban North. It should be noted, however, that the Black Power project was not a complete break from the civil rights movement in terms of the premium activists placed on racial justice and democracy. Yet Black Power conceptions of freedom and liberation went beyond the call for basic civil rights. Black Power activists, largely of the youth generation, focused on the racial aspects of oppression but understood their struggle in its larger historical, political, cultural, and economic contexts. Racism was understood as systemic, and rooted in the transatlantic slave trade period, making white supremacy an enormous impediment to self-determination. Guided by differing ideologies ranging from nationalist to Marxist, Black Power activists and organizations responded by employing varied strategies such as building autonomous black-controlled institutions and alliances with revolutionary struggles in the Third World. Because of their ancestral ties to the continent, Africa held special importance, and international travel to Tanzania became the means through which Black Power activists could explore Africa's meaning to their cultural and political identities.

Abbreviations

6PAC	Sixth Pan-African Congress
AAR	Afro-American Resources, Inc.
AFL-CIO	The American Federation of Labor and Congress of Industrial Organization
ALD	African Liberation Day
ALDCC	African Liberation Day Coordinating Committee
ALSC	African Liberation Support Committee
ANC	African National Congress
ASCRIA	African Society for Cultural Relations with Independent Africa
ASP	Afro-Shirazi Party
BRC	Black Radical Congress
BPP	Black Panther Party
CAP	Congress of African People
CBE	Center for Black Education
CORE	Congress of Racial Equality
DSB	Drum and Spear Bookstore
DSP	Drum and Spear Press
ELF	Eritrean Liberation Front
FRELIMO	Mozambique Liberation Front
FCC	Federal City College
FNLA	National Liberation Front of Angola
IBW	Institute of Black World
LCA	Liberation Committee on Africa
LCFO	Lowndes County Freedom Organization

Abbreviations

MFDP	Mississippi Freedom Democratic Party
MPLA	People's Movement for the Liberation of Angola
MMI	Muslim Mosque, Inc.
NAACP	National Association for the Advancement of Colored People
NAG	Nonviolent Action Group
NAIMSAL	National Anti-Imperialist Movement in Solidarity with African Liberation
NCNW	National Council of Negro Women
NJAC	National Joint Action Committee
NJM	New Jewel Movement
NOI	Nation of Islam
OAAU	Organization of Afro-American Unity
OAU	Organization of African Unity
OAU-LC	Organization of African Liberation Committee
PAC	Pan African Congress
PACST	Pan African Center of Science and Technology
PAIGC	African Party for the Independence of Guinea and Cape Verde
PASP	Pan African Skills Project
RAM	Revolutionary Action Movement
SCLC	Southern Christian Leadership Conference
SNCC	Student Nonviolent Coordinating Committee
SOAS	School of Oriental and African Studies
SWAPO	South West Africa People's Organization
TANU	Tanganyika African National Union
TFL	Tanganyika Federation of Labor
TYL	Tanganyika African National Union Youth League
TYL-UDSM	Tanzania Youth League, University of Dar es Salaam
TYL-UCD	Tanzania Youth League, University College of Dar es Salaam
UAACC	United African Alliance Community Center
UCD	University College of Dar es Salaam
UDSM	University of Dar es Salaam
UNIA	Universal Negro Improvement Association
UNITA	National Union for the Total Independence of Angola
USARF	University Students' African Revolutionary Front
UWI	University of the West Indies
UWT	Umoja wa Wanawake
ZANU	Zimbabwe African National Union
ZAPU	Zimbabwe African People's Union
ZNP	Zanzibar Nationalist Party

Encounters

Malcolm X, A. M. Babu, and the Seeds of Solidarity

> I wanted to show our brothers . . . the necessity of us forming a coalition, a working community, with our brothers of the African continent . . . I feel it is necessary for those of us who were taken from the African continent and who today are suffering exploitation and oppression in the Western Hemisphere to reach out our hands and unite ourselves with our brothers and sisters again, wherever we are, and then work in unity and harmony for a positive program of mutual benefit.
> —Malcolm X, founder of the Organization of Afro-American Unity (OAAU)

The speed with which the dismantling of colonialism occurred in Africa was cause for celebration among African Americans. Between 1957 and 1963, approximately twenty-six independent nations in Africa came into being.[1] For African Americans eager to identify and connect with African states and their leaders sympathetic to and supportive of their struggle for racial justice, Tanzanian President Nyerere's pro-civil rights and pan-Africanist positions put forward in the late 1950s and early 1960s left a favorable impression. Although he may not have received the same amount of veneration and media coverage as Kwame Nkrumah in Ghana, Patrice Lumumba in the Congo, and Jomo Kenyatta in Kenya, Nyerere's actions in both the domestic and foreign policy realms managed to convince African Americans of his genuine pan-Africanist credentials. However, African American civil rights and trade-union leaders evaluated African

Chapter One

decolonization through an ideological lens that lent itself to anticommunism and multiracialism. While this may have been the dominant trend, even among most African American journalists, the civil rights philosophy of nonviolence, and its agenda of racial integration at home and informal international ties abroad, did not entirely capture the sentiments and attitudes of black radicals. Hints of ideological differences within the black freedom struggle became more pronounced when a revolution broke out in Zanzibar, Tanganyika's neighboring country, in January 1964, followed by a series of army mutinies throughout East Africa.

Just thirty miles east off the coast of mainland Tanganyika lies Zanzibar, a Swahili island with a rich history of economic interaction and cultural exchange with the Indian Ocean world. A British colony since 1896, largely administered by an Arab ruling monarchy, Zanzibar was granted independence by the British in December 1961. Over the next two years, a coalition government between the island's two major political parties, the Zanzibar Nationalist Party (ZNP) and the Afro-Shirazi Party (ASP), tried to provide political stability to an island characterized by rivalries between Indians, Arabs, and Africans as well as between peasants, urban workers, petty traders, and big merchants. But the conservative factions within each party pursued repressive policies against trade unions, youth leaders, urban youth, and other progressive forces that marginalized a growing faction of Zanzibar leftists affiliated with ZNP and ASP. In September 1963, the Umma (People's) Party was formed by ZNP's former secretary general, Abdulrahman Mohamed Babu, and led by a Marxist cadre of educated, urban youth. In the face of mounting racial animosities, the Umma Party pushed to mobilize the working class, peasants, and youth across racial and ethnic lines. On January 11 and 12 of the following year, an uprising led by these political forces, including marginalized ASP youth members and enraged unemployed youth, had commenced. With the assistance of Umma Party members, who had received guerrilla warfare training in Cuba during the early 1960s, what had begun as an act of spontaneous revolt quickly transformed into a socialist revolution.[2] In a matter of hours, the prison, the police station, and the radio station were under the revolutionaries' control, and the sultan, his entourage, and members of his coalition government were fleeing the island. When the revolution was over, a new revolutionary government was created, calling itself the Revolutionary Council, an alliance between the ASP and Umma Party. ASP leader Abeid Karume was designated Zanzibar's new president while Babu was appointed the minister of foreign affairs.

Abdulrahman Mohamed Babu was born in 1924 and raised by his great-aunt after the deaths of his father and mother in 1925 and 1926, respectively, at a time when Zanzibar was a British protectorate. At the age of twenty, Babu worked as a "weighing clerk" and later as an assistant to the accountant at the Clove Growers Association, a colonial state corporation that exported the colony's primary commodity. In 1951, he set out to Britain to further his studies in accountancy, philosophy, and English literature. Moved by the Chinese revolution in 1949, Babu's professional interests shifted towards politics. "In the 1950s, it was almost obligatory for young radicals to read as much as possible about the Chinese revolution and its successes in 1949," Babu later wrote in the outline to his memoir. "This revolution had inspired many African and Asian youths who saw in it a promising way to alleviating the mass poverty in their respective continents."[3]

For the next six years, he was a fixture in London's radical political communities, drawn to the politics of anarchism, Marxism, and pan-Africanism. As a budding anticolonial nationalist, Babu went to great lengths to build a solidarity movement between Africans and Asians as well. Acting under the auspices of the East and Central Africa Committee for the Movement for Colonial Freedom (MCF), he helped launch *African Outlook*, a monthly journal dedicated to exploring the questions pertinent to the Bandung generation, those of national liberation, nonalignment, pan-Africanism, and socialism. At the same time, he also was an editor for the *Afro-Asian-Latin American Revolution*, a leftist magazine based in Paris. The revolutionary movements in Vietnam, Algeria, and the Gold Coast provided him with further inspiration and hardened a commitment to mass party political action.

Babu returned to Zanzibar in 1957 and became the secretary general of the Zanzibar Nationalist Party (ZNP), a position he held until 1962. As Babu mobilized workers, peasants, and youth, he also continued to pursue broad-based alliances with Africans and Asians beyond the island. He was a founding member of the PAFMECA (Pan-African Freedom Movement of East and Central Africa) and participant at the 1958 All-African People's Conference in Accra, Ghana. In late 1959 he accepted an official invitation to visit China, where he met and held discussions with Chairman Mao Tse-Tung and Foreign Minister Chou en Lai, among other Chinese communist leaders. It was a visit that led him to take on the position of African correspondent for the China News Agency, *Hshinhu*, which, in his words, gave him "an opportunity to contribute to their understanding of our continent and its complex politics."[4] This connection with communists also compelled the colonial government in Zanzibar to imprison him for two years for sedition. After he was released, the ZNP's radical shift to the right, particularly its role in fomenting racial tensions between Africans and Arabs, convinced Babu to go his separate way and form the Umma Party in 1963. Under his guidance, the Umma Party secured educational scholarships and military training for its members from independent Third World nations such as Cuba and Algeria, and went on to play a prominent role in the revolution in January 1964. The historian Thomas Burgess points to the significance that Babu and the Umma Party had on Zanzibar politics in the aftermath of the revolution:

> The prominence and activity of Umma youth during the "100 days" of the People's Republic of Zanzibar represented the temporary realization of Babu's theories of a vanguard generation bringing about socialist development. Umma merged with the ASP [Afro-Shirazi Party], and Umma youth came to occupy influential positions in the new army and bureaucracy, as officers and junior ministers. Their overseas training and education were essential to a new government absolutely serious about replacing as soon as possible a colonial civil service overwhelmingly staffed by British expatriates, Arabs, and Asians.[5]

Back on the mainland, President Nyerere recognized the extent of Babu's influence on the island. However, in the days after the revolution, Nyerere had little time to respond to what was transpiring politically off the coast of his newly formed nation.

On January 20, a week after the revolution, African soldiers staged a mutiny in Tanganyika, which spread to Uganda and Kenya as well. In Tanganyika, soldiers of the 1st Battalion Tanganyika Rifles stationed at the Calito barracks in Dar es Salaam demanded that Nyerere implement a policy of Africanization to ensure higher wages and promotions to replace expatriate British officers. To see that their demands were taken seriously, mutineers imprisoned their officers, set up roadblocks, and seized control of key government institutions in the city. Forced into hiding, Nyerere was only able to subdue the mutiny, which had spread to the towns of Tabora and Nachingwea and later to the countries of Uganda and Kenya, by calling for British military intervention. It was a decision that weakened Nyerere's credibility among pan-Africanists even after he tried to justify his actions at an emergency meeting of foreign ministers of the fledgling Organization of African Unity (OAU) held in Dar es Salaam on February 12. "The presence of British troops in Tanganyika is a fact which is too easily exploited by those who wish to divide Africa, or to dominate Africa," he told OAU member states.[6]

With the East African army mutinies suppressed, the world's attention again shifted back to Zanzibar. The leftist ideology of the post-revolutionary government stoked Western fears about the spread of communism in Africa. At first, a frantic round of memos by the U.S. State Department speculated that Cuba, China, and the Soviet Union were directly involved in the revolution. By February, however, the United States was forced to look to Zanzibar and the Revolutionary Council, mostly notably Babu, Zanzibar's new foreign minister. Described as the "prime mover in the coup," Babu was the "leading Zanzibar nationalist" and "the most outspoken critic of the West on the island."[7] By targeting Babu, the U.S. government had found its primary communist threat to peace and democracy in Africa. When Babu expelled the U.S. consul in Zanzibar in January, the Central Intelligence Agency (CIA) regarded it as a "significant victory for the Communists."⁸ The U.S. press followed this line of Cold War thinking and set out to discredit the new regime by targeting Babu. Stories of Babu's anti-West, leftist ideologies soon alternated with stories of government authoritarianism under Babu's leadership.⁹ Between January and April, over fifty articles on Zanzibar's "drift to the left" and Babu's consolidation of power littered the pages of the *Washington Post* and the *New York Times*.

African Americans did not see eye to eye on these political events in East Africa. African American anticommunists refused to endorse the revolution for its communist overtures evidenced in the coverage it received in leading black-run newspapers. In the *Chicago Defender* appeared two briefings that suspiciously questioned Zanzibar's ties to Cuba and China. Accompanying one of the briefings was a photograph of Babu and Karume with a caption that read, "friends of Red China?"¹⁰ The conservative African American journalist George Schuyler shifted attention away from Asia's impact on Zanzibar onto the United States' primary Cold War rival. Writing for the *Pittsburgh Courier*, Schuyler saw the revolution as a victory for the Soviets, who were "fast infiltrating the Dark continent" through communist ideology and military aid from other Eastern Bloc countries. He took the coverage further by morally condemning government-led executions of overthrown leaders with ties to the ZNP opposition.¹¹ In the opinion of another journalist, the revolution was a "massacre of still uncalculated thousands," which made it difficult to support from afar.¹² The army mutinies that broke out in Tanganyika, Uganda, and Kenya in the revolution's immediate aftermath proved to heighten their concerns over Nyerere's power and affirm their anticommunist outlooks.¹³

Revolutionary violence in East Africa, however, did not fail to dampen the mood of U.S. black nationalists. For those who saw their struggle as one of self-determination in direct opposition to Western imperialism, the Zanzibar revolution was to be commended not condemned. Max Stanford, a leader in the Revolutionary Action Movement (RAM), a black internationalist organization heavily influenced by Marxism and the Third World revolutionary struggles, came out strongly in support of the revolution. In an essay titled "The Relationship of Revolutionary Afro-American Movement to the Bandung Revolution," Stanford praises the revolution for its populist orientation and the post-revolutionary government for its firm stance against U.S. imperialism and its embrace of nonalignment and pan-African unity. As a result, Zanzibar was on the "vanguard of the Bandung Revolution" alongside Cuba and China.¹⁴

Black radical responses to the army mutinies also challenged the viewpoints disseminated by mainstream black and U.S. newspapers. The Liberation Committee on Africa (LCA), a New York City–based pan-Africanist group, used its local ties to an East African student organization at Columbia University to state its position on the matter. While the LCA found Nyerere's "counter-revolutionary" decision to sanction

British military intervention deeply disconcerting, the Nation of Islam (NOI), at the time the largest black nationalist organization in the United States, took an interest in the soldiers' race consciousness. Its media organ, *Muhammad Speaks*, sympathized with the soldiers' demands and urged Nyerere to promote black Africans to officer positions occupied by British expatriates. In some ways, the Zanzibar revolution and the East African army mutinies brought to the surface a growing ideological divide within the U.S. black freedom movement. In some political circles, Nyerere's image as a nationalist and pan-Africanist was tarnished. The image they held of him in other circles was that of a leader in a highly vulnerable position of power threatened by external and internal communist forces. However, these were two conflicting images not beyond repair. When Tanganyika unified with Zanzibar in April, only three months after the Zanzibar revolution, the perception of Nyerere as a leading, progressive African voice was restored.

In early April, President Nyerere initiated a private meeting with President Karume to discuss unification between their respective nation-states. On April 25, a "special meeting" of Tanganyika's national assembly convened to ratify an "Agreement of Union." The next day legislation was passed unanimously. "In no other part of the world is there so great an urge for unity as we in Africa," Nyerere wrote. "But whilst we are rightly proud of this aspiration, the sentiment of unity, we must remember that meaningful unity will not come simply by talking." Nyerere tried his best to frame unification with Zanzibar as an outgrowth of his pragmatism and expression of his commitment to state-centered pan-Africanism. He refused to entertain any kinds of arguments that claimed he was pressured by the West to curtail Zanzibar's leftward turn. "Unity in our continent does not have to come via Moscow or Washington. It is an insult to Africa to read cold war politics into every move towards African unity."

Nyerere's justification did little to sway the opinions of the U.S. government, which viewed the union as a shrewd act on the part of the Tanzanian president to block Babu and other Zanzibar radicals from a complete takeover of the island.[15] Even though Babu was incorporated into the union government and transferred to work out of Dar es Salaam, mainstream media identified him as the "chief loser" in "Nyerere's coup."[16] The union was met with equal fanfare from liberal and radical pan-Africanists in the United States, who all seemed to welcome any steps toward continental unity. African American anticommunists lauded the union, yet reasons had far more to do with their belief that communism was nothing more than a disruptive force in Africa. The *Tri-State Defender*, a black-run weekly newspaper based out of Memphis, Tennessee, ran with the headline "Tanganyika, Zanzibar to 'Fight Reds.'"[17] Black nationalists and radicals, however, chose to promote the union because it represented another step towards African unification.

The Seeds of Solidarity

As East Africa was embroiled in revolutionary upheaval, the United States' most popular and influential black nationalist leader at the time, Malcolm X, was undergoing a profound religious and political transformation. This set him on a course towards strategizing how African Americans could build stronger relations with African and Third World nations and their leaders. Born Malcolm Little in 1925 in Omaha, Nebraska, Malcolm X was the child of two parents who were members of Marcus Garvey's Universal Negro Improvement Association (UNIA)—the largest black nationalist organization in history, which flourished during the 1920s with its message of race pride, self-determination, and pan-Africanism. After the murder of his father and the psychiatric hospitalization of his mother, Malcolm's youth became defined by his experiences with northern urban racism, petty criminal activity, and drug abuse, which eventually led to imprisonment for larceny and breaking and entering at the age of twenty. While in prison, Malcolm Little, who was then known as "Red," was influenced by the Nation of Islam (NOI), a black religious nationalist organization founded in the 1930s and led by the Honorable Elijah Muhammad. He joined NOI while in prison and changed his last name from Little to X—a move that was meant to symbolize African Americans' unknown African ancestry. Between 1952 and 1963, while serving as the minister of Temple No. 7 in Harlem and later as the organization's national spokesman, Malcolm X helped to expand the NOI's membership by the thousands, largely because of his ability to relate to the lived experience of the black working class and underclass, and articulate a message of self-reliance, nationhood, and armed self-defense in clear and honest terms. It was this militant message that provided an alternative perspective and approach to black liberation at a time when the nonviolent, integrationist strategy of the civil rights movement ruled the day.

By 1963, however, Malcolm X had found himself increasingly marginalized within the NOI and within a black freedom movement wedded to "turn-the-other-cheek" strategies of the National Association for the Advancement of Colored People (NAACP), the Southern Christian Leadership Conference (SCLC), the Congress of Racial Equality (CORE), and the Student Nonviolent Coordinating Committee (SNCC). As the late Manning Marable notes in his richly detailed biography, Malcolm's activism was constrained by NOI's racial-religious philosophy that forbade its members from involvement in any kind of secularist-oriented civil rights activism. At a time when the struggle for civil rights and anticolonial nationalist mobilizations in Africa had intensified, Malcolm found it difficult to reconcile his loyalties to NOI codes of conduct with his desire to get more directly involved in a struggle he viewed in need of a black nationalist perspective. Malcolm later explained why he left the NOI in a speech delivered at the Tuskegee Institute in Alabama in February 1965. To a group of black college students who were engaged in such direct-action protest activities throughout the Deep South, he stated: "Elijah believes that God is going to come and straighten things out. I believe that too. But whereas Elijah is willing to sit and wait, I'm not willing to sit and wait on God to come. If he doesn't come soon, it will be too late."[18] Two years earlier, in 1963, before being suspended indefinitely by Elijah Muhammad for his comments about President Kennedy's assassination, Malcolm was already reevaluating his Islamic faith and entertaining the idea of a political life beyond the NOI.[19] Elijah Muhammad's sexual infidelities, coupled with a growing faction of NOI leaders adamantly opposed to Malcolm's position within the NOI hierarchy, were also contributing factors to his eventual defection from the organization.

By March 1964, Malcolm was determined to reinsert himself in the African American freedom struggle.[20] Much of his efforts were aimed at articulating Africa's importance to black people in the United States. On March 18, he delivered a speech at Harvard University that stressed the need for African Americans to claim as their own Africa's past of dynastic rule to challenge prevailing notions that their history began with enslavement in the Americas:

> We have to teach our people something about our cultural roots. We have to teach them something of their glorious civilizations before they were kidnapped by your grandfathers and brought over to this country. Once our people are taught about the glorious civilization that existed on the African continent, they won't any longer be ashamed of who they are. We will reach back and link ourselves to those roots, and this will make the feeling of dignity come into us; we will feel that as we lived in times gone by, we can in like manner today. If we had civilizations, cultures, societies, and nations hundreds of years ago, before you came and kidnapped us and brought us here, so we can have the same today. The restoration of cultural roots and history will restore dignity to black people in this country.[21]

Yet this psychological return to Africa was not an end in itself, but rather a stepping-stone towards forging political alliances with independent African states centered on combatting the problem of American racism. He continued: "We need help from our brothers in Africa who have won their independence. And when we begin to show them our thinking has expanded to an international scale, they will step in and help us, and you'll find that Uncle Sam will be in a most embarrassing position."[22] Underlying this message was a concerted attempt to grapple with the question of solidarity at home. Malcolm X rejected alliance building with the Democratic and Republican Parties as a strategy that would eradicate the social, political, economic, and cultural ills plaguing the African American community.

Between April 11 and May 21, while union proceedings unfolded between

Tanganyika and Zanzibar, Malcolm X took this message abroad. He visited Egypt, Lebanon, Saudi Arabia, Nigeria, Ghana, Morocco, and Algeria. From each country visited he wrote in his diary, revealing how travel had informed his ever-evolving political perspective. From Lagos, on May 10, Malcolm reflected on how Africans regarded African Americans as "long lost brothers of Africa . . . interested in every aspect of our plight."[23] A day later, while in Accra, Malcolm penned another letter that calls on African Americans to identify themselves as "Pan-Africanists" and return to Africa "culturally and philosophically" in order to develop a "working unity" with Africans in the "framework of Pan-Africanism."[24] Together, these letters capture how international travel served as a source of radicalization for Malcolm. He begins to identify a set of characteristics and approaches that would help him identify allies from enemies—friends from foes—in the international arena. In the same letter written from Accra, Malcolm points out how the United States was "bowing, grinning and smiling"—posing as a friend of Africa in an effort to stake claim to Africa's mineral wealth.[25] It is to youth/students and specific African states and their leaders, who have progressed to a stage of revolutionary consciousness, that Malcolm delegates the status of friends. On the one hand, he was encouraged to learn that Africans held a diasporic sense of selfhood expressed in the ways they acknowledged their historical-ancestral connection to African Americans. On the other, he recognized that the U.S. presence in Africa raised fundamental obstacles to his political project, and it forced him to prioritize a critical interpretation of the function of the print media in masking U.S capitalist interests in Africa and in blocking "direct lines of communication" between African Americans and Africans.

When he returned to the United States in late May, Malcolm X threw his energies into two new organizational projects: Muslim Mosque, Inc. and the Organization of Afro-American Unity (OAAU). The former was the outgrowth of his conversion to Sunni Islam and an effort to spread the faith among the African American community, especially the followers of Elijah Muhammad. The latter was inspired by the ways in which Africans sought to forge a coalition of independent states to end colonial rule and to work in cooperation on issues of mutual concern through the auspices of the Organization of African Unity (OAU), which was founded in 1963. The OAAU was envisioned as an umbrella organization for nationalist, civil rights, and leftist organizations led by African Americans. To advance the cause of self-determination, it sought to pursue and establish concrete links of solidarity with African and Third World nations and anticolonial nationalist movements—an approach to movement building that Malcolm X believed to be absent from the black freedom struggle.[26] For the OAAU, unity with Africa was one of its principal aims and objectives, pledging to "join hands and hearts with all people of African origin in a grand alliance by forgetting all the differences that the power structure has created to keep us divided and enslaved."[27] This did not mean that the OAAU had the definitive answer to how a successful black global united front could be formed. "This is our aim. It's rough . . . we have to smooth it up some. But we're not trying to put together something that is smooth," he admitted. "We don't care how rough it is. We don't care how tough it is. We don't care how backward it may sound."[28] Participating in the OAU's 2nd Summit of governmental ministers and heads of states was a good place to start to smooth out OAAU's approach to international black solidarity. In July, Malcolm traveled to Cairo as an uninvited delegate to this OAU gathering.

At OAAU's second official rally, five days before traveling to Cairo, Malcolm explained why he was traveling to Africa for an extended period of time. "We want the United States charged with violation of human rights and the African states can get it on the floor of the United Nations . . . If our problem does not come up then neither South Africa nor Angola nor Southern Rhodesia nor any other colonial issue should be discussed at the United Nations."[29] Since African Americans have "African blood in our veins," Malcolm reasoned, "and we've heard them say that Africa is not free until all Africans are free—we're Africans too, and we want them to be just as concerned at the governmental level with our problems as they are with the problems of our people in South Africa and Angola."[30] It was hoped that by cultivating allies, sympathizers, and supporters in the formerly colonized world, his organization could help transform the question of racial justice for African Americans into an international one. With OAU member states becoming a numerical majority in the United Nations, Malcolm saw the continental organization as a potentially powerful political force that could exert extensive pressure on the U.S. government.[31]

Before attending the conference, Malcolm made a pilgrimage to Mecca, which marked his conversion to the Sunni Islamic faith, and where he would take on the name El Hajj Malik el-Shabazz. His encounters with Muslims from different racial backgrounds forced him to rethink some of his views on racial separatism while enhancing his understanding of the nature of racism in the United States. "Each hour here in the Holy Land enables me to have greater spiritual insights into what is happening in American between black and white," Malcolm wrote from Mecca. "The American Negro can never be blamed for his racial animosities—he is only reacting to four hundred years of the conscious racism of the American whites. But as racism leads America up the suicidal path, I do believe, from the experiences that I have had with them, that the whites of the younger generation, in the colleges and universities, will see the handwriting on the wall and many of them will turn to the spiritual path of truth—the only way left to America to ward off the disaster that racism inevitably must lead to."[32] His experiences traveling abroad, in general, also led him to the conclusion

The Seeds of Solidarity

that alliances between African Americans and Africans were necessary if pan-African liberation was to truly occur.

Malcolm arrived in Cairo on July 9. He immediately began "lobbying" OAU delegates, speaking informally with them about the need to defend the African American struggle as an extension of the aims and objectives of the African decolonization movement. Once his presence became public knowledge, a controversy quickly erupted over whether or not the OAU should grant him official observer status. As this debate went on behind the scenes, conversations with anticolonial nationalists, presidents, prime ministers, foreign ministers, journalists, and intellectuals from all over the continent continued.[33] Five days later he believed he had made significant progress: "Everyone is aware and is interested in the Afro-Americans' plight," he wrote in his diary on July 14. Although he had the recent passing of the U.S. Civil Rights Act to contend with, Malcolm was convinced that he could show African anticolonialists the political hypocrisy of the United States "with just a few words and examples."[34] One example he used was a recent police killing of a black male youth in Harlem that sparked off a week-long confrontation between Harlem's black residents and the New York City police that occurred in July during his travels abroad. He believed this event could buttress his claims about the lack of racial progress in the United States. On July 15, however, Malcolm had changed his tune about how easy it was going to be to win support from African leaders, noting how "American propaganda ... has been powerful in influencing most of them to think we hate Africans and don't identify with them in any way."[35]

Abdulrahman Mohamed Babu was one of the many radicals whom Malcolm encountered in the lobbies and rooms of the Shepheard Hotel and the Hilton Hotel, as well as aboard the *Isis*, a yacht reserved for representatives of anticolonial nationalist organizations from northern and southern Rhodesia, Mozambique, Guinea-Bissau, and South Africa, and other special guests.[36] Babu came to the 2nd Summit as the minister of economic planning in the Tanzanian government. Although the union between Tanganyika and Zanzibar stripped Babu of his powerful position as Zanzibar's foreign affairs minister, he had come to the OAU as one of Tanzania's foremost pan-Africanists, an asset to the union government in shaping both countries' economic and foreign policies.[37] Many years later, he recounted the first time he met Malcolm X in Cairo:

> Malcolm came to my room in a very ambivalent mood because at that very moment Harlem was burning. The youth in the uprising was calling for Malcolm ... And Malcolm was in two minds. He wanted to go back—to come back and lead the struggle and be with the people in the struggle. But we wanted him to remain there in the conference so as to give us "the feeling of the struggle" and to convey to all the Third

29

>World leaders what America, the real America, were [sic] going through. I'm glad to report that we succeeded in detaining him there . . . Malcolm X had the vision to see the threat a united Third World would pose to imperialism.³⁸

Impressed with the seriousness and rigor with which Malcolm invested in pan-Africanism as a strategy of liberation, Babu also did not overlook the fact that Malcolm had traveled to Cairo while Harlem was awash in racial violence after another incident of police brutality.³⁹ In Cairo, Malcolm did not hold back in calling the United States an imperialist nation and the major threat to African sovereignty and unity—a perspective that Babu shared. For these reasons, Babu persuaded Nyerere to officially put Malcolm's petition on the OAU agenda so that the issue of racial oppression in the United States could be formally discussed.⁴⁰

On July 17, the first day of the conference for heads of state, Malcolm X was granted official observer status, which allowed him to submit an eight-page memorandum. Titled "Appeal to the Heads of State," Malcolm extends a hand of friendship while challenging independent African states to confront U.S. hegemony head-on by publicly condemning the U.S. government's role in the perpetuation of racial oppression. In his address, he critically examines the past and the present, drawing a link between the violence of transatlantic slavery and the violence meted out against civil rights workers in the South and African Americans in general. The image presented is one of African Americans under constant attack, historically neglected by a government claiming to be the torchbearer of human rights and multiracial democracy. The Civil Rights Act, he tells them, was not a response to black protest, but an attempt on the part of the U.S. government to "polish" its image abroad while masking a "deceitful" foreign policy towards Africa based on "'friendly' American dollarism."⁴¹

For Malcolm, Africans needed to embrace a diaspora consciousness. He refers to Africa as "the mother continent," African heads of state as "the Shepherd [sic] of All African peoples everywhere," and African Americans as "long lost brothers and sisters . . . living in a strange land . . . under the clutches of the imperialist Wolf."⁴² If Africans were to embrace a diaspora consciousness and view pan-Africanism not solely as a continental movement, then they would see that addressing the problem of racial oppression in the United States was just as important as combatting apartheid in South Africa, if not more so.

Malcolm ends his appeal with the question "What makes our African brothers hesitate to bring the United States government before the United Nations and charge her with violating the human rights of 22 million African-Americans?"⁴³ Answers to this question were articulated in an OAU resolution titled "Racial Discrimination in the United States." The document fell short of Malcolm's expectations. Essentially, the OAU declared that the Civil Rights Act of 1964 was sufficient evidence of the U.S. government's effort to solve its domestic racial crisis. However, the resolution further stated that it was "a sad reflection too, that 100 years has passed between the signing of the U.S. Proclamation of Emancipation and the new legislation—and that despite this long passage of time the problem is still far from resolved."[44] With this statement, African leaders made it clear that they were unwilling to endorse Malcolm's call for OAU support and outright condemn the U.S. government for its racist treatment of African Americans. Whether it was because they feared U.S. economic reprisals (i.e., the loss of foreign aid) or U.S. military intervention is not entirely clear. Judging from some of the comments made by African delegates, it appears that the OAU's position of neutrality was a combination of their belief in racial progress in the United States and a conception of pan-Africanism as strictly a continental movement. Egypt's head of state, Gamal Abdel Nasser, for example, cited the Civil Rights Act as an "encouraging" sign that needed to be praised, while one Ugandan delegate referred to Malcolm's proposal as a distraction to the OAU, "a continental organization" with its "own problems."[45] Taken aback by the latter's comments, Malcolm thought it necessary to respond, saying: "He should be ashamed of himself. Doesn't he know that two Ugandans were beaten up in New York last week? This [racism] is a world problem and not an internal United States problem. When trouble starts, the whites are not going to know an ambassador from me."[46]

The U.S. national press, including African American newspapers, treated the OAU resolution as a forceful denouncement of Malcolm's version of pan-Africanism. But Malcolm disagreed that it was a dismal failure, serving as proof that Africans and African Americans held little in common.[47] In an interview with Milton Henry, a black nationalist lawyer from Detroit, Malcolm saw the legitimization of the debate itself as a stunning success. "Afro-Americans in the United States are still Africans, and we felt that the African heads of state were as much responsible for us as they were responsible for the people right here on the continent. This was a sort of challenge to them and I think that most of them realize it today, more so than they did prior to the conference."[48] He understood that forging bonds of mutual understanding was not going to be a smooth process, and therefore did not feel so inclined to disparage publicly the OAU resolution on the African American question despite its shortsightedness.

In addition to addressing Africa's relationship to the diaspora, the conference facilitated an ongoing learning process for Malcolm X about the issues and debates most prominent in the continental pan-Africanism movement, which elicited some conflicting emotions and attitudes. He praised Africans for providing an official denouncement of Western imperialism in Africa. However, he was frustrated that racism in the United States was not brought up again as a topic of debate, and concerned about the public nature of the internal divisions within the oau. His strongest criticisms of the conference were reserved for African heads of state opposed to President Nkrumah's call for immediate continental unification. He took particular note of the debate that broke out between Nyerere and Nkrumah on the best course of action for African continental unification. President Nyerere criticized Nkrumah's immediate approach to African unity: "To say that the step to step method was invented by the imperialists is to reach the limits of absurdity. I have heard the imperialists blamed for many things, but not for the limitations of mankind. They are not God!"[49] In his diary, Malcolm sided with Nkrumah while adding, "I didn't like Nyerere's attacks on Nkrumah. It was pleasing only to the West and its stooges."[50] To Malcolm, the OAU resolution was a "reluctant" step in the right direction. At the same time, his participation at the summit proved to be a valuable teaching moment; he learned about the dynamics of inter-African state politics and about a growing sentiment of support for the African American freedom struggle.[51] The key contacts he made with African leaders also held enormous importance. In fact, it was at the conference that Babu invited Malcolm X to Tanzania.

The *Nationalist*, the English-speaking newspaper of the TANU Party, made public Malcolm X's presence in the country with a front-page headline that read "Malcolm Rips USA." After the OAU summit and before arriving in Tanzania, he had traveled to Ghana,[52] Nigeria, Saudi Arabia, Lebanon, Palestine, Sudan, and Ethiopia, where he spoke at universities; drank tea with heads of state and African political leaders and intellectuals; ate dinners with European, American, and African American expatriates; toured sites of cultural heritage; and granted interviews with various press agencies. He had come to Tanzania with an already favorable impression of some of its leaders and people, which was buttressed by his visit to Ethiopia. In Addis Ababa, he met with several Tanganyikan students as well as with Otimi Kambona, the younger brother of Tanganyika's minister of external affairs, Oscar Kambona, who was regarded by many as the country's most popular black nationalist leader in the government. On October 2, he met with Tanganyikan students for a second time, leaving the conversation impressed with how they showed "profound interest and support of the African American struggle for human rights."[53]

At the time of Malcolm's visit, Tanzania was a new nation gradually emerging out of a union between Zanzibar and Tanganyika that had occurred five months earlier. The contours of Tanzania's political landscape were increasingly being characterized by the consolidation of one-party state rule, an exploration of African socialist ideas of economic development, and a pan-Africanist orientation toward foreign policy affairs.[54] As early as 1962, when the government was still committed to a capitalist form of development, President Nyerere was exploring the socialistic underpinnings of traditional African societies and their relevancy to Tanzania nation-building. In a paper titled "Ujamaa—The Basis of African Socialism," published and released by the Tanganyikan government in 1962, Nyerere wrote: "Our first step, therefore, must be to re-educate ourselfs [sic], to regain our former attitude of mind. In our traditional African society we were individuals within a community. We took care of the community, and the community took care of us. We neither needed nor wished to exploit our fellow men."[55] Tanzania's most appealing feature of its pan-Africanist foreign policy came in the form of serving as a frontline state for African liberation groups fighting national wars of independence in southern and central Africa. By 1964, liberation groups were setting up bases of operation in Dar es Salaam for waging guerrilla warfare in Portuguese and settler colonies, a development Malcolm was fully aware of, having spent considerable time with African freedom fighters during the OAU summit in Cairo.

Unlike during his visit to Ghana, Malcolm did not have a small contingent of African American expatriates to serve as his official hosts while visiting Tanzania. This changed when Malcolm X met Bill Sutherland, the black expatriate community's de facto head, at a party thrown in his honor at the Algerian embassy.[56] Sutherland was born in 1918 and grew up in Glen Ridge, New Jersey, a majority white suburb. He was introduced to pacifism as a teenager. Yet his political awakening occurred between 1936 and 1940 when he was a student at Bates College in Lewiston, Maine, where he was the chairman of the Social Action Committee of the Christian Association and worked on issues of racism, warfare, and economic exploitation. In 1945, after a stint in a racially segregated prison for dodging the draft, Sutherland became an active member in a host of civil rights and pacifist organizations, including the American Friends Service Committee (AFSC), the Youth Committee Against War, Workers Defense League, Committee for Fair Employment Practices, Fellowship of Reconciliation (FOR), and the Congress of Racial Equality (CORE). Sutherland distinguished himself as a student of nonviolence philosophy, civil disobedience, and direct action. As a member of the Committee for Non-Violent Action, Sutherland cycled from Paris to Moscow to advocate for worldwide nuclear disarmament.

During the 1950s, Sutherland was drawn into the pan-Africanism movement. Inspired by the nonviolent mass movement in India led by Gandhi, and decolonization movements in Africa, he moved to the Gold Coast in 1953, believing that "Africa offered the greatest hope" for worldwide revolutionary social change. Between 1958 and 1962, he participated in the All-African People's Conference in Accra in 1958 and the Pan-African Freedom Movement of East and Central Africa (PAFMECA) while serving as the secretary to Ghana's minister of finance, K. A. Gbedemah. However, when Gbedemah had a falling out with President Nrkumah, Sutherland moved to Tanganyika.[57] As early as 1961, Sutherland had viewed Tanganyika as the new vanguard state in the African liberation struggle due to Nyerere's leadership. In an article for the *Jerusalem Weekly*

Post titled "Pan-Africanism and Democracy: Seed of Unity and Freedom Flowering in Dar es Salaam," he wrote: "The seed of continental African unity and freedom sown in Accra shows the most promise of bearing fruit in Dar-es-Salaam, where the leaders of East and Central African countries have joined forces, with the unassuming but powerful Julius Nyerere as host."[58] For the next two years, Sutherland positioned himself as a bridge between the African American freedom struggle, the antinuclear war, and the continental pan-Africanism movements. Despite the fact that Sutherland disagreed with Malcolm X on the topic of nonviolence, this difference in philosophy did not deter him from helping Malcolm spread his message of racial solidarity.

Sutherland became Malcolm X's "chauffeur," which afforded him the opportunity to gain a better understanding of Malcolm's politics and mission abroad. What struck a chord with Sutherland was Malcolm's willingness to converse with anybody. "In terms of general impression, Malcolm was a person who was constantly exploring, constantly alive, not afraid to talk with anyone," he later recalled. "He talked to everybody in his own quest for answers . . . He had the kind of confidence, a kind of vitality that was different from many other famous people."[59] Because of Sutherland's extensive network within the country, he was able to secure a series of private meetings with the Tanzanian and foreign press agencies, African American and white expatriates and students, foreign embassy officials, representatives of African liberation movements from southern and central Africa, and Tanzanian government officials.[60] Malcolm also met with Tanzanian government ministers and TANU leaders, most notably Oscar Kambona, the minister of foreign affairs, and Bibi Titi Mohamed, head of the women's wing of the ruling party, apparently winning them over with his sense of humor, open-mindedness, and intellectual acumen.[61]

Even though Malcolm did not have the opportunity to speak formally before an assembled audience as he had done in other nations, he used the country's national press as a public mouthpiece through which to talk about African Americans' desire for friendship with African nations. In an interview with the *Tanganyika Standard*, he reflected on the benefits of travel by commenting, "I am meeting Africans at all levels for the purpose of creating a better understanding of Africans here and of the 22 million African Americans. American Negroes are beginning to see that their relationship to Africa is something which cannot be denied."[62] Malcolm's message also offered a joint critique of U.S. domestic policies towards African Americans and U.S. foreign policies towards Africa in order to frame the U.S. government as a "common enemy."[63] In another interview published on October 13, he presents himself as a man inspired and humbled by Tanzania's nationalist project while at the same time he tries to make sharp distinctions between the sincerity of his motives and those of the U.S. government.[64] Therefore, the Peace Corps, the United States' Information Services

(USIS), and African Americans working for these government agencies, were to be treated with harsh skepticism: "The right type of Negro can make a great contribution in Africa, but the type that is being sent here now by the American Government is not designed to make a contribution to things African. They are designed to create an image that will make the African feel repulsive. It is my contention that they make Africans hate American Negroes."[65] This comment, in particular, prompted a response from an African American Peace Corps volunteer, who took offense to being labeled a "tool" of the U.S. government. In his letter to the editor, published weeks after Malcolm left Tanzania, he accuses Malcolm of "inciting hatred through his personal greed for publicity and self-acclaim."[66]

Not all African Americans living in Tanzania were put off by Malcolm's remarks. Some were simply curious and eager to meet and talk with him, while others expressed interest in establishing an OAAU chapter in Dar es Salaam. But creating such a chapter did not seem to occupy his time. Instead, Malcolm spent a considerable amount of time with Babu, who acted informally as his governmental host. This proved to be a pivotal moment in the consolidation of their political friendship, and where Malcolm was able to get to know Babu on a more personal level.[67] Although Malcolm's travel diary on his Tanzania visit is not incredibly detailed, he describes Babu as "friendly" and "well-informed." "An extremely alert man," Malcolm wrote, "and dedicated to what he believes."[68] As Malcolm would later reveal, Babu's hospitality manifested in rich, private conversations at his office, at the bar lounges of the Paradise Hotel and the New African Hotel where revolutionaries in Dar es Salaam socialized, and in the privacy of his home, where he was able to meet Babu's children. Babu also accompanied Malcolm on a trip to Zanzibar. For Babu, spending time with Malcolm only seemed to reaffirm the first impressions he held of the black nationalist leader when they first met in Cairo. As he did at the OAU summit, Babu sought out Nyerere, yet this time to orchestrate a meeting between the Tanzanian president and Malcolm X.

At a dinner with Babu and his family, Malcolm was informed of his meeting with the president. The news caused him to later write in his diary, "I was elated." By all accounts, President Nyerere did not hold the same feeling. In fact, it took consistent pleading from Babu as well as from Kambona. Nyerere finally relented and consented to a three-minute meet-and-greet. It is not altogether clear as to why Nyerere did not want to meet with Malcolm X. He was already aware of Malcolm's radical politics, having been the one to get Malcolm's "Appeal to African Heads of State" on the debating table of the Cairo conference. This did not mean he agreed entirely with Malcolm's point of view. Nyerere sided with the liberal civil rights strategy in the United States, differing with Malcolm on the sincerity and commitment of the U.S. government in eradicating its system of racial inequality. Nor did Nyerere subscribe to "racialist

Chapter One

thinking." Another point of contention had to do with the question of armed struggle. Malcolm X had never abandoned his belief in revolutionary violence even after leaving the Nation of Islam.[69] Despite his growing support of armed guerrilla struggles in white minority-ruled territories in central and southern Africa, Nyerere did not believe that African Americans had reached a stage in their struggle where revolutionary violence was necessary. But ideological differences with Malcolm should not have been a reason to decline a meeting.[70] What is apparent, however, is that Nyerere wanted to keep his distance for reasons that may be reducible to Cold War anxieties.[71]

Three minutes was all Malcolm needed to win over the Tanzanian president and transform a brief meet-and-greet into a three-hour conversation. The meeting took place at around 7 p.m. on October 13, the day China had successfully developed its very own nuclear capabilities. Babu, who was present at the meeting, later remembered part of their exchange: "President Nyerere said, 'Malcolm, for the first time today in recorded history, a former colonial country has been able to develop weapons at par with any colonial power. This is the end of colonialism through and through.' And Malcolm replied, 'Mr. President, this is what I've been thinking all the way as I was coming from my hotel to this house.'"[72] China's nuclear power, combined with its economic policy of communism, compelled Malcolm to later turn to his diary to reflect on the "importance of land. No one has the right to own land: it should be socialized." He added: "China has made a human being out of the white man . . . He is more frightened like all human beings—they are all banding together out for China.'"[73] Nyerere's interests in China, in socialism, even in African continental unity, seemed to take Malcolm by surprise. Again, he turns to his diary to describe his new impressions of the president: "He is very shrewd, intelligent, <u>disarming</u> [underlined by Malcolm] a man who laughs and jokes much (but deadly serious)."[74]

By all accounts, the meeting went extremely well. It was as much about breaking down "image" barriers than anything else. In the Western press, Nyerere was regarded as the "Darling of the West" while Malcolm was widely seen as a racial extremist. By conferring with Nyerere, such an image was turned on its head. Malcolm made a point of this later when meeting with African American expatriates in Paris. When someone asked him if Nyerere was an ally to the United States, Malcolm laughed it off, claiming that he "had conversations with some of these so-called moderates recently, and some of the things they said would make the hair stand up on the back of your neck."[75] The notion that Nyerere was beholden to the West was severely exaggerated. According to Malcolm, the conversation left him thinking about socialism as a viable economic strategy of liberation and China as a potentially powerful Third World ally. Most important, it left him convinced of Tanzania's importance to advancing OAAU's internationalist agenda.

The Seeds of Solidarity

Meeting with Nyerere and getting to know Babu were the high points of Malcolm's two-week stay in Dar es Salaam. Nyerere was an African head of state open to the idea of transnational exchange and solidarity, while Babu became a close friend with access to a large Third World network. Although this was Malcolm's first and last visit to Tanzania, it would not be the last time he connected with Babu. In late November, Babu was part of the Tanzanian delegation to the Sixth Ordinary Session of the United Nations General Assembly held in New York City. The UN session occurred right at the time when the postcolonial situation in the Congo had again grabbed international headlines. When Congolese guerrilla fighters opposed to the coalition government seized control of the city of Stanleyville, taking hostage 1,600 European expatriates, the United States and Belgium responded by sending in military forces in late November, resulting in both Congolese and European casualties. While the U.S. government perceived its military intervention as a humanitarian initiative, African American radicals and the Tanzanian state viewed it as another act of imperialist aggression that began with the assassination of Patrice Lumumba, the democratically elected prime minister, in 1961. To add insult to injury, the U.S.-backed Congolese prime minister who sanctioned the rescue mission was none other than Moïse Tshombe, the former secessionist leader who played an instrumental role in Lumumba's assassination.[76]

These latest developments in the Congo served as a political point of convergence. On the whole, African Americans and the Tanzanian government condemned the actions of the United States and Belgium.[77] Malcolm X and Babu were especially outraged at the two countries' complicity in the affair. With Babu in New York City, an opportunity to collectively scrutinize an American policy in Africa shaped by Cold War imperatives presented itself. Thus, Babu agreed to speak on three separate occasions at political rallies and forums held throughout the city, most of which were sponsored or orchestrated by Malcolm X's OAAU. Before packed crowds that ranged from a few hundred to a few thousand, he shared his views not only on the Congo situation but also on the history of the Zanzibar revolution, and how Africans started to view pan-Africanism as a movement inclusive of black people in the African Diaspora.

On December 13 Babu spoke at an OAAU rally in Harlem to an estimated crowd of 1,500.[78] He was running late that night, putting Malcolm in a position to extrapolate on his experiences abroad, making known how Nyerere assisted him at the Cairo conference: "And I'm proud to state that the one who was responsible for bringing that resolution forth and getting it agreed upon by the other African heads of state was probably the last one that you and I would expect to do it because of the image that he's been given in this country. But the one who came forth and suggested that the African summit conference pass a resolution thoroughly condemning the mistreatment of Afro-Americans in Africa and also thoroughly supporting the freedom struggle for human rights of our people in this country was President Julius Nyerere. I was honored to spend three hours with him when I was in Dar es Salaam, Tanganyika, shortly before it became known as Tanzania."[79] After explaining how the rally's purpose was to show how internationalizing struggle opens up a window to new allies that could speed up "progress," he moved into a more explicit discussion of friendship and the challenges in distinguishing friend from foe in American society. This allowed Malcolm to centralize the press as a primary agent in making false friend/foe distinctions in its characterization of global geopolitical affairs.[80] To elaborate on the function of this "image-making press," he used the crisis situation in the Congo as an example.[81] "You and I should practice the habit of weighing people and weighing situations and weighing groups and weighing governments for ourselves," he told the crowd. "And don't let somebody else tell us who our enemies should be and who our friends should be."[82] He closed his speech by introducing Babu: "I am honored to call him my friend. He treated me as a brother when I was in Dar es Salaam. I met his family, I met his children—he's a family man. Most people don't think of revolutionaries as family men. All you see him in is his image on the battle line. But when you see him with his children and with his wife and that atmosphere at home, you realize that revolutionaries are human beings too. So here is a man who's not only a revolutionary, but he's a husband—he could be yours; he's a father—he could be yours; he's a brother—he could be yours. And I say he is ours: Sheik Babu."[83]

Based on Malcolm X's comments after Babu's speech, Babu relayed an overarching message of friendship by showing that as "long as we think we're over here in America isolated and all by ourselves and underdogs, then we'll always have that hat-in-hand begging attitude that the man loves to see us display." He continued: "But when we know that all of our people are behind us—as he [Babu] said, almost 500 million of us, we don't need to beg anybody. All we need to do is remind them what they did to us; that it's time for them to stop; that if they don't stop, we will stop them. Yes, we will stop them."[84] The FBI was particularly concerned with Malcolm X's contacts with African leaders. Reporting back to the FBI office in New York City, one informant noted that Babu told the crowd how "all black people were united in opposition to the Congo."[85] Following the rally, informants were urged to continue to attend these rallies and report back on the African leaders and other foreign delegates in attendance, including Babu, Ahmed Hassan of Sudan, and Ernesto "Che" Guevara of Cuba.[86]

The following day Babu was the featured guest speaker at the Manhattan Center organized by the May 2nd Movement, a "radical student peace organization." The flyer that advertised the event contained a photograph of Babu looking straight at the camera with his trademark grin and with a caption that read: "BABU! Leader of the Zanzibar Revolution Speaks on the Congo." Joining Babu that night on stage was the

The Seeds of Solidarity

African American poet and playwright LeRoi Jones, the novelist and biographer Truman Nelson, and the writer and literary critic Mark Schleifler. Babu's speech specifically recounted the history of slavery and colonialism in Zanzibar and the spontaneous revolution that transpired in 1964. It was a revolution, he claimed, that shook the Western world at its very foundations. In protesting against Western intervention in the Congo, Babu further framed Tshombe as an archetypical African enemy from within. As he explained, "Africa will never consent to Tshombe and if there any renegades on this issue among the leaders of Africa they will have to answer to African people in their own country."[87]

On December 15, Babu was the featured speaker once again at a rally cosponsored by the OAAU and the Harlem Progressive Labor Club led by William Epton, an African American communist heavily influenced by the Chinese revolution. One journalist noted that before a politically diverse, interracial crowd of "nationalists, socialists, Muslims, communists and Garveyites," Babu addressed the Zanzibar revolution and the Congo crisis in a way that made these political lines "vanish." OAAU member Peter Bailey's report on the speech was featured in the OAAU's journal *Blacklash*. According to Bailey, Babu was relentless in his attack on the United States. "Imperialist countries," Bailey claims Babu said, "just don't understand that the African countries are determined to plan their own destinies."[88] While Babu sought to highlight U.S. imperialism in Africa, Malcolm X used the Congo to craft an analysis of the press and its function in advancing a statist conception of the friend/foe binary that stood in sharp opposition to the kind of solidarity model he was formulating in order to "internationalize" the African American freedom struggle.

During the month of December, Babu and Malcolm had engaged in a public performance of political friendship, which aimed to create an idiom of mutual understanding between the African Diaspora and Africa. In private, they debated a host of issues. In fact, they met for the last time at Babu's hotel room in early January 1965. In all likelihood, Babu shared his concerns with Malcolm about the Zanzibar-Tanganyika union. Only much later, in the outline to his autobiography, did he criticize the union, calling it "rushed" and "ill-timed."[89] Such a discussion may have taken place that night in his hotel room. Joining Babu and Malcolm were LeRoi Jones, the playwright, poet, and activist who would later become a prominent black nationalist leader in the United States, and members of the Revolutionary Action Movement (RAM). For twelve hours, "from 8pm 'til 8am," they discussed how a united front against colonialism and imperialism could be forged and whether race or class was the defining characteristic of any freedom struggle.[90]

Although increasing friction mounted between Malcolm X and the NOI after Babu left New York City in January, Malcolm X remained preoccupied with making

39

clear distinctions between allies and enemies to a wide-ranging audience. "Brotherhood is a two-way street," he said in a speech at Harvard Law School. "Brotherhood should hinge upon the deeds and attitudes of a man."[91] A closer look at other speeches and interviews also reveal some noticeable shifts in Malcolm's view on the African American relationship to Africa. Firstly, he appears to have abandoned the political project of a mass exodus to Africa as articulated by the NOI, which he still endorsed between December 1963 and March 1964.[92] After his extensive travels abroad, however, Malcolm attempted to articulate a more abstract conception in its place, calling for African Americans to return back to Africa "spiritually, philosophically and psychologically."[93] This was neither a rejection of travel nor of permanent repatriation. Malcolm was prepared to reconsider Africa's place in the black political imagination without rejecting the value of a diaspora consciousness as a constitutive element in forging solidarity with Africans.

Malcolm X was most effective in making a sharp friend/foe distinction when addressing external forces, especially the United States. But when it came to making such an important distinction in the context of Africa, his thoughts read incomplete. He was full of praise for how travel "broadened" his politically thinking—for which his conversations with African heads of state were responsible. He praised Kwame Nkrumah (Ghana), Gamal Abdel Nasser (Egypt), Ahmed Ben Bella (Algeria), Jomo Kenyatta (Kenya), Ahmed Sékou Touré (Guinea), and Julius Nyerere (Tanzania), but for a different set of reasons. Methods of resistance adopted to win independence and domestic policies that empower African women were two prominent identifiers of friendly African states. To Malcolm X, Tanzania, specifically, was "one of the most militant and uncompromising" independent states in Africa "when it comes to the struggle for freedom for our people on the African continent, as well as over here and anywhere else on this earth."[94]

Clearly, the emergence of independent state disrupted how pan-Africanism as an intellectual project was imagined and as a political project was practiced, but Malcolm was either not fully prepared or inclined to critique nation state formation in a way that posed specific leaders (with the exception of Tshombe) in a negative light. Instead, Malcolm saw African Americans as more of an obstacle to building a solidarity movement with progressive African states because of the psychic violence inherent in their experience with transatlantic slavery. He was insistent on this point.

Because Africans on the continent were gaining their freedom "by any means necessary" at a faster rate than African Americans, Malcolm surmised that colonial representations of Africans as savages had a greater cultural and psychological effect on African Americans than Africans.[95] In a speech given at the London School of Economics on February 11, he called this process a "chain reaction" where African Americans internalized racist imagery of Africa/Africans to create a collective black inferiority complex. "You can't hate the land, your motherland, the place that you come from, and we can't hate Africa without ending up hating ourselves."[96] He closed his speech with one of his most forceful statements on diaspora consciousness as a precondition to solidarity with Africa: "The same beat, the same heart, the same pulse that moves the Black man on the African continent—despite the fact that four hundred years have separated us from the mother continent, and an ocean of water has separated us from that mother continent—still, the same pulse that beats in the Black man on the African continent today is beating in the heart of the Black man in North America, Central America, South America, and in the Caribbean. Many of them don't know, but it's true."[97] Three days later, Malcolm X's home was firebombed. This attack by the NOI, however, did not deter him from traveling to Detroit, where he admitted to "fanatically stressing" what he learned from conferring with Africans while traveling abroad: nothing but "warmth, friendship, sympathy and a desire to help."

Less than a week later, on February 21, Malcolm X was assassinated during an OAAU rally held at the Audubon Ballroom in Harlem.[98] Babu was in Shanghai on a diplomatic mission with President Nyerere when he heard the news. As he explained many years later, "It was the end of an existing epoch in the Afro-American struggle for justice and equality."[99] Messages of condolences were published in Tanzanian newspapers and the journals and newsletters of African liberation groups. The Kiswahili-speaking newspaper *Ngurumo* featured an article that explained Malcolm's death not in terms of his rift with NOI or his promotion of armed self-defense, but rather as a consequence of a culture of violence in a supposedly democratic society:

> Sasi iwapi demokrasi ya America? U wapi ustaarabu wa Waamerica? Wa kwana? Akae mahali pema Malcolm X na iendele jitahada ya kajipatia haki Wanegro.
>
> [Where is democracy now? Where is America's civilization? For killing each other? Rest in peace Malcolm X and African Americans keep on struggling for your rights.][100]

Similar African nationalist constructions of Malcolm X as a Third World revolutionary martyr came from African anticolonial nationalist groups based in Dar es Salaam. They too refused to explain away his death as a direct consequence of Malcolm's advocacy of violence. South Africa's African National Congress (ANC) issued a statement that recognized its ideological differences with Malcolm X, but also "recognized in him a militant fighter for the recognition of the black man as a man." The ANC statement continued: "He recognized the roots of the Afro-American in Africa, and sought to weld closer ties between the black man of America and ourselves in the struggle for freedom." The South West African People's Organization (SWAPO) referred to his death as a "tragedy" because he "fought for his people in a land whose very core of existence is foul play and the glorification of gun play the natural way of life [*sic*]."[101] While the Pan-African Congress (PAC) of South Africa described Malcolm as "another Lumumba," anticolonial activists of the Comoro Islands believed "with no shadow of a doubt" that his assassination was "a plot by the imperialists."[102]

The months of December and January were a climactic moment for Malcolm X and OAAU. Babu's presence brought legitimacy to him and his organization's transnational agenda. His critics, coming at him from various ideological angles, be it civil rights leaders or white and black leftists or the U.S. government, could not claim that Malcolm lacked international support. Furthermore, as William Sales has argued, Third World nations started to see Malcolm X as an "asset" because of the ways in which he supported these independent states within the United States, raising their profiles within progressive political circles. But one can only speculate on the kinds of collaborative projects that would have come out of the relationship between Malcolm X and the OAAU and the Tanzanian government after 1965. What is for certain, however, is that Babu emerged as a primary political contact for U.S. pan-Africanists seeking to travel to and build solidarity networks with the Tanzanian government and TANU during the years following Malcolm X's death.

The decade following Malcolm X's death saw black nationalism and pan-Africanism reach new heights in the United States. Stung by Malcolm's assassination and impatient with the slow pace of racial progress despite civil rights legislation, a new generation of black radicals emerged to champion Malcolm's call to psychologically "return to Africa," to travel to Africa and broaden their thinking, and to find ways to collaborate with like-minded Africans around issues of mutual concern. More importantly, they too looked to Tanzania, which was being seen as an independent nation on the vanguard of the pan-Africanism movement due to the 1966 military coup in Ghana that sent Kwame Nkrumah into exile, and the passing of the Arusha Declaration in Tanzania in 1967, which put the nation on a path toward socialism. This new wave of activists on the forefront of the Black Power movement sought to deepen their ties with Tanzania, believing that the country was on the cusp of radical sociopolitical transformation. In taking a closer look at nation-state formation in Tanzania and how it impacted African American pan-Africanists, a discussion of the Student Nonviolent Coordinating Committee (SNCC) is the subject of the next chapter.

Chapter 2

Growth and Conflict in SNCC-Tanzania Relations

Black Power means that Black People must redefine themselves, that they must tell their history and have pride in their culture ... Black Power is not "racialism"; it is not about preaching the inferiority of whites and black superiority. It does not preach the exclusion of whites; it is about "respect" and partnership of races on equal power. We in Tanzania (and I mean the workers and the peasants) must take Black Power very seriously.

—Abdulrahman Mohamed Babu, Government Minister,
United Republic of Tanzania (1964–1972)

Malcolm X's assassination left many African Americans shaken, confused, and angry. Among those significantly wounded by his death were the young black organizers of the Student Nonviolent Coordinating Committee (SNCC, pronounced "snick"). Founded in 1960 after students in Greensboro, North Carolina, initiated a nationwide sit-in movement against racial segregation, SNCC emerged to channel that energy, spirit, and courage exhibited by the nation's young people into grassroots community organizing and nonviolent direct action campaigns in the southern United States. Between 1960 and 1965, SNCC activists operated as "the shock troops" of the civil rights struggle, a multiracial organization largely committed to local leadership development and empowerment, racial equality, and liberal civil rights reform. SNCC's relationship with Malcolm X grew

43

Chapter Two

over this time period. In the summer of 1964, SNCC leaders ran into Malcolm X while touring East Africa.[1] In that same year, Malcolm X's OAAU invited SNCC activist Fannie Lou Hamer to speak to the Harlem community. A year later, SNCC invited Malcolm X to speak to five hundred youth activists in Selma in February, three weeks before his assassination. His ability to galvanize and inspire southern African Americans with his message of armed self-defense and ties to northern urban ghettos interested SNCC. His pan-Africanist vision appealed to SNCC as well. Cleveland Sellars, a SNCC program director and early proponent of black nationalism within the organization, reflected on Malcolm's impact on SNCC in his autobiography *The River of No Return*: "SNCC members were becoming increasingly aware of the international implications of domestic black oppression. Malcolm X had a lot to do with this new awareness. Although we didn't have much personal contact with him, his ideas about the international struggle for human rights made a big impression on our thinking."[2] Sellars went on further to express his shock when he learned of Malcolm X's death, writing that his "charisma and brilliant insights" would have made him one of the "first men in history to lead a multi-continental revolutionary movement." By 1965, the influence of Malcolm X's political ideas on SNCC was more evident as SNCC activists frequently studied and discussed Malcolm's published speeches. In the aftermath of his death, SNCC would try to think critically about drawing a connection between the African American freedom struggle in the United States and African liberation. And like Malcolm X, the organization would come to view Tanzania as a vital ally in its effort to internationalize the U.S. black freedom struggle. Stokely Carmichael and James Forman—two prominent SNCC leaders—undertook this task of being the faces of SNCC's attempt to conceptualize and implement the organization's pan-Africanist agenda. Forman's efforts to build a sustainable, international office that led to SNCC's participation in a United Nations conference on apartheid and colonialism in Africa, the setting up of a technical-skill assistance program with the Tanzanian government, and then later Carmichael's visit to Tanzania offer three examples of how the fledgling Black Power movement attempted to forge a working relationship with the Tanzanian government and TANU Party.

Despite inroads made in civil rights legislation like the Civil Rights Act of 1964 and the Voting Rights Act of 1965 through nonviolent direct action, black independent political party formations on a local level, and mass voter registration, a change in attitude toward this tactical approach, combined with a growing sense of disillusionment with the federal government, was boldly expressed at the Meredith March Against Fear in June 1966. After being arrested again—his twenty-seventh time over the course of a six-year period—for protesting against racial inequality, Carmichael emerged from a Mississippi jailhouse to address a crowd of six hundred marchers and civil rights supporters gathered at Broad Street Park in Greenwood. "This is the twenty-seventh time that I've been arrested. I ain't going to jail no more. I ain't going to jail no more . . . We outnumber the whites in this county; we want Black Power. That's what we want: Black Power."[3]

This slogan would profoundly change the direction of the black freedom movement. The speech, and most important, the positive response from the crowd, laid the basis for the struggle over the meaning of Black Power—a meaning inextricably tied to understanding the function of race and racism in American society. From a national perspective, Black Power was defined as political, economic, and cultural self-determination through black-run institutions. From an international perspective, Black Power was conceptualized as an ideology and movement of solidarity aligned with Third World struggles against imperialism in Latin America, Asia, and most importantly, Africa.[4] In the midst of this heightened militancy, SNCC was undergoing many changes from within. Problems emerged, however, over the question of Black Power and the implications of its official adoption for SNCC's future. The controversial election of Carmichael as SNCC chairman in May 1966 and the banning of white membership in December 1966 provided some answers.

SNCC's radicalization was not only a product of their work organizing in black communities in the Deep South but also a direct result of their interest in world affairs. Could anticolonial nationalist movements and Third World governments serve as a potential source of new allies to compensate for the loss of domestic support from white liberals, the Left, and moderate black civil rights leaders who all viewed Black Power as a dangerous expression of anti-white racist violence? Throughout its transition from civil rights to a Black Power organization, SNCC struggled to reach a consensus on what constituted an effective strategy of transnational alliance building. This was to change in May 1967. At a national meeting to further discuss the practical meaning of Black Power, SNCC also addressed the need to craft a clear-cut foreign policy agenda, which produced two important outcomes. SNCC decided to apply for nongovernmental organization status on the United Nations Economic and Security Council, a decision that sought to give SNCC greater legitimacy in formal international-relations diplomatic processes. The other decision was to form the International Affairs Commission (IAC) to better coordinate SNCC's internationalist activities. Headed by James Forman, the IAC was designed to "inject an anti-imperialist position not only in SNCC but into the black movement as a whole."[5]

By 1967 James Forman was a seasoned SNCC veteran known for his sense of discipline. Prior to joining SNCC, he had served in the Korean War, enrolled at a number of universities to pursue a Bachelor of Arts degree, taught in Chicago public schools, and published articles on civil rights activism for the *Chicago Defender*. In his role as the executive secretary of SNCC between 1961 and 1965, Forman strengthened SNCC's organizational capacity by providing logistical support to fieldworkers, paying bills, and expanding the national office by hiring and training staff members. He stepped down from this position in 1965 due to exhaustion and a desire to study revolutionary theory. Studying the works of Lenin, Fanon, Mao, among other revolutionary theorists, during his brief sabbatical from SNCC occupied his time, leading him to come to the conclusion that the organization needed to have a clear class analysis on the nature of black oppression, especially if it claimed to be the voice of Third World opposition from within the United States. In addition, SNCC needed to actively participate in multistate institutions and their anticolonialist initiatives. Thus, IAC set up its office on Fifth Avenue in Manhattan to ensure consistent access to the United Nations headquarters and the Third World diplomats and activists who came through its doors.

SNCC's plan to gain a foothold at the UN occurred right at the time when Tanzania had gained a significant amount of authority over matters of African liberation within both the UN and the Organization of African Unity (OAU). Under Nyerere's leadership as president, the Tanzanian government carried out an aggressive foreign-policy campaign focused on "positive" nonalignment and African unity. The consolidation of Tanzania into a one-party state after the drafting of a new constitution in 1965 accorded Nyerere with a number of executive privileges and powers, allowing him to play active leadership roles in both TANU and the government, especially in shaping their ideological and pragmatic approaches to international affairs.[6] Although foreign policy ideas had to go through a set of state institutions, Nyerere faced little opposition from within in addressing a continental political landscape punctuated not only by the emergence of more independent African nations but also by military coups, post-independence civil wars, and the continued entrenchment of colonialism in Portuguese-ruled territories and apartheid in South Africa.

Two of many bold and fearless foreign-policy actions of the TANU government that best illustrate Nyerere's commitment to the principle of liberation no matter the consequences occurred during 1965 and 1966. In November 1965, the white minority-led government in Rhodesia, a self-governing British colonial territory since 1923, passed the Unilateral Declaration of Independence (UDI), an attempt to establish an independent nation that would keep the majority black African population in a subordinate position. At an OAU meeting held in Addis Ababa on December 2, Nyerere responded to this new development by calling on all OAU member states to break off diplomatic relations with Britain for not intervening in Rhodesia. The seriousness with which Nyerere took the proposal was driven home two weeks later when Tanzania matched its rhetoric with action by severing its diplomatic ties with Britain. "Africa maintains that Southern Rhodesia is at present a colony of the United Kingdom, and that ultimate responsibility for events there resides, in consequence, with the Government of the United Kingdom." He continued in an address to the National Assembly: "Britain has not shown serious determination either to get rid of those in Southern Rhodesia who have usurped British power, or to replace them by representatives of the people. For it is not the independence of Rhodesia that Africa is complaining about; it is independence under a racialist minority government."[7] To Nyerere, this issue was about the principle of anticolonialism and African unity. By severing ties with its former colonizer, Nyerere showed that Tanzania would not conform to standard behaviors of nonconfrontational diplomacy, especially concerning causes that represent a "betrayal of our country and the cause we are fighting for."[8]

Tanzania's leadership role in the continental pan-Africanism movement was strengthened through its participation as a member state in the OAU. Because of its geographical proximity to southern and central Africa and because of the absence of internal political disorder, Tanzania had been the headquarters of the OAU Liberation Committee since the OAU's founding in May 1963. By 1965, liberation movements had either sprung up or gathered strength in South Africa, Namibia, Mozambique, Angola, and Southern and Northern Rhodesia, transforming Tanzania into a vital frontline state that acted as a rear base for military operations. ANC, PAC, SWAPO, MPLA, FRELIMO, ZAPU, and ZANU camps were spread out over eight regions of the country while administrative offices were set up in Dar es Salaam. Despite Nyerere's misgivings about the effectiveness of the OAU in aiding the liberation movements due to the inability of member states to cooperate with each other in favor of competing for economic concessions from non-African, "wealthy" nations, he invested heavily in the institution with the hope that, gradually over time, the OAU would serve as a means through which member states would surrender their sovereignty in "favor of an All-African Government" envisioned with the framework of a federated state. At least this was Nyerere's attitude in the summer of 1965, when he penned the essay "The Nature and Requirements of African Unity": "For the purposes of African Unity what matters is the existence of one or many bodies in ultimate control of all relationships with outside powers. While national sovereignty persists there will be, as at present, many ultimate sources of power in relation to the external world. That is the practical meaning of African sovereignty. When Africa is united there can only be one source of ultimate power as far as non-African powers are concerned; national sovereignties have thus ceased to exist, and been replaced by sovereignty of Africa as a single unit, incorporating all the separate units . . . As far as the outside world is concerned Africa, too, must have a single source of power, and a single spokesman on external Affairs—The Government of Africa."[9] Nyerere's pragmatism, however, compelled him to view the realization of a "United States of Africa" as a gradual process of development. The first step was eradicating all remaining vestiges of colonial rule in Africa. As one of nine member states on the Liberation Committee, Tanzania positioned itself in the vanguard, attempting to fulfill a set of roles and responsibilities that included mobilizing resources for liberation groups, providing financial and material support for liberation groups, assessing and assisting the performance of liberation groups, and waging diplomatic offensives on behalf of these nationalist movements through conferences, international tours, and press and radio agencies. After the overthrow of Ben Bella in Algeria in June 1965 and Nkrumah in Ghana in 1966, Nyerere's leadership role took on added significance as a result of the loss of these two prominent leaders in the pan-Africanism movement that rippled across Africa and her diaspora.

The coup in Ghana, in particular, was a devastating blow. Between 1951 and 1966, the diaspora played an active, albeit restrictive, role in the decolonization movement in the Gold Coast and postcolonial nation-building in Ghana.[10] For pan-Africanists the world over, the coup forced them to think seriously about its implications for the pan-Africanism movement as well the diaspora's role in it. The overthrow of Nkrumah also marked the demise of Ghana's leadership role in the movement, which left a "great, aching void in Africa—an emptiness in which the masses are turning around and around."[11] Tanzania was regarded as the obvious choice to replace Ghana as the "matrix of pan-Africanism"—a responsibility Nyerere was more than willing to embrace while fully aware of the potential consequences. "When Ben Bella and Nkrumah were overthrown, the exploiters and enemies of Africa, the imperialists applauded . . . The freedom fighters of Africa will remain based in Tanzania until each oppressed territory on the continent is liberated"[12] According to TANU, the coup had made Tanzania more vulnerable to Cold War aggression from the West. "We are quite conscious of the fact," read one editorial in the *Nationalist*, "that now Dr. Nkrumah has been removed from the African political scene, all forces of disruption will be aimed at and concentrated upon Tanzania, because this republic's leader and Ghana's Nkrumah were two of the most painful thorns in the imperialists' flesh."[13] Military coups had swept across the continent during the first giant wave of decolonization, taking from the pan-Africanism movement three of its leaders: Patrice Lumumba of the Congo, Ben Bella of Algeria, and Nkrumah of Ghana. The loss of these three was a painful reminder to pan-Africanists of the significant challenges that lay ahead.[14]

If the Ghana coup meant that Tanzania was one of the few remaining independent African states with the leadership capacity to assume a more prominent role in the pan-Africanism movement, then the passing of the Arusha Declaration cemented this position. On January 29, 1967, the TANU National Executive Committee, which was responsible for policymaking, drafted the Arusha Declaration, a document detailing the socialist principles and values that were to guide the country towards postcolonial liberation. Six days later, the document was published in English- and Kiswahili-speaking newspapers, and a celebratory mass march and rally was held in Dar es Salaam. With Nyerere serving as the primary architect of this historic document, "Ujamaa na Kujitegemea," Kiswahili for "Socialism and Self-Reliance," was the name given to this socialist-oriented economic initiative.

Nyerere developed both an intellectual and pragmatic interest in the general concept of socialism during his time spent as a student in Scotland, where he was drawn to the Fabian school of thought. Later on, René Dumont, a French agronomist who wrote extensively on agricultural reform, influenced him as well.[15] And ever since his visit to China in 1964, Nyerere had become an active observer and student of the Chinese revolution. However, in a TANU pamphlet published in 1962 that he authored, titled "Ujamaa—The Basis of African Socialism," Nyerere identified an African version of socialism rooted in precolonial societies. In "traditional" African societies, he argued, there were no class tensions or conflict since "idea of 'class' or 'caste'" was nonexistent.[16] For Nyerere, "true socialism" was an "attitude of mind." "It is therefore up to the people of Tanganyika—the peasants, the wage earners, the students, the leaders, all of us—to make sure that this socialist attitude of mind is not lost through the temptations to personal gain which may come our way as individuals, or through the temptation to look on the good of the whole community as of secondary importance to the interests of our own particular group."[17] By providing a "definition of socialism in Tanzanian terms," Nyerere hoped to differentiate it from capitalism and European forms of socialism as a way to highlight its distinctiveness and reinforce Tanzania's status as a nonaligned nation. African Socialism "is opposed to capitalism which seeks to build a happy society on the basis of exploitation of man by man; and it is equally opposed to doctrinaire socialism which seeks to build its happy society on a philosophy of inevitable conflict between man and man."[18]

A number of national development issues factored into Nyerere's decision to steer the government, party, and people in an African socialist direction. Firstly, it was a direct response to a stagnant economy. Despite the implementation of minor socialist-oriented initiatives such as marketing cooperatives and public ownership of land and small companies, Nyerere was following a policy of capitalist development that ensured the country's subordinate position in the world capitalist economy of "exploitation of man by man." Decreases in the prices of its primary exports, limited industrialization to process its own raw materials, and a reliance on private investment led to virtually no increases in national income.[19] Secondly, Nyerere was concerned that the absence of a coherent socialist ideology to guide party leaders could facilitate internal class tensions within the country. The attitudes and behaviors of government and party leaders and members—their visibly affluent lifestyles and increasing support of an anti-Asian Africanization policy—suggested a crisis in political leadership characterized by a disconnection with the peasants and workers.[20] The Arusha Declaration of 1967 was a five-part document that takes into account these concerns over postcolonial underdevelopment and the lack of principled and committed leadership.

In requiring all of its citizens of every race, ethnicity, and class to adopt a "socialist attitude of mind" based on precolonial systems of democracy and communal social relations, Nyerere hoped this would foment a nationalist work ethic and loyalty to the state. In the declaration, the state was identified as the leading instigator for bringing about this imagined egalitarian socialist society of the future. The two last points of "The TANU Creed," part 1 of the declaration, read:

> (h) That in order to ensure economic justice the state must have effective control over the principal means of production; and (i) That it is the responsibility of the state to intervene actively in the economic life of the nation so as to ensure the well-being of all citizens, and so as to prevent the exploitation of one person by another or one group by another, and so as to prevent the accumulation of wealth to an extent which is inconsistent with the existence of a classless society.[21]

Nyerere realized that the attainment of these objectives relied heavily on the actions and attitudes of government officials and TANU Party members, and therefore introduced a leadership code of ethics that prohibited them from owning private property and shares in any corporation and holding directorships in private businesses. "The first duty of a TANU member is to accept these socialist principles, and to live his own life in accordance with them."[22] A "genuine TANU leader," he surmised, "will not live off the sweat of another man, nor commit any feudalistic or capitalistic actions . . . it is difficult for leaders to promote its growth if they do not themselves accept it."[23] The basic idea, then, was to provide ideological clarity and direction for the one-party state, to mobilize popular support, and to inspire the national citizenry to embrace the "socialistic" cultural values of "traditional African society" in order to build a modern African nation. In economic terms, this meant privileging the needs of the peasants through a policy that favored radical agrarian reform over urban industrialization. This emphasis on making a modernized agricultural sector the economic foundation of the nation would allow for the equal distribution of wealth. However, the Arusha Declaration was solely concerned with domestic policy. It also contained explicit positions on pan-Africanism. In addition to maintaining "the independence of this country and the freedom of its peoples," TANU would also "co-operate with all political parties in Africa engaged in the liberation of all Africa" and "see that the Government co-operates with other states in Africa in bringing about African unity."²⁴ These aims and objectives, as laid out by Nyerere for TANU members to follow, opened the gates for Tanzania to confront the issue of apartheid in South Africa.

Tanzania's approach to the OAU mirrored its approach to the United Nations. In the past, the Nyerere-led TANU Party used the United Nations on three separate occasions in the 1950s to lay the groundwork for a comparatively smooth transition process from colony to independent nation.²⁵ Nyerere wanted to continue to use the institution to the benefit of African liberation in the postcolonial era, hoping to wage part of its diplomatic fight against colonialism in Africa through the UN's Special Committee on Apartheid. Formed in 1963, this committee was designed to draw the world's attention to the ill effects of apartheid policies on black Africans and the violent nature of state repression against anti-apartheid activists and organizations, to isolate the apartheid government, and to foment a worldwide anti-apartheid solidarity movement. Chairing the committee was John Malecela, Tanzania's permanent representative to the UN. As a recipient of higher-education degrees from prestigious schools in India (Bombay University), England (Cambridge University), and the United States (University of Texas) between 1958 and 1962, Malecela engaged in TANU nationalist politics from afar, eventually joining TANU upon his return to Tanganyika in 1962. He was appointed by Nyerere as Tanzania's UN ambassador in 1964, a position he held for four formative years in Tanzania's foreign-policy history.

In May 1967, around the time SNCC had formed its international commission, Malecela helped to draft a UN proposal that called for a series of seminars that envisaged providing an "opportunity for consultations on means to intensify international efforts to eradicate apartheid, racial discrimination and colonialism in southern Africa."²⁶ Approved by the UN General Assembly, the seminars were scheduled for July and August. Fifty independent state and nongovernmental organizations were invited to Kitwe, Zambia, for the seminar.²⁷ On the list of NGO invitees were the most prominent U.S. civil rights and Black Power organizations, including the National Association for the Advancement of Colored People (NAACP), the Southern Christian Leadership Conference (SCLC), and the Congress of Racial Equality (CORE). Out of these organizations, Malecela chose SNCC to deliver a paper on the plight of African Americans in an effort to engage "militant elements in the United States' integration movement in larger international aspects of the drive against apartheid, racial discrimination, particularly in Africa."²⁸

The decision to allow SNCC this opportunity was a historic one. It would mark the first time in UN history when an African American–led political organization was permitted to speak before an international audience of independent states and anticolonial liberation groups about the state of American race relations in the context of the black freedom struggle. It was a decision met with hostility from civil rights organizations and the U.S. government, but for divergent reasons. To civil rights organizations like the NAACP and SCLC, SNCC's new black politics did not reflect the opinions of the majority of African Americans, nor did its strategy of liberation, which they believed advocated anti-white violence. To the U.S. government, the decision to allow SNCC to present a position paper that articulated its radical analysis of the racial problem in the United States to an international audience gave some legitimacy to the argument that racial oppression in the United States deserved serious international inquiry and possible interventionist action.

It is not altogether clear as to why Malecela identified SNCC as the featured nongovernmental organization at the seminars. Perhaps it was Malecela's encounters with racism as a university student in Texas that made him more sympathetic to SNCC's militancy. In looking at SNCC's and Tanzania's foreign-policy objectives, it is clear they shared a lot in common. They both held strong stances against the Vietnam War and, most important, they both were die-hard supporters of African decolonization and African unity. Moreover, SNCC prioritized internationalist work in such a way that it made greater inroads in the Third World political community than its civil rights counterparts. Whatever Malecela's justifications, the implications of the decision were not lost on Forman, who saw it as a chance for SNCC to engage in concrete internationalist work within the structures of state-to-state relations, a growing feature of pan-Africanism in the 1960s that placed nongovernmental organizations in positions to further their respective causes, albeit in subordinate ones.

Forman and Harold Moore, one of SNCC's lawyers and an IAC staff member, were the primary SNCC delegates to the UN Special Committee's seminar on apartheid. On the seminar's second day, following brief introductory remarks by Malecela, Forman delivered one of SNCC's most significant statements in the history of the organization. In a position paper titled "The Indivisible Struggle against Racism, Colonialism and Apartheid," Forman compares the black freedom struggle in the United States to the anti-apartheid struggle in South Africa, finding a common experience of racist oppression and state repression: "We can understand South Africa because we have seen the inside of the jails of Mississippi and Alabama and have been herded behind barbed-wire enclosures, attacked by police dogs, and set upon with electric prods—the American equivalent of the sjambok. There is no difference between the sting of being called a "kaffir" in South Africa and a "nigger" in the U.S.A. As the vanguard of the struggle against racism in America, SNCC is not unfamiliar with the problems of South Africa."[29] The lack of mutual understanding about their respective struggles was not as troubling as the threat of U.S. imperialism. Forman went on to argue this point, claiming that U.S. military interventions in Africa and Southeast Asia were the salient feature of U.S.

foreign policy. Indeed, SNCC questioned the capacity of the United States to serve as the disseminator of democracy abroad given its crisis in race relations and its passive approach to racial justice at home. Although remaining conscious of the urgency to address global racial oppression, SNCC recommended a gradual course of action that put the onus on the agency of the UN. For example, its first recommendation was to place decolonization on the "provisional agenda of the next session of the General Assembly" and "strenuously urge that a seminar be convened and held to study and investigate the nexus between racial, political, economic and cultural discrimination in the States, and racial discrimination in South Africa."[30]

SNCC's position paper did not deviate from the radical positions taken by other representatives at the seminar.[31] The tactic of nonviolence was routinely rejected in favor of revolutionary violence as the only viable option of anticolonial resistance in Africa. The U.S. government also did not escape scrutiny; its delegation was forced to confront a constant barrage of attacks over its role in supporting apartheid.[32] Forman was particularly enamored with the actions of Malecela, whom he described as a "man of tremendous energy and organizational ability" based on his performance at the seminar.[33] Malecela scolded U.S. officials on two separate occasions. The first came when a U.S. official claimed that sending aid to the victims of the Sharpeville Massacre of 1961 was a waste of time. And the other scolding was for the United States' reluctance to carry out a UN-sanctioned voluntary arms embargo. Malecela, Forman noted in his journal, delivered a "vicious counter-attack" that challenged the United States not as chairman of the committee but as a representative of Tanzania: "He says he hopes to avoid too much polemics, but he hopes there will not be a suppression of the facts."[34]

In the immediate aftermath of the seminar, Forman and Moore visited Dar es Salaam as invited guests of the TANU government. For Forman, the nation-building atmosphere of Dar es Salaam was electric as a palpable optimism in Tanzania's socialist future was hard to deny in the wake of the Arusha Declaration. "Our first days in Dar es Salaam lifted our spirits, as we wanted to remain in Africa for the rest of our lives," he wrote in his journal. "Everywhere people were working hard to build Tanzania, and we wanted to help. Earlier that year Tanzania issued the Arusha Declaration, calling Tanzania a country trying to build socialism. This declaration was under intense discussion in political circles. The freedom with which people talked socialism, armed struggle, the liberation of Africa, was a liberation in itself for Howard and me, coming as we did from the repressive atmosphere of the United States."[35] The romantic feelings Forman harbored for Tanzania were not unique. In the course of six years, from 1961 to 1967, Tanzania came to represent a political homeland for the African Diaspora. However, Forman's romanticism was short-lived. When he learned of accusations that directly associated the African American presence in Africa with CIA covert operations, he was emboldened to seek out other practical ways to collaborate with African governments in order to combat this false perception.

During his tour of Tanzania, Forman met privately with Nyerere to discuss the potential for other collaborative projects between SNCC and the government. At the meeting, he proposed the Afro-American Skills Bank, a transnational initiative that would address Tanzania's skilled labor shortage by recruiting African American skilled technicians to live and work in Tanzania on temporary government contracts. This initiative's ultimate aim was to help break Tanzania's dependence on white expatriates and Western aid agencies. The lack of skilled labor was regarded as "one of the most politically explosive problems confronting the new government,"[36] forcing the president to decide whether hiring Africans with inadequate technical-skills experience—a necessary policy of "racial discrimination" known as Africanization—was the correct approach to nation-building. "In Tanganyika it is not much help producing a scheme which requires an army of skilled or educated agricultural workers, because we do not have them now, and despite all of our efforts, will not have them for many years to come," Nyerere admitted in a speech delivered at a UN conference on Food and Agriculture held in Rome in November 1963. "Every change also needs skilled and educated power for both the administrative and technical work."[37] Four years later in 1967, little had changed, as Nyerere refused to follow a policy of rapid Africanization, which he believed was extremely impractical and unwise. The recruitment of African American skilled technicians with pan-Africanist commitments was one way to stem the tide of criticism directed at Nyerere from within the country for not adequately addressing the legacy of racism brought about by colonialism. To Forman, the skills bank idea was not about "control and co-optation," but rather a clear demonstration of the possibilities of "revolutionary unity." Not only would this project give African Americans an opportunity to sharpen their anti-imperialist and nationalist perspectives by living and working in Tanzania, but it would also contribute to Tanzania's socialist-oriented nation-building project. Furthermore, it would demonstrate to African skeptics wary of the African American presence in Africa their loyalty to postcolonial state-driven nation-building. Nyerere seemed to share Forman's enthusiasm for the project, and together they came to a "verbal agreement" of a partnership between SNCC and the President's Office.

Back in the United States, SNCC attempted to foment an anti-apartheid movement led by African Americans and implement the technical skills project with the aid of the Tanzanian government. In July 1967, SNCC sent a statement to the Africa and Asia Missions to the United Nations, requesting their moral support and that they formally condemn the governments of the United States, South Africa, and Portugal "on the grounds that racism in this country is a matter of international—not merely domestic—concern."[38] One month later, SNCC sent a letter to Oliver Tambo, head of South Africa's African National Congress (ANC) in exile in Tanzania, pledging its "moral support" for taking up arms against the apartheid regime. Angered over U.S. corporate investments in South Africa, the letter also informed Tambo of SNCC's intention to mobilize "Overseas Africans," especially in the city of Detroit, Michigan, the capital of the automobile industry, to "not buy new General Motors cars for the year 1968."[39] "While we are aware there are other United States companies operating in South Africa," the letter further stipulated, "we believe by calling for a selective boycott of 1968 General Motors cars we may in some small manner assist the struggle for the armed liberation of South Africa."[40] This call for a boycott was immediately followed up by another SNCC statement addressed to African Americans, urging that they perform specific acts of cultural and political solidarity with Africa. In addition to collecting and sending money and medical supplies to African liberation groups based in Tanzania and educating the public on U.S. corporate investments in South Africa, African Americans could express their cultural pride in Africa by wearing "national African dress" and going to the UN to observe the discussions on world affairs.

SNCC's efforts to internationalize the U.S. black freedom struggle were hampered by the enormous energies it took to confront both a multi-headed backlash as well as internal discord. The vilification of SNCC in the mainstream media showed no signs of abating. The lack of funds and other resources for programmatic expansion and the defection of activists also affected SNCC in critical ways. As civil rights leaders and white liberals continued to distance themselves from SNCC, the FBI intensified its covert campaign, leading to the arrest of SNCC's newly minted chairman, H. Rap Brown, for violating federal firearms laws and inciting "riots" in Dayton, Ohio, and Cambridge, Maryland, in 1967.[41] These developments, however, did not seem to severely damage its relations with the Tanzanian government. When Brown was permitted by federal authorities to travel to New York, his first stop was the diplomats' lounge of the UN to meet with Malecela. Initially, Brown was prevented from entering the lounge by security until Malecela intervened to chastise the guards before embracing the "fiery" SNCC leader before a curious media crowd. Malecela's subsequent statements to the press that his meeting with Brown was purely a social visit fell on deaf ears. A *Los Angeles Times* article described Malecela as one of the "more militant African diplomats." It went on to suggest that SNCC's diplomatic ties with African nations such as Tanzania could alter UN political landscape and culture, "counter balance the right wing campaigns of support for white supremacy regimes in South Africa," and "encourage more radical solutions to U.S. race relations."[42]

The Afro-American Skills Bank initiative helped to breathe new life into SNCC's national organizing efforts. The process began with a propaganda campaign. In one of three statements issued on African decolonization, SNCC, referring again to African Americans as "Overseas Africans," evidence of its growing diaspora consciousness and the importance placed on nomenclature to the movement, urged African Americans to learn "industrial skills" in fields such as engineering and medicine and take them to struggling African nations. "We must use the white man's schools to help our brothers in Africa," the statement read.[43] IAC also began recruiting African Americans with technical skills in and around New York City. Its first step was to identify community organizations and individuals who could assist in planning and recruitment. However, much to Forman's frustration, the absence of initiative on the part of the Tanzanian government halted SNCC's efforts to get the project off the ground. The IAC's response to letters of inquiry from potential recruits about the state of the exchange project suggests a complete breakdown of communication between SNCC and the government.[44]

Forman very much wanted the Afro-American Skills Bank to begin by June 1968, but refused to begin the application until word from the Nyerere administration. It never came. In one last-ditch effort to save the project from being shelved, Forman wrote an urgent letter to Abdulrahman Mohamed Babu, a close friend of the late Malcolm X, asking for any updates of importance. Ultimately, Forman's reports of the "fantastically favorable reaction" to the project among African Americans did little in reopening lines of communication between the two sides. Yet even if the Tanzanian government took on a more proactive role, it is clear that the project's success rested on SNCC's shoulders. Given that local SNCC offices were shutting down at a rapid pace by 1967 due to the depletion of funds and the intensification of state and local repression, it is highly unlikely that SNCC could have implemented and sustained the program on a nationwide level. By December, there were only ten SNCC offices in operation, and most of them were in a state of disarray.[45]

The Afro-American Skills Bank can be seen in part as a continuation of an ongoing but tentative process of transnational dialogue between the Tanzanian government and the Black Power movement in the United States that started with the efforts of Malcolm X and the Organization of Afro-American Unity (OAAU) in late 1964. Coming from the top echelons of the government, Nyerere's initial receptiveness to the project revealed the seriousness with which he viewed African Americans as an alternative source of foreign technical assistance. However, it was not until 1970 that an actual program of this kind was implemented through the auspices of the Pan-African Skills Project led by Irving Davis, a former SNCC activist. The reasons as to why there was no follow-up by the government remain unclear. In *In Search of Power: African Americans in the Era of Decolonization*, Brenda Gayle Plummer argues that the skills bank was not implemented due to a combination of negative press coverage of SNCC's Black Power politics and the TANU government's reluctance to devote its resources to "utopian" pan-Africanist projects with nongovernmental U.S. black political organizations.[46] While this may be true, Forman refused to give credence to any of these factors. By January 1968, he was convinced that Stokely Carmichael's controversial visit to Tanzania in October 1967 caused irreparable damage to SNCC's relations with the Tanzanian government.[47] This sentiment was echoed a year later in a letter from African American journalist Richard Gibson, who was living in Dar es Salaam at the time of Carmichael's stay: "I am told, however, that President Nyerere holds a very low view of Stokely, as a result of Stokely's call on the President when Stokely last visited Dar."[48]

Born in Port-au-Spain, Trinidad, on June 29, 1941, Stokely Carmichael immigrated to the United States when he was eleven years old, spending the remainder of his teenage years in New York City, where his exposure to the black protest tradition provided the basis for his early political development. In 1960, at age nineteen, he enrolled at Howard University, majored in philosophy, and joined the SNCC-affiliated Nonviolent Action Group (NAG), a student organization that engaged in civil rights protests throughout the D.C. area. While being mentored intellectually by an array of Howard professors such as Sterling Brown, Charles Hamilton, Alan Locke, Ralph Bunche, Rayford Logan, Chancellor Williams, William Leo Hansberry, E. Franklin Frazier, and Toni Morrison, Carmichael was also active in a southern-based civil rights movement that had gained tremendous momentum.[49] For example, he participated in the Freedom Rides, a desegregation campaign of the public transportation system in the southern United States coordinated by the Congress of Racial Equality (CORE). Carmichael became a full-time member of SNCC after he graduated from Howard in 1964, earning a reputation as a gifted organizer through his work with the Mississippi Freedom Democratic Party (MFDP) in Mississippi and with the Lowndes County Freedom Organization (LCFO), the original Black Panther Party, in Alabama. When he was elected to the post of SNCC's national chairman in 1966, Carmichael embraced his role as the voice of SNCC, embarking on a national tour to promote and explain SNCC's Black Power position through press conferences, speaking engagements at U.S. colleges and universities, protest rallies, meetings, and political conferences, oftentimes ignoring SNCC protocols. Within a relatively short time span, he became a national and international celebrity—labeled the heir to Malcolm X in the mainstream media.[50]

Before 1966, Carmichael held a sense of optimism for racial justice in the context of American democracy. By the close of 1966, he had come to believe that such an outcome was not possible. The United States, he argued, was an empire—the leading imperialist nation in the world. Thus, the U.S. government was incapable of acting as an agency of democracy and racial progress. In holding such radical beliefs, Carmichael spent the entire year of 1966 devoted primarily to attacking U.S. imperialism by drawing attention to the United States' involvement in the Vietnam War. He also weighed in on the pros and cons of interracial alliances, discussed the bankruptcy of racial integration and the tactic of nonviolence, and addressed the state of black oppression in northern urban ghettos.[51] January 1967 marked the end of his tenure as SNCC chairman, leaving him with more freedom to pursue on-the-ground grassroots organizing in his adopted home of Washington, DC. At the same time, he was also interested in the Third World moment, and the only plausible and effective way to connect with other struggles for liberation was through international travel. Like Malcolm X, he would travel extensively, visiting Puerto Rico, Canada, England, Cuba, China, Vietnam, Guinea, Algeria, and Tanzania over a ten-month period in 1967. International travel proved to be an incredible source of radicalization. "For me," Carmichael later recalled in his autobiography, "international struggle became tangible, a human reality, faces, stories no longer an abstraction."[52] His visit to Guinea, in particular, was incredibly important as he was taken under the wings of President Ahmed Sékou Touré and former Ghana president Kwame Nkrumah (who was exiled there after the 1966 coup). He met with them daily to discuss pan-Africanism, Black Power, and guerrilla warfare in Africa. During these meetings, which largely served as political education classes, Nkrumah urged Carmichael to visit Tanzania to gain a better understanding of the realities of anticolonial nationalist struggles and postcolonial state-building.[53]

Piero Gleijeses's *Conflicting Missions: Havana, Washington, and Africa, 1959-1976* maintains that Carmichael met with Amilcar Cabral, the military leader of the African Party for Independence of Guinea-Bissau and Cape Verde (PAIGC) during his visit in Conakry, Guinea's capital, where they came to an agreement to send African American volunteers to West Africa to fight with PAIGC freedom fighters on the stipulation they receive training in guerrilla warfare in Tanzania.[54] But according to Carmichael, it was the Pan-African Congress (PAC) not the PAIGC he intended to link up with, since it was the only African liberation group to respond to the letters of inquiry he sent while visiting Algeria. Whether it was PAC or PAIGC, Carmichael's mission was clear: he was en route to Tanzania to get President Nyerere's permission to allow him to "join one of the liberation groups" and participate in the pan-Africanism movement in Africa as a "frontline fighter."[55] Yet as a SNCC representative, Carmichael was expected to strengthen the "active relationship" between the organization and the Tanzanian government and TANU Party and to "tirelessly" show the U.S. Black Power movement's relevance to the struggles against imperialism in the Third World. It was a task that Carmichael completed with mixed results.

While the Tanzanian press did not offer extensive coverage of Malcolm X's visit in 1964, it took the opposite approach in its coverage of Carmichael, an indication of Tanzania's growing interest in the black nationalist views emanating from the African Diaspora. Part of the reason for this shift in perception had to do with the boost in coverage of U.S. race relations in Tanzania's most prominent English-speaking newspapers: the *Nationalist* and *Tanganyika Standard*. Prior to Malcolm X's visit, both were drawn to the nonviolent and multiracial character of the civil rights movement. Articles revolved around the leadership role of Martin Luther King and major events in the movement he led, such as the 1963 March on Washington for Jobs and Freedom, and often depicted the U.S. government as an ally in the struggle for racial equality.[56] However, Tanzania's exposure to Malcolm X's views, coupled with the explosion of urban rebellions in U.S. cities between 1964 and 1967, altered the ways in which the *Nationalist* and the *Tanganyika Standard* covered the racial problem in the United States. Because both newspapers published articles and editorials written in English, their readership largely consisted of the educated, urban elite that did not possess a singular view on race and racism. As the Tanzanian press continued to pay close attention to an emergent black nationalist consciousness among African Americans, it no longer could depict King as the leading spokesman of an ideologically and strategically unified movement. While the *Tanganyika Standard*'s coverage mirrored that of the *New York Times* and the *Washington Post* in viewing the rise of black militancy as a step backward, the *Nationalist* took a far more welcoming approach to Black Power's emergence.

Launched in 1963, the *Nationalist* was the organ of the TANU Party, focusing primarily on the state's foreign policy initiatives, particularly the leadership roles it took in the UN and OAU as well as its burgeoning relationship with China. The *Tanganyika Standard*, on the other hand, was a privately owned newspaper dominated by British expatriates, serving as the *Nationalist*'s primary rival due to its pro-West and pro-capitalist positions. In March 1966, Nyerere directly appointed Tanzanian national Benjamin Mkapa, a member of the TANU Youth League and "one of the most highly respected journalists in the country," managing editor of the *Nationalist*. Mkapa felt that since there was no leftist-oriented English-speaking national newspaper to counter the conservatism of the *Tanganyika Standard*, it was necessary for the *Nationalist* to fill that void by taking on a "left of center" identity, especially in its coverage of international affairs.[57] The addition of Abdulrahman Mohamed Babu's editorial column "Pressman's Commentary" in 1965, a year before Mkapa's appointment, had already helped to steer the *Nationalist* in this new direction. His editorials on Black Power helped prepare Tanzanians (and African political exiles) for Carmichael's visit.

Ever since his incorporation into the union government, Babu had enjoyed enormous popularity in Tanzania. He became known for living a modest lifestyle free of the corruption and class elitism that was beginning to characterize African government

Chapter Two

officials throughout the continent. Although his inclusion in the union government effectively isolated him from Zanzibar's political scene, he brought with him what one political scientist noted as an "aggressively nationalistic economic policy" that was "more insistent than Nyerere about the need for a bloc of underdeveloped countries to confront the West."[58] The potent combination of Babu's blending of Marxist, nationalist, and pan-Africanist leanings and professional background in journalism made him an asset not only to a government attempting to implement socialism, but also to the party's newspaper when it came to giving it a leftist ideological identity as advocated by Mkapa. His column became one of the most popular weekly features, especially within Tanzania's leftist political circles. For Babu, no subject was off-limits that concerned Africa and her strides toward unity. In these editorials he would don the mask of racial pan-Africanist and set out to expose Western imperialist press policies and their impact on Africa. "The imperialists use the news media," he wrote in October 1966, "as an instrument for diverting the world's attention away from the kind of situations which expose imperialism in its naked form."[59]

Because of Babu's friendship with Malcolm X, which brought with it a unique exposure to and deeper understanding of African Americans' black nationalist sentiments, he was in an advantageous position to discuss the meaning and significance of Black Power politics to an African audience. Through the pages of the *Nationalist*, Babu felt the need to discuss the meaning behind the rise of Black Power in the United States and its relevance to African liberation. In one column, Babu questions U.S. mainstream media distortions of Black Power as an expression of anti-white black supremacy, urging Africans to not take seriously such representations. The U.S. press, he argued, was reducing Black Power to an "obnoxious form of racialism" that had fractured beyond repair its alliances with moderate civil rights organizations and their leaders. He warned: "These reports are transmitted to us through the news media wholly dominated by the perpetrators of racial injustice in the U.S. who are highly accomplished in the art of propaganda and double talk."[60] In this editorial, SNCC was also addressed. Since SNCC was continually associated with Black Power, why was the organization considered such a threat to the "U.S. ruling class" and the "well-being of American society?" The answer to this question did not necessarily reside in the slogan of "Black Power" itself, since "slogans do not create a political climate—it is the other way around." In his estimation, Black Power exposed the fallacy of a color-blind U.S. capitalistic democracy, and therefore the movement constituted the "greatest struggle waging inside the great society," with SNCC serving as the embodiment of a new form of black resistance.[61]

Babu and the *Nationalist* had positioned the one-party state as an ally to the Black Power movement. Between May 1966 and September 1967, the *Nationalist* featured over twenty editorials and articles that sought out an alternative explanation for the intersection between urban rebellions and black nationalism. Its coverage of racial violence in Newark (New Jersey), Detroit (Michigan), and Chicago (Illinois) during the summer of 1967, two months before Carmichael's visit, implicitly questioned the progress made with the passing of civil and voting rights legislation. The ghettoization of black neighborhoods (i.e., deplorable housing conditions, under-resourced schools, the lack of job opportunities, and policy brutality) was one root cause for deteriorating race relations and the escalation of Black Power militancy. The kinds of analyses on the emergence of Black Power in the United States put forth in the *Nationalist* mirrored those of Carmichael's and SNCC's between 1965 and 1967. The *Tanganyika Standard*, on the other hand, published only seven articles and editorials over this same period, which categorized the Black Power movement as a youth-driven movement led by a SNCC organization that preached anti-white violence.[62] Throughout August and September alone, the *Nationalist* exceeded that number, publishing eight articles on U.S. race relations, half of which celebrated Carmichael's and SNCC's actions.[63] When Carmichael arrived in Dar es Salaam in late October, Black Power was not as foreign an idea in the country as one would think.

The Tanzanian press followed Carmichael's activities in the United States as well as his visits to Cuba and Vietnam, where he was treated like a de facto head of state of the African American nation.[64] Although the *Nationalist* had earlier described him as lacking political experience because of his youth, the twenty-six-year-old Black Power leader became Tanzania's star attraction, almost eclipsing Nyerere's historic march from his home village in Butiama to Mwanza to mobilize popular support for Ujamaa na Kujitegemea and kick off the TANU National Conference (reportedly one of the longest marches made by an African head of state). Soon-to-be wife Miriam Makeba, the internationally acclaimed, Grammy Award–winning South African singer and anti-apartheid advocate, visited Tanzania to perform at the same time as Carmichael's arrival in the country.[65] Although they tried to keep their budding romance a secret after it began in Guinea, their arrival and tour of Tanzania was their first public appearance together as a couple, which ended up having a far more negative impact on Makeba's music career.[66]

Sporting a short-cropped Afro hairstyle, white turtleneck, black coat and pants, and sunglasses, Carmichael arrived in Dar es Salaam on October 23. However, the first articles on Carmichael in Tanzania did not emerge until November 1. Over the next few weeks, Carmichael toured the country, spoke at the national university, and met with Tanzanian government leaders, TANU members, and African liberation groups. On November 2, upon the invitation of the University Students African Revolutionary Front (USARF), he spoke at Theater Hall on the campus of the University College of

Chapter Two

Dar es Salaam, where the speech was repeatedly interrupted with students chanting, "Black Power!"[67] Makeba, who accompanied Carmichael to the university campus, added to this atmosphere revolutionary fervor by following up Carmichael's speech with revolutionary songs.[68] His romantic ties to the South African songstress led to another positive experience as a result of her friendship with exiled leaders of PAC, a South African liberation group that held a strong black-nationalist philosophy and was seen as the ANC's chief rival. On November 11, he visited the Mgulani national service camp, where he posed for a photograph.[69] Surrounded by at least twelve smiling young men and women in military uniform, some looking at Carmichael while others face the camera, an exuberant Carmichael is wearing a dashiki and jeans with both arms raised at eye level and both hands clenched into fists. His meetings with African liberation groups and his visits to youth national service camps reflected a growing political interest in armed resistance as a tool of liberation. While the former provided insight into the state of African liberation movements in southern and central Africa, the latter showed him how Tanzania, as a frontline state, approached developing its military capacity through compulsory service.

Carmichael's presence in Tanzania aroused much interest from the Tanzanian press, whose journalists charted his every move and recorded his speeches about and answers to questions about a variety of hot-button topics. Yet with Carmichael assigned a TANU host, Chris Liundi of the party's youth league, the government had every reason to believe that Carmichael would not stir up trouble, feeling secure enough to hold the TANU National Executive conference in Mwanza, a long distance away from Dar es Salaam. That was until Carmichael was prompted by a question about African unity. Carmichael lashed out against the authoritarian rule of Mobutu Sese Seko in Zaire, formerly the Democratic Republic of the Congo, one of the men responsible for the assassination of Lumumba in 1961. Word that Carmichael had criticized an OAU member state and its head of state by name reached Mwanza, touching off a serious discussion about what to do with the young, brash militant leader from America. Some party members urged Nyerere to throw him out of the country, while others called for censorship. Both sides, however, agreed that remarks of this kind could damage Tanzania's standing within the OAU. Nyerere eventually sent word to Liundi, secretary general of TYL, to speak with Carmichael and inform him that he was not permitted to use Tanzania as a platform from which to launch attacks against specific independent African states.[70] Carmichael appeared to comply with this demand, but never relented in taking a confrontational approach towards African political leadership, a prominent issue he tackled over the course of his two-week visit. From all accounts, his visit was nothing short of controversial, informative, and entertaining as he crafted an image of himself as a serious intellectual and uncompromising revolutionary, and SNCC as the vanguard organization of a surging anti-imperialist movement in the United States.

Carmichael saw the opportunity to spread his Black Power message to a broad-based African audience through the pages of the *Nationalist* and the *Tanganyika Standard*. In one interview with the latter, he explained why he had come to Tanzania, making it a point to claim Africa as the homeland to all black people living and suffering in the African Diaspora:

> Well, number one I think that Africa is our Motherland. There are many African Americans who are willing to fight for Africa. We have to realize that the African today is 900,000,000 strong around the world. Our struggle lies in the unification of those 900,000,000 people. Our base of course will be Africa—it's our Motherland. And that would give support to us, to give us dignity in ourselves and a willingness to unite outside Africa wherever we are, to fight for our rights inside those countries and to give aid and assistance to the Motherland.[71]

This did not mean he was calling for an immediate mass repatriation movement—"at least not at this point," he disclosed. "The best protection for Africa today is the 50,000,000 African Americans inside the United States because when we start to move against South Africa if the United States dares to come into this continent, the African Americans will burn that country down to the ground."[72] Black Power, he explained, was "the coming together of black people around the world to fight wherever they are, for their dignity, and the regaining of their Motherland, and to fight for the benefit of the masses of our people who are oppressed around the world."[73] In addition to discussing pan-African unity, Carmichael addressed U.S. imperialism in Vietnam, interracial alliances, the U.S. civil rights movement, the global dimensions of racism, revolutionary armed struggle, international class formation in Africa, and Marxist theory—all in an effort to conceptualize "Black Power" as an ideology of African liberation and as an anti-racist and anti-imperialist movement.

On the issue of the Vietnam War, Carmichael vowed that African Americans were primed to resist the draft in opposition to the "master of the world." "We won't go," he announced. "We are fighting the same master, U.S."[74] Racism in the U.S. military, he argued, meant that African Americans were disproportionately represented on the frontlines of the war and therefore more prone to embracing an antiwar and anti-imperialist consciousness. Carmichael used the issue of the Vietnam War to proclaim his support of revolutionary violence as the only viable means to combat the United States, which "has spread its oppressive tentacles throughout the world."[75] "It is better to die at 26 years of age with a gun in your hand," he told one journalist for the *Nationalist*, "than die of malnutrition and disease at 56."⁷⁶

One of Carmichael's core arguments was that racism was a global phenomenon of greater concern than class exploitation:

> The first fight ... is the fight against racism. That is the fight that only the black man can fight. The black man around the world suffers from an inferiority complex. Everybody spits in our faces. The scum of the Western white society—Portugal—today inhabits our motherland and spits in our face. Everybody takes his turn with the black man. The fight against racism is our fight. We must fight it. We cannot depend on anybody to fight our fight for us. The first fight we are struggling for is BLACK POWER—POWER FOR THE BLACK MAN. The black man has no power in the world today.⁷⁷

He continued: "Our history has not been capable of transcending racism. When you talk about classes, when you talk about poverty to a white man he talks about color. It is impossible to bridge the gap." The position on prioritizing racial oppression over class oppression led him to conclude that alliances with whites constituted a dependency relationship that jeopardized any black-led political movement. "We will not depend upon anybody to fight for us. We will depend on our people. And we will fight with arms, with bottles, with bricks ... But we will fight."⁷⁸ He also held firm to the notion that the white working classes of the world lacked the kind of antiracist consciousness needed for interracial alliances to function effectively. "The reason the white west has been able to avoid the inevitable class conflict is that when their working class began to demand more money the rulers of those countries began to exploit the Third World. They got more money and gave the crumbs to the working class. The white working class accepted these crumbs, which were made from the sweat of the Third World, and kept their mouths shut."⁷⁹ Only when their economic security was challenged would the white working classes of the United States and Europe develop the "revolutionary consciousness" needed to wage an international and interracial struggle against imperialism. Until that time, Africans and black people worldwide must go it alone and demonstrate to the world their ability to be self-reliant.

Carmichael believed that dependency had two faces: a reliance on white allies and Western revolutionary ideologies. He therefore challenged Marxist definitions of the proletariat by redefining class as a marker of racial identity and stripping the white industrial laborer of its vanguard role. According to Carmichael, the world was comprised of the "Rich White Man" and the "Proletariat Black Man." In echoing Nyerere's views on "traditional" African societies, he further claimed that it was an ideology of white supremacy that gave rise to the transatlantic slave trade and European colonization of Africa and resulted in internal class formations that did not previously exist on the continent. These two historical processes had rendered black people and Africans the most "economically insecure" race in the world. "Any African leader who does not recognize this is at best a fool," Carmichael told one journalist of the *Nationalist*, "and any African leader who recognizes that and continues to create classes is a traitor."[80]

Although such categories prevented an analysis of women's oppression, it was nevertheless an attempt on Carmichael's part to stress the importance of international racial solidarity as a key ideological component of pan-Africanism. For Carmichael, the class struggle constituted, first and foremost, a struggle against racism. This struggle needed to be led by Africans on the economic, cultural, and intellectual fronts. Because the United States was seen as the major threat to African liberation, African Americans would play a supportive, advisory role since they were most familiar with the nature of U.S. racism. On many levels, it was an underdeveloped conception of class oppression shrouded in racially charged rhetoric of self-reliance. His insistence on prioritizing racism over class oppression, coupled with his confrontational tone and style, left him open to criticism, especially from the African leftists who viewed racism as a secondary concern.

One major liability to his message of international race solidarity, however, was the hard-line position he took on political leadership, an issue that prompted him on several occasions to lambaste independent governments and liberation groups. When asked about his views on the postcolonial situation in Africa, Carmichael brushed the question off, claiming there was "no point in indulging in bourgeois tea party revolutions."[81] During his speech at the university, however, he called African leaders "traitors" because they were "playing with the people's lives," taking particular issue with the accuracy of death toll statistics in colonial territories where guerrilla wars were being waged. "They disgust me," he added. "African leaders disgust me."[82] One particular exchange between Carmichael and a journalist for *Tanganyika Standard* unfolded as follows:

> VIEWPOINT: Going back to your present tour of Africa. You have been openly critical of some African leaders. Can you explain why?
>
> CARMICHAEL: Yes, I think many African leaders are clowns. They are betraying their people.
>
> VIEWPOINT: In what way?
>
> CARMICHAEL: They are not making true revolutions; they are selling their people out; they are more interested in big cars and white women than they are in facing the problems of their people. Many of them are not even concerned with the problem of South Africa and Zimbabwe. It is impossible for any African

living on this continent not to be concerned with that problem. Many of them are not concerned with a united Africa. And this is absolutely absurd.
VIEWPOINT: Will you name the leaders you feel that way about?
CARMICHAEL: I will not. You will never divide and conquer me![83]

These same sentiments were expressed in an interview with the *Nationalist*, where he again insisted, without naming names, that Africa was "ruled by clowns who are more concerned about big cars than the welfare of their people." "I don't name them because I don't want the white man to divide Africa further," he clarified. "But I think it is crystal clear to all that many African leaders today who are playing with the lives of their people are traitors."[84] While he seemed to comply with the restrictions imposed upon him by the TANU government in terms of not specifically identifying independent African states and African liberation groups and their leaders he had problems with, it did not stop him from repeatedly calling into question their capacity to lead. He did not let up in portraying them as out of touch with the masses, materialistic, and poor guerrilla-warfare tacticians. What seemed to trouble Carmichael the most was how African leaders had been so thoroughly "brainwashed" by the West to the extent that it signaled a loss of their African cultural sensibilities.[85] This line of thinking led Carmichael to challenge the notion that political exile was an effective tactic of resistance. "They are THE ONLY setback of the African liberation movements," he remarked. "Half of those leaders do not even know how to use a gun. The other half have never seen a jail inside their country and they are fighting revolutions."[86]

It mattered little that he never called out a liberation organization or leader by name. The ANC publicly rebuked Carmichael for "meaningless and arrogant demagoguery."[87] The U.S. national press picked up on the ANC response to Carmichael's visit, carrying headlines that read: "Free Africa Group Blasts Stokely View," "Africa Group Accuses Carmichael of Hatred," and "Carmichael Denied by Africans."[88] Although his underlying message was one of pan-African solidarity, his attempt to expose the crisis of the African political establishment certainly blunted the appeal of his message within Tanzania. But this is not to say that Carmichael and his ideas were widely rejected. Proponents of Carmichael's views did not perceive his comments on race or his comments on the hypocrisies of African leaders as being entirely inaccurate.

Richard Gibson, an African American pan-Africanist visiting Tanzania during Carmichael's visit, thought that the ANC's criticism of Carmichael had everything to do with the Cold War. Writing for *The Liberator*, an African American radical journal, Gibson claims that Soviet imperialism forced the ANC to denounce Carmichael's radical views because "Russia fears that militant Black nationalism, Black Power doctrines, might sweep through Africa, shutting the door on white revisionist communist "guidance" for African liberation movements."[89] He goes on to accuse the ANC of launching "a widespread word-of-mouth campaign against Afro-Americans in Africa, who are described viciously as "Black chauvinists" and paid agents of the CIA and Chairman Mao Tse-tung." At the same time, Gibson is reluctant to place all of the blame on the ANC. Carmichael's visit should serve as a lesson to black activists of the African Diaspora that they needed to study and understand "the intricacies" of African politics before making sweeping judgments on the state of the African revolution. Indeed, the ANC-Carmichael feud was a "rude reminder" that pan-African unity between the African Diaspora and Africa was neither automatic nor inevitable.

Carmichael's visit prompted a wave of responses by Tanzanian nationals as well, sparking a debate about race, nationalist identity, armed struggle, and colonialism. The Tanzanian press served as an outlet for critical debate where Tanzanians could publicly engage with Black Power ideas. Some chose to respond directly to Carmichael, while others sought to address Tanzanian opinions of Carmichael. Some shared his hard-line critique of leaders of African liberation movements, especially the claim that they had grown complacent while living in exile. One letter to the editor dubbed the ANC as "professional freedom fighters" that "hide back in the rear waiting to become Ministers after the struggle!!"[90] Yet criticism of Carmichael and his message was more prominent in the *Tanganyika Standard* than the party newspaper. One editorialist was not at all impressed with Carmichael. His "gratuitous and ill-formed insults" and penchant for "flamboyance and histrionics" was incredibly unappealing. Arguing that his provocative racial rhetoric clouded his sensible analysis of racism, the editorial columnist found Carmichael's calls for armed struggle extremely problematic:

> However, like all brash young revolutionaries he would change the world overnight, no matter the consequences or the harm that could be done to countless thousands of innocent victims in the process. He is clearly impatient with the comparatively quiet and calm methods by which we in Tanzania achieved our independence... The world is witnessing far too much bloodshed for any leader to lightly encourage the shedding of more. A little more thought and fewer fiery words would benefit Mr. Carmichael, his listeners and his cause.[91]

For this Tanzanian, Carmichael's youth and outsider status were two reasons as to why his views should be challenged and ultimately rejected. In another dissenting opinion, Vinad Nair took issue with the idea that Carmichael's views reflected the sensibilities and attitudes of "50 million" African Americans, and that the U.S. government was

Chapter Two

supportive of apartheid in South Africa. His views on race were equally disconcerting in the way they reminded Nair of German Nazism.[92] In responding directly to this less than flattering letter to the editor on Carmichael, Tony Cali refuted all of Nair's claims.

As already noted, Carmichael found a receptive audience at the University College of Dar es Salaam. Theater Hall was packed for his two-hour speech on the pitfalls of Western education and impact of cultural imperialism in Africa. Wasilwa Barasa, a university student who attended the speech, identified strongly with Carmichael's arguments on African dependence on Western forms of thought and systems of education and governance. He began his letter championing the Black Power slogan, arguing that it represented a "threat to collective neo-colonialism and gives white racists and their lackeys many sleepless nights." Barasa goes on to question the credibility of Africans reared in Western intellectual tradition who had become apologists of anti-black racism, who hid behind outdated notions of academic objectivity, and who refused to see the "contradictions of the white man." "I for one believe any honest man must support Black Power . . . Once we get the false concept of intellectualism out of the University College we will be able to create a revolutionary elite that exposes the selfish financial interests and imperial agents while affording the socialist revolution and regaining our humanity—Black Power."[93] Barasa's comments suggest that a Tanzanian youth intelligentsia was drawn to Carmichael's Black Power ideas about racism and knowledge production, and willing to raise important questions about the political function of the university in Tanzania in the context of socialist nation-building.

In two separate editorials on Black Power, Abdulrahman Mohamed Babu came out in defense of Carmichael, choosing to address prevailing opinions about Carmichael's lack of a serious analysis on class struggle in the pan-African world. In one editorial titled "African Revolution," Babu attempts to historicize African Americans' relationship to the communist movement, noting that the decade of the 1950s was awash in anticommunist hysteria and repression, so much so that it prevented African Americans from engaging fully with Marxist ideas. Black Power, Babu argues, constituted a generational shift in the black freedom movement that marked a trend of open-mindedness to Marxism.

> The main characteristic of this generation is that it is largely free from the fear of communism, having heard so much of it lost its original impact. In fact, the impact has been the other way around, rather than carrying them away from communism it brought them nearer to it . . . From fear of the communist bogey, this young leadership can convincingly use the Marxist-Leninist argument to describe the end of American capitalism.[94]

By arguing that young black radicals from the United States were gravitating toward Marxism in developing their critiques of U.S. imperialism, Babu was far more concerned with highlighting what the Black Power movement held in common with the African liberation movements than dissecting the inherent flaws of Carmichael's analysis of class struggle.

Babu put forth a similar argument in his second editorial on Black Power, published a month later in December. He believed that Carmichael was to be commended for accomplishing two important tasks during his visit to Tanzania. Firstly, he articulated the meaning of Black Power in domestic and international contexts and, secondly, he showed how the aims and objectives of the movement held commonalities with African (and Third World) struggles for liberation. "Black Power means that black people must redefine themselves, that they must tell their history and have pride in their culture," Babu wrote. "Black Power is not "racialism"; it is not about preaching the inferiority of whites and black superiority. It doesn't preach exclusion of whites. It is about "respect" and partnership of races based on equal power."[95] In concluding his editorial, Babu urged Africans to "pause and listen" to Carmichael's message if they were truly interested in understanding the "'true picture' of the internal situation in the U.S."

Carmichael left Tanzania on November 26, which meant he was present in the country as Africans debated the pros and cons of his message. In his last interview with the *Nationalist* he spoke candidly about his experience in Tanzania, offering the following assessment:

> I enjoyed myself immensely. I have learnt a great deal. I intend to use that which I have learnt to further help organize the 900 million Africans in the world today ... I am sure after I have gone there are those who will continue to preach that I am a hateful man. But I ask for them not to use ad hominem attacks but rather to dispute the facts and offer alternative solutions. Before I leave Tanzania, I wish to send a special message to the people of the country—primarily the youth—and that is: THE REVOLUTION MUST CONTINUE.[96]

Contrary to the prevailing perception that Carmichael was chased out of Tanzania, his message of international race solidarity resonated within the Tanzanian pubic sphere. Africans saw value in his critique of African leadership and the need for race consciousness. Not to mention that his anti-Vietnam war position and calls for self-reliance were very similar to Nyerere's political views as reflected in the Arusha Declaration.[97] Instead, it was his combative style, brashness, and overconfidence that left much to be desired.

Chapter Two

If bringing the issue of racism to an African audience was one of SNCC's goals, then Carmichael's visit proved a surprising success, largely due to the accommodationist attitude of the Tanzanian government. It permitted SNCC to use Tanzania as a platform from which to express an anti-imperialist and antiracist political philosophy despite restrictions. The same could not be said about SNCC's goal to collaborate with the one-party government on nation-building projects of mutual concern. While the UN seminar in Zambia revealed how Black Power organizations and African governments could act in solidarity with one another over the issue of apartheid and colonialism in Africa, the Afro-American Skills Bank represented aa squandered opportunity. Forman argued this latter point in July 1968, seven months after Carmichael's visit to Tanzania:

> We felt that this program would help break the backbone of dependency for recruitment on the European countries. It still maintains the African continent must consider us as overseas Africans and make provisions for us to spend some time in those countries helping to develop our continent.[98]

He continued:

> As an African living in the United States, we have the right, if not more than the right, to criticize what are the weaknesses in African Government on the continent. That continent belongs to us as much as it belongs to any African living anywhere in Africa. Those of us living will indeed be happy when we see African governments standing tall and responding to the conditions not only to us, to Africans living in the United States, but to the masses of people in Africa.[99]

Forman's insistence on the importance of African Americans to African liberation reflected a growing diaspora consciousness taking hold in Black America. In regarding Africa as their ancestral homeland, African Americans who came of age during the Black Power and African independence eras held a strong sense of entitlement and urgency based on enormous expectations for independent African states like Tanzania.

Despite the brief encounter between SNCC and Tanzania, the results and implications of their partnership were no less significant. Between 1965 and 1967, a transnational dialogue had expanded in a manner Malcolm X envisioned in 1964, raising questions about the possibility of sustainable collaboration. The TANU government believed Black Power activists could play a role in addressing foreign and domestic policy concerns, but the extent to which the government was invested in the African Diaspora was not yet clearly defined. Although the commitment and enthusiasm of Black Power activists could not be questioned, their ability to politically organize on an international scale could be. By 1969, SNCC was an organization in fast decline. Its community programs were barely operational due to inactive local chapters, the loss of veteran organizers, and infighting.[100] Carmichael left SNCC, and the United States for that matter, for Africa, living as a political exile in Guinea for the remainder of his life until his death in 1998, while Forman shifted his energies into the reparations movement as well as into pursuing advanced degrees in the 1970s and 1980s. However, Forman and Carmichael were not the only ones drawn to the ideas of Black Power and Ujamaa na Kujitegemea. Both ideas were championed in the Caribbean, compelling intellectuals and activists like Walter Rodney, a Guyanese Marxist historian, to move to Tanzania in 1968 and participate in its nationalist project within the context of higher education. It is to his experience teaching at the University College of Dar es Salaam (UCD) that we now turn.

PART 2

Doings

Chapter 3

Walter Rodney, African Students, and the Struggle to Define University Education

> We believe that a knowledge and understanding of African history is important for the growth of our continent.
>
> —Julius Nyerere, President of the United Republic of Tanzania

Malcolm X and Carmichael's visits to Dar es Salaam in 1964 and 1967, respectively, illustrated how international travel became an important practice of African solidarity work and represented a breakthrough in Black Power–Tanzania relations. For political activists in the African Diaspora, however, it became just as important to show solidarity in action through active participation in Tanzania's nationalist project by living and working in the country. In the period between 1968 and 1974, Tanzania became the epicenter of the pan-Africanism movement in large part due to the passing of the Arusha Declaration, which shaped Black Power activists' conceptions of African statehood in multiple ways. Could the Tanzanian nation-state initiate socialist changes while taking the lead in wiping out colonialism and white minority rule in the rest of the continent? Could black expatriates who possessed the technical know-how and pan-Africanist consciousness define for themselves a role in nationalist projects based out of the continent that would be equally attentive to the needs and aspirations of oppressed black peoples in the diaspora on one hand, and the nation-building demands of

Chapter Three

African governments on the other? These questions did not just speak to the interests of Black Power activists based in the United States like Malcolm X and Stokely Carmichael. Caribbean radical intellectuals and activists were drawn to Tanzania as well, carrying with them similar questions of how they could contribute to the pan-Africanism movement through direct, on-the-ground involvement in the country's Ujamaa experiment.

One intellectual-activist of note who would test the possibilities of this relationship was the Caribbean Marxist historian Walter Rodney. Born in Georgetown, Guyana, on March 23, 1942, Rodney's working-class consciousness was nurtured within a working-class family that was involved in the country's multiracial (African and Indian) nationalist movement during the 1940s and 1950s. Having excelled at school at an early age, he was awarded a scholarship to Queen's College, a prestigious secondary school in Georgetown where he developed a love for debating, history, and languages and won another scholarship to pursue advanced studies at the University College of the West Indies in Mona, Jamaica, in 1960. Three years later, after being awarded yet another academic scholarship, he moved to London, earning his doctorate in history at the School of Oriental and African Studies (SOAS) at the University of London.[1] Between 1960 and 1966, he honed his debating skills, studied the history of Africa, and devoured Marxism with a voracious appetite, resulting in a dissertation, "A History of the Upper Guinea Coast, 1545–1800," a historical-materialist interpretation of the deleterious effects of the transatlantic slave trade, particularly the process of social stratification and subordination, on West African societies.[2]

Growing political commitments counterbalanced these six years of intensive academic study. His political activities outside of the classroom were just as significant in his political and intellectual development as what he was learning inside multiple elitist universities. While studying at UWI, Rodney's pan-Africanist and internationalist politics were cultivated by the solidarities and networks forged with West Indian students from various Caribbean islands as well as from visits to Cuba and the Soviet Union. While studying in London, Rodney received political mentorship from C.L.R. James, the Trinidad Marxist and pan-Africanist; perfected his public speaking and debating skills at political gatherings in Hyde Park; deepened his theoretical understanding of Marxism via study groups; and participated in the West Indian Student Union, a student organization, where he protested against anti-black racism in Britain and raised awareness about political struggles in the Caribbean, the United States, and Africa.[3] By the time he received his PhD in 1966, at the age of only twenty-four, Rodney was poised to be, in his words, a "revolutionary intellectual"[4] right at a time when there was a growing demand for academically trained intellectuals to fill positions at emergent universities throughout the continent.

Which independent African state held the most potential for serving as a model of inspiration to others in imagining a postcolonial liberated future? By 1966, identifying progressive independent nations that were receptive to African diasporan radicals' presence in their countries was a difficult task. Since the Ghana moment had been a spectacular failure punctuated by the 1966 military coup that overthrew Nkrumah and led to both the forced and voluntary exodus of African American and Caribbean activist-expatriates, "an aching" void was created in the pan-Africanism movement. Many pan-Africanists in the African Diaspora were left searching for Ghana's replacement as the leading independent state committed to global African emancipation at a time when the coup d'état became the norm rather than the exception of postcolonial rule. The state of African politics was just one issue that factored into Walter Rodney's decision on where to teach after receiving his PhD. "The imperial nexus was more important and facilitated my move to Tanzania," he stated years later. "I would have preferred to go to West Africa, which was my special area of research. But as I looked at West Africa, I couldn't see a place where it seemed to me that I could go and live and learn while teaching. Other than Guinea, which I'm eliminating for cultural and historical reasons, I don't see that it would make much sense for me to go to Ibadan or Accra at that time . . . I don't think I could have learned anything from participation in the kind of politics being developed in Nigeria, or at that time in Ghana after Nkrumah. Hence the choice was to go to Tanzania."[5]

Rodney arrived at two conclusions. Coming from the English-speaking Caribbean, he felt that Guinea, with its history of French colonialism, would place too many restrictions on his academic research and political activities in the country due to these differences in language and history. Because Nigeria was embroiled in a civil war and Ghana was ridding itself of its pan-Africanist identity, the two countries carried little appeal. The appeal of Tanzania, then, mainly had to do with the leadership of Nyerere. Rodney kept abreast of the developments in Tanzania between 1964 and 1966 when it started to carve out more forcefully a leadership role in the continental pan-Africanism movement. What he saw from afar was a president who was articulating a postcolonial vision, attempting to align its domestic policies with a progressive foreign-policy agenda and reputation. Part of that vision entailed recovering African history and reorganizing education.

One year before Rodney's arrival in Dar es Salaam to assume the position of lecturer in history, Nyerere appeared at the International Congress of African History held at the University College of Dar es Salaam (UCD). Before an audience of Africanist historians from Africa and the world, Nyerere's comments placed emphasis on the importance of African history to the political, economic, and cultural growth of the continent as told from an African perspective:

> Most people who study our history at educational institutions throughout the world still learn the discovery of Africa and the journeys of the great explorers. They learn the slave trades and the European invasions; they analyze the economic motivations and effects on Europe of these events. The vital thing is that we should be able to develop a really African history... It is only when these things are looked at from Africa outwards that history will develop.[6]

Nyerere's words—the need to challenge the long-held notion that Africa was without a history and to formulate archival and methodological approaches to "erase" this misconception"[7]—spoke directly to Rodney's professional aspirations as a historian, as an intellectual, and as a pan-Africanist. However, despite making an immediate impression on the university college community, Rodney was never able to gain a foothold there, as he found himself back at his alma mater, UWI-Mona, to start off the 1967–1968 academic year once his one-year appointment at UCD came to an end.

Although Rodney served as a lecturer in history in the West Indies' premier academic institution for only two years, he nevertheless made a lasting impression there as well. At UWI, Rodney was continuing to define his intellectual work in political terms, and thus helped to galvanize not only university students and progressive intellectuals into action, but also oppressed segments of Jamaica's population, such as urban youth and Rastafarians, with his message of Black Power. After attending the Congress of Black Writers in Montreal in October 1968, Rodney tried to return to Jamaica to resume his teaching responsibilities, only to be denied entry by the Jamaican authorities. Apparently, the Jamaican Labor Party–led government under the leadership of Prime Minister Hugh Shearer faulted the young Guyanese lecturer for the emergence of political protests from below, so much so that the uprising became known as the "Rodney riots."[8] Having limited teaching options at his disposal given his disinterest in pursuing faculty positions in the United States or Europe, Rodney was able to return to UCD in Tanzania in 1969, in large part due to the intervening efforts of Terrence Ranger, the British historian who chaired the university college's history department and hired him in 1966.

A lot had changed in Tanzania in the two years that Rodney was away, particularly at UCD. Established in 1961, the year of Tanganyika independence, as an affiliate college of the University of London (1961–1963) and the University of East Africa (1963–1970), UCD was envisioned as an institutional space of higher learning that would train generations of skilled technicians and local and national government and party leaders. The main campus was located thirteen kilometers west, overlooking the city and thus popularly nicknamed "the Hill" because of its elevated location, which also gave it an aura of elitism. After 1961, the Nyerere government tried to invest its limited finances in educational development, managing to boost student enrollment by the thousands and expand the curriculum over a six-year period.[9] Yet in its first six years of existence, the nationalist consciousness of university students was hard to locate and define. This was especially the case in October 1966 when university students came out strongly in opposition to compulsory military service and salary reductions for graduates in Form IV and above. What was once a voluntary service program designed in 1963 to give students military, vocational, political, and agricultural training had become a mandatory youth policy in 1965. On October 22, close to four hundred university students dressed in red caps and gowns took to the streets and marched from the main campus to the State House in the downtown area in hopes of convincing the government and party to revoke the policy.[10]

The student protest, popularly dubbed "the National Service crisis," sent shockwaves throughout the entire nation, but not because of the number of students involved. Rather the negative backlash against the students was because of their audacious display of privilege and lack of patriotism. Government officials, party leaders, students, and, finally, the president all weighed in on the event. Vice President Kawawa, who was also the university college's vice chancellor, chided the students by attributing their ill-thought-out actions to their age and subsequent immaturity. "Should it be the habit to say these old men are unwise?" he asked rhetorically. "I would laugh at them because a youth hasn't got as much wisdom as an old man who has a lot of experience."[11] Babu chose to focus on the Western media's coverage of the protest, citing how it managed to make a protest of 400 out of 8,000 students a global event, despite the fact that compulsory service was a popularly accepted (and much needed) policy for a Third World country given the threat of external interference in Africa's cultural, political, and economic affairs. Put simply, and most likely unbeknownst to the student protestors, the Western "imperialist" media's sole interest in covering the student demonstration was to make Tanzania look "unstable."[12]

The protest certainly caught President Nyerere by surprise as well. Five months previously, he delivered an inspiring opening address at the General Assembly of the World University Service, held at UCD. He addressed the role of university education in newly independent nations with the following opening remarks:

> For I believe that the pursuit of learning can be a luxury in society; whether it is or not depends upon the conditions in which that society lives. Perhaps I am being foolhardy in making such a statement at a university gathering, but I am going to repeat it; when people are dying because existing knowledge is not applied, when the very basic social and public services are not available to all members of society, then that society is misusing its resources if it pursues pure learning for its own sake.[13]

The anti-National Service protest was not only an abuse of this "luxury," but also an affront to the cooperative ethos that should exist between students and the "Government and the people." For exercising autonomous collective agency outside the control of the state, particularly the TANU Youth League, Nyerere decided to reprimand the students in the severest way possible. On October 24, he announced that 393 students had been expelled—a decision met with wide applause and approval.[14]

The National Service crisis was part of the backdrop for the rise of leftist student-led activism at the university college that revolved around organizing, mobilizing, and educating students in a way that would challenge rather than reinforce elitist attitudes and behaviors. "Tanzania needs all of the efforts to fight with hands and brains to thwart the imperialist machinations against progress and socialism here," read one letter to the editor written by a self-identified "socialist" student. "Students must work with the people for the people."[15] Grant Kamenju, a Kenyan lecturer in literature at the university college, echoed these sentiments, arguing that the anti-National Service students were "products of an elitist and conservative education system." Reluctant to place all the blame on the students, Kamenju shifted the discussion to the institutional legacy of colonialism. How could the students be entirely at fault when they studied at a university college that subjected them to "esoteric discussion of the nonsensical British 'liberal' studies variety"?[16]

Student expulsions were the least significant of Nyerere's responses to the problem of postcolonial education. One month after the passing of the Arusha Declaration, Nyerere's "Education for Self-Reliance" was published as a TANU policy pamphlet that was widely distributed, assessed, and applauded. As many Africanists have noted, Mwalimu's passion for education was directly rooted in his experience as a student in Tanganyika, Uganda, and Scotland, and as a secondary-school teacher in Dar es Salaam, before he joined the anticolonial nationalist movement on a full-time basis in the 1950s.[17] "Education for Self-Reliance" began by drawing a clear distinction between European formalized education and the "lack of formality" yet the importance of precolonial African educational institutions, before analyzing the discriminatory education policies of British colonial rule. In highlighting postcolonial state interventionist initiatives in educational development, Nyerere identified increases in youth enrollments at all school levels, changes in the curricula where Tanzanian youth were learning more than British and European history, and expansion of educational facilities as three major accomplishments.[18]

The threat now posed so sharply to the future of education in postcolonial Tanzania was supporting a system that continued to induce "attitudes of inequality," that continued to promote elitism through low enrollment numbers at the secondary and university levels, that continued to be isolated from everyday society, and that continued to "over-value book learning."[19] Nyerere thus presented the next phase of the struggle against the legacies of colonialism as one geared towards envisioning an education system that would fully integrate students in the life of the dominant, rural community and foster "living together, and working together, for the common good." His ability to articulate a vision of Ujamaa-inspired education in clear and concise terms shines through in his closing remarks:

> The education provided by Tanzania for students of Tanzania must serve the purposes of Tanzania. It must encourage the growth of the social values we aspire to. It must encourage the development of a proud, independent, and free citizenry which relies upon itself for its own development, and which knows the advantages and the problems of co-operation. It must ensure that the educated know themselves to be an integral part of the nation and recognize the responsibility to give greater service the greater the opportunities they have had.[20]

Walter Rodney stayed abreast of these developments in Tanzania. Lured by the Arusha Declaration and "Education for Self-Reliance" and their implications for realizing socialism in Africa, Rodney published two articles on Ujamaa while teaching at UWI: "The Arusha Declaration—Problems of Implication" and "Education and Tanzanian Socialism." In the latter piece, he invokes Nyerere's critique of colonial education while dismissing entirely the importance of "book learning" as it relates to the application of ideas. In his estimation, a majority if not all African universities, including UCD, were institutions that had yet to break free of their colonial legacy in the postcolonial era. Although UCD was an outgrowth of a pro-democracy, anticolonial movement, it still perpetuated the political, cultural, and economic ideologies of the colonial education system. He further explains: "Few Africans raised fundamental challenges to the bourgeois ideology which dominated their school systems, and, wherever possible, the colonial peers handed over the reins of government to trustworthy products of their schools."[21] The Arusha Declaration and "Education for Self-Reliance," on the other hand, represented a reimagining of education—one that promoted students' integration into an agrarian-based society through socialist education. For Rodney, the role of the university professor was to provide the "ideological arms" for students, since "ideology . . . is the particular responsibility of the higher levels of the education system." And this task, as Rodney notes, was a "formidable one of actively combatting attitudes produced by colonial and neo-colonial schooling." He goes on to argue:

> This cannot be done by exhortation or admonition. The object must be to challenge the minds of the students to recognize the superiority of the socialist world-view as

it is applied to their particular fields of academic study. Courses on socialism, per se, are marginal to the achievement of victory in the realm of ideas. The two prerequisites for a successful orientation of students of the university and institutions of higher learning are, first, the need for committed socialist staff (especially within certain strategic social disciplines); and second, the need for a concerted effort to illumine the social realities of Tanzania and Africa, in a perspective that is hostile to imperialism and class domination.[22]

Two years after the publication of "Education and Tanzanian Socialism," Rodney was back in Dar es Salaam, serving as senior lecturer, at age twenty-seven, in the History Department at UCD. Though his reappointment took place under unforeseen circumstances, his essays on Tanzania's nationalist project reveal an interest in and vision of socialist education that echoed Nyerere's in parallel ways.

When Rodney arrived on the Hill for his second teaching stint, and the most important to his intellectual development, he was introduced to a radical student-led movement underway, led by a small contingent of progressive students and faculty known as the University Students' African Revolutionary Front (USARF). USARF was in part a direct response to the National Service crisis and the Arusha Declaration. In fact, it occurred out of an informal study group designed to combat a culture of political apathy and ignorance among the student community. In November 1967, USARF, formerly known as the Socialist Club, was formed. These radical students saw the TANU Youth League's lack of any meaningful presence on campus as an opportunity to seriously question the role of university students and faculty and the function of university education in relation to building a socialist, egalitarian society, but on their own terms. As much as these students were inspired by Nyerere's views on socialism and education, they were profoundly shaped by the European Marxism of Karl Marx and Frederick Engels as well as the Marxism of African and African diasporan intellectual-activists like Frantz Fanon, Amilcar Cabral, Abdulrahman Babu, and Walter Rodney, which they engaged with, embraced, and challenged to mixed results. In a way, the group's ideological position, combined with its autonomous identity, made it an automatic rival of TANU Youth League's university chapter (TYL-UCD) and, as a result, the one-party government.

USARF was comprised of students from different cultural, ethnic, racial, and national backgrounds, pursuing degrees in a range of fields such as political science, mathematics, law, sociology, and history. Their motivations for being active on campus varied. For Yoweri Museveni, a Ugandan student who arrived at UCD in July 1967, the pull of Tanzania was directly tied to its reputation as frontline state. Thus he was drawn to Dar es Salaam's "atmosphere of freedom fighters, socialists, nationalizations, anti-imperialism" more so than the "so-called 'academicians'" that fostered an apolitical study body at the university college. But once confronted with the lack of student militancy and how the "apathy towards, and ignorance of, many vital questions regarding the interests of the African people were the rule of the day," Museveni decided to get involved in the student movement. As a non-Tanzanian, he could not join TYL-UCD, leaving USARF as the best and most logical alternative.

The Arusha Declaration similarly inspired Henry Mapolu, a Tanzanian adult student who enrolled at the university college in July 1969. "I too had been captivated by socialistic ideals," he remembered.[23] Prior to enrolling, he was politically active in the Tanganyika African National Union Youth League (TYL), serving as a junior faculty member at Kivukoni College, TANU's political education institute. He joined USARF "immediately and enthusiastically" while also playing a prominent leadership role in TYL-UCD as the campus representative to TYL's national office. Mapolu and Museveni were joined by Charles Kileo, Issa Shivji, Karim Hirji, Kapote Mwakasungura, Bernard Mbakileki, Andrew Shija, George Hajivayanis, Patrick Oorro, Ramadhan Meghji, Salim Msoma, James Wapakhabulo, Eriya Kategaya, Munene Njagi, and Zakia Hamdani Meghji, among many others.

USARF was not exclusively a student organization for Tanzanians; its pan-Africanist orientation was reflected not only in its rhetoric but also in its membership, attracting black Africans from Tanzania, Kenya, Zimbabwe, Uganda, Malawi, Sudan, and Ethiopia such as Museveni, Mapolu, and Njagi; Africans of Asian descent such as Shivji and Hirji; and Tanzanians of mixed-race heritage such as Hajivayanis. For example, Hajivayanis was of African, Greek, and German descent, which exposed him firsthand to different kinds of racial discrimination as a child growing up in Dodoma in central Tanzania. He arrived on the university campus at the same time as Mapolu, and within the first weeks of his first semester he found himself attending Walter Rodney's public lecture on the Cuban Revolution held in the large assembly hall (Nkrumah Hall) and "filled to capacity."[24] He joined USARF immediately afterward.

Participation in radical student militancy appealed to women as well. A small number of African women joined USARF for similar reasons as their male counterparts. Zakia Meghji, who grew up in a Zanzibari political family, joined USARF in 1968, her first year at the university college, because she was "appalled by the misery of our peoples, and enthusiastically wanted to play my part in changing the world into a more just and humane place."[25] Meghji remained in USARF until she graduated in 1971. Within this campus climate of apathy and nationalist fervor, a number of university students felt compelled to band together to, in Museveni's words, "encourage revolutionary activities in the college, and to transform the college from being a center of reaction . . . to being a hotbed of revolutionary cadres."[26]

Though USARF was not bashful in articulating its Marxist-inspired ideas, it did not seek to solely expose the limits of Ujamaa socialism in order to replace it with European communism. Rather it attempted to convince political authorities of the nation, the university college administration, and students to adhere to the principles of the Arusha Declaration by genuinely championing the dual causes of the peasantry and working class as well as the colonized people of Africa and the Third World through debate, research, scholarship, community work, and nonviolent direct action. "It had always been our view that he [Nyerere] would go further than the Arusha Declaration," Museveni later recalled, "if he felt that popular pressure demanded it."[27] USARF was convinced of its role to apply that pressure, pushing the nationalist project further to the left in a manner and style that reflected its youthful idealism and uncompromising attitude.

USARF employed a number of tactics in its mission to raise students' awareness about a host of national and international issues. In utilizing the tactic of civil disobedience, one of its very first actions was sabotaging "Rag Day." This student activity was an annual philanthropic event, a "tradition carried over by British universities," whereby students dressed in "rags" and begged for money on behalf of the poor throughout the city. At a USARF meeting, the event was discussed at length, leading the group to conclude that it had to be opposed for its "mockery of the poor." Rag Day, USARF believed, symbolized a "band-aid, not a genuine solution to the problem of mass poverty."[28] On November 9, USARF sought to terminate "Rag Day" for its promotion of "bourgeois philanthropy" by barricading the lorries that were to transport students to the city center: As Issa Shivji recalled:

> Next day early morning tractors and lorries that were to carry the students to town for their begging spree arrived and were parked in the square near the post-office. There were about 200 students who were going to participate. When they came out of the cafeteria after their heavy breakfast they found that the tires of 'their' lorries had been punctured and that some 20 or so radical students had erected barricades across the exit of the square.[29]

Zakia Meghji remembers confronting pro–Rag Day students until police intervened, ultimately siding with USARF and canceling the event.[30] It was a small victory for USARF, one that brought immediate publicity to the fledgling organization on a national scale. Civil disobedience, however, was a tactic USARF rarely employed. Another time it was used was in July 1969 when USARF occupied the Faculty of Law building to protest the inclusion of military law courses in the core curriculum. On several occasions, it organized rallies and marches, usually concerning a global political event or issue.

In July 1968, USARF and TYL-UCD organized a mass march from the university college to the American embassy located in the city center to protest against U.S. militarized aggression in Vietnam. The protest was captured on film and in photographs by a U.S. news agency covering the activities of African American nationalist and fugitive-at-large Robert F. Williams, who had briefly settled in Dar es Salaam after six years of political exile in Cuba and China. Given the ominous title "'Let It Burn': The Coming Destruction of America," the news segment shows briefly a cluster of mostly African students chanting "Ho! Ho! Ho Chi Minh!" while jogging in military union past the National Hall of Commerce towards the U.S. Embassy.[31] USARF members took the lead in coming up with creative slogans for the picket signs. "For many activities, preparatory work was needed," Hajivayanis later remembered. "A demonstration had to have placards and banners . . . I made sure to contribute my share of the preparatory work. My close friend Ramadhan Meghji, a second-year student, was good at drawing and painting. He and I had a good time thinking up the slogans and phrases for the banners and drawing of the posters."[32] The end results help to illustrate the specific nature of USARF's anti-imperialism and antiwar stance. Examples included: "American Imperialist Society Is Rotten"; "Support the Vietnamese People for Independence"; "On Every Grave Will Rise a Raging Rice Field"; "Long Live Uncle 'Ho' and the Heroic People of Vietnam"; "Yankee! Go Home!"; "Create One, Two, More . . . Vietnams!"; "Johnson is a Murderer"; "Mmarekani ni Vampiri" (America Is a Vampire); and "The T.Y.L. University Branch and the University Students African Revolutionary Front Condemn U.S. Aggression in Vietnam."[33] The highlight of the demonstration occurred when U.S. ambassador Jon Burns allowed USARF and TYL-UCD to read out loud a joint statement shaming the United States for "sabotaging" the 1954 Geneva Accords that recognized Vietnam's right to national self-determination and independence.[34]

Other demonstrations and marches soon followed. Being based out of the university afforded USARF easy access to African liberation groups based in Dar es Salaam, and thus it set out to express its solidarity with their struggles against Portuguese colonialism and white minority rule in southern and central Africa. For example, on October 7, 1969, USARF organized "FRELIMO Day" in solidarity with the Marxist-inspired anticolonial nationalist group from Mozambique. The day began in the early evening with a campus-wide march that started at the cafeteria. About fifty students, joined by FRELIMO (Mozambique Liberation Front) representatives and others, marched in and around residence halls to the block of administrative offices while chanting in Kiswahili, "FRELIMO Oyee, Mreno zii, Kaburu zii (Kiswahili for "Up with FRELIMO, Down with the Portuguese Colonizers, Down with Apartheid"). After the march ended at Nkrumah Hall, the day concluded within the large assembly hall with a film screening on the life and work of Karl Marx, directed by a Cuban filmmaker, and speeches by representatives from FRELIMO and TYL-UCD.[35]

Between 1967 and 1969, African radical students had demonstrated their genuine excitement over the prospect of creating and sustaining a student movement that was aligned with yet critical of the government's foreign and domestic policies. In setting out to "rigorously" theorize a revolutionary alternative to Western-derived education and "traditional conservative scholarship," USARF used a Marxist framework of analysis to tease out the flaws of Tanzanian socialism in the name of national development and progress while gaining an understanding of the nature of struggles in other African countries as well as in Asia, the United States, Europe, Latin America, and the Caribbean. Infused with a new spirit of Third World internationalism and nationalism, USARF and TYL-UCD reached out to a faculty of "liberal, leftist, socialist, anti-imperialist, Pan-Africanist, or Marxist political orientation" for ideological mentorship and guidance. In an effort to broaden their thinking and their activism, USARF militants drew on the knowledge and resources of a contingent of progressive faculty, including but not limited to Guyanese historian Walter Rodney, Canadian political scientist Jon Saul, South African sociologist Archie Mafeje, Hungarian economist Tama Sventes, Tanzanian legal scholar Joseph Kanyiwanyi, Kenyan literary scholar Grant Kamenju, Italian sociologist/economist Giovanni Arrighi, British legal scholar Sol Picciotto, Ugandan political scientist Dan Nadubere; and British political economist Lionel Cliffe.

It first reached out to these mostly young faculty members when it began as a study group. In November 1969, USARF protested against the lecture of a visiting political scientist from the United States who appeared to have arrogantly dismissed and misconstrued Frantz Fanon's theory of revolutionary violence by organizing a symposium on Fanon. USARF called upon Rodney, Saul, and Kamenju to counter the American political scientist's "false interpretation." "In the process, we learn that it is as absurd to accuse Fanon of promoting violence or accuse Karl Marx of inventing class struggles as it is to accuse the doctor of spreading the case of malaria he has recognized."[36] Hirji further remarks:

> We learn the US State Department is waging an all-out global offensive to contain the spread of radical ideas, especially Marxist ideas, among university students, trade union and peasant movements. One way it does this is by dispatching a veritable army of pliant academics who articulate the US ideological line on world affairs. These scholars are ideological cold warriors in disguise and not simple academics.[37]

To keep a "constant vigilance against imperialist ideology and propaganda by every possible means," USARF also organized weekly "Ideological Classes" that further utilized the progressive faculty on campus. Held every Sunday morning, the inaugural session occurred on October 12, 1969, at the main lecture room in the Faculty of Law building, where they addressed the fundamentals of Marxism.

Over the course of the next five years, university professors, university students, and representatives of African liberation groups facilitated sessions on a range of theoretical issues. For example, at the 2nd Ideological Class of the 1969–1970 Academic Year, Sventes lectured on the core concepts and arguments of Karl Marx's *Das Kapital*, while Rodney's lecture explored the "political economy of African labor under capitalism and imperialism." USARF student Eriya Kategaya concluded the session with a talk on the long history of social transformation in human societies.[38] But these Sunday morning sessions went beyond lectures. A syllabus was created each academic year, and its reading list was as diverse as the range of subjects they studied for critical debate. Political economy and colonialism were the most popular subjects of inquiry, and they looked to the works of Karl Marx, Frederick Engels, Vladimir Lenin, Mao Tse-Tung, Frantz Fanon, Kwame Nkrumah, and Odinga Odinga for insight while supplementing them with writings by economists, agronomists, and novelists.[39] Indeed, one of the significant aspects of "Ideological Classes" is that progressive faculty followed the lead of the USARF students in making rigorous analytical study a salient feature of USARF's activism. By delivering lectures, suggesting books and articles to read, and tailoring curriculum to the needs of its students, progressive faculty like Rodney were giving students the tools to, in the words of Shivji, challenge the "bourgeois compartmentalization of knowledge" and understand how "knowledge cannot, and ought not to be divided."[40]

USARF attempted to balance academic, ideological study with political practice by engaging with nation-building work off-campus. Hoping to demonstrate its commitment to the government's policy of Ujamaa na Kujitegemea and to gain a deeper understanding and connection to the peasant lived experience, USARF students organized site visits to the Kongo Ujamaa Village in Dar es Salaam in 1969 and the Mpugunzi (Kiswahili for "revolution") Ujamaa Village in Dodoma in 1970. These visits were not just designed to observe at a closer distance the on-the-ground results of the government's villagization policy that sought to modernize and socialize agricultural production. Instead, USARF students actively participated in the agricultural labor by clearing, digging, and planting for "several hours" and forging interpersonal bonds with the people of the village community.

In his essay "The Spark Is Kindled," Hirji relies on his personal diary in revisiting his experience at Kongo: "Upon return to the Hill at 6:30pm, our arms and feet ache from the grind of the day. Yet we are upbeat in spirits. I feel the trip was an essential expression of solidarity with fellow humans. It is not enough to talk and theorize

Chapter Three

about socialism. We have to physically participate in the struggles on-the-ground as well."⁴¹ For USARF member Zakia Meghji, doing shamba (farm) work showed her the importance of making the issue of women's marginalization and oppression in African societies a key aspect of the African liberation agenda. As she recalled many years later,

> The situation of women in the rural areas was also of specific interest. I was touched by the atmosphere in the villages and soon became engulfed in their day to day activities. I was really touched by young children waking up before sunrise, carrying buckets of water on their heads, and walking long distances to and from their homes... Overall we tried to share the daily lives of the villages in every respect... I grounded with my sisters. I returned to the Hill as a new person, understanding much more the suffering of the people. In the academic classes on underdevelopment in Africa, I was more aware of the real situation and appreciated the arguments in relation to our concrete situation.⁴²

Hajivayanis's recollections of his shamba work at the Mpugunzi Village in Dodoma center on how Rodney, who accompanied the students, facilitated an enriching conversation between the students and the villagers about Ujamaa na Kujitegemea. "I still remember our work with the peasants in their plots at their homes," he remembered. "We had nocturnal discussions with the peasants about the policy of socialism and their future. They really appreciated him [Rodney]."⁴³ As these recollections suggest, USARF's work in socialist villages exposed students to the collective agency of the peasants, opened their eyes to the issue of women's oppression, made USARF a tighter-knit group, and brought them closer to progressive faculty on an interpersonal level.

USARF took seriously the notion that it was participating in an anti-imperialist struggle over ideas. It was not enough to share and exchange ideas through marches, film screenings, symposiums, and lectures, or by spending a few hours each week working with the peasants. USARF felt that the most effective way to participate in this ideological struggle was through producing its own student journal. At a USARF meeting held in November 1969, the group decided to produce a journal, *Cheche* (Kiswahili for "Spark"), naming it after the revolutionary journals that provided the ideological armor of the revolutions in Russia and Ghana. Through consultation with university faculty members Rodney and Kanyiwanyi, it was decided that *Cheche* would be dedicated to identifying the obstacles to African liberation in the context of neocolonialism, exploring the theoretical applicability and relevance of Marxism to Africa, assessing the successes and failures of Ujamaa socialist policy in Tanzania, and challenging "bourgeois" control over academic knowledge.⁴⁴

Although it had limited funds and supplies, USARF was able to produce three issues of *Cheche* between 1969 and 1970 in large part due to the extensive labor of its editorial team, comprised of Hirji, Mapolu, and Zakia Meghji. On the 26th of November, 293 copies of *Cheche*'s first issue were released and put on sale, with a handful mailed to African liberation groups, libraries, and secondary schools. In introducing the journal, USARF editors' declare:

> Thus far, the university has not played the role it should be playing in the construction of a socialist society. So we struggle to make that happen. That is why we do what we do. We are not saints, but inexperienced students with faults, failings and personal inclinations. But our dreams and strivings are for the total liberation of Africa, and for a humane, just and egalitarian society where no one will go hungry or lack the basic necessities of life.[45]

In many ways, *Cheche* managed to adhere to its initial vision by relying on the contributions of the university college's progressive faculty. Issue no. 1 features the work of John Saul, Archie Mafeje, Tama Szentes, and Walter Rodney. Rodney, for example, contributed a work-in-progress on class formation in Africa, after being sought out specifically by Mapolu. But the inclusion of progressive faculty never dominated the journal's pages. *Cheche* was a collaborative endeavor. Students were major contributors as well, showcasing what they were learning in the courses taught by progressive faculty. Its first two issues were largely internationalist in scope and content as *Cheche* featured analytical essays written from multiple disciplinary perspectives, exploring topics such as socialism in Sweden, Portuguese colonialism in West Africa, political leadership and African liberation groups, the role of youth in revolutionary struggle in Africa, and U.S. covert operations in Africa. Supplementing these sharp, well-researched essays were poems and cartoons that gave the journal artistic and comedic appeal.

The reviews were mixed. To some, *Cheche* was seen as an amazing accomplishment, evident in the letters of support that poured into its "office" after the release of its first issue. The government and party, on the other hand, sent a contradictory message to USARF students, publishing two articles over the course of one week in the *Nationalist*. While the first article praises the journal, the second review penned by the newspaper's editor in chief, Benjamin Mkapa, criticizes the ways in which *Cheche* emphasized international issues without discussing their relevance to Tanzania's conditions. Equally disconcerting was the use of Marxist language and "abstruse theories." Put simply, USARF reliance on "foreign ideologies" was regarded as a potentially dangerous development, and the government continued to use the print media to mount this conflicting message.

The Second Seminar of East and Central African Youth marked a major turning point for both USARF and Walter Rodney. For the first time since his arrival in Dar es Salaam, Rodney became a target of state repression (though in a mild form), which held implications for USARF's future. In the lead-up to the conference, he had made a profound impression on the university's political culture, garnering a following among radical students from his courses on African and African Diaspora history as well as his public lectures on topics ranging from the Cuban Revolution and its relevancy to Africa to the revolutionary theories of Frantz Fanon. Held at the Hill during the second week of December 1969, and sponsored by TYL, the seminar was viewed by many as an opportunity for youth to collectively envision a free and united Africa.[46]

TYL-UCD's secretary, A. S. Namano, invited Rodney to be the main speaker at the seminar and to share his views on the challenges facing the pan-Africanist movement on the continent.[47] Rodney readily obliged, and presented a paper titled "The Ideology of the African Revolution" that demonstrated his increased attention to internal class conflict and the emergence of political elites in post-independent African nations. Describing the African revolution as a "a process aimed at restoring the dignity and freedom of African people and at giving that freedom and dignity concrete expression through the eradication of poverty, misery etc.," Rodney goes on to identify the failures of anticolonial nationalist movements, particularly the inability of its leaders to attack capitalism and imperialism once formal independence was achieved. In the postcolonial context, these nationalist leaders who were once "genuine spokes[men] of the masses" had joined "the band of exploiters" and promoted a "narrow nationalism and tribalism."[48] It was a biting critique, but one that was not a total shock to the seminar participants. Hirji, a USARF member, later remembered Rodney's argument as a "statement of plain fact, a rewording of the false decolonization" argument put forth in Frantz Fanon's *The Wretched of the Earth* (1961).[49] To Hirji and fellow USARF comrade George Hajivayanis, though they both agreed with Rodney, they could see how his comments could be considered as transcending the "norms of diplomacy."[50]

Where Rodney seemed to have "crossed the line" is when he takes his analysis further by harshly critiquing the socialist projects spearheaded by unidentified African governments: "The petty-bourgeois ideology, however, has been framed with the knowledge that 'capitalism' is not an acceptable word to the African toilers, who understand (however vaguely) that Socialism speaks on their behalf. Therefore, the petty-bourgeoisie usually assert that they are choosing the virtues of both capitalism and socialism in order to produce something unique called "African Socialism"—a curious creature that has turned out to be neither African nor socialist. It is, in fact, nothing but the capitalist hyena dressed up in African petty-bourgeois clothes."[51] While Rodney maintained that postcolonial African governments' inability to "revolutionize" their economies was a continent-wide problem, the TANU government took offense to Rodney's suggestion that leaders of their type had taken the "word 'socialism' and used it as a bush behind which to hide their exploitative tendencies."[52]

The TANU government responded to Rodney's paper with an editorial titled "Revolutionary Hot Air," published in the *Nationalist* on December 13. After stating that Rodney's position "did not represent Tanzania's ideas about socialism," the editorial condemns Rodney's advocacy of overthrowing neocolonial regimes in Africa through violent means. "Completely unacceptable," it reads, especially coming from a foreigner who seemed to have abused "the hand of friendship" extended to him by the government after his ban from entering Jamaica a year before.[53] In drawing attention to Rodney's noncitizenship status, the government was explicitly reminding him of his precarious political position in the country.

> Both Tanzanians, and non-Tanzanians, in this country must accept two things. The subversion of our constitution, and the use of Tanzania facilities to attract other African states are both equally unacceptable here. Surrounding them with revolutionary jargon and the use of words like 'imperialist', 'neocolonialist', and 'capitalist', does not alter their unacceptability.[54]

It was widely believed at the time that President Nyerere authored the editorial. If true, this rebuke of Rodney's ideas is all the more significant, raising questions about the role of diaspora political activists in Tanzania. Clearly, from the state's perspective, a leftist's critical interpretation of postcolonial nation-building was unwanted and frowned upon.

Given the magnitude of the backlash to his paper, Rodney hoped to mend what was clearly a fractured relationship with the Nyerere government with an editorial piece of his own. In "Dr. Rodney Clarifies," published four days after "Revolutionary Hot Air," Rodney takes a conciliatory tone and approach, first clarifying that his argument was indeed his own and never put forth as the position of the government or party. More importantly, he then explains how an ideology of revolution was "effectively" being carried out "by the President, Party, and Government of the United Republic of Tanzania,"[55] and therefore Tanzania, in unequivocal terms, was not to be considered a neocolonial regime. As far as his using particular terms in his analysis of Africa's concrete conditions, Rodney remains unapologetic. The same can be said when addressing his foreigner status. He writes: "My indulgence in those terms is aimed at exposing a system which is barbarous and dehumanizing—one which snatched me from Africa in chains and deposited me in far-off lands to be a slave beast, then a sub-human colonial subject, and finally an outlaw in those lands. Under those circumstances, one asks nothing but to be allowed to learn from, participate in, and be guided by the African Revolution in this part of the continent; for this Revolution here is aimed at destroying that monstrous system and replacing it with a just socialist society."[56] In many ways, the government's attack on Rodney was an attack on USARF, of which Rodney was an honorary member. While USARF tried to err on the side of caution by deciding against publishing his seminar paper in the no. 4 issue of *Cheche*, the "Rodney affair," as it was called, did manage to become a contributing factor in USARF's rapid demise less than a year later.

The 1969-1970 academic year proved a difficult one for USARF. While the success of *Cheche* and other initiatives boosted the organization's profile within various political circles, the TANU government's attack on the students picked up steam. USARF visits to Ujamaa Villages, liberated zones in Mozambique and Angola, and public lectures did not test the boundaries of Nyerere's "tolerant yet paternalistic approach" to student and faculty radicalism at the university college.[57] What appeared most troublesome to President Nyerere and the TANU government was its militant student journalism. Although produced on a shoestring budget and limited resources, *Cheche* became an internationally distributed journal that gave a wide-ranging audience an alternative view of the Tanzanian revolution.

Much as in the anti–National Service protest of 1966, USARF had exerted their political autonomy and deviated from the state's conception of youth; yet in USARF's case, it had swayed too far to the left. While publicly admonishing USARF in the *Standard*, which was nationalized in the same year, the TANU government worked to urge the group to tone down its rhetoric and criticism. When Nyerere held a question-and-answer session at the university in October, USARF dominated the discussion, pressuring the president with calls for greater commitment to socialism among the political elites and against the hiring of nonsocialist lecturers and professors, only to have Nyerere publicly rebuke their politics in front of the entire university community. Two private meetings between USARF and Nyerere soon followed. However, the stalemate between USARF and the government did not last very long after the second meeting with the president. This was due in part because USARF did not heed his words after the first meeting. In addition, the prospect of USARF overtaking the student government in the coming elections was a major cause of concern. Finally, the special issue of *Cheche* that was released in October on the internal class struggle in Tanzania did not assuage the one-party government's fears about USARF's leftist politics.

The success of the group, especially when measured in terms of the autonomy with which USARF students operated, led the government and party to intervene and assert control over what constituted student activism in service of the nation by banning the organization. On November 12, at a meeting between USARF, TYL, and the university administration, USARF was informed that the organization had to cease all activities. Try as it might to justify the ban by claiming that USARF was redundant since TYL-UCD already existed, the government made it known that its decision was final.⁵⁸ USARF refused to accept this line of reasoning, and hastily organized an emergency meeting to develop a strategic response. After careful deliberations, however, it decided against mounting a protest to save the organization.

The ban did not entirely eradicate leftist politics at the university, as may have been intended. Many USARF members joined or remained members of the university's TYL branch. Perhaps the most significant consequence of the banning of USARF, however, was the marginalization of non-Tanzanian students. Membership in TYL's university branch, unlike USARF, required that a student was a Tanzanian citizen. With USARF banned, radical students from Kenya, Uganda, Malawi, Sudan, and Ethiopia found themselves alienated from a new campus political culture monopolized by TYL. USARF's principles, aims, and objectives were pushed within the structure of the party's youth wing, as radical students and progressive faculty continued to promote a Marxist critique of Tanzanian socialism and class formation as well as publishing these ideas via a radical student journal, but under a different name. As a response to charges of being brainwashed by foreign ideologies, this new contingent of TYL-UCD leftists (former USARF Tanzanian students) renamed *Cheche* to *Maji Maji*, after "the first 'multi-tribal' united front" against German colonialism in Tanganyika where Africans relied on a spirit medium for leadership; but, the journal felt it necessary to add: "Today the superstitions must be replaced by a scientific outlook" as Marxism's "usage of science is essential if our people are to conquer poverty, ignorance, and disease."⁵⁹

Former USARF students waged their final protest in the pages of its first and second issues, released January 1971 and July 1971 respectively, with a series of editorials. Its first issue featured a statement of support for USARF and was highlighted by an article that took to task the university curricula: "Bourgeois education is not designed to produce thinking and committed individuals. It aims to churn out upholders of the capitalist system that would question its irrationality." What were needed were books largely written by European and African Marxists. The highlight of its second issue was Hirji's "Militancy at the Hill," where he argues that the ban "isolated" USARF from student masses and "effectively de-radicalized" them. Indeed, the piece reads like an admission of defeat as Hirji claims that USARF got caught up in "petty-bourgeois intrigue" and was never able to develop any significant relations with peasants and workers it sought to represent. On a certain level, it was a fair critique in terms of USARF's tendency to indulge in rhetoric and sectarian politics.⁶⁰

The demise of USARF coincided with the university transitioning from an affiliate college of the University of East Africa to a nationalized university. In November 1970,

Chapter Three

UCD officially became the University of Dar es Salaam (UDSM). With Rodney and other leftist intellectuals under scrutiny, the nationalization of the university raised questions about the extent to which the state would tolerate academic freedom, particularly among its leftist faculty. It was no secret that the most conservative members of the TANU government and university administration were opposed to their presence, arguing that they had dominated the discourse on socialism at the university and adversely affected students with their foreign Marxist ideologies.[61]

Despite his rift with Nyerere and the TANU government in 1970, Rodney continued to define his active participatory role in Tanzania's nationalist project within the context of university education. This meant reforming core curriculum, advising and collaborating with radical African students affiliated with TYL-UDSM as an honorary Youth League member, and teaching undergraduate and graduate courses. As his reputation grew, so did the size of his classes—an array of course offerings that, he later recalled, presented "new formulations to students" on how "to address political questions in a very direct manner."[62]

In "Historians and Revolutions," for example, he provides an advanced course for master's students in the Department of History that explores the historiographies of the French and Russian Revolutions. The course was marked by its multiple intentions to introduce students to the praxis of historiography and to dialectical materialism as a methodological approach to writing histories of revolutionary struggles across the globe.[63] He impressed upon students that doing history was a politically interpretive and subjective act. Thus, they needed to rid themselves of the notion that objectivity was a prerequisite to writing history. For essay assignments, he posed questions that required students to think seriously about the applicability of Marxist theory and a comparative framework of analysis to understanding revolutionary moments, past and present.[64]

In another advanced course, "Black Peoples in the Americas," Rodney's primary goal was to provide students with a comparative lens from which to analyze the impact of the transatlantic slave trade on black communities in the Caribbean, Brazil, and the United States. This course was divided into three parts, where students learned about the varied processes of socialization during and after slavery, and modes of black resistance and accommodation during the postwar period. It was a course that challenged the restrictive categorization of history as nation-centric by "bourgeois" historians, maintaining that the history of black peoples tied to the transatlantic slave trade is best understood from an analysis that traverses national-territorial boundaries.[65] By examining plantation slavery systems and post-emancipation societies across geographic spaces, students could compare and contrast varied social formations.

Having at their disposal significant works of the black radical intellectual tradition—such as Eric Williams's *Slavery and Capitalism*, W.E.B. Du Bois's *Black Reconstruction*, E. Franklin Frazier's *Black Bourgeoisie*, to name but a few—students were asked to compose written essays that discussed and evaluated the effectiveness of passive forms of resistance; located African cultural survivals in diaspora communities and discussed their importance; analyzed the relationship between blacks and "mulattos" during the Haitian Revolution; charted the embarkation/disembarkation points of enslaved Africans and their specific slave-labor roles; and assessed the treatment of enslaved Africans and their descendants.[66]

In this same course, Rodney was equally interested in tracing the history and contours of U.S. black resistance to racial capitalism from the post-emancipation era to the Civil Rights/Black Power period. In order to answer questions about the possibilities and limitations of collective black political agency, the challenge put forth to students was to make sense of the multiple aims and objectives of black protest movements and the strategies and tactics black political actors employed. Reconstruction, black nationalism, pan-Africanism, race, class, segregation, and anti-black violence were concepts and categories to be taken up in order for them to view more comprehensively Black Power politics of the contemporary moment.[67] For Rodney, the postwar Black Power movement represented a tactical geographical shift from the rural South to the urban North, as well as an ideological shift as a result of mobilizing efforts in the urban ghettos. "To what extent," read one exam essay question, "did 'Black Power' mark a decisively new phase" in the black freedom struggle? To answer this question, students needed to account for the growing "lumpen" class awareness against "European bourgeois aspirations" occurring in impoverished black communities, and the centrality of repression and violence in shaping the black lived experience.[68] From a political perspective, the concern of this course was to expand students' notion of pan-Africanism to include the transatlantic diaspora.

On the whole, Rodney's teaching objectives were complex and multifaceted. He wanted to get students to identify "leading trends of change" and "the motion of history" by developing a habit of reading. Of equal significance was helping to transform students into effective public speakers and debaters. In discussing the latter's importance to students' intellectual and political development at a symposium held in Atlanta in 1974, Rodney proclaimed:

> One must understand that the purpose of debate is not to alienate and intimidate. The purpose is not to force certain other people to retreat into their shells and hence to stagnate. But it is to get out there and let people understand the power of one's ideas

and its relationship to their own lives and, at the same time, to be supremely confident that these ideas, if put forward in the clearest manner possible, will triumph against bourgeois ideas, assuming that the person to whom one is speaking doesn't have special class interests that will definitely tie him or her to a set of ideas.[69]

Rodney's pedagogy reflected his research interests and political activism, and offered clear examples of his belief that it was the duty of the university lecturer/professor, one committed to Tanzania's nationalist project, to develop students' critical consciousness of the history of capitalism and white supremacy on one hand, and the history of revolutionary struggle on the other. And through this process of learning, where ideology was openly embraced rather than dismissed under the guise of "objectivity," students would gain the necessary technical tools (i.e., skills in Marxist methodologies, empirical research, historical writing, public speaking) and a historical-political consciousness needed to critique actual policies of national development and formulate new ones that would genuinely empower "the producer classes" (i.e., peasants and workers). To "have a socialist society," Rodney argued, a nation needs "scientific socialist perspectives."[70] Above all, Rodney hoped that students would gain a deep appreciation of the "inseparable" link between theory and practice.

The impact of his unique teaching methods and style were indeed profound. USARF student Zakia Meghji, one of the few women in USARF, later recalled how attending Rodney's lectures made her realize "how erroneous my previous vision of African history had been."[71] His influence on students taking his courses stemmed from his "scientific and thoroughly-researched interpretation of history that challenged the colonial Eurocentric interpretation."[72] Meghji also noted how such courses were enhanced through Rodney's promotion of debate and dialogue:

> In the lecture, he presented the main points from it, giving us an opportunity to discuss them and give our own point of view. His lectures were extremely thought-provoking. In time, I became close to Rodney and his family—his wife Patricia, son Shaka, daughters Kanini and Asha. They would invite me and other students to their house on a regular basis. He loved to do this. After the meal, the comrades would continue to discuss and brainstorm about the world and local affairs until late at night. When later we walked back to our halls of residence that were about five minutes away from his house, we were well-fed and ideologically contented as well, looking forward to another day of struggle.[73]

As her recollections suggest, Rodney's impact and influence extended beyond the classroom as he forged enduring connections with students. This reflected a belief that their intellectual and political development required guidance, direction, and access to resources. For Rodney, he believed that one means of sustaining the pan-African movement was to create an approach to teaching and learning that emphasized dialogue and personal relationship building. He developed what he referred to as a "grounding" approach while at UWI in 1968, frequently leaving campus to converse and reason with Rastafarians and youth gangs in the poverty-stricken streets of Kingston.[74] In Dar es Salaam, very similar to his experience in Jamaica, "grounding" with students outside the classroom became an integral component of his political praxis.

His capacity to treat students as peers and "comrades-in-struggle" only further endeared him to the student community. For example, while Rodney was researching and writing his magnum opus, *How Europe Underdeveloped Africa*, he was having radical students read over drafts and provide comments. Like Meghji, Karim Hirji and George Mapolu of USARF (and then TYL-UDSM) forged kinship bonds with Rodney and his family and served as unofficial editors of his book. In his 2010 essay "Not So Silent a Spark," Hirji fondly remembers how on any given night one could find Rodney typing out "page after page" of *How Europe Underdeveloped Africa* in his office.[75] But what most impressed Hirji was how receptive Rodney was to their critiques, and the way he treated them as critical contributors to his research and writing process. "For several weeks he has given draft copies of the chapters, one at a time, to Henry and me. We read the drafts, and meet with him. Imagine a stalwart historian giving his manuscript to two upstart students, and sitting down for hours to listen to their comments."[76] Hirji and Mapolu's most pressing criticisms, Hirji much later recalled, had to do with getting Rodney to be more critical of Tanzanian socialism and to frame national independence in Africa as a "limited step forward."[77]

As the title suggests, *How Europe Underdeveloped Africa* is concerned with the question of Africa's postcolonial future by focusing on the impact of the transatlantic slave trade and colonialism on the social, cultural, economic, and political development of African peoples. In combining Latin American dependency with Marxist dialectics, Rodney argues that the transatlantic slave trade and colonialism constituted historic periods of economic exploitation and political subjugation that resulted in the social, economic, technological, cultural, and political development of Europe at the expense of Africa. When discussing the book a few years after its publication in 1972, he did not mince his words in explaining the book's political rather than historiographical purpose. The book, however, was widely embraced in academic and nonacademic circles alike, further catapulting Rodney and UDSM into the international spotlight. Its popularity ended up garnering for him a reputation as one of the foremost Black Marxists of his generation, and the university as an internationalist site of higher learning. One would be hard-pressed to argue against the fact that *How Europe Underdeveloped*

Africa was a direct outgrowth of the "militant leftist" movement and political culture that Rodney, African students, and others had fashioned over a short period of time. For Rodney, it gave him a broader platform to share his erudite knowledge of history and political views, evidenced in the enormous amount of invitation letters to speak at conferences, universities, and symposiums that filled up his office mailbox. For students, the book, especially their direct and indirect involvement in its making, gave legitimacy to their activism and ideological training.

■ ■ ■ ■

As previously noted, Rodney served as a liaison of sorts, an ambassador from the African Diaspora, intent on raising students' consciousness of the Black Power movement in the United States. Thus, he was one of many whose presence in the country ensured that Black Power was part of the political discourse on the Hill. For radical African students, ever since Carmichael's visit in November 1967, the *Nationalist* and the *Standard* were crucial sources of information on the African American freedom struggle, both its civil rights and Black Power elements. The *Nationalist*'s coverage primarily revolved around three core, interlaced issues: urban riots, the nature of domestic repression of movement activists by the U.S. state, and the activities of black political leaders. The various explosive episodes of unrest in American cities did much to dispel any notion of interracial harmony, while the arrest and assassination of black political leaders, particularly Martin Luther King Jr. in April 1968, served to reinforce the legitimacy of the struggle against racism for the *Nationalist*'s readers. After King's death, questions about a leadership void in the movement were raised, and the *Nationalist* would go on to introduce its readership to the movement's new political figures and organizations, such as James Farmer of the Congress of Racial Equality (CORE), H. Rap Brown and the Student National Coordinating Committee (SNCC), Huey P. Newton and Eldridge Cleaver of the Black Panther Party (BPP), Amiri Baraka of the Congress of African People (CAP), and Owusu Saduakai of the African Liberation Support Committee (ALSC).

In the spirit of pan-Africanism, USARF and TYL-UCD students committed themselves to learning about and engaging with black struggles in the African Diaspora not solely through the pages of the TANU Party's newspaper. Information sharing and exchange was realized through public lectures sponsored by the two student organizations. Often acting as cosponsors, USARF/TYL-UCD brought to campus high-profile African American political leaders, activists, and intellectuals such as Stokely Carmichael in 1967 (see chapter 2), Robert F. Williams in 1968, and Angela Davis in 1973.

As noted in the previous chapter, Stokely Carmichael made a huge impression on students when he was invited to speak at the university college under the auspices of the USARF, then known as the Socialist Club. As the national press noted, his comments on corrupt African political leadership and the racist underpinnings of Western educational institutions were met with the chant "Black Power!" From Williams's lecture, they learned about the state of the Cuban and Chinese revolutions based on his experiences in exile in both countries; the bankruptcy of reformist civil rights politics; the nature of U.S. government repression against U.S. black radicals; and how racism was an integral component of Western imperialism.[78]

In the journals *Cheche* and *Maji Maji*, radical students took a keen interest in the work of the Black Panther Party and the repression it faced under the Nixon administration. This form of identification with the Panthers had much more to do with the powerful Marxist currents of the organization than any simple notion of racial kinship. Having formed in 1966 in California, by 1969 the BPP emerged to incredible global prominence by espousing armed revolutionary violence and social-economic justice. It was no secret to the world that the U.S. government had identified the Panthers as the most dangerous Black Power organization in the United States, and went to enormous lengths to dismantle the organization through covert surveillance, harassment, imprisonment, assassination, and other means. USARF/TYL-UCD also appeared aware of the growing tensions within the U.S. Black Power movement between cultural nationalists, Marxists, and liberals. Yet, as Marxists were caught up in the ideological struggle within the continental pan-Africanism movement, they took an antagonistic stance against liberals and cultural nationalists. For instance, issue no. 3 of *Cheche* carried an article on the CIA and the Black Power movement that claimed the covert agency was primarily responsible for co-opting mainstream civil rights leadership and black cultural nationalists to "maintain a foothold in African states in order to emasculate black radicalism in Africa."[79] The repression meted out against African American radicals by the U.S. state, it further argued, served to redefine Black Power in the forms of African cultural romanticism and capitalism. "But Black Power hardly seems a revolutionary slogan today. It has been refined and domesticated, awarded a prominent niche in the American Dream."[80]

To further illustrate this point about its interest in understanding the perceived decline of Black Power because of state repression against its most radical elements, USARF/TYL-UCD students continued to follow and assess the activities of organizations and leaders they identified with on an ideological level. The assassination of George Jackson and the trial of Angela Davis between 1970 and 1973 offered an opportunity for African radical students to express their solidarity with the African American freedom movement as well as critically debate U.S. nation-state power. Radical students looked again to Rodney for guidance and insight. In "George Jackson: Black Revolutionary,"

Chapter Three

which appears in issue no. 5 of *Maji Maji*, Rodney introduces his targeted Tanzanian/African audience to the recently slain African American political prisoner and member of the Black Panther Party (BPP), one of the movement's most militant Black Power organizations, who was "incarcerated for years under the most dehumanizing conditions because he discovered that blackness need not be a badge of servility but rather could be a banner for uncompromising revolutionary struggle."[81] Rodney then gives a concise biographical sketch, telling of the circumstances that led to his incarceration at the age of eighteen; his one-year-to-life sentence for a minor, nonviolent crime; his radicalization in prison under the tutelage of Marx and Mao as well as the Panthers; the courageous but failed attempt by his younger brother, Jonathan, to free him by the use of force when on trial for murder of a prison officer (which led to Jonathan's death along with two others); the imprisonment and trial of one of George's closest comrades, Angela Davis, the Black Marxist professor, for allegedly aiding Jonathan Jackson; and ending with the assassination of George Jackson in August 1971. But Rodney's recounting of this chain of events is meant to illustrate what Jackson's life can teach the world about the racial and class character of black resistance in the "belly of the beast." Rodney sees the prison movement that Jackson initiated in the United States as a crucial component of the African American freedom struggle writ large for politicizing the "undesirable elements" of the black community, igniting an international solidarity movement to free Angela Davis, and spawning white radical resistance inside the United States.

For Rodney, George Jackson is to be regarded as the embodiment of black "lumpen-proletariat" militancy in the same vein as the late Malcolm X. "White racist policies have tended in the direction of transforming the whole of the black population into lumpen," Rodney argued. "Under these circumstances, black people in the U.S.A. who are unemployed or 'criminals' cannot be dismissed as white lumpen in capitalist Europe were usually dismissed."[82] Rodney's take on the African American condition was radically conceived from a class-based framework of analysis, challenging what many thought of as a race- and domestic-based struggle. "Conversely, the black struggle is internationally significant because it unmasks the barbarous social relations of capitalism and places the enemy on the defensive on his own grounds."

Maji Maji continued to highlight the contributions of George Jackson to the worldwide struggle against imperialism by reprinting an interview with Jackson from the *London Observer* and reviewing his book, *Soledad Brother: The Prison Letters of George Jackson* (1970). Authored by Issa Shivji, one of USARF's founding members, the book review lauds Jackson's prison writings, placing his theoretical insights and understanding of the capitalist system on the level of Marx, Lenin, Trotsky, Mao, and Fanon. "He sees capitalism as an international system," wrote Shivji. "His attack is permeated with internationalism which transcends nationalism and racism—and this in a thoroughly racist society."[83]

Coverage of the trial of Angela Davis, who was charged with conspiracy, kidnapping, and murder by the state of California, was framed in similar internationalist solidarity terms. A year later, an editorial piece in *Maji Maji* read like a statement of racial solidarity after Angela Davis was acquitted of all charges: "We would like to take this opportunity also to salute Comrade Angela Davis for winning gallantly her battle with the U.S. pigs. It is so rare for clear-minded people to be at large in that part of the world that all of us must be grateful that she has been released. She will certainly be a tremendous asset to the fighting black people in the United States at this juncture when they so badly need clear ideological guidance. We should of course have no illusions whatsoever, the pigs are after her and if they have failed to eliminate her 'legally,' they will certainly try their hand at illegal methods. Thus ultimately it is upon all of us to fight relentlessly against racism and reaction. Meanwhile, however, we wish Angela bright success in her oncoming trials!"[84] The following year, on August 24, Davis visited the university campus for a talk sponsored by TYL-UDSM and the university branch of Umoja wa Wanawake (UWT), the women's wing of TANU. As soon as she stepped to the podium to speak about socialism and political prisoners before a jam-packed crowd in Nkrumah Hall, she was greeted with cheers, hand clapping, and screams of "Dada" (Kiswahili for "Sister") Angela.[85] Courses, public lectures, books, Ideological Classes, and journalism represented the channels and processes through which African students developed an African Diaspora consciousness on the Hill. Partially because of Rodney's activities, African students, Tanzanian and non-Tanzanian, came to be allies of the Black Power movement.

■ ■ ■ ■

Shortly before the historic Sixth Pan-African Congress, which was held in Dar es Salaam in 1974, Rodney and his family left Tanzania for good. He settled in his home country of Guyana and became a leading figure in the working-class struggle against a Forbes Burnham-led government. Before resettling there, Rodney shared his reasoning for leaving Tanzania, for leaving Africa, at a symposium organized by the Institute of the Black World (IBW), a black radical intellectual think tank, pointing out his noncitizenship status as a key determining factor:

> I could have become a Tanzanian citizen, and indeed thought about it seriously. The question is, what does that really mean? You change your legal status, you become a new national and, therefore, hopefully you are open both to the advantages and disadvantages of being a national of that country. I say hopefully because there are

times when people have changed their nationality and the government in existence or perhaps the succeeding government still treats them as being apart. Because their citizenship was granted rather than being a matter of birth, it could be revoked.[86]

Rodney also felt strongly that cultural alienation impeded his nation-building work. As an outsider, he would never be able to fully grasp the cultural worldview of the peasants and workers whose needs and aspirations he passionately championed. It should be noted, however, that Rodney's activities did pose a problem to the TANU government in a manner that was reminiscent of the concerns it had with Carmichael during his visit in 1967. While it provided a space and forum for debate, it had a very clear idea of the boundaries within which black radical expatriates could operate in sharing their views and technical skills. Undoubtedly, it held minimal tolerance for their criticism of postcolonial nation-building projects and the economic interests of political elites. Rodney recognized this fact, and its implications factored into his decision to leave Tanzania as well. It was this marginal position of black radicals in Tanzania, combined with worsening economic conditions and increasing political repression in Guyana, that pushed him away from the East African nation and pulled him towards the country of his birth, which just so happened to be Tanzania's closest Caribbean ally.

Under the auspices of the Working People's Alliance (WPA), Rodney set out to topple a government through a working-class coalition of Afro-Guyanese and Indo-Guyanese peoples after Burnham denied him employment at the national university. Sadly, on June 13, 1980, Rodney was killed by a car bomb explosion. Back in Tanzania, after learning of his death, the radical community on the Hill moved into action. Their memorialization of Rodney was captured in a special issue of *Maji Maji* where they demanded that the university administration "confer upon Dr. Rodney an honorary degree posthumously" for his "dedication to committed scholarship and his unflinching devotion to the cause of the oppressed" that "inspired many a student and member of staff, and reverberated beyond the four walls of the University."[87]

Between 1969 and 1974, in the face of widespread criticism concerning the status and the role of the university in building a socialist society, students, lecturers, and professors seized on the value of theory and practice afforded by a political landscape of worldwide revolutionary struggle. Such developments brought intellectuals and students of like mind to the country's premier university, resulting in the cultivation of relationships of reciprocity that served as one defining characteristic of the alternative teaching and learning experience students and faculty created. Their interactions, both inside and outside the classroom, both formal and informal, translated into their mutual intellectual and political development.

Despite the negative impact of state censorship of radical student and faculty voices, their intellectual and activist work had a number of important consequences for the pan-Africanism movement. First, the collaboration between students and Walter Rodney represented an effective model of cooperation and reciprocity between Tanzanians and Black Power activists. Secondly, he cultivated a pan-Africanist consciousness among the next generation of Tanzanian nationalists by exposing university students to African Diaspora history, culture, and politics from books and authors historically excluded from university curricula. His experience in Tanzania was a part of a broader migratory trend, revealing how the diasporic relationship to Tanzanian nation-building was moving from theory to practice, from diplomatic visits and tours to long-term relocation. This transition from a rhetoric of political friendship to active participation within clearly defined labor roles was primarily due to the consistent demonstrations of committed leadership on the part of President Nyerere (i.e., the Arusha Declaration, "Education for Self-Reliance," and the TANU leadership code). The president had recognized that intellectuals had a role to play in the production of socialist, skilled technicians, and diaspora activists seized upon this developmental need.

While Rodney was working within the structures of advanced education in addressing the state's education policy, a group of former SNCC activists based out of Washington, DC, chose to address the educational needs of African diasporans and Africans from a different angle by publishing books about pan-Africanism and working closely with the state's Tanzania Publishing House (TPH). Rodney's intellectual life and political activism at the university showed how diasporan political activists could play an influential role in nation-building. At the same time, it revealed its limitations. Would other Black Power activists confront the same political experience of reciprocity and marginality? This question is taken up in the following chapter, which explores the cross-fertilization of the publishing movements in Tanzania and Black America.

Chapter 4

The Drum and Spear Press and the Cultural Politics of Book Publishing

> Books can break down the isolation of our lives and provide us with a friend wherever we may be. I think we have to try very hard in Tanzania to cultivate the habit of reading among our young people and among our newly literate citizens. It is a fact which we must recognize, that in dealing with the modern world children in Europe have two big advantages over our own children. One is the familiarity with mechanical things, the other, and perhaps even more important one, is familiarity with books.
> —Mwalimu Julius Nyerere, President of the United Republic of Tanzania

In the context of the Black Power movement in the United States, the publication of *How Europe Underdeveloped Africa* positioned Walter Rodney as one of the most important intellectuals of the era. For anyone interested in gaining a historical understanding of slavery and colonialism in Africa and the challenges that postcolonial states faced in ridding their nations of these legacies, Rodney's text became required reading and a part of a canon of revolutionary literature joining the likes of Malcolm X's *The Autobiography of Malcolm X*, Frantz Fanon's *Wretched of the Earth*, and Mao Tse Tung's *Quotations of Mao Tse Tung*, among many others. In the aftermath of *How Europe Underdeveloped Africa*'s publication, letters of congratulations and requests for signed copies poured into Rodney's office on the "Hill." The praise the book received among pan-Africanists had a lot to do with a long-held notion that literacy was a key vehicle to self-determination. As the 1960s passed to the 1970s, Black Power activists clung tightly to this notion of reading as a political practice, so much so they started to form independent bookshops to disseminate books like Rodney's on a grassroots level.

In 1967, five years prior to the release of *How Europe Underdeveloped Africa*, SNCC activist Charlie Cobb found himself inside the historic Présence Africaine bookstore and publishing house in Paris, standing in awe as he scanned over what seemed like an endless list of book titles about the African and African Diaspora experience. Located in the Quartier Latin in the 5th arrondissement of the city, the bookstore was founded in 1949 as a repository of knowledge to aid the pan-Africanist objectives of a cultural, political, and literary movement known as "Négritude." For almost twenty years, the bookstore provided access, naturally, to the writings of Aimé Césaire, Léopold Senghor, Léon Damas, and Frantz Fanon, among others of Francophone Africa and the Caribbean, as well as printed information that emphasized the cultural and historical diversity of the black world writ large. For Cobb, being in the bookstore brought up memories of his childhood, especially of his mother, whose intellectual interests in the Negritude movement stemmed from an academic background in literature. His father was a renowned reverend and activist who plied his trade in Washington, DC, Massachusetts, and Kentucky. Born in Washington, DC, in 1943, Cobb had a childhood that was shaped by a politically active family that exposed him to the value of education and trade-union and civil-rights activism. He also grew up at a time when decolonization in Africa figured heavily into his growing political consciousness:

> As I came of age, the things that are dramatic in my memory are the 1954 Supreme Court decision, the events in Little Rock, and the events in Montgomery, Alabama, and tangled in there are the independence of Ghana and the Mau Mau struggle in Kenya. I remember the *Pittsburgh Courier* used to run a little box on the front page that talked about the conflict in Kenya, the conflict in Congo, the Sharpeville demonstrations, Lumumba, Tshombe, Kasavubu, all of which were happening when I was in high school. These things were part of my consciousness, growing up.[1]

Thus, when Cobb enrolled at Howard University in 1962, he quickly fell into a friendship with Stokely Carmichael and other radical black students that gravitated towards the direct-action work of the Nonviolent Action Group (NAG), an anti-segregationist, national, and multiracial student organization that would end up producing some of the civil rights movement's most stalwart and inspirational young activists. Cobb soon joined SNCC, withdrew from Howard, and became a full-time fieldworker in the Deep South, working mainly on organizing voter-registration campaigns and conceptualizing and implementing "Freedom Schools," locally based civic education and political training schools, throughout the Mississippi Delta.[2]

How Cobb arrived at Présence Africaine had much to do with his role as communications secretary of SNCC, which proved an emotionally draining and time-consuming experience largely characterized by repeatedly combatting mainstream-media distortions of Black Power as an expression of white hatred and reactionary violence, and Carmichael as the devil incarnate. By 1968, Cobb was at a crossroads in his political life—suffering from activist's fatigue, yet interested in other pursuits outside of SNCC. Despite the fact that SNCC was making inroads in the international arena by embracing an anti-imperialist posture and fashioning a reputation as the leading Black Power organization in the United States through international travel, it was embroiled in a state of uncertainty that cast a dark shadow over the organization. The combination of federal government co-optation of the civil rights initiative in the southern states, and the rise of spontaneous urban rebellions in American cities since 1964 led to the outward migration of activists from the Deep South to cities like Philadelphia, Chicago, Detroit, and Washington, DC. However, the implementation of Black Power grassroots initiatives was slowed by internal disputes over white membership, ideological positions, and local and state repression. Eventually, SNCC merged with the Panthers to stem its gradual decline, but this partnership fell apart as quickly as it was put together. Thus, during the late 1960s, many activists, especially those who joined the organization in 1961, were confronted with the decision to envision life after SNCC. For Cobb, the question of whether to move into a new political-organizing direction inevitably overlapped with the question of whether to remain in the organization.

Cobb's brief visit to the Présence Africaine bookstore could not have occurred at a more auspicious time, as it marked the endpoint of a summer-long journey across three continents. Prior to his arrival in Paris, he was in Stockholm, Sweden, as part of a SNCC delegation to the International War Crimes Tribunal, an antiwar initiative organized by a group of European leftist intellectuals on U.S. military atrocities committed in Southeast Asia. This gathering brought Cobb briefly to Vietnam on a fact-finding mission. In the tribunal's aftermath, he delayed his return trip to the United States and, joined by fellow SNCC member Courtland Cox, traveled by ship down the coast of West Africa from Spain, conversing with African migrant laborers about nationalism and independence while making quick stops in Liberia, Senegal, and Guinea. It was a trip that proved to reinforce a commitment to the pan-Africanism movement that he felt needed to redouble its efforts in fostering transnational communication networks of solidarity between black transnational actors, and educating the masses of black and African peoples.

Chapter Four

Présence Africaine sparked an interest in political organizing in the context of institution-building and education. Cobb saw firsthand the power of information sharing and exchange, of providing access to a world of books written by and for Africans and people of African descent. With its stated aim of promoting African cultural identity and values, the bookstore came to symbolize something more than just a business enterprise.³ Instead, it offered an effective and tangible approach to rediscovering and connecting to Africa. At a time when African Americans were increasingly gravitating towards a black nationalist worldview, the collection and dissemination of the "right" books could address their cultural, political, and economic needs.⁴ Rather than remain in SNCC and rejoin the movement in Mississippi or Georgia, Cobb returned to Washington, DC, and threw himself into politicizing the book trade industry that eventually landed him in Dar es Salaam in the early 1970s. On January 11, 1968, he submitted an application to the Office for the Record of Deeds. He was seeking permission for his new nonprofit organization—Afro-American Resources, Inc. (AAR)—to operate in the D.C. area. Joining Cobb on AAR's board of directors were former SNCC activists Courtland Cox and Marvin Holloway.

The success of anticolonial nationalist movements in Africa convinced AAR that black-controlled institution-building linked with educational programming was an appropriate strategy for "dealing with either the psychological and practical needs of the black community" and combatting the "white-power complex" in the United States: "Afro-American Resources, Inc has witnessed the reassertion of black cultural legitimacy, the persistent attacks upon the distortions and self-defeating illusions concerning the Afro-American past. Members of the corporation . . . highly approve the impact of the independent states in Africa in enhancing the Black men of America's effort to achieve a positive re-orientation of their own lives. For these developments in Africa serve to underscore the American Black man's own potential for meaningful self-advance."⁵ Seeing itself as a local, national, and international resource center about the African and African Diaspora experience, AAR held the belief that the fundamental problem facing African Americans was the lack of a politicized racial consciousness and institutions to nurture its growth. AAR, therefore, embraced a mission that sought to establish "viable" institutions in the area of education and communications that sustained the black community's "struggle to foster an improvement in their collective quality of life." A major objective of AAR was to promote education-based programs designed to reject "white consciousness as human consciousness" and get African Americans to understand their African heritage and historical experience in the Western world.⁶

The United Church Commission for Racial Justice, a religious-based civil rights organization run by Cobb's father, provided AAR with necessary startup funds to implement its institution-building agenda. The $10,000 grant awarded to AAR was primarily used to set up AAR's first initiative: the Drum and Spear Bookstore. Initially located on the ground floor of an apartment complex called the New Amsterdam Hotel at 2701 14th Street and Fairmont in the northwest section of the city, the "heart" of the black community,[7] the bookstore was conceived as a community center of sorts where "the materials in stock . . . are those books that aid in understanding what social, political, and economic mechanisms are confronting black people in their struggle for freedom; and those books that give a positive understanding of the community."[8]

Washington, DC, was a city segregated by race and class dating back to the era of chattel slavery. Black Washingtonians experienced the severe effects of racist policies at the hands of city officials appointed by the president of the United States and administered by southern U.S. senators and congressmen who were known white supremacists. In the postwar era, D.C. underwent rapid changes due to white—and to a lesser extent black—middle-class flight and the subsequent ghettoization of largely all-black neighborhoods.[9] By the time the Drum and Spear emerged, decades of "separate but equal" politics had turned D.C. into a pseudo-colony where a white minority ruled over a black majority of largely working-class people.

This legacy and reality of systemic racial discrimination may very well explain why the Drum and Spear Bookstore was the city's first black-owned bookstore.[10] AAR's decision to organize in Washington, DC, was not solely because of some AAR members' ties to the area. Because of its 70 percent black majority, Washington, DC, offered a perfect opportunity for testing out a theory of black collective empowerment through local institution-building. The presence of Howard University, a historically black university formed in 1867 during the Reconstruction era, not to mention the city's rich history of black music, further added to the city's Black Power appeal. It was little wonder why the city was fondly nicknamed "Chocolate City" by the late 1960s. For AAR, basing its operations out of the 14th Street corridor, was a "conscious choice" to serve the community and "be near the large flow" of black Washingtonians.[11] Though the bookshop was not fully stocked with books on its first day of business, it opened up anyway in late April 1968 in what was later described as a "burnt out shop" on the corner of 14th Street and Fairmont Street.[12] By the end of its first week of business, the pungent smell of tear gas lingered throughout the entire store.

Few dispute the basic facts of what happened in the evening hours of April 29: SNCC leader Stokely Carmichael led a group of college-aged youth to the U Street Corridor, and entered businesses demanding they cease operations as a gesture of solidarity and respect for the slain civil rights leader Martin Luther King Jr. However, as numbers swelled and feelings of anger increased, things quickly escalated into acts of looting and arson for the next two days, spreading to other parts of the city.[13]

A state of emergency was issued and a curfew was set. The National Guard and local police occupied the city, putting out fires and arresting residents while doing little to protect the destruction of largely small-scale businesses. Signs of desperation posted on the doors and windows of stores that read "Very, Very, Very, Very Soul Brother" or just simply "Soul Brother" were ignored once this initial call for peaceful mourning escalated into spontaneous violence.[14] The damage done largely by 123 fires amounted to an estimated cost of $13.3 million.

The implications and impact of the event were assessed in a number of ways. Conservatives, liberals, and black militants all weighed in, feeding a national discourse on the racial and class dimensions of the urban crisis ignited by a series of black uprisings that began in 1964. Conservatives reduced the rebellion to a riot. Not only was it a manifestation of African American pathology, but it also was an example of how the Johnson administration had let white guilt for past racial injustices dictate a soft policy on crime. Law and order was replaced by a policy of impunity and racial-preference programs. For liberals, the uprising was once again proof of the extremes of urban poverty that framed rioting as an act of desperation. What was needed, in their view, was government intervention in housing, education, and business development.

Black Power activists, on the other hand, took an altogether different stance from the ones espoused by conservatives and liberals. For them the riots were rebellions—black working-class and underclass articulations of spontaneous violence. They were designed to force the government's hand in, at the very least, acknowledging the depths of economic exploitation and anti-black racism that pervaded U.S. society. What were the opinions on the acts of looting and burning? They saw these as revolutionary acts against capitalism and materialist consumption.[15] Black Power activists argued in this vein at the U.S. Senate Committee on the District of Columbia and the D.C. City Council, held throughout May 1968.[16] AAR was tied to this militant interpretation of the event, viewing the rebellion as an opportunity to think seriously about the city's redevelopment from the ground up. Because Washington, DC, was an urban space with a black majority, the formation of a black-run institution could potentially cultivate and wield enough collective power needed to foment structural change and racial equality.

Even though the federal and local government waxed poetic about urban-renewal plans, there was little economic investment to show for it all. Privately owned lots were left abandoned, with the exception of swelling piles of trash. By 1973, it was reported that "things are dragging still" and "all that has been achieved so far seems very small and disappointing."[17] Abandoned buildings and dilapidated public housing blended in seamlessly with the general dismal physical surroundings. As one journalist observed, "trashed clogged alleys and junked cars" became all too familiar visual reminders of President Nixon's "forgotten promise." Indeed, housing shortages, unemployment, and crime were all on the rise. At the same time, "the D.C. riot" displaced thousands of black workers, which swelled the ranks of the unemployed. For small business owners, the riots resulted in higher security costs and loan insurance rates, which inevitably raised prices of products and limited the number of storewide discounts. Owners had problems hiring people as well, due to a rising fear of crime in the area. This fear of crime was so widespread that businesses often closed before dark, leaving the streets virtually empty by evening time.[18] While these factors discouraged small business development, AAR saw in these federal and local acts of abandonment an opportunity to form and strengthen Black Power institutions during a period of urban crisis.

AAR's mission to promote political and cultural identification with Africa informed all aspects of the bookstore. It began with the bookstore's name. As Cox explained to one journalist: "The drum in the African world is a way of carrying information, the spear a method of defense. So the idea was the defense of the mind defending information."[19] AAR knew exactly what it was getting into when it entered the book trade industry. It held strongly to the belief that the inferiority complexes that so infected black people were a direct result of a "separate but equal" education—a deadly combination of the lack of book learning and access to resources and the consumption of books that projected a racist image of African people. In appropriating cultural and military symbols of precolonial Africa in the naming of the bookstore, AAR sought to connect the African past to the African American present, understanding their work as a means of protecting the mind against an ongoing onslaught of racist ideas about the black lived experience. After two years, in March 1970, the bookstore moved from its original location in a cramped, dark-lit space to a larger space around the corner at 1802 Belmont Rd.

The Center for Black Education (CBE), AAR's second institutional project, also grew out of AAR's frustration with the state of American education systems. "Education for us is meaningless," AAR argued, "if it does not attempt to train students to be servants of African people."[20] Initially, AAR tried to establish a presence at the newly formed Federal City College (FCC), a federally funded land-grant school for local residents of the urban working class founded in 1968. Its efforts to create a Black Studies program were immediately thwarted by the board of trustees, who had hired AAR-affiliated faculty members. As a response, they created CBE. Aware of the paucity of black-centered educational resource material and lack of institutional agency to generate such materials, the creation of the Drum and Spear Press (DSP) soon followed.

Based on the premise that the actual institutional organization of the black community was central to the degree to which individuals could achieve self-determination, the Drum and Spear Press had emerged as the final link to what would be known as the "Drum and Spear Complex." The Drum and Spear Bookstore, Center for Black

Education, and the Drum and Spear Press, though connected under the organizational umbrella of AAR, were autonomous institutions that sought to reinforce each other's respective aims and objectives. With this support network in place, the Drum and Spear Press entered into the world of American print capitalism, seeking to carve out their own sphere of influence guided by a vision of creating an autonomous Black Power print culture.

Its formation coincided with an unprecedented increase in independent book publishing activity.[21] In practically every major city, independent black book publishers emerged, serving as autonomous print-media businesses designed to stimulate a nationalist consciousness about racial identity and institution-building among people of African descent.[22] Through building independent black-run institutions, especially in poor urban communities that were systematically ignored by local and state governments, the Drum and Spear was determined to move against white-controlled institutions of communication, their monopolization of the industry, and reckless projection of degrading and dehumanizing images of black people. This black nationalist approach to publishing, grounded on a principle of self-reliance, attempted to make accessible to a wide, underserved audience books written predominately by black authors that refuted historically reproduced racist ideologies and practices.[23]

The DSP referred to itself as "Book Publishers for the Pan-African World," and it planned to publish six books a year, making available "books of historical significance, which generally sell at prohibitive prices, to the majority of the black community."[24] Its first publication was the reprint of C.L.R. James's 1939 classic *A History of Negro Revolt*, which was a fitting introduction and statement on what types of political and cultural messages the DSP sought to promote to a broad black audience. James, whose career as radical scholar and activist spanned decades, had resettled in the United States after being deported from the country for his political beliefs fifteen years earlier. Essentially, he had returned to an American political landscape that was literally and figuratively set on fire by black radical activity and outrage. Yet before this move from London to the United States in the spring of 1968, he visited Tanzania, met with President Nyerere, and delivered a lecture on the "rise and fall" of Nkrumah at the University of Dar es Salaam (UDSM).[25] Between 1969 and 1971, he gave lectures on Marxism, pan-Africanism, and Third World revolution at Howard University and Federal City College (FCC), a small land-grant college that catered to students of working-class backgrounds in Washington, DC. His exposure to the Black Power movement in the city seemed to give him renewed energy. In finding a "more sympathetic" audience to a "black revolutionary point of view," James quickly became a mentor to what he referred to as "the Drum and Spear people" that he came into close contact with as a visiting professor in literature and history at FCC.[26] His expertise in the history of worldwide revolutions, he believed, could serve to benefit a movement that lacked a historical consciousness. In a draft of his unpublished autobiography, he admitted that students influenced by Black Power were "very race conscious." However, not "in the ordinary sense of being aware of themselves as persecuted and suffering black people. No, black was beautiful, was not very historical, but was very contemporary... The average black student had little use for names like Frederick Douglass, and other famous names in the black corpus."[27]

With little resistance from James, the DSP renamed his text *A History of Pan-African Revolt*, a minor edit to signify a new engagement among black activists in positive acts of naming, and a clear reflection of its own political position. This new edition would also include a discussion of Ujamaa socialism, which was assessed in an extremely positive light: "The impact that the policies of Tanzania has made upon Africa and can in time make upon the rest of world, underdeveloped or advanced, has already established the African state of Tanzania as one of the foremost political phenomena of the twentieth century. Tanzania is the highest peak reached so far by revolting blacks and it is imperative to make clear, not least of all to blacks everywhere, the new stage of political thought which has been reached."[28]

As historian Robin D. G. Kelley noted, because booksellers in the 1930s tried their best to inhibit *A History of Negro Revolt*'s wide circulation, the DSP was correcting a past injustice by recirculating a groundbreaking book that was a "stinging indictment of colonialism" and a celebration of the political, religious, and cultural revolutionary spirit of Africans and peoples of African descent.[29] "This book is a double landmark," wrote CBE staff member Marvin Holloway in the book's introduction. "In these days when black people throughout the world are clamoring for self-knowledge, the Drum and Spear Press has recognized the need in servicing this rising concern."[30] *A History of Pan-African Revolt* highlighted the DSP's intention to service the intellectual needs of the black community by "providing channels through which black people can communicate with each other on issues vital to our lives."[31] Furthermore, by publishing texts of "black scholars of an earlier age" who historicized black social movements worldwide, the DSP understood the importance of instilling in its readers a sense of historical consciousness.

The books following this first publication covered a range of genres such as education, poetry, children's literature, history, and politics.[32] One could find advertisements and glowing reviews of its books in independent black journals such as the *Liberator*, *Black World*, the *Black Scholar*, and *Black Books Bulletin*. It also set up tables at teacher conferences and book fairs and advertised their products over its weekly radio program for kids. One other aspect of DSP activists' marketing strategy was taken out of the pages of their SNCC past. With flyers in hand, staff members visited the bars, street corners, barbershops, pool halls, and hair salons informing the community of the bookstore, press, and books available for purchase. While many scholars have stressed the importance of the rise of the Black Studies movement on college campuses, one issue that has not received the attention it deserves is how this movement fueled and sustained black bookshops throughout the United States.[33] The newly established Black Studies programs were the Drum and Spear's major sources of revenue. Black Studies programs at Cornell University, Stanford University, the University of California at Berkeley, and Howard University, for example, all bought their books from the Drum and Spear bookstore, which helped to fund the press.[34] By 1971, the DSP had an advisory board and possessed a computerized database of over ten thousand contacts and networks of support from the United States, Africa, and the Caribbean.[35]

As a black-owned small business run by activists, its organizational structure was roughly fashioned along the lines of SNCC: it was nonhierarchical, where positions were relatively fluid, giving staff members enough autonomy to creatively pursue and implement ideas. The AAR and its three initiatives (the bookstore, press, and educational center) were staffed by men and women who were full-time, part-time, or volunteer workers. Women were to play prominent roles in practically every aspect of the day-to-day operations of the bookstore and press. For example, Carolyn Carter was the first bookstore manager; Connie Austin was the bookstore's bookkeeper; Daphne Muse headed up the bookstore's children's books section. As far as the press was concerned, Anne Forrester was the first managing editor of the press; Jennifer Lawson was the press's art director and illustrator, and later the Drum and Spear representative in Tanzania; and Judy Richardson was the children's books editor. Other women such as Charlotte Featherstone, Wadine Henderson, and Gerri Stark were also "critical members of the team." Lawson later maintained that women played "pivotal roles," but stressed that this was not a conscious expression of their feminist consciousness.[36] Other women echoed Lawson's assertion, claiming that there was equality in terms of male and female roles and that the DSP men did a fairly good job at keeping their chauvinism in check after the issue was raised.[37]

A brief discussion of the SNCC experience partially explains the lack of gender-related tensions within the bookstore and press. The impact SNCC made on their notions of gender equality during their post-SNCC activism helps to distinguish the DSP's cultural nationalism from the prevailing cultural nationalist tendencies of the time. Black cultural-nationalist organizations such as Us Organization and the Committee to Fund a NewArk (CFUN), which later became known as the Congress of African People (CAP), among many others, subscribed to notions of patriarchy and women's submissiveness broadly defined within an African "tradition" cultural context.[38] The DSP men expressed ambivalence towards these sexist black cultural-nationalist practices and attitudes born out of their encounters with assertive black women organizers. They were exposed to women taking on vocal leadership positions and speaking out against male chauvinism. For the DSP women formerly of SNCC, like Richardson and Lawson, their involvement in SNCC consisted of challenging notions of middle-class femininity, taking on leadership roles, and advocating for gender equality within the organization.[39] Though drawn to certain cultural-nationalist ideas, the DSP's outlook on gender relations set it apart from dominant black cultural-nationalist organizations. Consequently, the DSP's ideological distinctiveness played itself out against some of the contradictions of a dominant stream of black cultural-nationalist thought.

Opposition to some cultural-nationalist ideas did not mean that the DSP books did not envisage a popular embrace of African cultures and values. In forging a new national culture in Black America, the DSP played a significant role in advancing the cultural reawakening that took hold in black communities. By the late 1960s, African Americans were in the process of creating a modern African American cultural identity largely informed by a strong identification with all things African. Various strategies were employed—namely, adopting African names; wearing Afro hairstyles, clothes,[40] and jewelry; and learning African languages.[41] In turn, these aesthetic choices sought to challenge Western cultural norms and values. The DSP emerged to publish and distribute books that guided African Americans in their search to understand and articulate their Africanness.

To satisfy this need, the Drum and Spear Press published Chief Osuntoki's *The Book of African Names* in 1970. Regarded as a "psycho-cultural return to Africa," *The Book of African Names* is more than just a list of African names for males and females. By providing an introduction, these names were placed in an African cultural and historical context by its author, "Chief Osuntoki," who encourages his African American readers to embrace their hidden or lost African identity—an identity transformed and tarnished as a result of the transatlantic slave trade.[42] Indeed, it is a powerful introduction in the ways in which it speaks directly to the diasporic longings of African Americans. However, one interesting fact about this book helps provide deeper insight into how the press's cultural nationalism converged with its business practices: Chief Osuntoki never existed; Anne Forrester and her husband Marvin Halloway were the coauthors of the text.

Forrester was one of the few DSP members who did not come out of the SNCC organizing experience in the South. Born in Philadelphia, Forrester attended schools in Massachusetts and Vermont. In 1962 she worked in Uganda and Kenya under the auspices of Operation Crossroads Africa, a U.S.-based volunteer organization. She later returned to the Northeast to teach African and African Diaspora history. Anxious to escape the white liberal world of New England, Forrester moved to Washington,

DC, in 1966, where she enrolled in a master's program in African history at Howard University and became a founding member of AAR, Inc. "Chief Osuntoki" was a fictional character meant to represent the DSP's new policy of collective authorship of introductions of all its books, its pan-Africanist politics, and its business acumen. Written in the first person, "Chief Osuntoki" establishes his African cultural authority as a "traditional" African chief skilled in the art of storytelling and eager to provide African Americans with knowledge of their "lost" African heritage. He also describes the birth of children as essential to the survival and continuation of African culture. The naming ritual "placed upon the children the whole sacred trust of African heritage ... It is the naming of the child also that first brings upon the child some general recognition by the community at large."[43] In turn, this ritualistic practice is depicted as an act of cultural resistance only when armed with the knowledge of its symbolic meanings. "Chief Osuntoki" serves as that critical link between Africa's precolonial past and postcolonial present—the source of information that gives the act of naming cultural and political value. "Chief Osuntoki's" commitment to pan-Africanism was evident in his view of African Americans as Africans, yet in desperate need of breaking away from their survivalist tendency towards assimilation into the dominant white culture. "It is strange," laments "Chief Osuntoki," "indeed, it hurts my heart that brothers from afar often come greet me bearing such names as 'Willie' ... So I, Osuntoki will tell them of their birthright and how they may seek their names. And the lessons I give you now, let them be written so that all may see."[44] What then follows is a comprehensive list of African names for boys and girls covering the entire African continent, including popular East African names such as Bomani and Njonjo for boys and Wambui and Njeri for girls.

Both Forrester and Holloway were graduate students in African studies at Howard University while working for the DSP, and the research involved in putting together the book is no doubt a testament to their knowledge of Africa. Relaying this sort of information through the character of "Chief Osuntoki" was also a shrewd business move, one that gave the book a form of African authenticity that boosted its mass marketability while staying true to DSP's policies and politics. Such a move to legitimize the text proved to be a success. For example, when the black maternity staff at the Wilmington Medical Center in Delaware noticed a trend among young black couples in giving their newborn babies African names, they started to give *The Book of African Names* to these new parents as a gift.[45] In many ways, it is telling that close to ten thousand copies of *The Book of African Names* were sold, the press's highest-selling publication. Such a publication and the warm reception it received nationwide proved to validate DSP's role as information providers on a national scale.[46] It mattered very little that a lot of the Drum and Spear members did not shed their "slave names" for African ones. What this merely points out is the extent to which the press acted as an activist-oriented enterprise and saw the political and economic potential in promoting a cultural-nationalist ideal that, for better or worse, called for them to "slant things" a bit.

The DSP's core ideological position was pan-Africanism, one that prioritized the global fight against racial oppression and promoted global black unity. In doing so, it adopted a cultural-nationalist perspective in its critical analysis of white supremacy and Western imperialism. Thus, one of the weapons it chose to free minds from the psychological inferiority complexes created by centuries of white supremacy was Tanzania's nationalist project. Indeed, the DSP's reprint of *A History of Pan-African Revolt* contained a new essay on socialist developments in Tanzania where James heaps praise upon Nyerere for his principled leadership and sees Ujamaa socialism as the embodiment of the political and cultural revolutionary spirit of Africans and people of African descent.[47] A closer look at the press's other publications reveals how its attack on racial and cultural oppression was heavily aided by the "Africa-centered ideas" coming out of Tanzania.

The DSP gained access to the guiding principles of Ujamaa socialism largely through Nyerere's *Freedom and Socialism*, published by Oxford University Press in 1968. Although Ujamaa was an expression of Tanzanian nationalism, the DSP members were easily won over by the universalistic quality of its concepts. Concepts like unity (*umoja*) and self-reliance (*kujitegema*) spoke directly to the press's aspirations, and subsequently the Black Power movement's aspirations. The attractiveness of the Ujamaa notion that the development of people took precedence over the development of the means of production, in many ways, reiterated the vital role books were to play in building a new nation. Moreover, Ujamaa was proof that Africans could be autonomous agents of radical social change devoid of an ideological dependence on Western liberal or communist traditions.[48] Nowhere was this made more evident than in the state's aggressive policy to make Kiswahili Tanzania's national language. While Tanzania's government was embarking on a mass literacy campaign that emphasized the production of Kiswahili books, Black Power activists were pushing for the Kiswahili language to be taught in U.S. schools.[49]

Originally a coastal trading language of Bantu origin, it was German and British colonialists, missionaries, and scholars who helped to spread Kiswahili into the interior during the early nineteenth century. Kiswahili became Tanzania's national language in 1962, only one year after formal independence. The Drum and Spear took an interest in promoting Kiswahili for both its symbolic and practical importance. As Anthony Bogues argues, the nationalization of a non-European language spoke directly to African nationalist conceptions of colonialism as a "knowledge regime," whereby decolonization came to symbolize a psychological break from a culturally oppressive European colonial past.[50] On a more practical level, Kiswahili was already spoken in numerous African regions across colonial territories and national borders—over 60 million Kiswahili speakers.[51] For African Americans who could not trace their African ancestry to any specific location or ethnic group, Kiswahili's attractiveness as the potential language of a black international community lay with how it transcended class, ethnic, and territorial boundaries, particularly in Tanzania, which comprised over 120 different ethnic groups.[52] By possessing a pan-African quality, and as a policy pursued in one of the most progressive African states, Kiswahili as a language of the Africa Diaspora was given further politico-cultural validity.

The DSP would name its newsletter *Kuhusu Vitabu* (Kiswahili for "About Books") and its weekly radio show for children *Sia ya Watoto* (Kiswahili for "The Children's Hour"). However, it was the publication of Bernard Muganda's *Speaking Swahili* (also known by its Kiswahili title, *Kusema Kiswahili*) that illustrates the press's ideological engagement with Kiswahili and Ujamaa socialism through book publications. In the introduction to the book, Forrester cogently explains the Drum and Spear's political interest in the language: "In the rising thrust of African peoples towards liberation from the cultural influences of varying European states, Swahili has been in the forefront of forging a language of nationalism . . . At this point in the history of African peoples, it is important that such a language, Swahili, is increasingly spoken by us. For its lingual contribution helps both to engender and to define our own efforts towards political consciousness and understanding of cultural priorities. Words and concepts such as Ujamaa [African Socialism], Uhuru [Freedom], and Kujitegemea [Self-Reliance] are meaningful to us in shaping the responsibilities of our actions."[53]

Muganda, a Tanzanian professor of Kiswahili at Howard University, echoed Forrester's assertion by claiming that the book "is intended not only to acquaint the Swahili student with Swahili reading but more importantly with the current and up-to-date African political ideologies, African history, education and economic philosophy."[54] Thus, *Kusema Kiswahili* was not solely a basic introduction to Kiswahili words and phrases but also an introduction to the aims and objectives of the state's socialist-inspired nationalist project. For example, in section 2 of the book, excerpts of speeches and writings, mostly by Nyerere, one of the "most outstanding Swahili speakers," are republished and followed by a set of questions ranging in linguistic and conceptual difficulty. One of the first exercises of this kind centers on TANU, mainland Tanzania's only nationalist party:

> Umoja ni nini?
> Shabaha ya kuunda TANU ilikuwa nini?

Kazi ya TANU ya leo ni nini?
Raia wa Tanzania ni nani?

[What does unity mean?
What were the goals of TANU??
What type of work is TANU doing now?
Who are the citizens of Tanzania?][55]

In another exercise based on a different Nyerere speech, a step up in conceptual difficulty than the previous exercise mentioned above, the questions that follow seek to offer its readers a clearer definition of Ujamaa socialism and how it differs from and is more suitable to Tanzanians than European models of socialism and communism:

Ujamaa nia nani?
Je, unaweza kuendesha nchi kwa kutumia Ujamaa?
Kuna tofauti gani kati va ujamaa wa kiafika na "Scientific Socialism" and Marxism?

[What is the purpose of African socialism?
Are you able to develop the country using the African Socialism program?
What are the differences between African Socialism and "scientific socialism"
or Marxism?][56]

As this lesson suggests, learning Kiswahili became closely interwoven with learning about the nation-state and its role in nation-building. The information provided in this book affirmed the legitimacy of the interventionist role of the state in carrying out the country's socialist strategy. At the same time, the Drum and Spear took it a step further by presenting Ujamaa as a nation-building model for the Black Power movement. As two sources used to transform black conceptions of African culture and nationalism, *Kusema Kiswahili* and *The Book of African Names* familiarized African Americans with the political uses and cultural value of Kiswahili, one-party state democracy, nonalignment, and forms of socialism, serving as a key locus of African American contact with Tanzanian nationalist discourse.

The DSP did not want to make its black cultural-nationalist impact felt strictly within the United States. By 1969, Black Power activists found it difficult to dispute the radical image of Tanzania with its policies of nonalignment and socialism and its swelling community of foreign political exiles. The DSP's interest in Kiswahili inevitably led it to consider publishing books in African languages and distributing them on the continent, and Tanzania was a logical choice. Through Forrester's contacts at

Chapter Four

the African Studies department at Howard University, especially Muganda, whose Tanzanian government contacts went all the way up to the president's office, the DSP orchestrated a meeting with Walter Bgoya of the Ministry of Foreign Affairs, and Benjamin Mkapa and Ferdinand Ruhinda, editors of the *Nationalist*, to discuss the possibilities of extending its publishing efforts to Tanzania. The meeting took place in late August 1969, a few weeks after some of the DSP members attended the Pan-African Cultural Festival in Algiers, Algeria. In a Dar es Salaam hotel, the DSP met these three close friends who were members of the TANU Youth League. At the meeting, Bgoya, Mkapa, and Ruhinda did not need that much convincing and urged the DSP to open an office in Dar es Salaam, and informed the press that government and party would sanction such an effort.[57] A few months later, discussions with Bgoya resumed during his visit to the United States as a Tanzanian delegate to the UN General Assembly.

Of all the three Tanzanians involved in these planning meetings, Walter Bgoya made the strongest connection with the Drum and Spear. Perhaps this can partly be attributed to his experience living in the United States as a college student at the University of Kansas from 1960 to 1964. He was one of over 113 Tanzanian nationals enrolled in American universities at the time. Initially, he had a difficult time building meaningful relationships with African American students, who he thought were not particularly welcoming to Africans. The fact that African Americans still held stereotypical misconceptions of Africa only further distanced him from the black student community. It was not until he began organizing with politically like-minded African Americans around issues of housing discrimination at the university and voter registration in the black urban enclaves of the Midwest that Bgoya began to cultivate cross-cultural friendships. Participating in voter registration drives exposed him to black urban poverty that was strikingly different from the rural poverty he experienced as a child growing up in Tanzania. After a group of concerned African Americans rescued him from a potential lynch mob for driving in a car with a white woman in the wrong part of town, Bgoya possessed a sober understanding of the realities of American racism and established a feeling of complete solidarity with black people in America.[58]

Bgoya returned to Tanzania in 1967 and joined the TANU Youth League because of his favorable impression of the socialist ideals articulated in the Arusha Declaration. In Dar es Salaam, he became a contact for the growing diaspora expatriate community while serving in the Ministry of Foreign Affairs. For instance, he fostered connections with Bill Sutherland, resulting in Bgoya sharing his poetry with the renowned black poet Langston Hughes on his visit to Dar es Salaam in 1967.[59] Bgoya even helped get former head of SNCC-Chicago Monroe Sharp settled in the country when he suddenly appeared in Tanzania looking for a place to stay. In September 1969, Bgoya traveled to the United States as a Tanzanian delegate to the United Nations General Assembly, where he also visited Drum and Spear bookstore and again encouraged DSP to internationalize their work. These series of meetings gave rise to the idea of an "Information Village," an educational center based in Dar es Salaam that would replicate the "Drum and Spear Complex" in Washington, DC.

The Drum and Spear Press left these meetings with TYL with the impression that it had the verbal support and approval from elements of the Tanzanian government and party to independently produce and distribute books that promoted its nationalist project. After a few internal discussions, it was decided that an office would be established in Dar es Salaam, managed by Cobb and Jennifer Lawson. Jennifer Karen Lawson was raised in Fairfield, Alabama, in 1946 in a middle-class family. Her father, William, was a small business owner while her mother, Velma, was a school teacher. Like many black students of her time, Lawson put her scholarship at Tuskegee Institute on hold and joined the civil rights movement in 1964. As a SNCC activist for four years, she worked on voter registration campaigns throughout the Deep South and enjoyed a reputation as an artist in the organization.[60] Disillusionment with the nature of SNCC's decline, especially with the rise of Black Power male chauvinism, led her to join the National Council of Negro Women (NCNW) in 1968. Around the same time, she became director of an adult education program in Whitman County, Mississippi, before taking on the position of art director for the Drum and Spear Press in 1969 after being recruited by Cobb and other former SNCC members associated with the press.[61] Like Cobb, traveling to Tanzania was not her first time visiting Africa. In fact, her visits to West Africa inspired the way she decorated the Drum and Spear bookstore, one of her first job assignments. While it is not altogether clear if Cobb and Lawson traveled to Tanzania together, Ruhinda was at the airport to greet Cobb upon his arrival in Dar es Salaam in April 1970. Reporting for the *Nationalist*, Ruhinda spoke with Cobb about the Drum and Spear's mission in Tanzania. "If Africa's position is strengthened," Cobb explained, "the position of black people elsewhere would have also been strengthened."[62] Cobb saw the DSP's Tanzania initiative as an example of an African American organization fulfilling its obligation "to contribute towards the achievement and consolidation of complete independence for the African continent." By 1971, the Drum and Spear was officially working in Tanzania for the cause of pan-Africanism and Tanzanian nation-building. Its immediate task was to publish books in Kiswahili that conveyed messages of international black solidarity, cultural pride, self-reliance, and self-determination—themes inspired by Nyerere's philosophy of Ujamaa.

By the time Lawson and Cobb settled in Dar es Salaam, the city had taken on a vibrant political, cosmopolitan character. Dar es Salaam of Tanzania's post-Arusha Declaration period can be described as undergoing a fourth stage of transformation and development shaped by its founding as a trading city by Arab Muslims in the late nineteenth century, then as a colonial city under the control of German and British colonialists in the early twentieth century. In the post-independence period of the 1960s, Dar es Salaam remained the political capital and financial hub of the country. With the coming of Ujamaa socialism, with the emergence of "the Dar School" at UDSM, and with the establishment of offices of OAU Liberation Committee and African liberation groups, Dar es Salaam also became the locus of the pan-Africanist struggle. A wide range of leftist and nationalist-oriented exiles, freedom fighters, refugees, writers, artists, students, embassy officials, and intellectuals from Mozambique, South Africa, Angola, Zambia, Kenya, Malawi, Ghana, Nigeria, the Congo, Uganda, Namibia, Zimbabwe, as well as from Eastern Europe, Asia, and the Caribbean islands migrated to, and lived and worked in the city for various political reasons. And the sheer political and cultural diversity immigrant communities brought to the city proved to lay the basis for transnational exchanges, interactions, and collaborations as an everyday occurrence.

As a result of the Cold War, it was evident that a cloud of suspicion hovered over Dar es Salaam's transnational political scene, but not to the extent that it kept African Americans from socializing with others. For Cobb, the small size of the city meant that day or night you could run into someone at a café and end up talking for hours about the state of African liberation. The Kilimanjaro Hotel and Paradise Hotel where Malcolm X and Stokely Carmichael conversed with revolutionaries, dignitaries, and diplomats during their visits in 1964 and 1967 still remained central meeting places for intense political discussions. Lectures from visiting scholars and activists at UDSM were routinely attended as well as the independence celebrations such as Saba Saba Day and African Liberation Day.[63] When looking to take a break from the city, they often toured the rest of the country, visiting islands located off the coast of the mainland, such as Zanzibar and Mafia; the Mikumi National Park for safari; and the town of Bagamoyo, a former trading port in the Indian Ocean slave trade. African American expatriates also organized and attended events on African American history and culture in hopes of better familiarizing Tanzanians with their experience.

It is important to point out that political-intellectual enrichment also came in very informal ways. When living in the Ilala district of the city, Cobb remembers socializing with Cubans who were never short on rum and always open to talking about race. He routinely conversed with South Africans for similar reasons by tapping into Bgoya's network of contacts. Moreover, the vitality of the black expatriate community was no doubt due in part to the presence of Walter Rodney, whose university flat quickly gained a reputation as a party pad and place to meet and interact with Dar es Salaam's Caribbean community.[64] Lawson also found in Dar es Salaam a community of radical expatriates forged through a common passion for the arts. Lawson and Cobb made fast friendships with Ayi Kwei Armah of Ghana and Ngugi wa Thiong'o of Kenya, two young novelists who had temporarily settled in Dar es Salaam and shared an apartment in Ilala located on the outskirts of the city center. They ended up forming a study group with Walter Rodney and Grant Kamenju, a Kenyan novelist, that aimed to provide collective support for each of their respective writing projects, from short stories to poems to novels to children's books to academic histories. Later, her connection with Ruhinda and Mkapa, who both recognized her creative skills and pan-Africanist point of view, landed her a job with the *Nationalist* as a political cartoonist. The nightlife was equally appealing. Outdoor bars and cafés also littered the urban landscape along with a slew of nightclubs concentrated in the downtown area that played live Swahili jazz music from the likes of the Dar es Salaam Jazz Band, NUTA Jazz Band, Milimani Park Orchestra, and Vijana Jazz, among others.[65]

The African American presence added to Dar es Salaam's heterogeneous political and cultural milieu, and their growing visibility in the city, and the country writ large compelled many to try to understand the aims and objectives of the African American freedom struggle and to define their role in Tanzania's nationalist project. What new arrivals like Cobb and Lawson could not ignore were conversations about nation-building that implicated African Americans in direct and indirect ways. Much of the Tanzanian citizenry saw African Americans as a technical labor force ideologically committed to postcolonial economic development, but arrived at this position over a period of time. Between 1961 and 1968, soldiers and TANU black nationalists largely confronted President Nyerere on the issue of Africanization, a term used to describe a government policy that focused on replacing Europeans with black Africans in various professional fields, in hopes of speeding along what they regarded as a slow process of implementation.[66] In spite of the nature of these various critical stances that questioned Nyerere's leadership, the president knew the government was making little headway in the production of indigenous skilled labor. When the Ministry of Economic Affairs published its annual report, it stated that 1969 was another "discouraging year" in the training of skilled Tanzanians. The ministry warned President Nyerere: "Until Tanzania is able to provide an adequate supply of properly trained and experienced personnel from its own resources the gap between development requirements and local resources must be bridged by importing the necessary skills from abroad ... failure to bridge this gap by an adequate overseas recruitment program had represented their major constraint of Plan implementation."[67]

In lieu of this skilled-labor shortage and in casting the foreign technical skills as a form of economic and racial imperialism, the Tanzanian state took greater notice of African Americans as an untapped pool of technical assistance. One editorial in *The Nationalist* urged the government to pursue a policy of African American recruitment, writing that since African Americans regarded Africa as their "land of cultural heritage" and possessed a wide range of technical skills, this could be used to the country's advantage.[68] On the other hand, this was not to say that African Americans did not need coaching on the socialist, anticapitalist, and anti-imperialist ways of being (i.e., humanistic) in Tanzanian society:

> Our Tanzania has no room for hang-ups of capitalism—and Afro-Americans who set foot on this soil must understand it. The people of this country are not striving for Coca-Cola values, they are striving for man's loftiest value—a fuller life for all. I am aware that Afro-Americans come to the United Republic for many reasons and may not arrive here as socialists or loyal supporters of our Party, TANU, but they should be willing to learn, as all true revolutionaries and avoid to take anti-people postures.[69]

In the 1970s, both the party and government were interested in a new way of approaching the question of foreign technical-skills assistance. Since attacks against expatriate recruitment were largely aimed at those of European descent, racial solidarity underlined their interest in seeking out African Americans to temporarily fill vacant positions. As mentioned in chapter 2, SNCC leader James Forman tried unsuccessfully to implement a technical assistance program in cooperation with the TANU government in 1967 known as the Afro-American Skills Bank. Three years later, under the leadership of Irving Davis, SNCC revisited Forman's idea and launched the Pan-African Skills Project (PASP). As the 1960s gave way to the 1970s and civil rights was taken over by Black Power, debates swirled around two central questions: Who was actually making the trek to Africa under the premise of lending their skills? In what ways were their actions, attitudes, and behaviors in Africa a hindrance to effectively living and working there? While the U.S. state sought to dismiss African Americans traveling and settling in Africa, suggesting that their motives were grounded on the faulty premise of romanticized racial kinship, Tanzanians challenged this assumption, demonstrating a critical sympathy towards African Americans' plight as descendants of enslaved Africans. Generally speaking, this sentiment is best captured in their referring to African Americans in Tanzania as "Wawerreaji"—Kiswahili for "returnees"—a label that illustrates their increasing awareness and acceptance of African Americans' diaspora consciousness.[70]

Tanzania's critical sympathy towards the African American freedom struggle gained even more currency as a result of the assassination of Martin Luther King Jr. in April 1968. The racial violence in the United States that had captured the attention of many Tanzanian nationalists ever since the Birmingham church bombing of 1963 was appalling, and feelings of anger reached a tipping point when King was gunned down in Memphis, Tennessee. They took to the press, releasing statements of solidarity combined with sharp denouncements of U.S. imperialism. One editorial called King's assassination the "greatest crime committed against black people in recent years" that gave credence to Black Power arguments on the myth of racial progress and the tactical and philosophical bankruptcy of nonviolence.[71] Indeed, King's assassination gave Tanzanians justification for supporting African Americans and their fight for racial justice. "The United States Government must understand that counter-revolutionary violence against a struggling people only helps to ignite revolutionary violence from the ranks of the people," read one statement signed by "Revolutionary Youth." "In the end, it is not the fascists and racists but the people who will win."[72]

Though King's death produced many skeptics about the state of U.S. race relations, the Tanzanian press also continued to play a role in disseminating information about African American achievements with coverage of the racial barriers overcome by actors, athletes, and musicians. The actor Sidney Poitier and the boxer Muhammad Ali enjoyed continuous media coverage and fanfare, but their influence paled in comparison to James Brown and the soul music craze that hit Dar es Salaam by storm and ushered in a contentious debate concerning the impact of African American cultural-nationalist politics on Tanzanian national culture. Soul music, it was argued, invoked indigenous African rhythms and dance forms that reflected the pro-African politics and aesthetics on the part of the African American national community. While a good portion of Tanzanian youth in their teens and twenties (as opposed to their thirties and forties) celebrated soul music, the Tanzanian state took issue with this form of youth appropriation of diasporic cultural styles and used the TYL as its vehicle to prevent the use of certain fashion/clothing items and the listening to soul music, popularly known as "soul digging," as forms of Western imperial brainwashing and thus anathema to Ujamaa socialist ideals.

In 1968 and 1969, the state took swift action in its attempts to define youth nationalist identity and culture. On January 1, 1969, the TANU-Youth League launched "Operation Vijana," a campaign designed to rid all forms of "indecent" and "decadent" dress from popular consumption, which included miniskirts, short shorts, tight pants, and skin-lightening creams. Next, the government's attack on Western cultural imperialism took aim at soul music, with its official ban occurring in November of the same year.[73] "Whatever can be said about soul music, one thing is quite certain: the more our youths have been "digging it," the more they have been wanting to become American," claimed one proponent of the ban in the *Nationalist*. "We are Tanzanians and we must remain so."[74] Lurking under claims to renewing "socialist morality" among youth was a sharp rebuke of identifying with the African Diaspora along racial and cultural lines, especially with a "trance-like" form of dance requiring the "dangling of limbs" in ways

Chapter Four

that resembled the movements of drug addicts.⁷⁵ Indeed, the implications connected to the consumption of not only the rhythms of soul music but also its lyrics' variant messages of black pride raises an interesting set of questions about the development and nature of Tanzanians' diaspora consciousness among youth and how receptive they were to notions of blackness and identity promulgated by Black Power activists, artists, and musicians.⁷⁶ In showing both sides of the argument, the *Nationalist* featured an editorial, "Black is Beautiful," that explained how African Americans' embrace of soul music, the Afro hairstyle, and African clothing indicated a "new cultural consciousness" and a "quest for non-assimilation."⁷⁷

What can be generally stated about African Americans' response to Nyerere's ban on soul music is that there were competing opinions. From afar, J. K. Obatala, an African American expatriate student at the University of Ghana in Accra, penned an article on the ban, which was originally published in the South African Communist Party's *African Communist* in 1970 and then later reprinted in the U.S. Black Power journal the *Black Scholar* in 1971. Arguing that he was compelled to write "U.S. 'Soul' Music in Africa: Has Charlie Got a Brand New Bag?" after visiting a student lounge and watching James Brown on TV, Obatala saw "nothing less than a visualized Myth of Afro-American Affluence which is widespread in Africa and which carries with it some serious implications for the future of Africa itself as well as for relations between Africans and Afro-Americans."⁷⁸ Nyerere's decision to ban soul music was not so much a "slap in the face" to African Americans' or Tanzanians' inability to either understand or recognize soul music's African roots. Rather it was an acute awareness of how African American culture was easily subjected to corporate co-optation. The commodification and global dissemination of African American culture as American culture in order to promote capitalism was a dangerous conflation no doubt, but one not without merit.

Living in Tanzania and witnessing firsthand the impact of the implementation of the ban on Tanzanian young people and African Americans caused black radical expatriates to view the banning from a different angle. The postcolonial government's actions in policing the musical tastes of its youth were incredibly disheartening because they illustrated an authoritarian nature of the state that African Americans were all too familiar with, having experienced U.S. state repression. Equally disconcerting was a policy that gave five hundred male TYL members the authority to publicly shame young women for wearing miniskirts, both verbally and physically. Cobb, a "soul digging" youth himself in his mid-twenties, was deeply bothered by these acts of state authoritarianism, so much so that he often confronted and argued with youth league members in the streets about the logic of their anti-soul and anti-miniskirt messages and how it was a gross misuse of their time. Other times he invited Tanzanian youth "soul diggers" to his apartment to listen and dance to the music of James Brown.⁷⁹ The soul music debate, therefore, must be understood in a broader context of Tanzanian engagement with African American culture and politics.

Other Tanzanian critics of the African American presence shifted their attention away from concerns about U.S. cultural imperialism to the questions about Cold War politics and national security and economic development. In addition to having to confront a national-cultural project that outright rejected certain diasporic expressive cultures like soul music, African Americans had to attend to continuous rumors and charges of espionage. A common argument disseminated and recycled largely by African and white leftists and conservative TANU members in Dar es Salaam was that African American expatriates were CIA agents, "day and night operating in our economic, political, religious and cultural spheres in the name of friendship to destroy our hard gained independence."[80] In "The C.I.A., Black Power and Africa," one TYL leftist student at UDSM viewed as imperative to call attention to the decline of Black Power radicalism. "It has been refined and domesticated, awarded a prominent niche in the American Dream," he stated. And through a "surprising alliance with certain forces of black militancy," he further argued, Nixon's regime had gained a "foothold in African states in order to emasculate black radicalism in Africa."[81] While positive assessments of African Americans as an alternative source of skilled labor dominated the national public discourse, especially due to the modest successes of the Pan-African Skills Project, there were some naysayers who argued that the use of foreigner expatriates, no matter their race, nationality, or anti-imperialist politics, merely reinforced their nation's economic dependency on the West. These above-mentioned concerns forced African American expatriates like Cobb and Lawson to be more aware of the implications of their presence in the country. Ultimately, they focused much of their attention on the book-publishing aspects of Tanzanian nation-building, but understood that one challenge was fully understanding the conflicting ideas about the African American expatriate in the economic, cultural, and political contexts of Tanzania.

The DSP operation in Dar es Salaam coincided with an intense period of national-socialist development activity. From 1969 to 1974, Tanzania was immersed in its Second Five-Year Development Plan, a plan intended to expand the state's control over its economic surplus through the nationalization of the key industrial, financial, and commercial businesses.[82] While nationalization, popularly nicknamed "nizations," did not transform Tanzania into a socialist state overnight, it nevertheless allowed the government to address the economic, political, and cultural imperatives of the state. Through its financial institution the National Development Corporation (NDC), the government attained majority ownership over key institutions. Government control of the book industry (publishing, printing, distribution) was no doubt a strategic move that would amount to considerable savings in foreign exchange, and thus lessen its dependence on the world capitalist economy. More importantly, it would aid the state in the mass dissemination of its socialist principles.[83]

Nyerere began taking note of the importance of book publishing in Tanzania years before the Arusha Declaration and the DSP came into existence. In November 1965, the president delivered a speech celebrating the recent opening of a printing works and book warehouse outside Arusha, the country's second largest city. At the ceremony, the question of book education was clothed in a language of postcolonial modernization. In order for Tanzania to deal with the newly emergent cultures of modernity throughout the world, Nyerere argued, a "habit of reading among our young people and among our newly literate citizens" was of primary importance.[84] Government ministers would follow suit in subsequent years. Years later, Tanzania's Minister of Information D. Mwakawago echoed a similar sentiment: "Since we are in the long march towards socialism it is true that the ideology could only be shaped in the minds of people through reading books which are relevant and conducive to the country's policy of socialism and self-reliance."[85]

The Tanzanian state had put forth an argument about the centrality of books for the consolidation of Ujamaa ideology, and though raising literacy rates was pursued with particular enthusiasm and determination, building and stocking libraries, schools, and bookstores, and creating profitable book publishing companies never took precedence over increasing agricultural production in the "mashamba" (i.e., the rural areas). Nevertheless, considerable progress was made in the book trade and education sectors after independence. In 1961, illiteracy in Tanzania was over 90 percent, but with the implementation of the adult literacy campaign spearheaded by the University of Dar es Salaam's Institute of Adult Education, it dropped to 39 percent in 1974.[86] Tanzania's Library Services increased its books stacks from 49,000 in 1964 to 900,000 in 1974 and attempted to make them available by establishing local libraries in all of its major towns, and "mobile libraries" for the countryside. Printpak, Tanzania's oldest printing company, was equipped with new technology to quicken the production process, and publishing companies regularly sponsored writing competitions and workshops for local Kiswahili writers.[87] But complaints about book selection and the shortage of Kiswahili publications during Tanzania's mass literacy campaign continued to signal a "book famine."[88]

During their time in Dar es Salaam, working for the DSP meant conversing with government officials, ruling party members mostly in the TANU Youth League, students, and African political exiles. By learning Kiswahili at the University of Dar es Salaam, Cobb and Lawson wanted to take an active part in the translation process of English books into Kiswahili. They became more knowledgeable about Tanzania's book needs after conducting a general survey of the books available in and around

Dar es Salaam. It was upon visiting the public libraries and bookstores that they discovered another disappointing peculiarity: While pleased to find books in Kiswahili as a popular commodity, they were dismayed when realizing that Kiswahili literature was largely being produced for and distributed by European missionaries. For them, this constituted an act of linguistic colonialism that explicitly contested the symbolic function of Kiswahili as a non-European national language.

In framing the problem as a manifestation of cultural imperialism with far-reaching political consequences, Cobb and Lawson thought it imperative to translate the press's 1970 children's book *Children of Africa: A Coloring Book* into Kiswahili. "The definition of language in its grammatical structure is totally in the hands of Europeans," Cobb lamented in a staff meeting held back in Washington, DC, one year into Drum and Spear's Tanzanian initiative. "The point is that the *Watoto wa Afrika* book we're producing in Swahili implies that Africa is still controlled by Europeans. Essentially Europe never ceased running Africa." The DSP's publishing mission in Africa became more clearly defined. It now saw itself as tapping into a market dominated by Kiswahili textbooks "for europeans [sic] coming to Tanzania as either colonial administrators or as missionaries."[89] *Children of Africa*, with its overriding message of pan-African unity, offered a counternarrative to dominant colonial and Christian themes of African subservience and submissiveness that flooded the Kiswahili book market in Tanzania.

The choice to translate and republish *Children of Africa* came at a time when there was increasing interest in children's literature about Africa as well. Such literature no longer constituted a singular obsession with Africa's wildlife, but instead a concern with the peoples who populated the continent.[90] However, in Tanzania's case, children's literature remained in a state of lack during its period of growth in education due to the fact that most books available were written in English while primary education in the country was taught in Kiswahili. The fact that Tanzania did not have a preschool-education or childcare system that could purchase and provide such books added to the difficulty in popularizing the genre.[91]

In addition to the low supply of Kiswahili books, the content of these books was also cause for major concern. TANU continually expressed the fear that Tanzanian children were becoming "estranged" from their African cultural heritage, and thus called for more books on African culture while calling on mothers to play a greater role in developing a habit of reading among their children.[92] "Colonialism had done all it could to destroy the confidence of Africans so as to justify the colonialist practices," Nyerere argued in 1968. "They taught us that our values were primitive, that our culture and dances were savage. It is now our duty to teach the truth of our culture and values."[93] For these very reasons, circumstances seemed highly favorable for a popular

Chapter Four

reception of *Watoto wa Afrika*, which would further shed some light on the efficacy of expanding its publishing activities outside the United States.

A glowing review of the first-edition English version appeared in the *Black Books Bulletin*: "Have your children take out their crayons especially the deep colors like red, green, and black, and get ready to work in the most intense color book ever published."[94] Lauded as a book with "Pan-African and black unity" themes that brought the parent and child together, *Children of Africa* puts forward a historical narrative of Africa and its Atlantic Diaspora linked by culture and imperial conquest, promoting one of the basic tenets of pan-Africanism: Black people all over the world shared a common experience and common struggle as a result of the transatlantic slave trade and its aftermath. In this vein, the DSP was trying to produce books that stressed a pan-Africanist cultural, political, and economic mode of being while filling a void in literature that lacked such an engagement.

The book's pan-Africanist impulse was best expressed in the following statement: "We often think of our interests and problems as a people are unique to the places in which we now live . . . All over the world the interests and problems of black people are the same."[95] Such statements appeared on the left-hand side of every page, which contained only written text to "provide the older reader additional information as he accompanies the child."[96] The right-hand side of each page contained images and written text that simply put these statements for adults in language children could visualize and understand. It is imperative that we appreciate how *Children of Africa* projected a positive image of Africa. Its humanistic portrayal of the continent challenged dominant myths of African primitiveness. Against the notion of Africa having no precolonial past to speak of with a sense of pride, the book positioned Africa as a historical point of origin for cultural formations in the African Diaspora. Putting forth such an argument was meant to instill a feeling of unity and sense of historical consciousness and purpose among its readership.

The idea of egalitarian communal relations was another Ujamaa theme that shaped the pan-Africanist politics of the Drum and Spear. Though there is no direct reference made to Tanzania's Ujamaa ideology, it appears that *Children of Africa* is filled with images that promote a "socialist attitude of mind" among contemporary Africans. For instance, the idea of "family-hood" (the literal meaning of Ujamaa) is best captured in a series of images of intergenerational cooperation—namely, between mothers and daughters and fathers and sons.[97] Ultimately, *Children of Africa* can be credited with contributing to the theorization of an African Diaspora of the Black Atlantic, an introduction to the philosophy of pan-Africanism, and a promotion of Ujamaa as a model of human development. Indeed, producing an accessible children's book that posed some complicated questions about history, culture, and contemporary politics represented a tremendous breakthrough in children's literature about Africa—for there were not too many children's books on the market relaying a message to black people worldwide that the struggle for freedom did not end with independence from colonial rule.[98]

The Tanzania Publishing House (TPH) published *Watoto wa Afrika* in 1972, the year the United Nations dubbed "International Book Year." By that time Walter Bgoya had left the Ministry of Foreign Affairs and taken on the position of managing editor of TPH.[99] Founded in April 1966 as a joint venture between Tanzania's National Development Corporation (NDC) and the Macmillan publishing company of Britain, TPH was one of the five major book publishers in Tanzania.[100] In its first six years of operation, it published seventy titles and sold over one million copies. TPH was determined to emerge at the forefront of publishing in Africa. For its manager editor Robert Hutchinson, a British expatriate, to "begin to transform the publishing house into a recognized center for socialist creativity," TPH needed to hire new editors, preferably Tanzanians who were committed to the goals of socialist development, nonalignment, and African liberation.[101] In 1972, his final year as managing editor, Hutchinson managed to move TPH in this anti-imperialist, nationalist direction by collaborating with Bogle-L'Ouverture Publications to publish Walter Rodney's groundbreaking text *How Europe Underdeveloped Africa*.[102] Immediately following the release of Rodney's work, and after a two-month training seminar in London, Bgoya returned to Dar es Salaam with a vision of totally radicalizing this formerly British-owned press with a reputation for "production for profit over production for need."[103]

Under Bgoya's editorship, TPH was transformed into the mouthpiece of the anti-imperialist struggle in Africa. The state-owned publishing company published nationalist and leftist texts covering multiple genres that further added to Tanzania's image as Africa's primary revolutionary vanguard state. His political contacts with the Marxist-oriented intellectuals and leaders of national liberation movements from Mozambique and Angola led to the publication of their work throughout the decade of the 1970s. These works, including Tanzanian law student Issa Shivji's *Class Struggles in Tanzania* (1975), a leftist critique of Ujamaa socialism, forced many activists and intellectuals around the globe to reconsider the dangers of Africa's economic relationship to Western imperial powers and the rise of intense internal class conflict in Africa.[104] Like the Tanzanian government, TPH was also concerned with developing Kiswahili books for mass political education. Agreeing to partake in the republication of the Drum and Spear's *Watoto wa Afrika* signaled a new direction for TPH only in the sense that this would be their first time working with independent black publishers from the United States since it started publishing children's books as early as 1970. *Watoto wa Afrika* was one of three children's books TPH published in 1972 at a combined total of 33,000 copies.

Chapter Four

A look at the national discourse about the state of the Tanzanian book industry in the early to mid-1970s helps us to better measure the overall impact of the DSP-TPH copublishing efforts in Tanzania. The DSP was able to meet some, but not all, of the expectations and needs expressed by nationalist book advocates. In general, government ministers, publishers, council directors, and students all found some specific problem to voice their concerns around. While Chairman Minwyi of the National Swahili Council called for more Kiswahili books to "fill the vacuum that still exists in Swahili literature," secondary student Freddy Macha chastised the government for importing "American-type books" that celebrated the achievements of the CIA. According to Macha, to combat these CIA adventure stories, "bourgeois sex stories" and "treasure island–type stories" polluting the minds of his young peers, access to books written by revolutionaries such as Mao Tse-Tung, Ernesto "Che" Guevara, Amilcar Cabral, and Eldridge Cleaver could reverse this dangerous trend. The director of TLS responded to Macha not by repudiating his Third World radical claims, but by echoing some of his sentiments. Because of lack of funds, Kiswahili writers, skilled manpower, and foreign publisher interest, Tanzania was still experiencing a "book gap."[105]

Tanzania's poor economic situation provides one answer to why the Drum and Spear was only able to publish one book with minimal distribution over a two-year period. In a report on the history of Tanzania's book industry published by UNESCO in 1987, Bgoya put forth a range of explanations for what he saw as the failures of the book industry in reaching the popular masses during the twenty years after the Arusha Declaration.[106] The development of a mass reading culture in Tanzania was dependent on the state of the nation's economy. Later on, the worldwide energy crisis of 1973 only exacerbated preexisting problems plaguing Tanzania's export-oriented economy, striking a particular blow to its book industry and the prospects of creating a mass culture of reading. The lack of paraffin for use in oil lamps, poor housing conditions, and the absence of bookshops located in the countryside and "working class districts" in the cities made reading "simply not possible." Put simply, Tanzanians just did not have the money to buy books, nor did the TANU government have the resources to build up a book trade infrastructure.

To its credit, the DSP succeeded in fulfilling multiple goals of Tanzania's nationalist project as expressed by the TANU state: *Watoto wa Afrika* was a Kiswahili publication for children (and adults) and about pan-Africanism and African socialism. In the end, however, the press's failures in functioning at a sustainable, profit-making level reflected the internal weaknesses of the press itself. DSP possessed neither the funds nor manpower capacity to establish itself as a viable publishing enterprise. Most of its members were novices in the book publishing trade and often viewed the press as a political and cultural organization as opposed to a business enterprise.

Part of the reason why the Tanzanian government agreed to allow the Drum and Spear to work in Tanzania was because the press promoted key nation-building concepts. It was also free of charge. Without either expecting or receiving Tanzanian government funding, combined with its inability to continue to rely on its financially strapped office in Washington, DC, the DSP admittedly could not sustain its publishing activities abroad, let alone set the groundwork for the establishment of the "Information Village." Perhaps this best explains why the Tanzanian government denied the DSP's application for land, and forced them to reapply "in triplicate" and endure another long bureaucratic processing period.[107] By not having "enough capitalization" and skilled expertise, the DSP encountered numerous obstacles in slowly building an institutional base with meager resources in an unfamiliar political and cultural environment. It no doubt halted further collaboration with TPH and other Tanzanian publishers. Yet despite being a short-lived and under-resourced project, the DSP took away some valuable lessons. Its desire to internationalize and reach an Africa-based audience helped its members to gain a better understanding of the nature of black international activism as it related to the complex processes of nation-state formation in Africa.

Critical insights into the complexities besetting African states in their struggles against capitalism, imperialism, neocolonialism, and racism were given their fullest expression when, in late 1971, Cobb returned to Washington, DC, to attend an AAR board meeting. The topic of discussion centered on the implications of DSP's publishing activities when understood within a context of Tanzania's postcolonial situation. The minutes of the AAR meeting throws considerable light upon the extent to which Black Power activists grappled with opposing visions of African unity, the difference between the rhetoric and reality of Ujamaa, the effectiveness of the African American expatriate presence in Tanzania, and the character of African state formation. In opening the discussion on the challenges of African independence, Cobb offered these cautionary words:

> The first thing being the tendency in the United States among black people is mostly because of the kinds of conditions that exist in the United States and leads to the development of a fairly romantic view of the Continent, which prevents us from really looking at what there is and what the implications of what there is means in terms of the kind of work we have to do. That's one of the points I'd like to build my description of what there is around . . . Even being in Tanzania for a year is neither enough time nor allowance for a fair assessment of a number of details about the Continent. But that aside, the main thing is the complexity of the place is really something that needs to be understood.[108]

Chapter Four

What follows is a glimpse into Cobb's experience living abroad as an African American committed to African liberation. Even though he warned that his ideas were not entirely coherent, Cobb explores Tanzania's post-independence realities from a perspective of a neocolonialist takeover crippling the state of pan-African solidarity on the continent. "You're only five minutes there before you realize Africans don't control the place," Cobb lamented. "The reality is that Europeans run these places."[109]

After Cobb briefed AAR on the vision and day-to-day challenges of the DSP operation in Dar es Salaam, the discussion took an interesting turn that would come to frame a question-and-answer session that sought to identify the obstacles to greater pan-African unity. The Ugandan coup of 1971 led by Idi Amin that ousted Milton Obote from power, a head of state considered to be an ally in the anti-imperialist struggle, was fresh in the minds of AAR members. What was particularly enraging about this latest military coup in Africa, similar to the 1966 coup in Ghana, was that no progressive African state, including Tanzania, entertained the possibility of using military force to restore Obote to power.

AAR members questioned the Organisation of African Unity (OAU) principle of noninterference in the domestic affairs of its member sovereign states, and Cobb took issue with progressive independent states such as Tanzania not using armed force to resist imperialist acts, which he believed impeded the steps toward continental unity. "There is no ideology even, no political line, no political program. There is nothing which makes those kinds of projections, militarily, economically, educationally, socially at any level—nothing . . . I'm willing to accept the regional concept myself as a first step, assuming a regional concept that leaves open a possibility of a Continental concept. There is no discussion of that. It doesn't exist in East Africa, or, as far as I can tell, in any country in Africa. All that means is that questions of military defense cannot be effectively considered."[110] According to Cobb, the vision of African unity, which was so forcefully articulated in the early 1960s, was virtually abandoned in the 1970s as a result of state inaction.

An interesting exchange between Cobb, Courtland Cox, and Jean Wiley illustrates how the recurrence of the military coup d'état in Africa exacerbated preexisting fears about Tanzania's national security. Both Cox and Wiley were attempting to get at how influential was Ujamaa rhetoric within the country. Was the concept of self-reliance so widespread and embraced on a mass scale as to prevent a military takeover in Tanzania from internal and external forces? On this question, Cobb temporarily assuaged their fears, claiming that Nyerere's cult of personality and the mass support he received for Ujamaa within the country would secure his leadership role. But Cobb was not without criticism of Ujamaa in the context of Nyerere's leadership. One problem with Ujamaa was its confinement to Tanzania alone. Tanzania regarded it as a state policy rather than a liberatory pan-Africanist ideology. The major weakness of Nyerere, he surmised, was an underestimation of his domestic power base that could permit him to not only promote Ujamaa throughout Africa but also take steps to safeguard the prospect of African unity through military means. On both accounts, Nyerere was falling victim to a "trick of not being able to extend beyond the boundaries that Europe drew for us for arbitrary reasons."[111]

Adamant about drawing a distinction between Nyerere on the one hand and the Tanzanian government and TANU on the other, Cobb was drawing attention to how Nyerere was the embodiment of the state, and that Ujamaa's success was directly tied up with the foreign and domestic policy decisions made by the Tanzanian president in respect to African affairs.[112] Cobb urged AAR members to understand that a huge gap existed between Ujamaa rhetoric and its application. When Cobb spoke of Tanzania's dependence on economic aid from imperialist nations, particularly the United States, and the dangerous rise of African and Indian elite classes, he was hinting at the notion that Tanzania was not self-reliant, nor was Ujamaa a policy adequately addressing the issue of postcolonial class formation in Africa, a viewpoint that was dominant within the Tanzanian Left.

AAR members continued to pose questions concerning the possibility of a coup in Tanzania, but this time to ascertain its implications for African American activism abroad. Cobb tried to tie in these concerns when speaking about his own feelings of cultural and political estrangement as an African American expatriate who, voluntarily or not, had embarked on a personal journey to discover both the "African" and "American" sides of his identity. For Cobb, his assessment of Tanzania's nation-building project was profoundly influenced by how he conceptualized identity formation in the African Diaspora. To be stateless, without a nation, forced African Americans to think beyond the interests of any postcolonial state. He asserted: "Blacks from the states tend to go to Africa as Africans, generally, with a general concept of Africa. But they go to a specific state that has been created by Europe, and it's a problem because you have a view of Africa as a Continent, you have a commitment to Africa as a continent, and you're ordering yourself in terms of that commitment . . . However, your commitment to Africa don't coincide with the particular interests of the state. In one sense, you're trying to transcend the state. However, wherever you are, you are there because the state is saying it's okay for you to be there."[113] The African American pan-Africanist imagination of temporary African states found it difficult to accept a permanent territorial nation-state concept being pursued by progressive African governments such as Tanzania.

The question concerning African Americans' role in Africa proved to be much more difficult to answer. Based on numerous conservations with Tanzanian government officials and TANU Party leaders who viewed African Americans as an alternative source of committed, skilled technical labor that could be used "to break the grip" of European, Indian, and Lebanese expatriates, Cobb was ultimately convinced of the necessity of African Americans in Africa. Their unique historical experience with racial oppression, combined with their ancestral ties to the continent, made it imperative for them to pursue black transnational linkages. But this did little in fleshing out what exactly other roles besides a labor one entailed. He provided an answer that included a short-term and long-term vision, attempting to convey the point that there existed multiple roles, yet he still struggled in defining the specifics of such roles under a rapidly changing political environment.

If pan-Africanist solidarity could be approached from a number of angles, what was the most realistic and pragmatic angle for African Americans who shared in a common tendency to politically and culturally romanticize Africa and also held views of pan-Africanism that oftentimes ran counter to those of the African state? At the same time, Tanzania's cultural and economic dependence on Western imperial powers dictated African American activism inside the country in more fundamental ways than language barriers.

The meeting could not disguise an undercurrent of disappointment both in the state of African affairs and Black Power romantic perceptions of Africa's postcolonial situation. The views and attitudes of AAR towards postcolonial nationalism and state-building are important because the discussions reflected strong anti-imperialist views and, most importantly, recurring concerns over the fragility of the African state and its capacity to act as an institution of global black liberation. Certainly, this meeting allowed Cobb to work through such various dilemmas associated with modes of African American identification with Africa, opposing visions of pan-African unity, and the contradictions of postcolonial state formation while in the company of like-minded peers from similar cultural, ideological, and political organizing backgrounds. Though his report back on Tanzania's nationalist project deepened his sense of uncertainty, Cobb concluded the meeting by portraying Tanzania as still holding revolutionary possibilities. "Despite all the contradictions, and no one knows where Tanzania is going to go," Cobb remarked, "it offers the clearest program of action for an organization of African people around the question of self-reliance, and that's not a total thing, but a minimal survival in the face of total control which Europe has over Africa."[114]

While it is not entirely clear how much impact this meeting had on the direction of the DSP's international publishing efforts, the challenges Cobb brings up hint at why the press could not get its project off the ground in Tanzania. If anything, the AAR meeting illustrated the importance of international travel, drawing attention to the fact that political communities in the African Diaspora felt increasingly isolated from the developments in Africa, and how they tended to look at African states from a core-periphery dependency framework, not just in economic terms, but cultural terms as well. In the final analysis, the DSP's presence in Tanzania allowed it to come to terms with some uncomfortable truths about the complexities that characterized the political, cultural, and economic realities of Tanzanian society. As a result of international travel, the DSP's image of Tanzania as one of the few remaining radical states left in Africa, and Ujamaa socialism as a universal ideology, was brought under serious reconsideration.

From its inception, the Drum and Spear Press was financially strapped, a characteristic reality of the everyday struggles of small publishing companies. Small book-publishing companies needed at least $125,000 to compete with other press corporations both small and large.[115] By 1970, DSP had amassed roughly $80,000. By 1973, the year both the bookstore and press ceased operations, it was $24,000 in debt. FBI harassment only added to its decline, as it did for many black radical organizations of the Black Power era.[116]

Given DSP inability to sustain itself as a profitable business enterprise in the recession era of the 1970s, one could easily downplay its contributions to the Black Power movement. After all, the books available for purchase were far from pricey, rarely exceeding a price of $2.50. Added to the fact that they sought to do business in a community slowly recovering from the 1968 rebellion and plunging headfirst into urban stagnation, the DSP held no illusions about making a serious profit.[117] However, its anti-profit motive did not bode well for them, especially when advocating economic self-reliance. Although the DSP published books for their political and cultural statements rather than for their potential in generating mass sales, it is precisely this approach that is significant for our understanding of the development and character of black independent institutions.

The DSP's contributions and achievements lie in the realms of politics and culture. By believing that black people do read, especially books that reflect their own lived experiences, the press introduced to an untapped audience a vast array of radical ideas from all corners of the globe. The political and cultural awakening in Black America provided the press with an opportunity to cater to African American demands for books that could aid in the formation of African diasporic identities. By attempting to open up one's imagination to the possibility of radical social change and self-transformation, the DSP promoted reading as a prerequisite to political action.

When the Drum and Spear sought to expand its operations to the African continent, its political idealism clouded its weak economic standing. However, its publications helped frame a Black Power print culture that gave special attention to African liberation in the overlapping contexts of postcolonial nationalism, cultural identity, and state formation. Embracing Tanzania's nationalist project, evidenced in the publication of *Kusema Kiswahili* and *Watoto wa Afrika*, simultaneously met specific nation-building needs of the Tanzanian government and the Black Power movement. For black internationalists who placed the black freedom struggle in a global context, settling in Tanzania in no way constituted a political contradiction, especially since the state prioritized book education as well. The DSP and the state-owned TPH found a mutually reinforcing reason to pursue collaborative ties, yet their collaboration was never adequately supported with the necessary manpower and capital. The challenges of organizing in Tanzania compelled the DSP to reassess the diasporic relationship to the continent and its political, cultural, and economic realities.

The DSP's publishing efforts in Tanzania left a lot of questions unanswered about the diaspora's role in African liberation. Is such a role strictly reducible to active participation in specific nation-building projects in postcolonial African countries, or advocacy from within one's home country? Can the Organization of African Unity, the continent's primary institution of pan-Africanism, help to usher in complete decolonization in Africa and cultivate African and African Diaspora unity? To what extent do independent African states obfuscate rather than clarify the solidarity practices of diasporic political activists? In engaging with these questions, I now turn to the Sixth Pan-African Congress, organized by Black Power activists in the African Diaspora and held at the University of Dar es Salaam in 1974, and the ways in which the marginalization of diasporic agency and participation in the pan-Africanism movement by postcolonial African states marked the decline of Black Power engagement with Tanzania's nationalist project.

Flyer: "Babu! Leader of the Zanzibar Revolution Speaks on the CONGO." Courtesy of Tamiment Library and Robert F. Wagner Archives, New York University.

Cartoon of Stokely Carmichael featured on the cover of Anti-Apartheid News, *a Britain-based newsletter. Courtesy of Archives of the Anti-Apartheid Movement,* Anti-Apartheid News.

Stokely Carmichael with National Service Youth of Tanzania, November 1967. Courtesy of the Daily News Photograph Archives.

LEFT: *U.S. Black Nationalist leader and political exile Robert F. Williams in Tanzania, 1968. Courtesy of the* Daily News *Photograph Archives.*

BELOW: *Angela Davis delivers speech at an event sponsored by the Union of Women of Tanzania, University of Dar es Salaam, 1973. Courtesy of the* Daily News *Photograph Archives.*

Front of the Drum and Spear Bookstore, 1970. Courtesy of Jennifer Lawson Personal Papers, private collection.

Inside the Drum and Spear Bookstore, 1970. Courtesy of Jennifer Lawson Personal Papers, private collection.

ABOVE: The Drum and Spear Bookstore business card. Courtesy of Jennifer Lawson Personal Papers, private collection.

LEFT: Jennifer Lawson, Dar es Salaam, 1971. Courtesy of Jennifer Lawson Personal Papers, private collection.

LEFT: Walter Bgoya, editor of the Tanzania Publishing House, 1969. Courtesy of the Daily News Photograph Archives.

BELOW: Queen Mother Audley Moore and President Julius Nyerere, Sixth Pan-African Congress, Dar es Salaam, 1974. Courtesy of the Daily News Photograph Archives.

PART 3

Undoing

Chapter 5

Convergence and Rejection at the Sixth Pan-African Congress

Although the Pan-African Movement was originally confined to black people, our particular struggle for dignity has always been one aspect of the worldwide struggle for human liberation. That is why if we react to the continued need to defend our position as black men by regarding ourselves as different from the rest of mankind, we shall weaken ourselves, and the racialists of the world have scored their biggest triumph.
—General Declaration of the Sixth Pan-African Congress

Through much of the late 1960s and early 1970s, the Black Power movement continued to put on display its internationalist sensibilities. Though various efforts were made to boost black popular and political support for African liberation, activists identified the lack of functional unity between Africa and its diaspora as a problem of increasing importance. In a context in which regions in Africa were still under colonial rule and white minority control, not to mention independent nation-states having little to show for their ambitious efforts at nation-building, Black Power activists feared that the commonalities between these various black struggles were being greatly overlooked or dismissed, especially the voices of non-state actors.

Movement activists adopted an anti-imperialist stance against a U.S. Cold War foreign policy and reached the conclusion they needed to play a more direct role in addressing African affairs by establishing and strengthening ties with African leaders on the continent. Of equal concern was a growing sense of marginality in the pan-Africanism movement. With their influential role dating back to the movement's emergence in the late nineteenth century, African Americans and West Indians were operating along its margins in the decolonization era. The emergence of the OAU as the primary pan-Africanist institution drove a statist definition of pan-Africanism, while independent states such as Tanzania positioned themselves as major players in shaping a politics specific to continental issues.[1] Decolonization led Africa to become the geopolitical locus of state power and anticolonial struggle, leaving many in the diaspora to ponder where they stood.

Black Power activists hoped that by organizing an international conference on pan-African unity, greater inclusion, decision-making power, and a more clearly defined role in African affairs were to come. As political scientist Ronald Walters noted, the Sixth Pan-African Congress (6PAC) would be "an attempt by the diaspora movement to express itself more and more within the context of African continental politics; there it confronted the tensions already existing among various political ideologies championed by one state or another."[2] Moreover, such an initiative would demonstrate that their commitment to a free and united Africa extended to nation-states and black political struggles in the diaspora. Thus, in June 1974, such an expression was realized at 6PAC. Held at the University of Dar es Salaam, it proved to be a historical moment of black transnational dialogue and exchange.

But what was imagined as a congress for the masses was marred by ideological sectarian and state interventionist politics, which seemed to cement African independent states' privileged position in the pan-Africanism movement. A closer look at the history of 6PAC provides another illustrative moment to examine in greater detail the inclusionary and exclusionary practices of the Tanzanian state when it came to its approach towards working with Black Power activists. On the one hand, by allowing the congress to be held in Dar es Salaam and legitimizing their leadership role, the TANU government and party helped to facilitate a temporary degree of autonomy and decision-making power in African political affairs. On the other hand, TANU placed some constraints on their mobilizing and institution-building efforts. The one-party government made sure to protect national governments from criticism and to push forth an agenda that favored their authority based on an OAU model. This statist position undermined Black Power efforts to hold a conference that strengthened popular participation. During this five-year process, from 1969 to 1974, the Tanzanian state exerted just enough influence to reconfigure the framework of the congress in a way that prevented Black Power organizers from realizing this vision.

Participants at the June 1969 Black Power Conference held in Bermuda first proposed the idea of a Sixth Pan-African Congress.[3] Between 1969 and 1971, a series of planning meetings were held in the Caribbean and the United States led by Roosevelt Browne, a member of the Bermuda parliament. However, it was not until 1971, when Browne convinced C.L.R. James to get involved, that the 6PAC idea was given much-needed momentum. At the time, James was still living in Washington, DC, lecturing throughout the country and making himself available to Black Power student activists who sought him out for political guidance, education, and informal mentorship.[4]

Although James was at odds with certain ideological tendencies of Black Power, this did not deter him from working with this younger generation of radical activists. In fact, as early as 1969, he was arguing that the African American freedom struggle served as the cornerstone of U.S. political culture and was an integral component to the worldwide socialist revolution.[5] At times, he was dumbfounded by Black Power uncompromising attitudes towards authority, but admired the autonomy of their organizations and youthfulness of their leaders. A planning meeting in 1971 marked James's involvement in the Sixth Pan-African Congress as advisor, historian, mediator, and mentor. He would especially embrace his role as historian, providing a historical perspective on black struggles and the shifts and ever-changing character of pan-Africanism. Indeed, the Black Power movement offered James an opportunity to politically educate activists by placing 6PAC in its proper historical context:

> I wish to give the impression that Black Americans today feel there is a great absence of political and historical ideas which can lead them in a political direction and they feel a great need for it, and what they are very much interested in hearing from me is my approach to the problems of the present-day, where they have come from and where they are going. Not that they accept what I say. Some do, some don't, but they like my approach because they feel that they will be able to find the answers to the questions that are troubling them.[6]

What James found was a committed group of activists, intellectuals, and students who were just as passionately invested as he was in seeing the end of colonial rule in southern Africa and the development of socialist societies in independent African countries.

This political sentiment was particularly strong with the activists he met at the Center for Black Education (CBE), a Black Power organization whose members largely staffed the main 6PAC organizing body, the Temporary Secretariat. As discussed in the previous chapter, the CBE was an educational institution created by Afro-American Resources, Inc., and emerged out of a confrontation with the board of trustees of Federal City College (FCC) over the control of the Black Studies curriculum. Rather than compromise their black nationalist-internationalist approach to education, Black

Chapter Five

Power activists decided to form the CBE as an independent institution. CBE activism revolved around political education, curriculum development, and publication of textbooks aimed at providing its students with an "in-depth understanding of the ideology of Pan-Africanism."[7] Its mission statement read: "We seek by dedication and struggle the total independence, sovereignty, and unification of all African People, on the African Continent and the Afro-Caribbean; the transportation of our people from European states to successful integration into Africa."[8] James, who had worked with the Drum and Spear Press in its effort to republish *A History of Pan-African Revolt* in 1969, became a frequent lecturer for the CBE's weekly seminars.[9]

From 1969 to 1970, the CBE played a minor role in the organizing process. However, this changed the following year. By 1972, when CBE member Courtland Cox assumed the position of secretary general of the Temporary Secretariat, CBE's role became more prominent.[10] A former SNCC activist, Cox had both the experience and political outlook that made him an ideal candidate for this leadership position. Born in 1941 in New York City, the son of Trinidadian immigrants, Cox enrolled at Howard University in the early 1960s and soon became politically active in the Nonviolent Action Group (NAG), where he worked closely with the likes of Charlie Cobb and Stokely Carmichael. After the lunch-counter sit-in movement was launched in 1960, he made his way to the Black Belt South, became a founding member of SNCC, and organized direct action campaigns, voter rights drives, and community empowerment programs. He also helped organize the 1963 March on Washington for Jobs and Freedom. Later, he relocated to Alabama to help form the Lowndes County Freedom Organization, the original Black Panther Party.[11]

Like Carmichael and his Afro-American Resources, Inc. (AAR) peers, Cox was part of the militant faction of SNCC who ushered in the organization's turn to black nationalism/pan-Africanism and northern urban activism (see chapter 4). When his friend Charlie Cobb traveled to Cambodia on an antiwar fact-finding mission in 1967, Cox was by his side even during Cobb's ship journey to West Africa. Back in Washington, DC, Cox funneled most of his energies into the CBE, serving in the "political unit," which developed curriculum and courses that promoted a stringent pan-Africanist agenda.[12] Because it was basing its operations out of Washington, DC, CBE members, including Marvin Holloway, Jimmy Garrett, Gerri Stark, and Edie Wilson, largely made up the staff of the Temporary Secretariat.[13]

The Temporary Secretariat knew that various factors would determine its success in bringing together such a wide range of people of African descent with various ideological outlooks to exchange ideas and engage in constructive dialogue. One of those factors rested on its ability to articulate clearly the general purpose and significance of the congress. Thus, after they were formalized as the lead organizers, a series of local and national meetings soon followed where they sought to answer three primary conceptual questions: Why the need for such a congress? What issues are to be discussed? And what does the congress seek to achieve?

Inspired by Tanzania's nationalist project, "Self-Reliance" was to be the overarching theme of the congress under which three primary issues were to be addressed. Most important and of "immediate relevance to the domestic struggles of Black People everywhere" was the question of the total liberation of southern Africa.[14] By 1971, Portugal still held firm to its colonies in Mozambique and Angola (and Guinea-Bissau in West Africa), while white minority rule was being entrenched in Rhodesia, Namibia, and South Africa. African liberation groups such as the ANC, MPLA, FRELIMO, ZAPU, ZANU, SWAPO, and PAC were engaged in armed struggles at various levels of intensity and were being supported by the OAU Liberation Committee. At the same time, with the minor exception of Mozambique, nationalist movements from the same colonized territories were consumed by infighting.[15] This was the situation in Angola between UNITA, FNLA, and MPLA, as well as in Rhodesia between ZAPU and ZANU.[16] The ANC, PAC, and SWAPO achieved small gains in their armed struggle against apartheid in the early 1970s due to the effectiveness of colonial state repression.[17] No matter what the status of these liberation movements, Black Power activists correctly believed they were in need of support and worldwide recognition.

Of further cause for concern, especially for African Americans, was the role of U.S. imperialism in Africa. U.S. foreign policy in Africa under the Nixon administration showed how the question of decolonization could not be divorced from U.S. Cold War imperatives rooted in the ongoing belief that African majority rule would only concretize both Soviet and Chinese influence in southern Africa. But under the guise of this Cold War rationale, President Nixon also gave priority to capitalist interests.[18] The rise in military aid and foreign capital investment to colonial and white minority-ruled regimes and the recent passing of the Byrd Amendment in 1971, which bypassed UN sanctions on the import of chrome from Rhodesia, fueled Black Power discontent over Nixon's Cold War policy agenda. As the Temporary Secretariat declared: "The white capitalist world is solidly behind the anti-African forces in Southern Africa. Their solidarity is expressed through institutions like the multi-national corporations that reap super profits from the abominable exploitation of African mineworkers. It is also expressed in institutions like N.A.T.O. which provide the bombs and the planes which bring death and destruction to crops, livestock and African lives."[19]

In line with advancing a discussion on decolonization, 6PAC organizers wanted the issue of postcolonial state formation to be a "subject of serious review." In their analysis of nation-statehood in Africa, they often stressed the limitations of political independence and framed the postcolonial situation in dependency terms.[20] African

Chapter Five

states' inability to move out of a peripheral position in the world capitalist economy—as an exporter of raw materials and importer of manufactured goods—was only compounded by an absence of the technological resources needed to do so. In addition, the prevalence and growth of military regimes in Africa made it impossible to not want to address the "internal" question of failed political leadership and systems.[21]

Finally, "the peculiarities" of the black situation in the United States also required serious discussion. Just as Africans on the continent were under the constant threat of imperialism, so too were African Americans who were "under the assault by the coercive machinery of the white racist state—its police, courts and jails."[22] However, just as the African liberation movements were racked by internal discord, so too was the African American freedom struggle. This ideological disunity was most evident at the National Black Political Convention held in Gary, Indiana, in 1972.[23] In addition to resolving issues of internal disunity, 6PAC organizers were poised to respond to the consistent requests from African governments for African American skilled technicians in hopes of arriving at a clearly defined role for African Americans in the sphere of international relations.

With the political climate among African Americans firmly set against colonial rule and U.S. imperialist intervention in Africa, 6PAC organizers had a base of domestic popular support from which to galvanize interest in the congress. The Congress of African People (CAP) and the African Liberation Support Committee (ALSC) were two radical organizations during this time that reflected this growing consciousness. Formed in 1970 and led by Amiri Baraka, CAP sought to pursue a black united-front agenda in the United States and promote and implement concrete programs that would bridge the gap between "the various wings of the black freedom movement."[24] The ascendancy of ALSC was an outgrowth of the African Liberation Day celebration of May 1972 and the work of the African Liberation Day Coordinating Committee (ALDCC).[25] Led by Owusu Saduakai of Malcolm X University in Durham, North Carolina, the ALSC's aims and objectives were internationalist in character through advocating concrete support to Africans still embroiled in armed conflict, participating in African nation-building, raising awareness about African decolonization, and pressuring the U.S. government for substantive change in U.S. foreign policy.[26] Thus, in the early 1970s, the ALSC and CAP were two indispensable black nationalist organizations that advanced Black Power's pan-Africanist agenda and helped forge popular anti-imperialist attitudes among the U.S. black population.

Black Power activists' call for a Sixth Pan-African Congress resonated with a tone of urgency because of their acute awareness of the exigencies of the times. It also grew out of anxieties that stemmed from their marginal involvement in African affairs. While there was a desire to emphasize the racial character of imperialism, 6PAC organizers also understood the situation in its broader economic context. Colonial and white racist rule in southern Africa, fragile unity within the African American and African freedom struggles, U.S. imperialist interests, and the misrule of African and Caribbean ruling elites provided powerful reasons for Africans and black peoples of the diaspora to not view their respective struggles in isolation: "Every African engaged in combat against the ancient structures of imperialism or the newly emergent forms of neocolonialism will not succeed if he disassociates his combat from the struggle waged by all other Africans."[27]

When it came to the question of who was to be invited, 6PAC organizers foresaw a "people's congress" where states would not hold a dominant position in the discussion on pan-African unity and its future directions. "It will not be a gathering of Heads of States," read one of their first written statements. Instead, participation was to be open to those "who adhere to the historical principles of African unity, common interests and common struggles."[28] The underlying principle of participation, they further argued, was the desire to see Africa and its diaspora move with greater speed toward functional unity. In a 1971 internal memo, the Temporary Secretariat argued that if the congress was to be truly an all-inclusive affair, then "no group of African people can be excluded or included because of the policy of their respective governments."[29] Though perhaps not as intentional as it appeared, it was a direct indictment of the OAU and its policies of noninterference and exclusion of a handful of liberation groups from recognition. Later, as the planning intensified, this very conception of 6PAC as a "nongovernmental affair" aroused the suspicions of Caribbean and African governments to such an extent that it forced the Tanzania government to intervene. Against the backdrop of "authoritarianism, military takeovers, and general socio-political instability," postcolonial governments were not going to be cleared of any wrongdoing, as the congress would aim to address both internal and external oppressive forces.[30]

All of these concerns, desires, and stated goals were articulated in a position paper titled "The Call." First published on February 5, 1972, the introductory paragraph to the edited and reissued version, which was released in August 1972, reads: "The 20th century is the century of Black Power. It has already been marked by two dynamics. First, a unified conception of all peoples who have been colonized. They are known by friends and enemies as members of the Third World. And the most significant members of the Third World are those who strive for power to the people and Black Power to the Black People. On the one hand, white power, which ruled unchallenged for so long during this very century, is marked by unparalleled degeneration, first by two savage and global wars such as the world had never before seen. The same mentality prepares for a third war. Its barbarism unpurged, European power strives at all costs to maintain that domination from which the formerly colonial peoples are breaking. That is the world white power seeks to maintain at a time when the colonial peoples have begun one of the greatest movements toward freedom that the world has ever known. The SIXTH PAN AFRICAN CONGRESS, to be held in the United Republic of Tanzania in June 1974, is part of that movement."[31] What follows is an attempt at highlighting the historical significance of the pan-Africanism movement from the colonial through the postcolonial eras.

"The Call" locates the movement's origins to 1900, the year of the First Pan-African Congress, which helped launch pan-Africanism as an idea and movement. Four others followed between 1919 and 1945, culminating in the Fifth Pan-African Congress in Manchester, England. What was going to distinguish 6PAC from the previous five was that it was going to be held for the first time on the African continent, to emphasize the needs and aspirations of the working class and peasantry, and to probe the limits and challenges of nation-statehood. Beyond the congresses, "The Call" gives mention to Marcus Garvey and the Universal Negro Improvement Association (UNIA) movement, as well as the International African Service Bureau (IASB) and its fight against colonialism and fascism in Ethiopia, because of their pan-African character, anti-imperialist politics, and mass-based political agendas. By providing this detailed background, the "Pan-African world" would understand 6PAC's historic role, pan-Africanism's autonomous organizing traditions, and the African, Caribbean, and African American contributions to its development. Therefore, although 1974 marked a new historical moment that ultimately differentiated 6PAC from the previous five Pan-African congresses that were held between 1900 and 1945, it would still represent "the continuity and acceleration of Black struggle"[32]

The last two sections of the "The Call" prioritized "complete and absolute" liberation in southern Africa and the development of a pan-African science and technology center and agenda. As a call for mutual understanding, "face-to-face planning," and most of all, coordinated action, the Sixth Pan-African Congress was imagined as an epic gathering of the minds where the idea of self-reliance would mean the "fullest utilization of our own human resources instead of continued dependency" on the West.[33]

The Temporary Secretariat was to serve as the "moving political force behind the Congress."[34] "We want to mobilize the progressive and revolutionary elements in the African world against those who are holding up the progress," James said at one meeting.[35] It would also function in an administrative capacity, working on a "day to day basis in various regions of the world" through setting up and overseeing regional committees in North America, Europe, the Caribbean, and Africa. Within each region, subcommittees were formed to determine delegate representation and draft papers on politics, economics, agriculture, health, technology, etc. According to the Temporary

Secretariat, it was believed that creating an organizational structure based on regions rather than nation-states would keep 6PAC framed as a people's conference.[36]

Although its all-inclusive vision was partially intended to carve out a space for debate about postcolonial state authoritarianism, the Temporary Secretariat still relied on the bulk of the funds to come from national governments. The potential problem was that nation-state funds would come with too much government meddling in the organizing phase. To prevent state intervention of this kind from happening, "sponsors" were created. These were "people of note" who had "toiled long in the vineyard" of the pan-Africanist struggle, such as Amy Jacques Garvey, Chancellor Williams, Shirley Graham Du Bois, Julius Nyerere, Walter Rodney, and C.L.R. James.[37] It was believed that these sponsors would provide the ideological perspective, and offset any kind of potential government control or manipulation of the congress's agenda.[38]

By 1972 the Temporary Secretariat had outlined the basic trajectory and goals of the congress, which proved useful in rallying popular support and securing financial backing from individuals, organizations, and postcolonial governments. Above all, these young pan-Africanist organizers had C.L.R. James. As they would soon learn, James's involvement added instant credibility to the congress idea and the leadership behind it due to the respect he had earned around the world as one of the preeminent radical activists and political thinkers of the twentieth century. When he advised them to first seek out Nyerere for support, they found themselves in Dar es Salaam at the State House for a meeting with the president, which James had orchestrated. Temporary Secretariat members needed little convincing from James on why Nyerere was the right choice of an ally and host of the first Pan-African Congress on "African soil." As already noted, the "Drum and Spear Complex," which included the CBE, were heavily invested in the Tanzanian revolution. These Black Power activists viewed it as a model of nation-building in terms of political leadership and the implementation of progressive foreign and domestic policies. James had made such a case in the revised *History of Pan-African Revolt*, published by the Drum and Spear Press, and continued to do so while advocating for the congress.

The meeting between James, Cox, Julius Nyerere, John Malecela, and Bernard Muganda of the Ministry of Foreign Affairs took place in mid-May 1972. Nyerere agreed to host the conference, provide logistical support, and help mobilize Africans on the continent. The president was attracted not only to the idea of supporting anticolonial armed struggles, but also the building of autonomous international institutions that would address technological underdevelopment. With Nyerere's full backing, the legitimacy of the congress could not be challenged, especially by the African government and liberation-movement representatives who knew very little about the Black Power organizers behind the event. When Cox later met with President Touré of Guinea, whom many Black Power activists also considered a progressive proponent of pan-Africanism, he left the meeting with the Guinean government's full support.[39] However, it was not until the Temporary Secretariat received support from the Tanzanian state that planning for the congress truly picked up steam, for it put them in a better position to garner support, mobilize participants, and secure more financial backing.

For close to two years, 6PAC organizers traveled the globe. They sent delegations to conferences; held private meetings with heads of state, government officials, and anticolonial nationalist leaders; and presented papers and delivered speeches at regional planning meetings. On May 11, 1973, they found themselves in Ohio for the North American Regional Planning Conference. Held on the campus of Kent State University, the famous site of the 1970 anti-Vietnam war student protest that resulted in the deaths of four students by national guardsmen, this meeting led to the formation of the North American delegation. One hundred and seventy-five people attended and forty-five organizations were represented. There was also a sizable group of African representatives sent from embassies and consulates in the United States, including Nigeria, Sierra Leone, Tanzania, and Libya.

James kicked off the proceedings with a speech that did not deviate from his primary role as political educator and historian. He made it clear that an emphasis on capitalist exploitation and the voice of workers and peasants would be lost if too much time was placed on the "race question." Only then would 6PAC truly become a people's conference and be considered a historical event similar to the Fifth Pan-African Congress. "The freedom and independence of the African people must be done by African people themselves," James explained, "and that is the essence of the Sixth PAC."[40]

The following day Cox addressed the audience, tailoring his speech to the large group of "Africans in the West" in attendance. He came out strongly against the U.S. government and multinational corporations and their complicity in Africa, seeing it as nothing more than evidence of a new scramble for Africa's abundant natural resources. "We state categorically that the major battle of the 21st century will be for the resources of the world," he began. The rise of the U.S. imperialist and neocolonialist power required that "Africans in the West" view their struggles in an internationalist context. "While we are looking around the block, America is telescoping around the globe . . . we have to ask ourselves which new world power forces—potential and actual—do we want to link up to . . . we have a responsibility to assist in the struggle against a new penetration of Africa," he explained. "But moreover, our own possibilities in the West become expanded in direct relationship to the strength and growth of Africa. We have a self-interest in the future of Africa."[41] Cox then laid out the five major objectives of the congress: increasing political unity between Africa and its diaspora; developing concrete support for the liberation of southern Africa; forming independent institutions to boost intercommunication; encouraging an attitude of self-reliance; and mobilizing skilled manpower.

Despite having a clear, stated vision, the planning stage of the conference was not without tension or unresolved questions. Owusu Saduakai, one of the national leaders of the ALSC, spoke quite forcefully about how the ALSC, and the Black Power movement more generally, should not follow OAU-LC protocol in only supporting the liberation movements that it recognized. He also made an impassioned plea to African representatives about the need for more reciprocity, suggesting that support among African states for the black freedom struggle in the United States left a lot to be desired.[42] This prompted a sharp response from the Ghanaian ambassador, who claimed that no African government was willing to throw its support behind a congress that did not adhere to an OAU model.[43] While the planning intensified, the threat of replicating an OAU framework often lurked just under the surface.

On May 17, four days after meeting at Kent State University, Cox, James, Edie Wilson, and Fletcher Robinson, 6PAC coordinator of health and nutrition, flew to Addis Ababa to attend the tenth anniversary celebration of the General Session of the OAU. For close to two weeks, they sought out African representatives of governments, liberation movements, and press agencies with the stated goal to formalize contacts, gain an understanding of the "African political climate," and collect information concerning the technical needs of independent African nations. According to Cox, "the objectives" of the meeting "were achieved in a very limited way."[44] Some of the more positive outcomes of their lobbying efforts were found in the contacts made with eleven nations and eight liberation movements, including groups not recognized by the OAU. In addition, editors of four African publications expressed their willingness to provide press coverage before, during, and after the congress. "Everyone with whom we spoke was very enthusiastic about the Congress," Cox explained in a monthly report, "and seemed to know that efforts are being made to have an international meeting for a historic, clearly-defined and much-needed purpose."[45]

Following the OAU session, Cox and James traveled from Ethiopia to Canada to attend the British Commonwealth meeting of Heads of State. Again, taking on the role of lobbyists, they held brief discussions with many African leaders. Yet their most promising results came from their meetings with Prime Ministers Forbes Burnham of Guyana and Michael Manley of Jamaica, which had netted them $20,000 of financial support along with Burnham's assurance that the Guyanese government would host a meeting of the Caribbean region in early November.[46] Although Cox and James were aware of the Caribbean nongovernment groups adamantly opposed to their home governments, little did they know that the greater involvement of these governments would later come to haunt them on the eve of the congress.

Initially, the Temporary Secretariat saw the ruling party acting in a more logistical capacity, especially on the African continent. "We see TANU, with its prestige and experience," read one internal memo, "doing the coordination on the African continent . . . Although we have made contacts with Africans in various regions of Africa, we think that TANU ought to make the contacts for and extend the invitations to Western and Northern Africa and Eastern and Southern Africa."[47] For Nyerere, he still displayed the desire to stay in positive leadership standing in the struggle to emancipate southern Africa at Tanzania's expense. Moreover, with the congress's emphasis on intensifying awareness and support for decolonization in southern Africa, President Nyerere believed 6PAC would boost Tanzania's credibility and generate favorable publicity for liberation movements and the African governments that supported them.[48] At a time when the other forty member-states of the OAU remained inconsistent in their required monetary contributions to the OAU-LC while Portuguese, South African, and Rhodesian governments, and their NATO allies, were boosting up their counterinsurgency military capacities to curb anticolonial dissent, convening pan-Africanists could only aid, not hurt the cause. Thus Nyerere's advocacy of the conference was strongly influenced by a desire to cement his pan-Africanist leadership in Africa and its diaspora and to further legitimate the state's influential role in continental affairs.

In planning for the conference, the TANU Party played the role of active collaborator and selective interventionist. Tanzanian ambassador to Canada Abbas Sykes took on an active, participatory role when the congress was merely an idea being floated around in 1969.[49] Sykes, for example, attended the first two planning meetings and then later accompanied a secretariat delegation to Europe in January 1972. He was fairly effective in bringing early credibility to the congress. Bomani's appointment as the new ambassador in December 1972 marked a period of internal reorganization that opened up communication channels between the state and Pan-African Skills Project (PASP) leadership. Paul Bomani, Tanzania's ambassador to the United States, also played an important 6PAC planning role. Bomani was one of the founding fathers of TANU, earning his anticolonial-nationalist credentials as a cotton-farmer organizer.[50] Later he was appointed as a representative to the colonial state's Legislative Council in 1954 and 1958, which set the stage for the dismantling of British colonial rule. When Tanganyika became a sovereign nation, he enjoyed the spoils of national independence, heading up a number of high- to mid-level ministries, including the Ministry of Agriculture and Cooperative Development and the Ministry of Finance.[51] Although he was defeated in the country's first one-party state general elections of 1965, Nyerere did not accept this loss of an "exemplary" TANU member and government official, and thus saw fit to intervene by granting Bomani a seat in the National Assembly as minister of economic affairs and development planning. This legal executive decision made him the first National Assembly member without a constituency in Tanzania's young history.[52] Two years later, Bomani held the position of minister of commerce and industry until his appointment as ambassador to the United States. Bomani's eighteen years of government experience afforded him intimate knowledge of Tanzania's developmental needs, particularly its shortages of skilled labor, which informed the nature of his involvement in the planning process.

Bomani's proactive participation was also partially a response to the ruling party's own official policy. As laid out in its guidelines of 1971, it became the policy of TANU to "establish fraternal revolutionary relations with those (Black) American citizens fighting for justice and human equality."[53] While there was division within TANU over cooperating with Black Power activists specifically, President Nyerere saw 6PAC as an opportunity for the one-party state to engage in another concrete form of collaboration with Black Power activists, one that could still meet the expectations and objectives of Tanzania's nationalist project. He remained drawn to the technical assistance initiative articulated in "The Call," aware that the absence of modern technology and know-how was an obstacle to economic and social transformation in Africa. The fact that the Pan-African Skills Project was still underway during the early 1970s meant that Nyerere saw little fault in promoting an idea already being implemented in his own country. And on many occasions Bomani relayed this sentiment to African Americans. Indeed, he displayed an enthusiastic willingness to speak at local and national Black Power gatherings, where he used the language of pan-Africanism to describe the significance of the African American technical assistance to Africa. At the "African Cultural Weekend" in Youngstown, Ohio, he spoke on African Americans' and Tanzanians' shared commitment to eradicate anti-black racism throughout the world: "I don't see any difference between my brothers and sisters in America and my brothers and sisters in Tanzania. We are all the same. It has taken a long time to establish a useful linkage between black people in this country and in Africa. It is high time we correct the mistakes and begin to vigorously pursue all means possible to establishing a meaningful link . . . Our major objective must be to free all black people wherever they are. We in Africa are willing to work shoulder to shoulder with you to correct injustices in the world."[54] From Newark to Brooklyn, South Bend to Chicago, San Diego to Boston, where he was flanked by assigned Black Power bodyguards and greeted by enthusiastic crowds of African American supporters, Bomani remembered being treated "like a king."[55]

In 1973, when interviewed by Cox and Stark, who described Tanzania as "one of the most important working models of self-reliance,"[56] Nyerere talked about how 6PAC would set in motion a dialogue that would strictly foster mutual understanding. He

Chapter Five

claimed that the Sixth Pan-African Congress would push forth the idea that the "liberation of the Black man has got to be seen as the liberation of the Black man wherever he is, and wherever he's not free. This awareness must be universal among African peoples."[57] He noted that African Americans could "provide skills and attitudes, and an experience" that would give Africa the technological strength needed for economic development.[58]

In order to avoid any potential backlash from Caribbean and African governments, Nyerere made the party, not the government, responsible for organizing the congress and working closely with the Temporary Secretariat. But since Tanzania was a one-party state, 6PAC organizers soon learned that there was a thin line between the two. However, the formation of the Dar es Salaam Coordinating Committee, nicknamed the "Dar Committee," in 1972 was an important development that illustrated the Nyerere government's concerns over African Diaspora domination of the 6PAC organizing phase. Bill Sutherland, who had the strongest ties to Nyerere among African American expatriates, was part of the committee, along with TANU members of various ministries, including foreign minister John Malecela, the Tanzanian foreign minister who facilitated SNCC's participation in the UN seminar in Zambia in the mid-1960s. The committee was most effective in carrying out TANU's various logistical duties of fundraising, organizing the Tanzanian delegation, setting up security at the conference, and providing accommodations (housing and food) to delegates, translating systems, a public address system, and facilities for the press and Permanent Secretariat.[59] By the beginning of 1973, the committee was serving as the "Temporary Secretariat in Africa" until the Cox-led Temporary Secretariat in Washington moved its office to Dar es Salaam in November of the same year.[60]

TANU held no reservations about making special appeals to the Temporary Secretariat, first by agreeing to host and finance the congress and then by granting it permission to set up an office in Dar es Salaam. This latter gesture also resulted in the provision of housing and transportation. In November 1973, the office moved from Washington, DC, to Dar es Salaam.[61] It was located in the downtown area of the city while the two houses provided by TANU were on Bagamoyo Road, five short blocks from the Indian Ocean.[62] This kind of TANU assistance allowed the Temporary Secretariat greater mobility and easier access to various African constituencies, fostered more efficient communication, and contributed to a greater sense of involvement in African affairs.

Among those who accompanied Cox to Dar es Salaam were Edie Wilson and Gerri Stark, two young black women who also played important leadership roles in the organizing process. As a college student, Wilson gravitated to the CBE by attending James's lectures and eventually joined its staff while working full-time in the U.S. Department of Health, Education, and Welfare.[63] While Wilson remained conference secretary in charge of practically everything from "protocol to passports,"⁶⁴ TANU created a special position for Stark. Stark was somewhat of a late addition to the Temporary Secretariat, having played no role in the planning that took place between 1969 and 1971. It was not until CBE took hold of the organizational apparatus in November 1972 that she became more actively involved.

Born in Cleveland, Ohio, Stark attended Howard University beginning in 1996, where, as a seventeen-year-old, she got heavily involved in the nationwide student movement that championed the creation of Black Studies programs on university and college campuses. This activist experience led her off campus to the Center for Black Education, where she worked in communications. She served as a coeditor of CBE's newsletter the *Pan-African*; host of CBE's radio show *Sauti* (Kiswahili for "voice"), where she wrote scripts and read book reviews; and a journalist for the Nation of Islam's newspaper *Muhammad Speaks*.⁶⁵ Of all the black activists involved with the "Drum and Spear Complex," she grew closest to C.L.R. James while he was living and teaching in Washington, DC. Because of her fluency in French, James took a particular liking to her. Stark frequented his apartment every Sunday to read to him English- and French-language newspapers about domestic and global events, which were always followed by intense discussion and analysis, usually over food cooked by either James or Stark.⁶⁶ It was this personal relationship with James that resulted in him asking her to became involved in 6PAC. Her first responsibility as the new communications secretary was to accompany James, Cox, and Garrett to Tanzania to meet with President Nyerere in 1972.

In 1973 Stark, and her newborn son, moved to Dar es Salaam once the office space was secured there. In Tanzania, her role changed from communications secretary to the official liaison with the anticolonial nationalist movements headquartered in the city. Created by TANU, her primary task was carrying out the interests and objectives of the Tanzanian government. Through working closely with the Ministry of Foreign Affairs, Stark traveled with Tanzanian government officials to OAU and OAU-LC meetings that were held in various African nations to garner support for 6PAC among African liberation groups and make sure to inform political groups not recognized by the OAU-LC that they were welcome to attend as observers, but not delegates.⁶⁷ This kind of diplomacy was done in an effort to keep them abreast of 6PAC developments and to show them how decolonization was going to be a central issue of the 6PAC agenda. These TANU efforts at incorporating Stark proved to be an effective strategy of mobilization that generated the impression that Black Power organizers had made official linkages with the postcolonial state. It represented one concrete form of legitimacy while also functioning on a personal level. Stark's activities allowed her to gain deeper insight into the complexities of the southern African liberation movements and challenges of state-to-state cooperation. Once again, the Ministry of Foreign Affairs served as an important state institution for the Black Power activism in the international arena.

Although TANU allowed the Black Power organizers to act in a relatively autonomous fashion, it intervened in ways that ended up ensuring the conference would neither fall into an excessive debate about "racial superiority," nor question the authority of the nation-state role in constructing an international black solidarity agenda. It publicly stated such a position in an early report on the first meeting between the secretariat and President Nyerere in March 1972. The *Nationalist* made it known that TANU was concerned about 6PAC and the black nationalist outlook of the African American organizers behind it. With an understanding of the need for race consciousness among African people, TANU members were nevertheless "insistent that they will not stage a Congress for the sake of racism or to prove that black is beautiful."[68] Furthermore, certain African heads of state were not to be excluded from participation because of their "reactionary politics." North African states were also not to be barred from attending because of their cultural and political ties to the Arab world. Rather than a congress meant solely to promote "Afro-Tanzania" relations, or "apartheid-type" ideas, the TANU state embraced a congress that spoke to its "own policies."[69] The extent of the accuracy of the report of this meeting is debatable, for there is no evidence to suggest that Cox, James, and other secretariat members envisioned a conference that excluded Malawi and Liberia based on their pro-West politics. The same could be said for Algeria, Egypt, Morocco, Libya, and other North African nations based on culture and race.[70] And with priority placed on mobilizing international support for liberation groups and promoting economic development, 6PAC was to be far from an empty celebration of blackness. TANU soon came to understand this position over the next two years. Nevertheless, TANU believed it was in its best interest to watch closely the activities of these Black Power activists based on a general suspicion that radical pro–Black Power elements had "infiltrated the ranks." This view became more pronounced as 6PAC approached.

Throughout the organizing phase, the Temporary Secretariat and TANU's Dar Committee struggled to see eye to eye. Even Sutherland's role as liaison to the Tanzanian government in the coordinating committee could do little to combat a mutual feeling of distrust. Sutherland's reputation among Black Power activists was partially to blame. In the past, some black radicals had questioned his relationship with white expatriates. This time around, African Americans and Tanzanian nationalists questioned his allegiances once he was appointed to the committee as the voice of the TANU government. This tension put Sutherland in a no-win situation, resulting in a pattern of miscommunication that marred the collaborative efforts between the Temporary Secretariat and TANU coordinating committee.[71] Some TANU and government officials were wary of 6PAC's bottom-up vision. For instance, behind the scenes Bomani expressed his frustrations with how the Black Power activists with questionable résumés dominated in the making of the 6PAC agenda. Equally frustrating was the lack of distinguished African American leaders like U.S. Congressman Charles Diggs in the planning process. In a letter to U.S. Ambassador to Tanzania W. Beverly Carter, Bomani gave his assurances that the Tanzanian government would not allow a Black Power takeover of the congress.[72] From a Black Power perspective, as much as TANU proved an ally, there was a general, lingering fear that too much government involvement could derail the congress from serving as a "nongovernmental affair."

This fear was realized in the immediate aftermath of the second Caribbean Regional Meeting. Held in Georgetown, Guyana, in December 1973 and sponsored by the Guyanese and Tanzanian governments and the Temporary Secretariat, the conference forced Tanzania to clarify its position on who was allowed to attend and receive delegate status.[73] It was a decision mainly based on two ongoing conflicts: the conflict between the Caribbean nongovernmental and government forces, and the conflict between Ethiopia and Eritrea. Ever since the International Black Power Conference of 1969, tensions had only increased between Caribbean activists and the governments of Jamaica, Guyana, and Trinidad-Tobago, making planning for 6PAC under a regional structure virtually impossible. At the second Caribbean Regional Conference, oppositional groups called for two separate delegations, one made up of government officials and the other comprised of "revolutionaries opposed to those states." This led Burnham to write to Nyerere, questioning the purpose of 6PAC, which prompted a swift apology from the president.[74] Efforts by Cox, James, and Geslier Mapunda, the political education secretary of TANU, to quell the conflict failed. For the first three months of 1974, then, Cox and the secretariat were in limbo, having failed to come to any resolution over the situation in the Caribbean. This impasse led the TANU government to postpone the conference for a fifth time, pushing the date back to June 19, which allowed the OAU to meet in Kampala, Uganda, in May to discuss the congress, among other, more pressing issues.[75]

It was at this same meeting where the conflict between Eritrea and Ethiopia took center stage. A former Italian and British colony, Eritrea was annexed by Ethiopia on the eve of the founding of the OAU, a clear violation of UN Resolution 390, which federated Eritrea with Ethiopia. Eritreans initially responded through a strategy of nonviolent protest (i.e., petitions, strikes, demonstrations, etc.), but later abandoned this strategy in favor of armed resistance led by the Eritrean Liberation Front (ELF), setting off an armed struggle that lasted until Eritrea gained independence in May 1991. Throughout the 1960s, Emperor Haile Selassie, one of the founding fathers of the OAU, did an expert job in convincing OAU member states that the Eritrean independence movement had secessionist aspirations.⁷⁶ As a result, TANU evoked the OAU principle of noninterference in the domestic affairs of member states to justify its decision to appease Selassie and bar the ELF from attending the conference as delegates.

Due to similar complaints aired by Caribbean governments, the OAU member states officially formed a committee consisting of representatives from Algeria, Guinea, Tanzania, Egypt, and Nigeria. It was telling that Cox was the only nongovernmental representative to serve on the committee. Accorded decision-making power that usurped that of the Temporary Secretariat, the committee decided to change the criteria for delegation status to only governments, African liberation movements (recognized by the OAU) and ruling parties, and "delegates and guests who are found not objectionable to governments or ruling parties of states from which they began."⁷⁷ This decision meant that political organizations such as the African Society for Cultural Relations with Independent Africa (ASCRIA) of Guyana, the New Jewel Movement (NJM) of Grenada, and the National Joint Action Committee (NJAC) of Trinidad, among others, were excluded from the Caribbean delegation.⁷⁸

Although it was a collective decision made by OAU member states, the change in delegate criteria really came down to the host country, Tanzania. President Nyerere recognized the possible damage to Tanzania's leadership standing in the OAU if he were to side with these diaspora and African resistance movements.⁷⁹ To prevent this from happening, Nyerere relied on an OAU principle of territorial integrity that was applied consistently throughout the 1960s and 1970s.⁸⁰ The decision met with little protest from Cox. As far as Nyerere was concerned, avoiding the Eritrean question and maintaining the alliances built with Caribbean governments were of greater importance to ensuring Tanzania's cultivated position of national state authority in pan-African affairs. The decision no doubt echoed some burgeoning fears Black Power activists harbored about the effectiveness of the OAU to foster a more expansive vision of African unity. What became apparent was that the conference was not going to be a platform from which governments were to answer for nondemocratic rule and state repression. Instead, as Jimmy Garrett later explained, the decision completely altered the framework in which 6PAC began: "From a non-governmental Congress with government participation, the Congress had become a governmental Congress with open participation from Blacks from non-Black states and qualified participation by progressive leaders from Black States."⁸¹ The question raised throughout 1973 and 1974 was: Can a nongovernmental organization have a voice at 6PAC when such a voice routinely lambasted national governments in the Caribbean and Africa?

In certain cases, the one-party state was willing to make special appeals and concessions to African Americans that extended to both potential attendees and lead organizers (as well as the organizers of the North American delegation). Such contributions were invaluable to the congress actually taking place. But when it came to the question of delegate status and non-statist participation—the vision of a "people's congress"—the TANU government refused to compromise. Instead, it wanted to work within the familiar structure of state-to-state international relations that privileged the authority and decision-making power of national governments. This move to invoke the OAU model would hold enormous implications for why the congress unfolded in the manner that temporarily demobilized the pan-Africanist politics of the Black Power movement.

There were other internal controversies worth noting. Back in the United States, the enormous North American delegation, which had only received observer status (with the exception of a handful of African Americans), was being racked by lack of cohesion. While leading figures such as James Turner, Sylvia Hill, and Fletcher Robinson, among many others, worked tirelessly behind the scenes, the production of a unified platform never materialized.[82] Part of the reason for this difficulty was the delegation's sheer size, numbering close to two hundred participants. Another reason stemmed from the ideological factionalism emerging within the movement as CAP and ALSC had moved closer to a leftist position during the organizing phase and ultimately disrupted the planning process with attacks on black nationalism and the compromised position of the Temporary Secretariat.[83]

Among these controversies, which were inevitable in any given political-organizing event of such scope and breadth, by far the most damaging was the exclusion of Caribbean opposition groups. In a response to Tanzania's decision on delegation requirements, C.L.R. James resigned from his informal role in the Temporary Secretariat and his formal role as sponsor. He also refused to attend the congress. Having worked closely with him for almost five years, secretariat members viewed his resignation as the loss of a major source of inspiration and guidance. Beyond the emotional impact, the loss of James was a harsh blow to the image and legitimacy of 6PAC. If one of the living stalwarts of pan-Africanism refused to attend, then what did that say about the congress itself? It was a question that hovered over the head of the secretariat. Calling off the conference was simply out of the question; it was too far along after being delayed five times. Resigning was an option that many members thought seriously about, but in the end decided against it largely on James's insistence that they finish the task.[84] Many simply moved forward, disappointed but hardened by this lesson of postcolonial state politics at work.

On a public relations level, Cox mishandled the situation by claiming that the nongovernment Caribbean political groups were not attending due to their failure to secure funding for the trip, a claim that later became a source of critique of Cox's leadership role.[85] Nevertheless, after James's resignation and Tanzania's refusal to reverse its decision, the Temporary Secretariat could do little to alter this course of events. From its new office in Dar es Salaam, it continued carrying out its major responsibilities of fundraising, media promotion, and involvement in regional conferences, planning sessions, and meetings with heads of state and African anticolonial nationalist leaders. While the blow of James's departure is often measured as a total loss of legitimacy, it also sheds some light on the problems of state intervention. The fundamental tension between 6PAC organizers and the TANU state rested on a conception of pan-Africanism that held different views on the role of the state. African Americans' inclination towards taking pan-Africanism beyond the framework of the OAU contrasted sharply with African state leaders who were less inclined to move outside an OAU model.

After close to five years of intense international organizing and five postponements, the Sixth Pan-African Congress got underway on June 19, 1974. For the twelve days, over 400 delegates, observers, and guests from close to thirty independent states and seven southern liberation movements engaged in what was to be a defining moment for the Black Power movement. On the eve of this historic gathering, the TANU state issued a statement, welcoming delegates to the country. This editorial, appearing in Tanzania's *Daily News*, reminded them of their arrival in a nation that "after realizing their appalling conditions have risen up to engage in the struggle for total liberation." What followed was a celebratory editorial composed in a distinctive language of racial kinship:

> Indeed in view of recent attempts by the enemies of African liberation to spread propaganda and dampen the atmosphere of the Congress, we would in particular like to assure all our brothers and sisters that Tanzania is a revolutionary base area of the struggle for the liberation of Africa. As soon as all delegate brothers and sisters set foot on Tanzanian soil, they should feel free. This is their home.[86]

As this passage suggests, the TANU state held no reservations about proclaiming its vanguard position in the African revolution, promoting Tanzania as a model modern state and geopolitical center of African liberation. The wave of black worker strikes in South Africa and the nationalist victory of the PAIGC (African Party for the Independence of Guinea and Cape Verde) in Guinea-Bissau only added greater enthusiasm for 6PAC as a mouthpiece of international solidarity for the African anticolonial revolutionary parties of South Africa, Mozambique, Namibia, Zimbabwe, and Angola.

The conference opened with statements from Africa's two most important leaders of pan-Africanism: President Nyerere and Guinean President Sékou Touré. Speaking in typical charismatic fashion, Nyerere first paid tribute to pan-Africanism's forefathers from the African Diaspora. Saving his final honors for one of the intellectual giants of the twentieth century, W.E.B. Du Bois, "a man of ideas, of intellect, and organizing ability,"[87] it was clear that Nyerere made it a point to highlight the contributions of black people of the diaspora to the development of pan-Africanism. But it was his discussion of race and racism that followed these remarks that proved most noteworthy. He stated:

> The Pan African Congresses were thus a recognition by the peoples of African descent, and those of Africa, that only by proclaiming the human rights and dignity of all black men could any of them demand their humanity. They all had to fight against policies and attitudes which made blackness or African ancestry into social, economic, and political disadvantage everywhere in the world. And they all had to fight for the freedom of nations inhabited by African people. Thus color became a uniting factor among peoples otherwise divided by nationality, political creed, religion and culture. The Pan African movement was born as a reaction to racism. And racism still exists. Nowhere has it been completely defeated.[88]

However, Nyerere stressed his opposition to "racialist thinking," urging delegates against viewing oppression from a narrow racial lens. "For if we react to the continued need to defend our position as black men by regarding ourselves as different from the rest of mankind we shall weaken ourselves, and the racialists of the world will have scored their biggest triumph."[89] He continued: "Yet in economic matters, the real problem is not color. Both within nations, and between nations, the problem is basically that of oppression arising from an exploitative system. We are neither poor, nor are we kept poor, because we are black. We remain poor because of the world trading and monetary systems—and these whatever the disadvantages, are color blind. They adversely affect the whole of the Third World."[90] The opening remarks of President Nyerere underscored his pragmatic leadership style. Certainly, he did not wish to alienate African Americans who held strong to their race-conscious perspectives by pointing out the limitations of such thinking.

Just as Nyerere paid tribute to African Americans and their role in the Pan-African Congress movement, so too did Touré. In contrast to Nyerere, Touré was much more explicit in his ties to Marxism when he denigrated Negritude, a black cultural-nationalist movement most prominent among French-speaking Africans and West Indians, by referring to it as "metaphysical obscurantism" and a movement without a revolutionary mission that serves "the interests of the same enemy."[91] What also set his speech apart from Nyerere's was the way Touré discussed the implications of state formation for pan-Africanism: "Pan Africanism . . . is not based on the strong will of a few States . . . Pan Africanism basically refers to an Africa of Peoples, it is in its interests to uphold the

Chapter Five

primacy of Peoples as against States . . . But when States are of the exploiting classes, they constitute the instrument for carrying out decisions against the people; and we cannot but observe that the States in the area covered by Pan Africanism are far from being those of the People or being faithful to the People."[92]

Their separate speeches set the ideological tone for the conference.[93] Together, they were welcomed with wide applause from congress participants and adopted as official documents. However as much as Guinea or Tanzania attempted to wipe themselves clean of any kind of tampering that went on behind the scenes during the organizing process, neither Touré nor Nyerere could truly deny the fact that they had already intervened in a way that established consolidated state authority at the congress. Most important, both speeches further reflected how pan-Africanism and the role of African Americans in Africa were going to be up for serious debate. Ultimately, the two African presidents called on all those in attendance to look beyond race and support a symbolic and practical united front based on traditions of resistance rather than a history of racial oppression.

The first three days consisted of plenary sessions that allowed delegations and guests to deliver their opening remarks. Various leftist delegations representing anticolonial movements seized the opportunity, making it a point to tie class struggle to scientific analysis and racism to emotionalism. The Sixth Pan-African Congress was not to be a forum to "sing the hymn of the black 'diaspora,' to share a great moment of superficial emotion," argued the Congolese delegation, which ended its remarks with a resounding support of the OAU model and the holiness of its charter.[94] The same went for the delegates of Somalia, who warned that any discussion of "black fraternity" simply confused the issue, and isolated Africa and its diaspora from "other progressive forces of the world, notably the socialist countries and the working class of the capitalist countries."[95] The African liberation movement too followed suit in its condemnation of black nationalism. The FRELIMO delegation referred to black nationalism as a "superficial and emotional analysis" and urged African Americans to seek solidarity with the working classes of the United States.[96] The isolationist argument was also pushed by the ZAPU delegation in claiming that pan-Africanism lacked conceptual clarity:

> It must be understood that blackness alone cannot serve as a political direction. Here we only want to convey that the Congress will have done greater services to future generations if we come out with a clear-cut concept, a revolutionary progressive concept, taking cognizance of the material world we live in, the class nature of the world community and of the fact that the existing conflict in the world is not black versus white; it is progress versus reaction . . . Pan Africanism, therefore, cannot exist

in isolation in a dynamic world of interdependence in almost every field, and we should not blame others for our failures.[97]

African Americans of the North American delegation were given their chance to respond to this litany of criticism mainly coming from Africans.

The speeches of African American delegates—Amiri Baraka, Owusu Saduakai, Lerone Bennett—fed the debate on race, class, and nationalism sparked by the statements of various African delegations, and raised a new set of questions about postcolonial nation-statehood. Baraka was convinced that black nationalism had been co-opted by black "petty bourgeois opportunists," that cultural nationalism constituted an ill-informed celebration of a feudalistic African past, and that "scientific" socialism was the only path to economic freedom. The task of pan-Africanists, then, was to identify the "reactionary" and "revolutionary" aspects of African culture so as to combat forces of European cultural and economic imperialism and to chart a path towards socialist liberation. In the first part of his paper, titled "Revolutionary Culture and the Future of Pan African Culture," it appears Baraka was intent on highlighting CAP's Marxist turn in an effort to show a similar ideological outlook with the African Marxist faction at the congress. "It is reactionary to present that there is no class formation and resultant strife, i.e. class struggle, throughout the African world," he argued. "To say otherwise at this point in history is to be innocent of reality or mischievous for profit."[98] To him, independent "radical political sectors" must be wary of the power wielded by African ruling elites through the nation-state apparatus. If anything, they demonstrated a willingness to consolidate their "economic and political dependency relations with monopoly capitalism."[99] Baraka believed that one of the foremost challenges to achieving pan-African unity was thinking through and solving the "contradiction of nation-statism." Pan-Africanism was undergoing a drastic transformation due to the nation-state seeing itself as the "protector of the national hegemony of a developing African petty-bourgeoisie."[100]

In many ways, Saduakai's speech echoed Baraka's concerns over the failures of black nationalism in the United States. He also identified the obstacles to coming to a functional unity in a global context. One difference was the greater emphasis placed on thinking about concrete forms of pan-Africanist collaboration between African Americans and Africans. As the national spokesman for the ALSC, Saduakai distanced himself from the U.S. black nationalist trend, pointing out how there was "very little agreement at this point as to the exact nature of our struggle in North America." With various nationalist expressions in competition, the ALSC stood firm in its conviction that any discussion about the "liberation of black people must speak to the question of the transformation of the American state to a socialist society."[101]

Although he recognized the erosion of unity within the African American struggle and the limits of black nationalist thought and practice, Saduakai was not willing to abandon an analysis of the intersection between racism and imperialism. To him, "capitalism provided the material basis for the existence of racism," a racism that is imprinted in the "superstructure" and its "legal machinery that is again overtly instituted to enforce the existence of racism."[102] In order to "see the connections," Saduakai proposed a national organizing campaign that targeted the U.S. black worker. This approach would "give the support to the movement against imperialism" by educating the black working class on how monopoly capitalism exploits them and others of African descent.[103]

The statements by Baraka and Saduakai were declarations of their Marxist positions and, in turn, the political organizations they represented. Both revealed as much in the use of Marxist language. Terms such as "modes of production," "productive relations," and "monopoly capitalism" were readily employed throughout their speeches, which are supplemented with references to Lenin and the African Marxist and leader of the PAIGC Amilcar Cabral.[104] Both activists were skeptical of what they saw as a pan-Africanism movement being led by a glorified nation-state run and administered by Africans with capitalist interests. But if they were inspired by using Marxism as a tool to critique modern state formation in Africa, this did not blind them to the struggles of black people against racism.

While the comments of Baraka and Saduakai reflected the reemergence of the Marxist tendency of the Black Power movement, it would be a mistake to characterize Lerone Bennett's speech as representing the black cultural-nationalist perspective. In fact, Bennett, a historian and editor of *Ebony* magazine, did not wed himself to a clear-cut Marxist position, but still emphasized the issue of class exploitation. But he also refused to say that the racial character of imperialism and anti-imperialist resistance should not be a subject of critical inquiry. In addressing the internal dynamics of the black freedom struggle and the precarious state of African political affairs, Bennett devoted his energies to explaining how Africans, wherever they might reside, were "menaced by the same system." "We want to make it clear here that we are opposed to the foreign policy of all governments whose foreign policy is opposed to the fundamental aspirations of Africans and peoples of African descent," he continued. Most importantly, Bennett expressed a firm belief in the concept of pan-Africanism, viewing it as a "product of the interaction between Africans in Africa and Africans in the Diaspora, and that it has existed for some seventy-five years in a living dialectical tension between the poles of Africa, the West Indies, and African-America."[105] On one level, these three opening speeches simply revealed the ideological heterogeneity of the African American freedom struggle. Yet none of the speeches gave much indication if African Americans could work together across ideological lines, but rather of their willingness to at least give it try. In examining the opening remarks of plenary sessions, one can see how an intriguing ideological debate over race and class was set to consume the congress. In addition to special receptions, dinner gatherings, and nation-building tours, the remainder of the congress consisted of workshop committee caucuses in economics, politics, and science and technology. These committees, which were dominated by the important African leftists of liberation movements as well as independent states, were responsible for drafting the final resolutions.

If inside Nkrumah Hall was reserved for the delegates with voting power, then outside resembled the spirit of a people's congress. Caucuses to discuss domestic situations, poetry performances, and soapbox speeches were on display while rumors swirled of a right-wing TANU conspiracy against African Americans. A few weeks prior to the conference, a group of African Americans living near the village of Butiama, Nyerere's home village, were caught with guns and ammunition, leading to the mass arrest of African American expatriates. Known as the "Big Bust," the TANU government debated whether this incident was a CIA plot, an attempt by Black Power radicals to connect with African leftist militants in Zanzibar, proof of Black Power's promotion of violence, or simply an isolated incident of criminal behavior.[106] African American expatriates were still imprisoned by the time the conference started, which led many to question their solidarity with the Tanzanian state or even their naïveté about African political realities.[107] Two days before the congress began, the black expatriate community penned a letter to Rashidi Kawawa, Tanzania's prime minister, in response to these mass arrests: "Recent events in Dar es Salaam have given us the impression that it is clearly on the side of the Tanzanian Government . . . we pledge our unwavering support for the investigation now underway. If we can be of any help in providing information on individuals and contacts for further clarification we stand ready."[108] Yet the "Big Bust" did not seem to damage Nyerere's standing with African Americans. It was all the more difficult to critique the president extensively, especially when he made it a point to accommodate the North American delegation.[109] Outside Nkrumah Hall, Nyerere could be found granting interviews with black journalists, holding private meetings with African American delegates and observers, and posing for pictures with African American political leaders, making it incredibly difficult to challenge his image as the preeminent champion of pan-Africanism.

For those who ventured outside onto the university campus, they were also able to get ahold of and read two popular position papers: Walter Rodney's "Towards the 6th Pan African Congress: Aspects of the International Class Struggle in Africa, the Caribbean and America," and the "Communique [sic] from the Caribbean Steering Committee Which Has Been Excluded from This Congress." These position papers were heavily circulated and provoked both unease and enthusiasm because they raised a question that hovered over the congress, but still seemed to be ignored: Are nation-states in Africa and the Caribbean impediments to constructive dialogue and coordinated black transnational action? Indeed, both Rodney and the Caribbean Steering Committee recognized that the tensions in the relationship between state and civil society had been left unexplored. Differences over the role of the national governments and the motives of state leadership led them to believe that state involvement in pan-Africanism muted potential criticism of state policies and actions.

Rodney did not attend the conference but wrote a position paper that was published in *Maji Maji*, a radical student journal of the University of Dar es Salaam. Rodney grabbed the attention of many participants searching for answers about the role of independent states in the pan-Africanist struggle. On an indirect level, the paper was a farewell to the Tanzanian revolution, as his eyes were set on returning to Guyana to wage an interracial struggle against the Burnham government—the same government that blocked the participation of Caribbean opposition movements (with the support of Nyerere).

Rodney's position paper made no clear distinction between progressive and "neocolonialist" independent states. He was mainly concerned with the direction of the pan-Africanism movement while in the hands of the African ruling elites. Similar to Baraka's speech, he was critical of the role of the African state in defining the terms and practices of pan-Africanism. The postcolonial situation was marked by "a conflict between the majority of the black working class and a small African possessing class."[110] The latter of the two had seized control of state institutions, using them as a source of personal enrichment and a force to suppress the political will of "the masses." And through the auspices of the OAU, African ruling elites elevated a conception of continental pan-Africanism that maintained "the separation of African peoples implicit in the present territorial boundaries."[111] By ignoring internal class conflict or softening its stance on dangers of state formation, 6PAC was, therefore, walking a "tightrope," legitimizing postcolonial rule at a time when such legitimacy had to be called into serious question. "Our conclusion at this point," Rodney wrote, " is that the African petty bourgeois leadership since independence has been an obstacle to the further development of the African revolution."[112] On one level, the state became a principal object of concern for the way it functioned as "negation of Pan-Africanism" rather than one of its agents.

The "secret communiqué" issued by the Caribbean opposition groups was another important "unofficial" document that sharpened the critical consciousness of 6PAC participants who were concerned with this question of nation-state power. The Caribbean nongovernmental delegation (i.e., the Organization for Black Cultural Awareness, the New Jewel Movement, ASCRIA, the People's Progressive Movement, the National Joint Action Committee, and the National Front for the Liberation of Cayenne) thought it imperative to tell their side of the story. "Of great significance is the fact that the membership of the Caribbean Steering Committee comprises organizations long commitments [sic] to Pan Africanism and social revolution," the statement read. "They are organizations which have come into conflict with the regimes because they, as organizations, dared to uphold the very principles of *The Call*."[113] The statement went on to blame the TANU government and the Temporary Secretariat for offering to congress participants a different vision of pan-Africanism. Because of their exclusion and the role played by the TANU government in preventing their attendance, they viewed 6PAC "not as a meeting of African people and their allies, but as a Government-dominated meeting, which is not the meeting as conceived by any of the Sponsors."[114]

For African Americans like P. Bai Akridge, the ideological debates over race, class, and nation-statism forced him to reassess his views on 6PAC, but not to the extent that this negatively impacted his overall experience. In 1970, Akridge enrolled at DePauw University in the small town of Green Castle, Indiana, where he was exposed to anticolonial nationalist literature (most notably Frantz Fanon's *The Wretched of the Earth*), befriended African students, and partook in campus activism over issues of divestment and decolonization in southern Africa. From 1971 to 1973, he spent time in Kenya at the University of Nairobi and then later in Uganda as an English teacher during the beginnings of Idi Amin's brutal reign. He also managed to travel to Tanzania, where he became entranced by its socialist experiment. Thus, at only twenty-one, his experience in East Africa not only contributed to rapid intellectual development, but also shaped him into an ardent pan-Africanist.[115]

Akridge was especially attracted to Tanzania's vision of a socialist society and the idea of skilled technical assistance to African nation-building. During the organizing process, he regularly attended Midwest regional meetings of the North American delegation. He even wrote a position paper titled "The Sixth Pan African Congress: Chaos or Community?," borrowing the title of Dr. Martin Luther King Jr.'s *Where Do We Go from Here: Chaos or Community?*, a compilation of essays published before his death in 1968 that addresses questions about the future and direction of the African American freedom struggle and American democracy. In sharp contrast to King, Akridge felt that to raise questions about the future of the black community meant addressing the entire pan-African world, and thus searching for ways to create mutual relations between Africans and African Americans.

Like most African American pan-Africanists, Akridge, in his position paper, pushed forth the idea that technical skilled-labor assistance could lead to more effective nation-building for Africa. "The year 1974," he wrote, "does locate Africans [sic]

Chapter Five

in America possessing the highest level of technical and scientific skills ever known to African [sic] people anywhere."[116] The task then was to harness those skills "for the consolidation of institutions which will ensure the welfare and security of Africans [sic]." For Akridge, a historic gathering like 6PAC could also alleviate the tensions in the Black Power movement over the "class-race analysis controversy" and push African American activists in the direction of legitimizing their claim that they constitute a nation within a nation. The congress could help challenge their own romantic notions of Africa while at same time encourage African Americans to "speak with one voice" on the "crucial issues affecting Afrikans [sic] internationally."[117]

As the proceedings shifted from opening remarks to specific formal committee sessions, Akridge became a bit bored and confused by its parliamentary jargon and protocol. This led him to frequently venture outside Nkrumah Hall into an atmosphere he later remembered as being incredibly festive.[118] It was outside where Akridge came across the documents produced by Rodney and the Caribbean opposition groups. He was impacted by their critiques to such an extent that he set out on a mission to collect as many documents as possible (forty-two in total) for his personal archive, which simply added to what he recalled as an already enriching experience.[119]

Other African American participants who were on the margins of the ideological debate measured the success of 6PAC in similar individualized terms. The opportunity to engage in animated and friendly conversations and learn about various black and Third World struggles was one of the undeniable strengths of the congress.[120] However, back inside Nkrumah Hall, African Americans with the power to implement change as delegates with "full status" experienced more setbacks than successes due to the general backlash against black nationalism. Nowhere was this tension between African Americans and African representatives more pronounced than with the efforts of the Committee on Science and Technology to push forth the creation of the Pan African Center of Science and Technology (PACST).

Largely comprised of black scientists out of Howard University in Washington, DC—namely, J. Fletcher Robinson, William Douglass, and Neville Parker—PASCT's primary function was that of "dealing with the material needs of the Pan African community" by developing a pool of "skilled Pan Africans," researching ideas that would lead to "sensible applied technology," and disseminating "shared information to Africans at home and abroad through courses, workshops and institutes."[121] Heading up the congress, the science and technology proposal held great promise on account of its emphasis on institution building and mobilizing skilled technical assistance. The 6PAC organizers harbored a deep attachment to an idea that would raise questions and provide solutions to issues of agriculture, health and nutrition, water resources, transportation, and communications, among others, seeing it as the most efficacious way for African Americans to insert themselves in African political, social, and economic affairs.[122]

This committee came up against strong opposition from Guinea and Egypt, as well as African liberation movement representatives, for being regarded as "bourgeois science."[123] While these Howard University scientists were proposing that African governments should commit their resources to a long-term strategy for technological development, whereby immediate gains would not be realized until the early 1980s, they quickly learned that the black nationalist stigma attached to African Americans mainly fueled African opposition to their proposal. In addition, their lack of familiarity with and control over parliamentary protocols such as points of order, etc., put them into a subordinate position to African governments and liberation movements.[124] Regardless of their motives for blocking the proposal, which they succeeded in doing, the defeat proved an enormous disappointment for the members of the committee who had devoted considerable energy over the previous five years in formulating the science and technology initiative.[125]

After approximately ten days of intense debate and transnational exchange, a General Declaration was produced along with resolutions on economics, politics, and science and technology. The significance of the declaration was twofold. Firstly, it advocated the view that combatting the force of racism was a secondary concern and embracing one's blackness was counterproductive. Secondly, it advanced a far more Marxist-inspired anticapitalist and anti-imperialist position. After chronicling the historical background to pan-Africanism, the declaration goes on to portray pan-Africanism as a concept in need of revision, requiring a "correct analysis" for a contemporary era more defined by class exploitation than by racialized oppression. What was needed in the postwar era was a more expansive strategy of alliance building: "That is why if we react to the continued need to defend our position as black men by regarding ourselves as different from the rest of mankind, we shall weaken ourselves, and the racialists of the world have scored their biggest triumph."[126]

The General Declaration even addressed the domestic struggle in the United States by calling on African Americans to ally with the white working class and rid themselves of "the utopian idea of returning to promised lands."[127] Moreover, to suggest that African Americans did not possess an "advanced class consciousness" was just another way to convey the point that they advocated an outdated conception of pan-Africanism that ran "the risk of falling into a racism which was intended to be anti-racist."[128] In the end, a new definition of pan-Africanism was put forward, one that was stripped of its racial solidarity underpinnings:

Chapter Five

> Pan Africanism must essentially be a dynamic force for the liberation of the colonized peoples as well as for the liberation of the oppressed peoples and classes, and liberation necessarily means eradicating the symptoms of exploitation and building societies based on the power of the exploited working class . . . Skin color—be it black, white, yellow or brown—is no indication of the social class, ideology, nature, behavior qualities or abilities of men or peoples . . . We must therefore define ourselves not in terms of skin color, which is a static element, but solely in terms of our aims of progress which are dynamic, just and noble . . . Revolutionary Pan Africanism inscribes itself within the context of class struggle.[129]

The declaration read as a triumph for the Marxists. And as Ronald Walters argues, this "hard-line definition of Pan Africanism," precisely because of its narrowness, helped to alienate advocates of U.S. black nationalism, Negritude, and African socialism while in the process leaving many delegates and observers wondering where do we go from here.[130]

On the last day of the conference, Courtland Cox stepped to the podium to deliver his closing remarks as secretary general. He could not help but admit that 6PAC did not turn out to be a "People's Congress" as initially envisaged: "Hindsight is always better than foresight. In retrospect, I am keenly aware of the mistakes made in organizing this Congress."[131] While Cox devoted the rest of his speech to pointing out the "positive contributions of the meeting itself," such as the ways in which 6PAC had "ratified the validity of African people meeting to chart a political course for our common problem" and emphasized the liberation of southern Africa, it was clear that he desired so much more than mere conversation. "I believe the major and most serious shortcoming of this Congress has been that some who should have been here were not," he concluded. "There should have been more people's movements represented, more women represented, more young people participating. That gap in participation in the Sixth Pan African Congress mirrors very real contradictions at work in the African World."[132]

Cox's speech was far more introspective and hinted at an uncertain future. On the other hand, the closing remarks made by Aboud Jumbe, Tanzania's first vice president, proved just the opposite. Rather than offer up any kind of criticism concerning the exclusion of certain groups at the last minute, or state control over an important aspect of the organizing phase, Jumbe saw this as an occasion to reiterate the vanguard role of the Tanzanian state in Africa's struggle for total emancipation. Also noteworthy was how Jumbe left out any reference to this new pan-Africanist struggle embarking on a path towards liberation that would eliminate all forms of racism: "Henceforth, any measure of success achieved or drawback sustained by our brothers and sisters in one part of the world must rally us together and spark off great incentive among the rest of us, until the struggle sweeps away all vestiges of imperialism, capitalism, exploitation, suppression and humiliation. The starting point for such a great revolution must first and foremost be within ourselves... I would like to feel that we have heralded and are entering a new era which will lead to complete emancipation of all oppressed people."[133] Taken together, the contrasting nature of the two speeches aptly reflected the political differences between Africa and its diaspora.

■ ■ ■ ■

As early as July, the *Chicago Defender* put forth what became a prevailing sentiment of disappointment with 6PAC. One major failure of the congress was the delegates' inability to put an institutional mechanism in place to implement policies and resolutions due to their obsessions with having the correct political ideology.[134] Earl Ofari Hutchinson, an independent journalist and author of *The Myth of Black Capitalism* (1970), wrote in the *Los Angeles Times*: "I was struck by what appeared to be militancy for militancy's sake on the part of some African delegates." Furthermore, he continued, the "'black first' politics" of the majority of African American participants "diminished the value" of the congress and served as a "source of amusement" to African delegates. With "no practical approaches" offered or agreed upon, 6PAC became a gathering that highlighted the "petty factionalism" that had consumed the pan-Africanist movement of the 1970s.[135]

On the whole, most criticisms of the congress continued to reflect the ideological struggle that engulfed African Americans and Africans. Brenda Paris, secretary of ALSC, lauded the opening remarks of Nyerere and Touré for the way they guided the congress towards a "scientific analysis" of the "class struggle against racism, imperialism, and capitalism."[136] Anthony Monteiro, a black Marxist and North American delegate who served as the acting executive secretary of the National Anti-Imperialist Movement in Solidarity with African Liberation (NAIMSAL), praised the anticapitalist and anti-imperialist tenor of 6PAC resolutions. He urged Black Power activists to implement them in the United States to address "the problem of monopoly capitalism" and "reverse the posture of the United States in Africa."[137] Monteiro also praised the correctness of the political line drawn at 6PAC, arguing that the congress was a "smashing repudiation of narrow black nationalism, black capitalism, and cultural nationalism."[138]

In stark contrast to those participants who understood racism as a secondary concern to the opposition against capitalism, imperialism, and colonialism, other African Americans viewed the congress as a forum to disparage black nationalism and pan-Africanism. Lerone Bennett found that the African liberation movements that espoused a Marxist line and played significant roles in drafting the content of the resolutions exaggerated what did or did not constitute the nationalist desires of Black

Power activists. The delegations of Guinea, Somali, Congo (Brazzaville), Tanzania, Cuba, Egypt, Algeria, along with the liberation movements of FRELIMO, SWAPO, ZANU, and PAC constituted a leftist bloc that before "the rest of the delegations could get their bearings, the leaders of this bloc fired two thunderous artillery rounds that virtually ended the contest." While he agreed that African Americans tended to suffer from romanticizing Africa, the leftists, "in their zeal to see-no-race, hear-no-race and speak-no-race, carried their arguments to incredible extremes."[139] The Committee on Science and Technology expressed similar disappointment in the Marxist faction and frustration over having "unrealistic expectations."[140]

Assessments of the congress were not only confined to African Americans. African intellectuals at *Transition Magazine: An International Review*, an intellectual journal founded in Uganda in 1961, banned by the Idi Amin regime in 1971, and revived in Ghana under the editorship of Nigerian novelist, playwright, and activist Wole Soyinka, were disillusioned by the congress for two major reasons. First, the Marxist-nationalist debate was viewed as unproductive: "For the 'internationalization' of pan-Africanism, the expression itself was emptied of content. Nothing remained but a sentimental attachment to a historic mood of black assertiveness. Was it necessary to summon a Congress to preside over the liquidation of a concept?"[141] Secondly, and even more problematic, they were concerned about the social and political implications of unchecked state power. The participation of African military regimes from Ghana, Uganda, and Nigeria represented the core of the problem. In their eyes, it was pure comic relief in all of its tragedy to see officials of nondemocratic governments flaunt their material wealth while masquerading as advocates of African liberation. Their presence alone turned 6PAC from a "platform for the African peoples" into "a platform of endorsement for questionable regimes."[142] "The Pan Africanist movement today," the editorial concluded, "should be nothing but a meeting of individuals and representatives of the organic groupings of black society—cooperatives of farmers and workers, trade union movements, writers, intellectuals, youth organizations, architects, engineers, scientific researchers, women's emancipation movements, liberation fighters, etc. etc."[143]

Back in the United States, ideological lines were being further drawn in the sand in the pages of the *Black Scholar*. Haki Madhubuti, director of the Institute of Positive Education and publisher of Third World Press out of Chicago, provided the most vitriolic assessment of the congress from a black cultural-nationalist perspective. He mainly argued that 6PAC proceedings showed how black nationalism and pan-Africanism were "under attack from the white left" and black Marxists. In particular, black radical organizations like the ALSC and CAP, black nationalists turned "turncoats," were "pushing a European socialist analysis of Black Nationalism and Pan Africanism" that ultimately skirted the issue of anti-black racism in favor of a narrow view of class struggle and promotion of an abstract notion of Third World internationalism.[144] He wrote: "This is a most important point because the marxist [sic] line is to subordinate Black Nationalism and Pan Afrikanism [sic] for world internationalism, which is to white people only a voiced principle that is/was never practiced. Universalism, internationalism, and one world-ism as defined specifically by Europeans."[145] For Madhubuti, the rhetoric of "scientific analysis" had successfully made any critical interrogation of the ideology of white racism an inexplicable afterthought even though its very historical roots preceded the emergence of capitalism.[146] In discussing the 6PAC proceedings, he also believed that the white presence from "Cuba, Egypt and other areas of the diaspora" played the role of spoilers. If anything, 6PAC revealed that "the Black World" must look inward, and come to an understanding that the *"highest stage of white supremacy is imperialism whether it's communist or capitalist."*[147]

The attacks unleashed by Madhubuti prompted a series of responses. One notable one came from Amiri Baraka. Though targeted in Madhubuti's response, Baraka only mildly gloated over the victory of the Marxist perspective at the congress. He spoke favorably on how 6PAC emphasized the class question, and was satisfied to see this clearly expressed in the content of the General Declaration and subsequent resolutions. For Baraka, to emphasize the class struggle in the pan-African world was to expose the "native agents of imperialism" from Joseph Mobutu in Zaire, to Idi Amin in Uganda, to Forbes Burnham in Guyana, to Kenneth Gibson, the black mayor of Newark, New Jersey.[148] Rather than go into enormous detail about the limits of black nationalism, Baraka was more interested in locating 6PAC's failures in the organizing process itself and assigning blame to the Temporary Secretariat. He believed it did a poor job in the logistical organizing and failed to fully explain the congress's political purpose. He was especially critical of the TANU state and the way it "dominated policy decisions" and used "Cox's coterie" to act in the interests of African and Caribbean governments at the expense of nongovernment political groups in the diaspora.[149]

Some 6PAC organizers also offered their own assessments. Jimmy Garrett published an article in *Black World* in March 1975 detailing the major events that took place during the organizing phase. Sensing that the post-6PAC debate was riddled with inaccuracies and misinformation, Garrett hoped to clarify a few things. He notes some of the failures of the secretariat, but makes clear that the failures of the congress were caused by the interventionist role of governments at the OAU meeting in May 1974. In his estimation, the complexities of what went on behind the scenes meant that it would take years before a "thorough analysis of the Congress" could be made.[150] In his own report on the congress, Sutherland echoed a similar concern in claiming that 6PAC was "not a Congress of people's organizations." But he also pointed out that the "two-line struggle" was an accurate reflection of the political realities of the time. For

Chapter Five

practical considerations, he proposed that meetings take place "by a group relatively free from diplomatic and protocol pressures, but who would have access to peoples' organizations of similar ideological persuasions."[151] No such meetings ever happened. Although the Temporary Secretariat and the Tanzanian government began publishing and distributing 6PAC documents, the conference "rejected the concept of establishing an ongoing PAC structure."[152]

If we simply base our assessment of 6PAC on its ideological struggle for the sake of unity or to implement a Permanent Secretariat, we will certainly miss out on the ways 6PAC impacted those Black Power activists in attendance. For some, it represented a climactic moment in their political careers. Queen Mother Audley Moore, a former communist turned cultural nationalist, had little to say about the "two-line struggle," choosing to emphasize the importance of being a part of a mass gathering of black people. "I am 76 years old. For 56 years I have been in the struggle. I have lived and worked—yes worked—for this great day," she told a reporter for Tanzania's *Daily News*. "This is the most historic occasion that has happened in the world as far as the African people are concerned. To me it is rewarding, for I have lived to see the fruits of our efforts. We are happy that such a large delegation of Africans from the U.S. has been invited. All from the platform have expressed the desire for total freedom and for the elimination of imperialism. Africans tell us, this is your home—Come and live with us."[153]

For P. Bai Akridge, the close ties he forged with the British delegation led him to travel to Britain upon their invitation to learn more about the black political struggles there.[154] For many other organizers and participants, 6PAC would launch careers in the U.S. solidarity movement for African liberation as activists, writers, journalists, and policymakers. These efforts culminated in the independence of Zimbabwe in 1980 and the end of apartheid rule in South Africa in 1992.[155] Neville Parker chose to live and work in Tanzania. After the rejection of the Science and Technology Proposal, Nyerere invited him and the Howard University professors for a meeting at the State House.[156] Sensing their disappointment, the president urged them not to dwell on the failed proposal and its outcomes. He then asked Parker to become chair of the Engineering Department at the University of Dar es Salaam. Parker accepted and went on to live in Tanzania for five years.[157]

Members of the Temporary Secretariat were impacted in similar ways. Gerri Stark remained in Tanzania and joined the editorial staff of the Tanzania Publishing House, working closely with Walter Bgoya in publishing radical texts. Stark eventually married and became heavily immersed in the anti-apartheid struggle in South Africa.[158] Edie Wilson completed her doctorate work in the United States, then in 1976 moved to Tanzania permanently to lend her technical skills to Ujamaa nation-building. She has been living there ever since.[159] Courtland Cox returned to Washington, DC, and the work of CBE. In the late 1970s, he joined a nonprofit policy think tank, where he wrote extensively on African foreign-policy issues.[160] Indeed, for Temporary Secretariat members, 6PAC was a turning point in their lives.

Between 1970 and 1974, a group of Black Power activists played a leadership role in the pan-Africanism movement. In organizing the Sixth Pan-African Congress, they brought together blacks and Africans of different political persuasions from across the globe to discuss the burning transnational questions of the era: total liberation in southern Africa, economic development and nation-building, and black unity—all under the banner of Tanzania's nationalist slogan of "Self-Reliance." Organizing the congress was an enormous task. The fact that the congress happened at all was a victory for pan-Africanism and the Black Power movement.

For its part, the TANU state brought legitimacy to 6PAC and the Black Power organizers behind it, facilitating the latter's entry into African liberation politics. Without such backing (financial, moral, material), 6PAC arguably could not have taken place. The TANU government and party held no reservations about backing a congress that promoted its own domestic and foreign policies, especially when it came to issues of decolonization and foreign skilled technical assistance. Moreover, supporting such an endeavor demonstrated its continued interest in cultivating an image of progressive nation-statehood. At the same time, this did not mean it was not going to have a say in shaping the aims and objectives of the congress, even if it meant going against those of the Black Power organizers.

The Sixth Pan-African Congress represented a promising moment for African Americans to forge working relationships with African liberation groups and independent states. Yet the congress also revealed that Black Power activists and organizations did not have the power to determine the nature of their role in the movement. Thus, 6PAC achieved fostering the black transnational dialogue it had envisioned to a certain extent, but also sharpened the ideological fissures within the Black Power and pan-Africanism movements. The manner in which black nationalism and the global character of racism were dismissed by Africans, and ways in which national governments took control of the framework of the congress, gave illumination to the difficulties Black Power activists encountered in their international organizing efforts. On one level 6PAC provided African Americans with an incredible access to nation-state power. On another, the interventionist actions made by TANU, African and Caribbean governments, and Marxist liberation movements cemented the marginal role African Americans were subjected to play during this era. While they recognized that political differences existed over the meaning of pan-Africanism, they never imagined it would be delegitimized.

Chapter Five

One could certainly argue that 6PAC, with its emphasis on solidarity with African liberation movements, helped to sustain the momentum of the April 1974 military coup in Portugal, which took place a few months before 6PAC and eventually set in motion national independence in Mozambique, Angola, and Guinea-Bissau in 1975, and the end of white minority rule in Rhodesia in 1980. Even though the future of pan-Africanism was unknown after the congress, African Americans continued to advocate on Africa's behalf, as evident in the anti-apartheid solidarity movements that emerged in the 1980s. However, the mid-1970s mark a critical historic juncture in the African American freedom struggle, especially for Black Power advocates.

Two major shortcomings emerged from 6PAC. Firstly, there was no Permanent Secretariat established to carry out resolutions as a functionally independent pan-Africanist institution. Secondly, it did not contribute to a renewed sense of cohesion within the Black Power movement. However, these failures should also be considered a reflection of Black Power's decline. Black Power advocates found solace in their ideological camps, while black electoral politics and new social movements emerged with momentum and militancy reminiscent of Black Power's glory days.[161] Yet in this context, it is also telling that the years following the congress did not witness any significant attempts by Black Power activists to forge collaborative ties with the Tanzanian state, thus marking an end to an evolving black transnational relationship that lasted for a decade.

Conclusion

By the mid-1980s, the enthusiasm for pan-Africanist activity surrounding Tanzania's nationalist project had considerably waned. The Pan-African Skills Project continued to send African American skilled technicians to Africa until 1980, but the project's expansion to other nations and its attempt to implement other projects also hindered the progress and growth of the skilled-labor project in Tanzania.[1] President Nyerere, perhaps sensing the shift in mood among Tanzanian citizens, decided against running for reelection in Tanzania's general elections slated for October 27, 1985. Approximately eighteen years had passed since issuing the Arusha Declaration that sent the nation and its peoples on a path towards socialism six years after achieving formal independence. While Ujamaa na Kujitegemea forged a sense of national cohesion and cultural pride as well as made substantive improvements and gains in the social sector, it was extremely difficult to locate its concrete success and outcomes as a vision and policy of economic liberation.

The economic failure of Ujamaa socialism has been well documented.[2] The one-party state's villagization scheme went from voluntary to forced removals that sowed seeds of antigovernment sentiments among the peasantry. This top-down attempt to increase and diversify agricultural production fell considerably short of expectations as it was also marred by mismanagement and lack of committed socialist leadership within the government and party. Riddled with issues of implementation, Ujamaa villages could only account for less than 5 percent of the country's agricultural output, which facilitated the country's downward spiral into severe economic depression during the late 1970s and early 1980s. Interventions by the International Monetary Fund (IMF) and World Bank only affirmed the elusiveness of self-reliance and the realities of postcolonial Africa's dependency on Western nations and institutions. In the end, neither an emphasis placed on rural development nor the nationalization of the finance and industrial sectors led to sustainable economic growth and prosperity.

But is eighteen years enough time to reverse or solve the economic and political legacies of labor and resource exploitation brought on by decades of colonial rule? Such a question was posed to the former president in the aftermath of the 1985 Tanzanian general election as he followed political developments in his country from the comforts of his ancestral village in Butiama. Interviewed by African American expatriate Bill Sutherland,[3] Nyerere spoke candidly about his presidency and the challenges of nation-building in Africa. At one point, he proclaimed: "The history of the continent that was expected to take place after independence actually did not take place. We had too much interference. I mean, it would have happened in any case, but I have to talk about history as it is. And history as it was. Africa again was not allowed to develop in freedom because the Cold War took over and we had these externally supported dictatorships everywhere over the continent. And so we ran into trouble. We did not develop. I naturally resent some of the implications I get about the 'wrong things' that are happening on the continent of Africa. We were never allowed a chance!"[4]

External interference was only one aspect of this exchange. Sutherland steered the conversation in a different direction, asking Nyerere to look internally and discuss "the structure of the nation-state" and its "built-in repressions"—a question that proved to occupy the minds of many political activists in the African Diaspora. For Nyerere, the postcolonial state was somewhat of an enigma: "I know the problems of nation-state, I don't know the answer! I know the problems of the bureaucracies, I became a bureaucrat . . . One can say the nation-state is a problem—not simply the problem against the individual, it's a wielder of power against society. At the international level, it prevents great linkages between people because it's not an instrument of integration."[5] At this intimate meeting between two elder statesmen of pan-Africanism whose friendship dated back to the 1958 All African Peoples Conference in Accra, Nyerere seemed to arrive at a similar conclusion put forth by Black Power activists who attempted to forge pragmatic working relationships with Tanzania's one-party state. Indeed, as an "instrument of integration," the state managed to open up avenues for pan-African alliance building while closing off access to others.

Nyerere's post-presidency years were largely marked by his efforts to end apartheid in South Africa, a cause he championed dating back to his days as a young, anticolonial nationalist until his death. On October 14, 1999, Mwalimu Julius K. Nyerere died of leukemia in a London hospital.⁶ He was seventy-seven years old. News of his death prompted a wave of condolence messages from around the world. The Black Radical Congress (BRC), a political organization formed in 1998 that claimed to represent the "new black radicalism" in the United States, issued a message of solidarity to the Tanzanian government and people. Some of its signatories were representatives of the Black Power movement of the 1960s and 1970s, including Amiri Baraka and Angela Davis, two black radicals who had visited Tanzania during the heyday of its socialist experiment. It was hardly surprising, then, that the BRC would issue a message that saluted Nyerere's leadership and policies, from his stance against African dictatorial rule, to his decisions to nationalize Kiswahili and provide universal health care and education, to his unconditional support of decolonization in southern Africa. Nyerere's treatment of African Americans, of course, was also noteworthy. An excerpt reads:

> Africans born in the USA who were fighting for civil rights always found a home in Tanzania when they were persecuted in the USA. The decision of Tanzania to be the Home of the Pan-African Skills Project that welcomed African Americans to the African continent was an act of solidarity that will not be forgotten. Many members of the BRC participated actively in the Sixth Pan-African Congress that was hosted by Tanzania in Dar es Salaam in 1974. Despite the relative poverty of the people, the government of Tanzania was making resources available for progressive and revolutionary forces from all over the world to find a common meeting point in Tanzania. Nyerere was partisan to Pan-Africanism but he was also an internationalist who supported the struggles of the Vietnamese, the Cubans and all those who opposed imperialism.⁷

Twenty-five years removed from this period and African American activists had little trouble articulating the reasons why Tanzania's nationalist project took hold of their political and cultural imaginations.⁸

Tanzanians have equally memorialized the Black Power movement in the contemporary moment. The continued presence of African American expatriates of the Black Power era is indeed a reminder of this increasingly forgotten past. For example, Pete and Charlotte O'Neal, former Black Panthers of the Kansas City chapter, settled in Tanzania in 1972, after living in political exile in Algeria. In 1991, they settled in Imbaseni village, populated by the Wameru ethnic group, in northern Tanzania and formed the United African Alliance Community Center (UAACC). Located on the slopes of Mt. Meru, Africa's third largest mountain, UAACC has spearheaded community service programs reminiscent of the "survival programs" of the Black Panther Party. Over the years it has initiated grassroots development projects that have addressed issues such as clean water, youth leadership development, arts education,

Conclusion

health and fitness, computer literacy, HIV/AIDS awareness, malaria prevention, and vocational training.[9]

By providing access to a recording space and beat-making software and equipment, the O'Neals' youth development work has helped to shape the radical politics of the local hip-hop movement in the Arusha region. Groups and artists such as River Camp, Joe Makini, Watengwa, JCB, Ukoo Flani Mau Mau, and Nako 2 Nako have given homage to the revolutionary activism of the Panthers and demanded that the U.S. government free the African American political prisoner Mumia Abu Jamal.[10] Dar es Salaam–based artists have also produced lyrics of solidarity with the African Diaspora that celebrate U.S. black radical leaders and organizations of the past. In 2005, the Tanzanian public was made aware of the issue of African American political prisoners imprisoned during the Black Power era when the Malcolm X Grassroots Movement (MXGM), a U.S.-based organization dedicated to securing the human rights of black peoples, held its annual Black August hip-hop concert in Tanzania. Political hip-hop artists from the United States shared the stage with Tanzanian hip-hoppers as a demonstration of pan-Africanist solidarity among the global hip-hop generation. This led to collaboration between dead prez, a U.S.-based black radical hip-hop group, and Nakaaya, a Tanzanian singer. In 2009, they released "Mr. Politician," a song about post-Ujamaa government corruption, to wide acclaim.

In 2011, shortly after the death of Geronimo ji Jaga, the former Black Panther who was a victim of the FBI's counterintelligence program and served twenty-seven years in prison for his revolutionary activism, Tanzanian rappers JCB, Fid Q, Dunga, and Lavotsi, along with Charlotte O'Neal (aka Mama C), produced "Rest in Uhuru" [Rest in freedom].[11] As a tribute to Geronimo, Tanzanian rappers reflected on the importance of his life, the Black Power movement that nurtured him, and the friendships they forged with him after he settled in Tanzania upon his release from prison in 1997. JCB's verse reads:

> His ideas will last like Tupac's in the streets
> And in the hearts of defenders of justice!
> He was an activist who fought for the rights of the black and oppressed
> During the reign of the oppressor
> He is gone
> We won't have image like Mjema
> But his precious ideals live on
> Rest in Peace our hero
> Respect!
> The candles will be lit forever

in memory of your greatness
You were in jail 27 years
Not different from what Mandela endured
What I remember about ji Jaga
He was a good fellow
The shadow of justice
like an umbrella in a scorching sun!
Rest in peace wherever you are
We will remember you
from January to December
We will build on what you started!
Rest in Peace, bro

Fid Q's verse reads:

Old soldiers never die, nor fade away
Keep hope alive, never go astray
Strategize, Sacrifice
Every step of the way
Analyze, Sanctify
At the end of the day
Our brother G
I know you are forever free
You are rested in peace
And have met Nyerere
Though you've left us
You're alive in our hearts and thoughts
The world without you
Is like Rock City with no rocks!
For writers and speakers
You are their quotes and quips
For the doubters and naysayers
Heed this Malcolm speech
Like Marcus Mosiah with
The Blackman's speech
Strive to go higher
because the sky ain't the limit
You told me I am the best

Conclusion

> Never to settle for less
> And that I am special
> Without a doubt
> let my ghetto lesson be a blessing
> So that I can stand in front
> And be on point like decimals
> You and the revolution remained attached
> Just like the snows and Eskimos

A year later, Nikki Mbishi released *Malcolm XI*, a reference to the iconic African American leader Malcolm X. To close his album, Mbishi samples from one of Malcolm X's most famous speeches, "The Ballot or the Bullet," relaying a pointed message to disenfranchised Tanzanian urban youth intent on fleeing to the United States for a better life about the hypocrisy of American democracy and the "American Dream." Over a jazz-infused beat, Malcolm X relays a message about American racism that he tried to convey to Tanzanians during his visit to Dar es Salaam almost fifty years earlier. The sample in its entirety is as follows:

> I'm no politician. I'm not even a student of politics. I'm not a Republican nor a Democrat nor an American and I got sense enough to know it. I am one of the 22 million black victims of the Democrats. One of the 22 million black victims of the Republicans. And one of the 22 million black victims of Americanism. When I speak I don't speak as a Democrat or a Republican nor as an American. I speak as a victim of America's so-called democracy. You and I have never seen democracy. All we've seen is hypocrisy. When we open our eyes today and look at America, we see America not through the eyes of someone who has enjoyed the fruits of Americanism. We see America through the eyes of someone who has been a victim of Americanism. We don't see an American Dream. We have experienced an American nightmare. We haven't benefited from America's democracy. We've only suffered from America's hypocrisy. And the generation that is coming up now can see it and are not afraid to say it. If you go to jail so what? If you are black, you were born in jail. If you black, you were born in jail."[12]

Other Tanzanian memorialization gestures have occurred on a grassroots level. Afriroots Adventures, Inc., a Tanzanian-owned ecotourism company that promotes environmental awareness and small business development, recently implemented the "Dar Liberation Tour," which takes Tanzanians, expatriates, and tourists on a walking tour of downtown Dar es Salaam to learn about "the role of the city in the

Conclusion

liberation struggles of Sub Sahara Africa—visit FRELIMO and ANC buildings, learn about Malcolm X and Che Guevara in Tanzania, what they did here and how they helped in the struggle for independence."[13] For Mejah Mbuya, cofounder and co-owner of Afriroots, whose historical consciousness of the Black Power movement and its relationship to Tanzania's nationalist project was nurtured by his frequent visits to the O'Neals' UAACC in Arusha, Tanzanians needed to know about this history of solidarity, the good and the bad. In an interview with NDTV, a Hindi news channel based out of India, he remarked: "Tanzania was like a candle. It gave light to others that needed hope but in the process it burned itself down."[14]

These fragments of collective memory when pieced together begin to capture the power of Tanzania's nationalist project—its global appeal and psychological, cultural, and political impact on black communities in the African Diaspora. In a historical moment marked by a multiplicity of overlapping struggles for black, African, and Third World liberation, I have sought in this book to draw attention to the collaborative ways in which Black Power activists, intellectuals, and organizations from the United States and the Caribbean islands conceptualized Tanzanian nation-statehood; built transnational networks and alliances with Tanzanian (and African) nationalists; imagined a liberated Africa free from colonial rule, economically independent, and united; and looked to Tanzania's revolution as a source of racial and cultural pride. This historical study of the respective dynamism of the Black Power movement and Tanzanian nation-building reveals points of convergence and difference that would prove difficult to assess without exploring the international dimension of Tanzanian, African American, and Caribbean histories.

Under Nyerere's leadership, both symbolic and real, Tanzania gained credibility in pan-Africanist circles before national independence in the 1950s and was given a boost of legitimacy in the aftermath of the Ghana coup in 1966. By 1967, an image of Nyerere and the Tanzanian one-party state as models of revolutionary leadership in the pan-Africanism movement had been firmly established in part due to the activities of Malcolm X and the Organization of Afro-American Unity (OAAU) in 1964. The humanistic principles underlying the Arusha Declaration, combined with its progressive foreign policies, enticed black radicals to seek out Nyerere and the TANU state as an ally through which they could partake in the country's nation-building program. Thus, the period between 1967 and 1974 witnessed Black Power activists and organizations attempting to open up channels of communication and work closely with the one-party state on unprecedented levels. James Forman and Stokely Carmichael of the Student Nonviolent Coordinating Committee (SNCC); Walter Rodney of Guyana; C.L.R. James of Trinidad; and Drum and Spear's Charlie Cobb, Jennifer Lawson, Anne Forrester, and Judy Richardson, found common ground and sense of purpose on dismantling the

Conclusion

apartheid system in South Africa, nationalizing university education, and publishing nationalist and pan-Africanist-oriented books.

The self-determination ethos of Black Power fueled the movement's efforts to tackle a host of local, national, and international issues, giving birth to numerous organizations, ideologies, and strategies. On the level of political organizing in the international arena, the TANU state allowed Black Power activists a measure of political autonomy while providing access to anticolonial liberation movements and state actors and institutions. It also allowed them to acquire firsthand knowledge of the challenges of nation-building and continental unity. Furthermore, the TANU state allowed Black Power activists the opportunity to internationalize the aims and objectives of their movements, which included educating the Tanzanian public about the phenomenon of worldwide systemic racism and the threat of U.S. imperialism in Africa.

Though Nyerere was in no way fully supportive of all Black Power ideas, strategies, and tactics, he nonetheless believed that the African Diaspora had a role to play in his vision for building a modern African nation under the auspices of a one-party state system. In this context, black diasporans from the United States and the Caribbean would exercise their individual and collective agency by traveling to, and settling in, Tanzania and performing specific nation-building roles that required their technical skills and know-how as well as their pan-Africanist consciousness.

The Black Power–Tanzania moment reached its peak in 1974, amid the intensification of anticolonial nationalist struggles in the Portuguese-ruled territories of Mozambique, Angola, Guinea-Bissau, and the Cape Verde Islands. However, in organizing and participating in the Sixth Pan-African Congress, Caribbean and African American activists and organizations found themselves increasingly alienated within the pan-Africanism movement. Black Power advocates were wary of entrenching nation-state control of pan-Africanism, but ultimately found they could do little in ensuring nonstate actors' equal participation in determining the movement's future directions. Yet 6PAC was just one episode that illustrated this tension. A critical study of the Tanzanian state response to Black Power brings into sharper focus the limited boundaries within which Black Power activists could operate. The capacity of the one-party state to facilitate Black Power pan-Africanist activity was counterbalanced by its ability to structure such activity. Censorship of Carmichael's public criticism of postcolonial African leadership, the banning of the University Students' African Revolutionary Front (USARF) and leftist politics at the University of Dar es Salaam, the mass arrest of African American expatriates, and the exclusion of Black Power organizations from the Caribbean at 6PAC are a few examples addressed in this study that show how the Tanzanian state cautiously engaged with Black Power politics and pursued alliances of mutual concern, yet on its own terms. At a time when the threat of Western imperialism put fragile independent nations in precarious positions, Tanzania could not always match its rhetoric of solidarity with the Black Power movements in the African Diaspora with full, practical support—particularly the kind of support expected from Black Power leaders and organizations. At the same time, the state did not always want to do so, because Tanzanian nationalist leaders did not always hold similar views on race and class struggle and strategies for continental unification. Diaspora marginalization within the pan-Africanism movement, as experienced through active participation in Tanzania's nationalist project, forced them to reexamine the nature and efficacy of their political philosophies and transnational activities. While Black Power activism abroad owed much to the state's facilitator role, the contingencies of this relationship and collaboration undermined Black Power activists' ability to act as equal partners in shaping Africa's liberation agenda.

By traveling to and living in Tanzania, however, Black Power activists had reinscribed political meaning into the diaspora concepts of "homeland" and "returning home," forging an African Diaspora identity and consciousness in the process. While they held internationalist sensibilities, which were expressed in their identification with the Chinese revolution and Vietnamese struggle for self-determination, Africa was given privileged status as a result of an acknowledgment of their ancestral connection to the continent. Nyerere and the TANU government responded in a reciprocal fashion by viewing them apart from other expatriates and utilizing not only their technical skills but also their assumed loyalty to the state in fulfilling domestic and foreign policy objectives. As a result, Tanzanian nationalists such as Abdulrahman Mohamed Babu, John Malecela, Walter Bgoya, Paul Bomani, and students associated with the USARF, such as Karim Hirji, Issa Shivji, Henry Mapolu, and Zakia Meghji, emerged as important political contacts, bridges, and friends. As Bgoya later recalled: "African Americans coming to Tanzania often arrived with names of individuals and institutions to contact, including in some cases the foreign ministry, and I was privileged to be one of the individuals who was contacted. It was a period of mutual discovery between those African Americans and Tanzanians, with unresolved questions and frustrations but also fulfillment."[15]

Yet the Black Power–Tanzania encounter raises questions about the ever-changing relationship between Africa and the transatlantic Africa Diaspora and the ways in which the nation-state concept complicates African Diaspora and African conceptions of freedom, belonging, and revolutionary struggle. Dating back to the postemancipation and colonial eras, African diasporans and Africans formed part of a broad transnational community where the exchange of ideas and the making of kinship bonds lay at the heart of their movement-building activities. Although conditions and circumstances have changed drastically over the course of fifty years, postcolonial

Conclusion

government repression and Western economic dependency in Africa and the Caribbean, and antiblack violence and racial exclusion in the United States continue to define the experiences of historically oppressed peoples. These are recurring themes in the long history of Pan-Africanism—themes around which a narrative about how African Americans, West Indians, and Tanzanians developed positive understandings of one another is possible.

Notes

INTRODUCTION

1. Julius K. Nyerere, *Freedom and Unity (Uhuru na Umoja): A Selection from Writings and Speeches, 1952-1965* (Oxford: Oxford University Press, 1966): 142-143.
2. "Inauguration of the Republic of Tanganyika and of Julius Nyerere as its First President: December 8-10, 1962—State Department—Unclassified A-355," Box 38, Folder 4, William K. Leonhart Personal Papers, John F. Kennedy Library, Boston, MA [hereafter cited as Leonhart papers].
3. George Houser, "Brief Comments on Recent East African Events," 5 February 1964, 3, Leonhart papers.
4. Julius K. Nyerere, "It Is Up to Us: Uhuru na Kazi," *Africa Today* 8, no. 10 (December 1961): 4-5.
5. Ikaweba Buntin, "The Heart of Africa: Interview with Julius Nyerere on Anti-Colonialism," *New Internationalist Magazine*, no. 309 (January-February 1999), http://newint.org/features/1999/01/01/anticolonialism/.
6. Thomas Molony, "Nyerere: The Formative Years," in *Julius Kambarage Nyerere: Life, Times, Legacy* (London: FIRST, 2009), 32-33.
7. Buntin, "The Heart of Africa: Interview with Julius Nyerere on Anti-Colonialism."
8. Ibid.
9. For more in-depth case studies of decolonization in colonial Tanganyika, refer to the following: John Illife, *A Modern History of Tanganyika* (Cambridge: Cambridge University Press, 1979); Frederick Cooper, *Decolonization and African Society: The Labor Question in French and British Africa* (Cambridge: Cambridge University Press, 1996); Susan Geiger, *TANU Women:*

Gender and Culture in the Making of Tanganyikan Nationalism, 1955-1965 (Portsmouth, NH: Heinemann, 1997); Andrew Burton and Michael Jennings, eds., *The Emperor's New Clothes: Continuity and Change in East Africa, 1950-2000* (London: James Currey, 2004); Andrew Burton, *African Underclass: Urbanization, Crime and Colonial Disorder in Dar es Salaam, 1919-1961* (Athens: Ohio University Press, 2005); Gregory Maddox and James L. Giblin, eds., *In Search of a Nation: Histories of Authority and Dissidence in Tanzania* (Athens: Ohio University Press, 2006).

10. See James Meriwether, *Proudly We Can Be Africans: Black Americans and Africa, 1935-1961* (Chapel Hill: University of North Carolina Press, 2002), 124-180.

11. Komozi Woodard, *A Nation within a Nation: Amiri Barka (LeRoi Jones) and Black Power Politics* (Chapel Hill: University of North Carolina Press, 1998), 57-59.

12. Yevette Richards, "African and African-American Labor Leaders in the Struggle over International Affiliations," *International Journal of African Historical Studies* 31, no. 2 (1998): 307. Also see Yevette Richards, *Maida Springer: Pan Africanist and International Labor Leader* (Pittsburgh, PA: University of Pittsburgh Press, 2004); Yevette Richards, *Conversations with Maida Springer: A Personal History of Labor, Race, and International Relations* (Pittsburgh, PA: University of Pittsburgh Press, 2004).

13. See Peter Weiss, "American Committee on Africa: Rebels with a Cause," *Africa Today* 10, no. 9 (November 1963): 38-39; George Houser, "Meeting Africa's Challenge—The Story of the ACOA" (ACOA, 1976).

14. Ibid.

15. George Shepherd, "Profile: Mr. Julius Nyerere," *Africa Today* 2, no. 1 (March-April 1955): 14-15.

16. Ibid., 15.

17. *Africa-UN Bulletin*, no. 2, American Committee on Africa (28 December 1956): 1-4, http://www.aluka.org/action/showMetadata?doi=10.5555/AL.SFF.DOCUMENT.acoa000082.

18. Randy Weston and Willard Jenkins, *Africa Rhythms: The Autobiography of Randy Weston* (Durham, NC: Duke University Press, 2015), 91-92.

19. For further background to the making of *Uhuru Afrika*, see Robin D. G. Kelley, *Africa Speaks, America Answers: Modern Jazz Revolutionary Times* (Cambridge, MA: Harvard University Press, 2012), 53-64. The impact of African decolonization on other jazz musicians of Africa and the African Diaspora has also been chronicled in the works of Penny M. Von Eschen, *Satchmo Blows Up the World: Jazz Ambassador Plays the Cold War* (Cambridge, MA: Harvard University Press, 2006); Ingrid Monson, *Freedom Sounds: Civil Rights Call Out to Jazz and Africa* (Oxford: Oxford University Press, 2007); and Njoroge Njoroge, *Chocolate Surrealism: Music, Movement, Memory, and History in the Circum-Caribbean* (Jackson, MS: University Press of Mississippi, 2007).

20. "Africa, where the sun shines brightly / Africa, where the world came first / Africa, out of yesterday's night: Freedom! / The Freedom wind! / The freedom wind blows!" Translation by author.

21. Randy Weston, "Introduction: Uhuru Kwanza (Part One)," *Uhuru Afrika*, Roulette Records, 1960, CD, 0:09-2:00.

22. Randy Weston and William Jenkins, *African Rhythms: The Autobiography of Randy Weston* (Durham, NC: Duke University Press, 2015), 89-90; "Black History Special: Jazz Legend Randy Weston on His Life and Celebration of 'African Rhythms,'" *democracynow.org*, 20 February 2012, http://www.democracynow.org/2012/2/20/black_history_special_jazz_legend_randy.

23. "Tanganyika White Rule to Be Ended by Britain," *Washington Post*, 16 December 1959, A6.
24. "The Key to Tanganyika: Julius Kambarage Nyerere," *New York Times*, 11 February 1960, 12; "An African Leader," *New York Times*, 14 February 1960, E8.
25. Jay Walz, "Africa: The Search for Unity," *New York Times*, 26 June 1960, E5.
26. "Tanganyikans Stride towards Independence," *Washington Post*, 4 September 1960, A4.
27. "Williams Is Impressed by Tanganyikan Leader," *Washington Post*, 26 February 1961, A11.
28. Warren Unna, "Nyerere Visit Here Plans Independent Tanganyika Role," *Washington Post*, 17 July 1961, A20.
29. "New African Leader," *Afro-American (Baltimore)*, 15 April 1961, 4; "Tanganyika 1st Multiracial African State to Achieve Independence," *Chicago Defender*, 11 December 1961, 5.
30. "Julius Nyerere: East African Moderate," *Negro Digest* 11, no. 5 (March 1962): 31–36.
31. Milton Bracker, "African Leader Going to London," *New York Times*, 22 June 1959, 11.
32. "Nyerere Expects U.S. to Cure Racial Ills," *New York Times*, 22 July 1963, 6.
33. "National Press Club Luncheons and Other Events: Summary Luncheon Addressed by the President of Tanganyika," 15 July 1963, unpublished sound recording, National Press Club Collection, Library of Congress, Washington, DC.
34. "Nyerere Pledges Fight 'til All Africa Is Free," *Washington Post*, 16 July 1963, A2.
35. Dorothy McCardle, "Pledges Peaceful Right to March," *Washington Post*, 18 July 1963, D1.
36. Letter from President John F. Kennedy to President Julius Nyerere, 14 June 1963, Box 162, Folder 7, Leonhart papers.
37. Department of State telegram from G. Mennen Williams to William K. Leonhart, 29 September 1963, Box 162, Folder 7: Tanganyika general 1963, Leonhart papers.
38. "African Nations Join in Mourning," *Chicago Defender*, 25 November 1963, 8. In a letter to President Kennedy months before his assassination, Nyerere wrote: "Although until independence relations between Tanganyika and America were entirely indirect, the friendship which has been developed since that time is a source of great pleasure to us." Letter from Julius Nyerere to President and Mrs. Kennedy, 2 January 1963, Box 162, Folder 7, Leonhart papers.

CHAPTER 1. MALCOLM X, A. M. BABU, AND THE SEEDS OF SOLIDARITY

1. New nations included Ghana, Guinea, Cameroon, Senegal, Togo, Mali, Madagascar, Democratic Republic of the Congo, Somalia, Benin, Niger, Burkina Faso, Côte d'Ivoire, Chad, Central African Republic, Congo-Brazzaville, Gabon, Nigeria, Mauritania, Sierra Leone, Tanganyika, Burundi, Rwanda, Algeria, Uganda, and Kenya.
2. Thomas Burgess, "An Imagined Generation: Umma Youth in Nationalist Zanzibar," in *In Search of a Nation: Histories of Authority and Dissidence in Tanzania*, ed. Gregory Maddox and James L. Giblin (Oxford: James Currey, 2005), 228. Also see Amrit Wilson, *The Threat of Liberation: Imperialism and Revolution in Zanzibar* (London: Pluto Press, 2013).
3. A. M. Babu, "Memoirs: An Outline," in *Babu: I Saw the Future and It Works*, ed. Haroub Othman (Dar es Salaam: E&D Limited, 2001), 18.
4. Babu, "Memoirs: An Outline," 16.

Notes

5. Burgess, "An Imagined Generation," 240.
6. Julius K. Nyerere, *Freedom and Unity (Uhuru na Umoja): A Selection from Writings and Speeches, 1952-1965* (Oxford: Oxford University Press, 1966), 288.
7. Central Intelligence Agency, *Zanzibar Revisited*, 18 September 1995, Lyndon B. Johnson Library, https://www.cia.gov/library/center-for-the-study-of-intelligence/kent-csi/vo111no2/html/v11i2a01p_0001.htm.
8. Central Intelligence Agency, *Special Report: Tanzania Taking the Left Turn*, 21 May 1965, Central Intelligence Agency's Freedom of Information Act Electronic Reading Room, www.cia.gov/library/reeadingroom/docs/DOC_0000126865.pdf.
9. Examples include "U.S. Embassy Aide Seized at Gunpoint by Zanzibar Officers," *Washington Post*, 17 January 1964, A1; "Zanzibar Regime Seizes U.S. Consul at Gunpoint," *New York Times*, 17 January 1964, 1; "Chaos in Zanzibar," *Washington Post*, 18 January 1964, A10; "Stories of Bloodbath Filter from Zanzibar," *Washington Post*, 20 January 1964, A11; "Arab Reds Begin Coup on Zanzibar," *Washington Post*, 31 January 1964, 1; "U.S. and Britain Envoys Expelled by Zanzibar," *Washington Post*, 24 February 1964, E4; "Zanzibar I—Behind the Clove Curtain," *New York Times*, 25 March 1964, 40; "Zanzibar II—An African Cuba," *New York Times*, 28 March 1964, 18; "Thousands Tote Anti-U.S. Signs in Zanzibar," *Washington Post*, 8 April 1964, A28.
10. *Chicago Defender*, 14 January 1964, 2.
11. George S. Schuyler, "The World Today," *New Pittsburgh Courier*, 25 January 1964, 1; George S. Schuyler, "The World Today," *New Pittsburgh Courier*, 11 April 1964, 1.
12. Max Lerner, "African Violence," *New Pittsburg Courier*, 15 February 1964, 9.
13. George S. Schuyler, "Views and Reviews," *New Pittsburgh Courier*, 29 February 1964, 8.
14. Max Stanford, "The Relationship of Revolutionary Afro-American Movement to the Bandung Revolution," *Black America* (Summer-Fall 1965), Reel 1, The Black Power Movement: Part 3: Papers of the Revolutionary Action Movement, Schomburg Center for Research in Black Culture, New York, NY. For a historical overview of RAM, see Robin D. G. Kelley, "Stormy Weather: Reconstructing Black (Inter)Nationalism in the Cold War Era," in *It's Nation Time: Contemporary Essays on Black Power and Black Nationalism*, ed. Eddie Glaude Jr. (Chicago: University of Chicago Press, 2002), 67-90.
15. Central Intelligence Agency, *Special Report: Tanzania Taking the Left Turn*, 21 May 1965, Lyndon B. Johnson Library.
16. "Tanganyika, Zanzibar to Merge," *Washington Post*, 24 April 1964, A1; "Matter of Fact . . . Irony in Zanzibar," *Washington Post*, 29 April 1964, A23.
17. "Tanganyika, Zanzibar Merge to 'Fight Reds,'" *Tri-State Defender*, 2 May 1964, 7.
18. John Henrik Clarke, ed., *Malcolm X: The Man and His Times* (New York: Macmillan, 1969), 22.
19. Ibid., 235-293.
20. Ibid., 264.
21. Archie Epps, ed., *Malcolm X: Speeches at Harvard* (New York: Paragon House, 1991), 142.
22. Ibid., 144.
23. George Breitman, ed., *Malcolm X Speaks: Selected Speeches and Statements* (New York: Grove Weidenfeld, 1965), 61.
24. Ibid., 63.

25. Ibid., 62.
26. William Sales Jr., *From Civil Rights to Black Liberation: Malcolm X and the Organization of African Unity* (Boston: South End Press, 1994), 97-132.
27. "Basic Unity Program, 1965," in *Modern Black Nationalism: From Marcus Garvey to Louis Farrakhan*, ed. William L. Van Deburg (New York: New York University Press, 1997), 109; Manning Marable, *Race, Reform, and Rebellion: The Second Reconstruction in Black America, 1945-1982* (London: Macmillan, 1984), 341-351.
28. Deburg, "Basic Unity Program, 1965," 104-105.
29. Ibid., 104-105; "Malcolm X seeks UN Aid against U.S. Bias," *Chicago Defender*, 13 July 1964, 3.
30. Betty Shabazz, ed., *Malcolm X by Any Means Necessary* (New York: Pathfinder Press, 1970), 87-88.
31. Roderick Bush, *We Are Not What We Seem: Black Nationalism and Class Struggle in the American Century* (New York: New York University Press, 2000), 189-190. Also see "U.S. Racialism under Fire," *Nationalist*, 23 July 1964, 1.
32. Malcolm X, *The Autobiography of Malcolm X as Told to Alex Haley* (New York: Ballantine Books, 1965), 341.
33. Sales, *From Civil Rights to Black Liberation*, 101.
34. "Diaries Notebook," Reel 9, The Papers of Malcolm X, Schomburg Center for Research in Black Culture, New York, NY [hereafter cited as MX Papers].
35. Ibid.
36. Breitman, *Malcolm X Speaks*, 77-87; "Kiongozi wa Wanegro Atuma simu kwa Telli," *Mwafrika*, 30 July 1964, 6.
37. Julius Nyerere, *Freedom and Unity: A Collection of Writings and Speeches, 1952-1965* (Oxford: Oxford University Press, 1967), 291-293.
38. Salma Babu and Amrit Wilson, eds., *The Future That Works: Selected Writings of A.M. Babu* (Trenton, NJ: Africa World Press, 2002), 84.
39. "More Shots as Harlem Unrest Smolders On," *Tanganyika Standard*, 22 July 1964, 1; "Looters Shot in New York Race Riots Flares-Up," *Tanganyika Standard*, 23 July 1964, 1; "Guns Roar in New York Riots," *Tanganyika Standard*, 27 July 1964, 1.
40. "Malcolm X Fails with Africans," *Chicago Defender*, 27 July 1964, 6.
41. Breitman, *Malcolm X Speaks*, 77.
42. Ibid., 72-78.
43. Ibid., 75.
44. "Racial Storm," *Tanganyika Standard*, 27 July 1964, 2; Organization of African Unity, *Resolutions Adopted by the First Ordinary Session of the Assembly of Head of State and Government Held in Cairo, UAR, from 17 to 21 July 1964*, http://archive.au.int/collect/auassemb/import/English/FIRST%20ORDINARY_E.pdf.
45. "Take Larger Role in U.N., Africa Urged," *Chicago Tribune*, 18 July 1964, 22; "Background to Cairo Conference: O.A.U. Leaders Seek Louder Voice from African Nations in Affairs of the World," *Nationalist*, 18 July 1964, 4.
46. "Malcolm Rips U.S. Government," *Chicago Defender*, 14 July 1964, 3.
47. "Malcolm X Fails with Africans," *Chicago Defender*, 27 July 1964, 6; "Malcolm X Bids Africans

Take Negro Issue to U.N.," *New York Times*, 18 July 1964, 2; "Malcolm X Seeks U.N. Negro Debate," *New York Times*, 13 August 1964, 22; "Malcolm X Rips U.S. Government," *Chicago Defender*, 14 July 1964, 3; "Take Larger Role in U.N., Africa Urged," *Chicago Tribune*, 18 July 1964, 22; "Background to Cairo Conference: OAU leaders Seek Louder Voice from African Nations in Affairs of the World," *Nationalist*, 18 July 1964, 4.

48. Breitman, *Malcolm X Speaks*, 83-84.
49. Nyerere, *Freedom and Unity*, 302.
50. Travel Diary entry, 20 July 1964, Reel 9, MX Papers. Tanzania's supportive effort did not go unnoticed by Malcolm X. While Malcolm left the conference still uncertain about Nyerere's politics, he was sufficiently impressed with Babu. During Malcolm's second tour of the continent, he took up Babu's invitation to visit Tanzania.
51. Travel Diary entry, 14 July 1964, Reel 9, MX Papers; "African Intrigue of Malcolm X," *Chicago Defender*, 7 August 1964, 5; Breitman, *Malcolm X Speaks* 86-87; "Malcolm X: Success at African Summit," *Blacklash*, 14 September 1964, 1, 4.
52. His visit to Ghana was mainly orchestrated by the "Malcolm X Committee" made up of members of Ghana's black radical expatriate community. For an insightful case study of the African American experience in Ghana from 1957 to 1966, see Kevin K. Gaines, *American Africans in Ghana: Black Expatriates and the Civil Rights Era* (Chapel Hill: University of North Carolina Press, 2006), 179-209. Also see Dayo F. Gore, "From Communist Politics to Black Power: The Visionary Politics and Transnational Solidarities of Victoria "Vicki" Ama Garvin," in *Want to Start a Revolution? Radical Women in the Black Freedom Struggle*, ed. Dayo F. Gore, Jeanne Theoharis, and Komozi Woodard (New York: New York University Press, 2009), 72-94.
53. "Travel Diary," Reel 9, MX papers.
54. Nyerere, *Freedom and Unity*; Julius K. Nyerere, *Ujamaa—Essays on Socialism* (Oxford: Oxford University Press, 1971).
55. Nyerere, *Freedom and Unity*, 166.
56. Gaines, *American Africans in Ghana*, 179-209.
57. "Letter from Bill Sutherland to Unknown," n.d., Box 1, Folder 5, Muriel S. & Otto P. Snowden Papers (Freedom House, Inc.), 1911-1990, Boston, MA [hereafter referred to as Snowden Papers].
58. Box 1, Folder 4, Snowden Papers.
59. Bill Sutherland and Matt Meyer, *Guns and Gandhi in Africa: Pan African Insights on Non-Violence, Armed Liberation Struggle, and Liberation in Africa* (Trenton, NJ: Africa World Press, 2000), 211.
60. Sutherland and Meyer, *Guns and Gandhi in Africa*, 210-212. Also see Jan Carew, *Ghosts in Our Blood: With Malcolm X in Africa, England, and the Caribbean* (Chicago: Lawrence Hill Books, 1994).
61. Flora Kambona interview with author; Susan Geiger, "Tanganyikan Nationalism as 'Women's Work': Life Histories, Collective Biography and Changing Historiography," *Journal of African History* 37, no. 3 (1996): 464-478.
62. "We're One with You, Says 'Evil' Malcolm X," *Tanganyika Standard*, 13 October 1964, 1.
63. "Malcolm X Rips USA," *Nationalist*, 12 October, 1964, 1.
64. "We're One with You, Says 'Evil' Malcolm X," *Tanganyika Standard*, 13 October 1964, 1.
65. Ibid.

66. "Peace Corps Leader Replies to Malcolm X," *Tanganyika Standard*, 2 November 1964, 2.
67. Walter Bgoya interview with author.
68. Travel Diary, 12 October 1964, Reel 9, MX Papers.
69. Sales, *From Civil Rights to Black Liberation*, 104.
70. Marable, *Race, Reform, and Rebellion*, 240-254. Nyerere was particularly enamored with President John F. Kennedy. While Malcolm X referred to Kennedy's death as an example of "chickens coming home to roost," Nyerere viewed it as tragic, claiming that JFK was "a man whose civility and sincere beliefs in human equality and dignity had given new hope to millions of people in Africa and elsewhere"; Julius K. Nyerere, *This Is the Way Forward: Republic Day Broadcast by President Nyerere, 9th December 1963* (Dar es Salaam: Kimetulewa na Idara Kuu Ya Habari, 1964), 8.
71. Marable, *Race, Reform, and Rebellion*, 317.
72. Babu and Wilson, *The Future That Works*, 86.
73. Travel Diary entry, 13 October 1964, Reel 9, MX Papers.
74. Ibid.
75. Steve Clark, *Malcolm X: February 1965: The Final Speeches* (New York: Pathfinder, 1992), 229.
76. For an exhaustive case study of the assassination of Lumumba, see Ludo De Witte, *The Assassination of Lumumba* (London: Verso, 2001). African American activists kept abreast of the Congo situation in 1960-1961, culminating in a major protest at the United Nations. For a discussion of this protest and political actors involved, see Brenda Gayle Plummer, *Rising Wind: Black Americans and U.S. Foreign Affairs, 1935-1960* (Chapel Hill: University of North Carolina Press, 1996), 303-304; James H. Meriwether, *Proudly We Can Be Africans: Black Americans and Africa, 1935-1961* (Chapel Hill: University of North Carolina Press, 2002), 233-234; Komozi Woodard, "Amiri Baraka, The Congress of African People, and Black Power Politics from the 1961 United Nations Protest to the 1972 Gary Convention," in *The Black Power Movement: Rethinking the Civil Rights-Black Power Era*, ed. Peniel E. Joseph (New York: Routledge, 2006), 55-60; Cedric Johnson, *Revolutionaries to Race Leaders: Black Power and the Making of African American Politics* (Minneapolis: University of Minnesota Press, 2007), 51-52.
77. In August, the TANU Youth League organized a mass protest at the U.S. Embassy in Dar es Salaam against U.S. intervention in the Congo. Protest signs read: "Stop killing our brothers in the Congo"; "Congo is no place for you"; "You Yankees smell Lumumba's blood"; "To hell with imperialism headed by American Yankee"; "Yankee hands off Congo." "Hands off Africa!," *Nationalist*, 21 August 1964, 1. A month later, at the OAU council of ministers meeting in Addis Ababa, Tanzania took a defiant stand on the Congo, questioning the legitimacy of Moïse Tshombe and decrying the actions of the United States and Belgium. "Tanzania Stand at Addis Talks," *Nationalist*, 5 September 1964, 1. And in the same month, students at the University College of Dar es Salaam staged a protest over the Congo crisis, which was again held at the U.S. Embassy. "Dar Students Demonstrate," *Nationalist*, 27 November 1964, 1. Also see Okwudiba Nnoli, *Self Reliance and Foreign Policy in Tanzania: The Dynamics of Diplomacy of a New State, 1961-1971* (New York: NOK Publishers, 1978), 90, 116-118, 194-195.
78. David Herman, "Hands off the Congo!," *The Militant*, 15 December 1963, 1.
79. Breitman, *Malcolm X Speaks*, 101.
80. Ibid., 90.
81. Ibid., 93.

Notes

82. Ibid., 102.
83. Ibid. Babu arrived late to the event, forcing Malcolm to talk extemporaneously until he arrived. When he did, he came bearing a note of solidarity from Ernesto "Che" Guevara, the Cuban leader and guerrilla warfare theoretician who had also come to New York to attend the UN General Assembly. Four months later, Che would find himself in Tanzania leading a cadre of Afro-Cuban guerrilla fighters across Lake Tanganyika into the Congo to lend military support to a rebel force under the leadership of Laurent Kabila. For insight into Che's experience in Africa, see Ernesto "Che" Guevara, *The African Dream: The Diaries of the Revolutionary War in the Congo* (New York: Grove Press, 1999); and Piero Gleijeses, *Conflicting Missions: Havana, Washington, and Africa, 1959-1976* (Chapel Hill: University of North Carolina Press, 2002), 101-123.
84. Breitman, *Malcolm X Speaks*, 103.
85. "Organization of Afro-American Unity," dated 15 December 1964, FBI File, OAAU [microfilm], Schomburg Center for Research in Black Culture, New York, NY.
86. "To Director of FBI from SAC-NY," dated 15 December 1964, FBI File, OAAU [microfilm], Schomburg Center for Research in Black Culture, New York, NY.
87. "A Revolutionary Pays Call," *National Guardian*, 9 January 1965, 12; "Tanzania Asserts Tshombe Is Outcast," *New York Times*, 15 December 1964, 18.
88. Peter Bailey, "Sheikh Babu Speaks at OAAU Rally," *Blacklash*, 22 December 1964, 4.
89. A. M. Babu, "Memoirs: An Outline," in *Babu: I Saw the Future and It Works*, ed. Haroub Othman (Dar es Salaam: E&D Limited, 2001), 17-20.
90. Babu and Wilson, *The Future That Works*, 88; Woodard, "Amiri Baraka, The Congress of African People, and Black Power Politics," 65. Also see *Death of a Prophet: The Last Days of Malcolm X*, DVD, directed by Woodie King Jr. (1981; La Crosse, WI: Echo Bridge Home Entertainment, 2006).
91. Epps, *Malcolm X: Speeches at Harvard*, 164-165.
92. Ibid., 140. While speaking at Harvard University in March 1964, Malcolm stated: "The only real solution to our problem, just as the Honorable Elijah Muhammad has taught us, is to go back to our homeland and to live among our own people and develop it so we'll have an independent nation of our own. I still believe this."
93. Shabazz, *Malcolm X by Any Means Necessary*, 145.
94. Breitman, *Malcolm X Speaks*, 101.
95. Clark, *Malcolm X: February 1965*, 53-54.
96. Ibid., 53.
97. Ibid., 55.
98. The assassination of Malcolm X can be attributed to the actions of the Nation of Islam, the Federal Bureau of Investigations, and the New York Police Department. While works such as Claude Clegg III, *An Original Man: The Life and Times of Elijah Muhammad* (New York: St. Martin's Press, 2000), 228-232; Karl Evanzz: *The Judas Factor: The Plot to Kill Malcolm X* (New York: Thunder's Mouth Press, 1992); and George Breitman, *The Assassination of Malcolm X* (New York: Pathfinder Press, 1991) are useful readings on his assassination, Marable's research on the subject is one of the best analyses out there. See Manning Marable, *Malcolm X: A Life of Reinvention* (New York: Penguin Books, 2011), 388-449.

99. Babu, "Memoirs: An Outline," 20.
100. "Kifo cha Malcolm X," *Ngrumo*, 24 February 1965, 2; translation by author.
101. "Malcolm X Is Killed in Harlem Ballroom," *Tanganyika Standard*, 23 February 1965, 1.
102. "Grieving for Malcolm," *Tanganyika Standard*, 25 February 1965, 5.

CHAPTER 2. GROWTH AND CONFLICT IN SNCC-TANZANIA RELATIONS

1. For an examination of Malcolm's visit to Kenya, where he met with SNCC members, see Howard Rudnick, "A Coincidental Cup of Kenyan Coffee: SNCC and Malcolm X Recast the Struggle in Nairobi," http://webfiles.wulib.wustl.edu/units/spec/filmandmedia/images/Rudnick_William_Miles_Prize_winner_2011.pdf.
2. Cleveland Sellars, *The River of No Return: The Autobiography of a Black Militant and the Life and Death of SNCC* (Jackson: University Press of Mississippi, 1990), 187–188.
3. Quoted in Clayborne Carson, *In Struggle: SNCC and the Black Awakening of the 1960s* (Cambridge, MA: Harvard University Press, 1995), 209–210.
4. Black Power's call for an African Diaspora consciousness was explained in more detail when Carmichael and Charles Hamilton, an African American political scientist, coauthored *Black Power: The Politics of Liberation in America*, which was published in 1967. See Stokely Carmichael and Charles V. Hamilton, *Black Power: The Politics of Liberation in America* (New York: Vintage Books, 1967), 38–39.
5. James Forman, *The Making of Black Revolutionaries* (Seattle: University of Washington Press, 1985), 481.
6. See Okwudiba Nnoli, *Self-Reliance and Foreign Policy in Tanzania: The Dynamics of Diplomacy of a New State, 1961–1971* (New York: NOK Publishers, 1978), 59–96.
7. Julius K. Nyerere, *Freedom and Socialism* (Oxford: Oxford University Press, 1968), 117.
8. Ibid., 132.
9. Julius K. Nyerere, *Freedom and Unity* (Oxford: Oxford University Press, 1968), 340–341.
10. A number of scholarly works about the impact of Ghana independence on African Americans have been published. See Ronald Walters, *Pan-Africanism in the African Diaspora: An Analysis of Modern Afrocentric Political Movements* (Detroit: Wayne State University Press, 1993); David Levering Lewis, *W.E.B. Du Bois: The Fight for Equality and the American Century, 1919-1963* (New York: Henry Holt & Co., 2000); Kevin E. Gaines, *American Africans in Ghana: Black Expatriates and the Civil Rights Era* (Chapel Hill: University of North Carolina Press, 2006); Dayo F. Gore, *Radicalism at the Crossroads: African American Women Activists in the Cold War* (New York: New York University Press, 2012); Leslie James, *George Padmore and Decolonization from Below: Pan-Africanism, the Cold War and the End of Empire* (London: Palgrave Macmillan, 2015).
11. Shirley Graham Du Bois, "What Happened in Ghana? The Inside Story," in *Freedomways Reader: Prophets in Their Own Country*, ed. Esther Cooper Jackson (Boulder, CO: Westview Press, 2000), 131.
12. "Mwalimu Slams Coups," *Nationalist*, 1 March 1966, 1.
13. Quoted in Opoku Agyeman, *Nkrumah's Ghana and East Africa: Pan-Africanism and Interstate*

Relations (London: Associated University Press, 1992), 151.

14. Between 1957 and 1966, military coups occurred in Senegal, Togo, Congo-Brazzaville, Dahomey, Algeria, Congo-Leopoldville, the Central African Republic, Upper Volta, Ghana, and Nigeria.
15. Irene and Roland Brown, "Approach to Rural Mass Poverty," in *Mwalimu: The Influence of Nyerere*, ed. Colin Legum and Geoffrey Mmari (London: James Currey, 1995), 10–13.
16. Julius K. Nyerere, *Ujamaa: Essays on Socialism* (Dar es Salaam: Oxford University Press, 1968), 11.
17. Ibid., 8.
18. Ibid., 12.
19. Chachage Chachage, "Socialist Ideology and the Reality of Tanzania" (PhD diss., Glasgow University, 2002), 350–355.
20. Nyerere, *Ujamaa: Essays on Socialism*, i–ii.
21. "The Arusha Declaration: Socialism and Self-Reliance," in Nyerere, *Freedom and Socialism*, 232.
22. Ibid., 249.
23. Ibid., 234–235.
24. Ibid., 232–233.
25. K. Matthews, "Tanzania and the United Nations," in *Foreign Policy in Tanzania, 1961-1981*, ed. K. Matthews and S. S. Mushi (Dar es Salaam: Tanzania Publishing House, 1981), 205–211.
26. *External Affairs Bulletin: An Official Recommendation of Foreign Policy of the United Republic of Tanzania* 3, no 9 (January 1967): 32–33.
27. U.N. General Assembly, *Report of the Special Committee on the Policies of Apartheid of the Government of the Republic of South Africa, 18 October 1967* (A/6864) (New York: United Nations, 1968), 48–59. Also see U.N. General Assembly, *International Conference or Seminar on Apartheid, Racial Discrimination and Colonialism in Southern Africa* (A/AC.109/236) (New York: United Nations, 1968), 4–5.
28. "U.N. Plans Parley on Bias in Africa," *New York Times*, 2 May 1967, 15.
29. "The Indivisible Struggle against Racism, Colonialism and Apartheid," in James Forman, *High Tide of Black Resistance* (Seattle: Open Hand, 1994), 101–102. This position paper was crafted by James Forman and Harold Moore with help from the African American scholar St. Clair Drake.
30. Ibid., 106.
31. See Brenda Gayle Plummer, *In Search of Power: African Americans in the Era of Decolonization, 1956-1974* (Cambridge: Cambridge University Press, 2013), 180–182.
32. "SNCC/United Nations," Reel 52, Student Nonviolent Coordinating Committee Papers [microfilm], Schomburg Center for Research in Black Culture, New York, NY [hereafter cited as SNCC Papers].
33. Forman, *The Making of Black Revolutionaries*, 487.
34. James Forman, *The Political Thought of James Forman* (Detroit: Black Star Publishing, 1970), 80.
35. Forman, *The Making of Black Revolutionaries*, 484.
36. J. Clagget Taylor, *The Political Development of Tanganyika* (Stanford, CA: Stanford University Press, 1963), 194.

37. Nyerere, *Freedom and Unity*, 238-239.
38. "An Urgent Message from New York SNCC" and "SNCC Appeals to the United Nations," Reel 51, SNCC Papers. The July statement, which was sent to African and Asian missions to the United Nations, also asked for support in charging Chase Manhattan Bank, the "pillar of the South African economy and thus of the apartheid system."
39. Ibid.
40. "A Message from Chairman H. Rap Brown," Reel 11, SNCC Papers.
41. Carson, *In Struggle*, 255-257.
42. "Judge Lets Brown Leave Jurisdiction to Make Speeches," *New York Times*, 26 August 1967, 23; "U.S. Negroes' African Allies," *Los Angeles Times*, 1 September 1967, A4.
43. "A Message from Chairman H. Rap Brown," Reel 11, SNCC Papers.
44. "Afro-American Skills Bank," Reel 51, SNCC Papers.
45. Sellars, *The River of No Return*, 184-187.
46. Plummer, *In Search of Power*, 246.
47. James Forman letter to Bobby Seale of the Black Panther Party, Box 5, Folder 2, Julian Mayfield Papers, Schomburg Center for Research in Black Culture, New York [hereafter Julian Mayfield Papers]. As SNCC was struggling to stay afloat as well as trying to expand its work to the urban ghettos, it sought to forge an alliance with the nascent Black Panther Party based out of Oakland, CA. For the BPP, its interest in the merger had largely to do with SNCC activists' organizing experience. However, this merger did not last very long as SNCC and BPP clashed over the race question, particularly concerning strategic alliance building with white liberals and progressives. Forman believed that Carmichael's black nationalist politics were to blame for the SNCC-BPP alliance eventually falling apart. See Carson, *In Struggle*, 278-286.
48. Letter from Richard Gibson to Robert F. Williams, 4 January 1969, microfilm, Reel 4, The Black Power Movement: Part 2: The Papers of Robert F. Williams, University of Michigan, Ann Arbor, MI.
49. Peniel E. Joseph, *Stokely: A Life* (New York: Basic Civitas Books, 2014, Kindle edition), 673-735.
50. Ibid., 161-162.
51. Carson, *In Struggle*, 215-228.
52. Stokely Carmichael (Kwame Ture) with Ekwueme Michael Thelwell, *Ready for Revolution: The Life and Struggles of Stokely Carmichael (Kwame Ture)* (Scribner: New York, 2005), 331.
53. In reflecting on the impact Ture and Nkrumah had on him during this visit, Carmichael wrote in his autography: "All the things I would learn from them, politics, ideology, revolution, how to organize, study, and prepare, were invaluable. But of all the things I learned from them, it is their values that most endure. The integrity of their example: the fearlessness, the selflessness, the incorruptibility, the underlying love of our people." See Carmichael (Ture) with Thelwell, *Ready for Revolution*, 332.
54. Piero Gleijeses, *Conflicting Missions: Havana, Washington, and Africa, 1959-1976* (Chapel Hill: University of North Carolina Press, 2002), 193-194.
55. Given Nyerere's views on the civil rights movement, it is highly unlikely that he granted Carmichael the permission to be trained as a guerrilla fighter in this country.
56. Examples include "'Remove Tarnish' Call to U.S.," *Tanganyika Standard*, 1 March 1963, 1; "800 Negroes Held in U.S.," *Tanganyika Standard*, 4 May 1963, 1; "Negroes Pack the

Jails," *Tanganyika Standard*, 8 May 1963, 1; "Truce Is Called—Then Negro Leaders Jailed," *Tanganyika Standard*, 10 May 1963, 1; "Segregationists Demonstrate," *Nationalist*, 30 June 1964, 6. Kiswahili-speaking newspapers also covered the civil rights leader in a similar vein. See "Ahutubia Waandishi wa habari," *Mwafrika*, 8 May 1964, 2; "'Kalamu Hii . . . ,'" *Mwafrika*, 14 July 1964, 8; "Dr. King Asifiwa Afrika Kote," *Mwafrika*, 19 October 1964, 6; "Bado Twaliia Haki Zetu," *Mwafrika*, 19 November 1964, 6; "Dr. King ni bingwa wa Amani," *Mwafrika*, 14 December 1964, 6.

57. Chachage, "Socialist Ideology and the Reality of Tanzania," 368–377.
58. Henry Bienen, *Tanzania Policy: Party Transformation and Economic Development* (Princeton, NJ: Princeton University Press, 1970), 222–223.
59. "Pressman's Commentary: The Student's Demonstration and the Imperialist World," *Nationalist*, 28 October 1966, 4.
60. "Pressman's Commentary: Black Power," *Nationalist*, 22 July 1966, 4.
61. Ibid.
62. "Americans Await the Long Hot Summer," *Tanganyika Standard*, 2 May 1967, 2; "Curfew after Negro Violence in U.S.," *Tanganyika Standard*, 13 May 1967, 5; "Racial Violence Spreads in U.S.," *Tanganyika Standard*, 16 June 1967, 1; 'Negro Crowds Ignore Plea for Calm," *Tanganyika Standard*, 21 June 1967, 1; "U.S. Race Riots Explode to Gun Battles," *Tanganyika Standard*, 12 June 1967, 1; "Black Power Leader Free on Bail," *Tanganyika Standard*, 20 September 1967, 3; "Negroes Go on the Rampage," *Tanganyika Standard*, 21 September 1967, 5.
63. "Violence in America Spreads," *Nationalist*, 1 August 1967, 1; "Black Rebellion Graver than Vietnam War," *Nationalist*, 1 August 1967, 3; "Murder, Violence in U.S.," *Nationalist*, 2 August 1967, 1; "Black Power Chief Vows to Destroy Yankee Imperialism," *Nationalist*, 4 August 1967, 2; "SNCC Chief Warns Johnson," *Nationalist*, 5 August 1967, 2; "Black Power Seeks Change to U.S. Regime," *Nationalist*, 2 September 1967, 5; "Problem of Black Man in U.S. Is to Survive," *Nationalist*, 4 September 1967, 8.
64. "Black Power Seeks Change to U.S. Regime," *Nationalist*, 2 September 1967, 5.
65. "Makeba raia Tanzania," *Ngurumo*, 27 October 1967, 3. In 1964, Makeba visited Tanzania to perform. After meeting with President Nyerere, Makeba was given a Tanzanian passport as recognition of her exiled status as a South Africa anti-apartheid freedom fighter. "President Julius K. Nyerere, one of the founding fathers of African Nationalism, greets me," she recalled in her autobiography. "He knew that I am in exile. Within an hour he gives me a Tanzanian passport. I am so happy that I weep . . . For the first time I feel that I am not only a South African native, but also a native of all of Africa." See Miriam Makeba and James Hall, *Makeba: My Story* (New York: Dutton Adult, 1988), 109–110. In the same autobiography, Makeba suggests that her romance with Carmichael began after the Tanzania visit, but Carmichael's recollections claim that it began in Guinea and blossomed in Tanzania. See Carmichael (Ture) with Thelwell, *Ready for Revolution*, 621–623.
66. Once married to Carmichael, Makeba's music was censored in the United States due to her affiliation with the Black Power leader. See Tyler Fleming, "A Marriage of Inconvenience: Miriam Makeba's Relationship with Stokely Carmichael and Her Music Career in the United States," *Journal of South African and American Studies* 17, no. 3 (2016): 312–333.
67. "Fight Call to Students by Carmichael," *Tanganyika Standard*, 4 November 1967, 3.
68. Ibid.

69. "Leaders Must Go without Luxuries," *Tanganyika Standard*, 12 November 1967, 1.
70. Christopher Liundi interview with author.
71. "Viewpoint Meets the Leader of Black Power," *Tanganyika Standard*, 5 November 1967, 4–5.
72. Ibid.
73. Ibid., 4.
74. "'Fight' Call to Students by Carmichael," *Tanganyika Standard*, 4 November 1967, 3.
75. "Black Power Leader Speaks Out," *Nationalist*, 1 November 1967, 8.
76. Ibid.
77. "On Third World Revolution," *Nationalist*, 6 November 1967, 2.
78. Ibid., 2.
79. Ibid., 3.
80. "On Third World Revolution," *Nationalist*, 6 November 1967, 2.
81. "Black Power Leader Speaks Out," *Nationalist*, 1 November 1967, 8.
82. "You Will Have to Fight," *Standard*, 1 November 1967, 1.
83. "Viewpoint Meets the Leader of Black Power," *Tanganyika Standard*, 5 November 1967, 5.
84. "On Third World Revolution," *Nationalist*, 6 November 1967, 2.
85. "Leaders Must Go without Luxuries—Carmichael," *Tanganyika Standard*, 12 November 1967.
86. Ibid.
87. Richard Gibson, "South Toms Denounce Stokely," *Liberator*, no. 12 (December 1967): 10.
88. "Free Africa Group Blasts Stokely View," *Chicago Tribune*, 5 November 1967, 12; "Africa Group Accuses Carmichael of Hatred," *New York Times*, 5 November 1967, 24; "Carmichael Denied by Africans," *Washington Post*, 5 November 1967, A28.
89. Gibson, "South Toms Denounce Stokely," 10.
90. "Letter to the Editor: Freedom Fighters," *Nationalist*, 17 November 1967, 6.
91. "Sunday News Opinion: Mr. Carmichael," *Tanganyika Standard*, 5 November 1967, 4.
92. "Carmichael Is Right," *Nationalist*, 7 November 1967, 4.
93. "Letter to the Editor: Black Power," *Nationalist*, 9 November 1967, 4.
94. "Pressman's Commentary: African Revolution," *Nationalist*, 10 November 1967, 4.
95. "Pressman's Commentary: Carmichael and Black Power," *Nationalist*, 1 December 1967, 4.
96. "Carmichael Returns to 'Hell,'" *Nationalist*, 27 November 1967, 8.
97. On October 16, Nyerere delivered a foreign policy address at a TANU conference, where he referred to the Vietnam war as the "most vicious and all enveloping war which has been known to mankind. The U.S.A. must recover from the delirium of power and return to the principles upon which her nation was founded." See *Address by the President Mwalimu Julius K. Nyerere at the Tanganyika African National Union National Conference*, 16th October 1967 (Dar es Salaam: Ministry of Information, 1968), 5–6.
98. Letter to Bobby Seale from James Forman, 21 July 1968, Julian Mayfield Papers, Box 2, Folder 2.
99. Ibid.
100. Carson, *In Struggle*, 290–295.

CHAPTER 3. WALTER RODNEY, AFRICAN STUDENTS, AND THE STRUGGLE TO DEFINE UNIVERSITY EDUCATION

1. Rupert Lewis, *Walter Rodney's Intellectual and Political Thought* (Detroit: Wayne State University Press, 1998), 13–46.
2. Ibid., 43–44.
3. Ibid., 31–39.
4. Walter Rodney, *Walter Rodney Speaks: The Making of an African Intellectual* (Trenton, NJ: Africa World Press, 1990), 19.
5. Ibid., 32–33.
6. "Need to Understand Africa," *Nationalist*, 27 September 1965, 1.
7. "African History," *Nationalist*, 28 September 1965, 4.
8. See Michael O. West, "Seeking Darkly: Guyana, Black Power, and Walter Rodney's Expulsion from Jamaica," *Small Axe* 1, no. 2 (February 2008): 93–104; Rodney, *Walter Rodney Speaks*, 74–79.
9. Andrew Ivaska, *Cultured States: Youth, Gender, and Modern Style in 1960s Dar es Salaam* (Durham, NC: Duke University, 2011), 130.
10. Ibid., 129–135.
11. "White Paper Approved," *Nationalist*, 5 October 1966, 1.
12. "Pressman's Commentary: The Students' Demonstration and the Imperialist World," *Nationalist*, 28 October 1966, 4.
13. Julius K. Nyerere, *Freedom and Socialism* (London: Oxford University Press, 1968), 179–180.
14. "Students' Protest Snubbed," *Nationalist*, 24 October 1966, 1. Less than a year later, in April 1967, he pardoned all 393 students and allowed them to re-enroll at UCD.
15. "What Is Wrong with the Hill?," *Nationalist*, 15 October 1966, 4.
16. "Reshape Education System," *Nationalist*, 29 October 1966, 4.
17. Also see Philemon A. K. Mushi, *History and Development of Education in Tanzania* (Dar es Salaam: Dar es Salaam University Press, 2009).
18. Nyerere, *Freedom and Socialism*, 271: Tanzania's prioritization of educational reform centered on ending racial and religious discrimination and expanding school. Primary school enrollments increased from 490,000 in 1961 to 825,000 in 1967, while secondary school enrollments went from 11,832 to 25,000; curricula reform: "No longer do our children simply learn British and European history."
19. Ibid., 269–278.
20. Ibid., 290.
21. Walter Rodney, "Education and Tanzanian Socialism," in *Tanzania: Revolution by Education*, ed. Idrian Resnick (Arusha, Tanzania: Longmans, 1968), 71–84, 73.
22. Rodney, "Education and Tanzanian Socialism," 83.
23. "Students' Protest Snubbed," *Nationalist*, 24 October 1966, 1.
24. George G. Hajivayanis, "Night-Shift Comrades," in *Cheche: Reminiscences of a Radical Magazine*, ed. Karim F. Hirji (Dar es Salaam: Mkuki Na Nyota, 2010), 83–98, 87.

25. Zakia H. Meghji, "Sisterly Activism," in *Cheche: Reminiscences of a Radical Magazine*, ed. Karim F. Hirji (Dar es Salaam: Mkuki Na Nyota, 2010), 77-82, 78.
26. Yoweri Museveni, "My Three Years in Tanzania," *Maji Maji*, no. 2 (July 1974): 13.
27. Yoweri Museveni, "Activism at the Hill," in *Cheche: Reminiscences of a Radical Magazine*, ed. Karim F. Hirji (Dar es Salaam: Mkuki Na Nyota, 2010), 11-16, 15.
28. Meghji, "Sisterly Activism," 78.
29. Issa G. Shivji, "Rodney and Radicalism on the Hill," *Maji Maji*, no. 43 (August 1980): 32.
30. Meghji, "Sisterly Activism," 78; Shivji, "Rodney and Radicalism on the Hill," 32.
31. Radical Films, "'Let It Burn': The Coming Destruction of America: Robert Franklin Williams Interview by Robert Carl Cohen," YouTube video, 00:29-01:39, 9 July 1968, https://www.youtube.com/watch?v=sjGVWQRCa90.
32. Hajivayanis, "Night-Shift Comrades," 87.
33. "Robert Franklin Williams and Mabel Williams Gallery: Havana Cuba 1963—Dar es Salaam Tanzania 1968," radicalfilm.com, http://radicalfilm.com/Robert_Franklin_Williams_Gallery.html.
34. "Militant Youth Protest against U.S.," *Nationalist*, 22 July 1968, 8; Robert Cohen, *Black Crusader: A Biography of Robert F. Williams* (Secaucus, NJ: Lyle Stuart, 1972), 344. While attending the demonstration, Robert Cohen, a U.S. journalist and later one of Williams's first biographers, conducted what would become over fifty hours of taped interviews with Williams.
35. Karim F. Hirji, "The Spark Is Kindled," in *Cheche: Reminiscences of a Radical Magazine*, ed. Karim F. Hirji (Dar es Salaam: Mkuki Na Nyota, 2010), 17-34, 26-27.
36. Ibid., 22.
37. Ibid.
38. Karim F. Hirji, "Tribulations of an Independent Magazine," in *Cheche: Reminiscences of a Radical Magazine*, ed. Karim F. Hirji (Dar es Salaam: Mkuki Na Nyota, 2010), 35-52, 35-37.
39. Issa G. Shivji, "The Life and Times of Babu: The Age of Liberation and Revolution," *Review of African Political Economy* 30, no. 95 (March 2003): 111.
40. Ibid., 12.
41. Hirji, "The Spark is Kindled," 20-21.
42. Meghji, "Sisterly Activism," 81.
43. Hajivayanis, "Night-Shift Comrades," 97.
44. Hirji, "The Spark is Kindled," 29.
45. Hirji, "Tribulations of an Independent Magazine," 51.
46. Hajivayanis, "Night-Shift Comrades," 92.
47. Letter to Walter Rodney from A. S. Namano, Box 5, the Walter Rodney Collection, 1960-1987, at Atlanta University Center, Robert W. Woodruff Library, Atlanta, Georgia [hereafter referred to as the Rodney Collection].
48. Hirji, "Tribulations of an Independent Magazine," 39.
49. Ibid.
50. Ibid; Hajivayanis, "Night-Shift Comrades," 92.
51. Walter Rodney, "Ideology of the African Revolution," *Nationalist*, 11 December 1969, 4-5.

Notes

52. Ibid., 5.
53. "Revolutionary Hot Air," *Nationalist*, 13 December 1969, 4.
54. Ibid.
55. "Dr. Rodney Clarifies," *Nationalist*, 17 December 1969, 4.
56. Ibid.
57. John S. Saul, *The Next Liberation Struggle: Capitalism, Socialism and Democracy in Southern Africa* (Toronto: Between the Lines, 2005), 150. In the introduction to this collection of papers, Saul reflects fondly on his time at UCD and involvement in the student movement on campus. He writes: "In the heat of debates over the theory and practices of Tanzania's vibrant and challenging radical initiatives of the time, many of us, teachers and students, expatriates and locals alike, first cut our political teeth on the question of Africa's contemporary circumstances and possible future . . . What, as expatriates, we did seek to do—alongside Tanzanians similarly inclined—was to help tease out, even reinforce, socialist possibilities from within the contradictory reality of the Tanzania of the time." See Saul, *The Next Liberation Struggle*, 8–9.
58. "Students' Front," *Nationalist*, 14 November 1970, 4; "Ban Claim by USARF," *Standard*, 13 November 1970, 4.
59. "Editorial," *Maji Maji* 1 (January 1971): 1.
60. Karim Hirji, "Militancy at the Hill," *Maji Maji* 2 (July 1971): 6-13.
61. "TANU Youth League—UDSM: TYL (University District) Memorandum on the University Crisis," 20 October 1971, Box 4, Rodney Papers.
62. Rodney, *Walter Rodney Speaks*, 35.
63. "UDSM-1970-71: Historians and Revolution," Box 9, the Rodney Collection, 1960-1987.
64. "UDSM-1970-71: Historians and Revolution (syllabus)," Box 9, the Rodney Collection.
65. "UDSM: Black Peoples in the Americas: Introduction," Box 11, the Rodney Collection.
66. "UDSM: Black Peoples in the Americas: Lecture Notes," Box 11, the Rodney Collection.
67. Ibid.
68. Ibid.
69. Rodney, *Walter Rodney Speaks*, 97.
70. Ibid., 98.
71. Meghji, "Sisterly Activism," 79.
72. Ibid.
73. Ibid., 80.
74. See Walter Rodney, *The Groundings with My Brothers* (London: Bogle L'Ouverture Publications, 1969). Also see Michael O. West, "Walter Rodney and Black Power: Jamaican Intelligence and US Diplomacy," *African Journal of Criminology and Justice Studies* 1, no. 2 (November 2005): 12-13.
75. Hirji, "The Spark Is Kindled," 18. In describing the atmosphere of the university, Hirji writes, "It is a cool breezy Friday evening. Books and notes are cast aside; high spirits permeate the air. Soothing tunes of Congolese and local bands echo in the residence towers. Reggae or Calypso enlivens a few floors. The cafeteria side is packed. Students with budgets on the low side are glued to the gossip postings in the walkway tunnel nearby. Some do their laundry; a few try to catch up on lost sleep. And more jostle in Ubongo and Mwenge—the neighborhoods nearby—

Notes

for food, fun, and dancing while others visit relatives and friends across the city... A narrow bridge connects the residential and academic areas at the Hill... only a handful of staff offices are lit. Walter Rodney types out page after page of *How Europe Underdeveloped Africa*."

76. Karim F. Hirji, "Not So Silent Struggle," in *Cheche: Reminiscences of a Radical Magazine*, ed. Karim F. Hirji (Dar es Salaam: Mkuki Na Nyota, 2010), 61; Karim Hirji interview with author.

77. Karim Hirji interview with author. He goes on to say: "So our criticism was mainly directed at pushing him more towards developing a class analysis, a more theoretical turn."

78. Cohen, *Black Crusader: A Biography of Robert F. Williams*, 335–347.

79. "The C.I.A., Black Power and Africa," *Cheche* 1, no. 3 (September 1970): 8.

80. Ibid.

81. Walter Rodney, "George Jackson: Black Revolutionary," *Maji Maji* 5 (November 1971): 4.

82. Ibid., 5.

83. Issa G. Shivji, "Book Review," *Maji Maji* 5 (November 1971): 12.

84. "Editorial," *Maji Maji* 6 (August 1972): v.

85. Christopher Liundi, "When Angela Davis Visited Our Campus," *Maji Maji*, no. 14 (February 1974): 19. Davis's trial was continuously covered in Tanzania's *Daily News* as well. See "Legal Row on Angela's Diary," *Daily News*, 27 April 1972, 2; "Angela Bought 'Killing' Gun, Claim," *Daily News*, 5 May 1972, 1; "Angela First Witness Speaks," *Daily News*, 24 May 1972, 2; "Angela's Defense Winds Up," *Daily News*, 26 May 1972, 1; "Defense Pleads for Angela," *Daily News*, 3 June 1972, 1; "All-White Jury Acquits Angela," *Daily News*, 6 June 1972, 1; "Angela Plans Major Tour," *Daily News*, 9 June 1972, 2; "Letter to Angela Davis," *Daily News*, 12 June 1972, 9; "The Kiss of Death," *Daily News*, 14 June 1972, 9; "Angela Davis' Case People's Victory," *Daily News*, 19 June 1972, 9; "To Angela Davis," *Daily News*, 20 June 1972, 9.

86. Rodney, *Walter Rodney Speaks*, 42.

87. "Statement to Vice Chancellor," *Maji Maji*, no. 2 (July 1980): 1.

CHAPTER 4. THE DRUM AND SPEAR PRESS AND THE CULTURAL POLITICS OF BOOK PUBLISHING

1. John Rachal, "Oral History with Charlie Cobb," 21 October 1996, Mississippi Oral History Program of the University of Southern Mississippi, http://digilib.usm.edu/cdm/ref/collection/coh/id/15294.

2. Ibid.

3. It was a movement connected with, but independent of, the Harlem Renaissance. Notable writers from the movement include Aimé Césaire, Léopold Sedar Senghor, and Léon-Gontan Damas. See Brent Hayes Edwards, *The Practice of Diaspora: Literature, Translation, and the Rise of Black Internationalism* (Cambridge, MA: Harvard University Press, 2003).

4. Ibid.

5. Afro-American Resources, Inc., "Social Resources and Institutional Development Projects in the Black Community," Report, F.B.I., "Drum and Spear Bookstore," September 25, 1969, Bureau File 7-0000-264.

6. Ibid.
7. See Seth Markle, "'Book Publishers for a Pan-African World': Drum and Spear Press and Tanzania's Ujamaa Ideology," *Black Scholar* 37, no. 4 (Winter 2008): 16-26.
8. Afro-American Resources, Inc., "Social Resources and Institutional Development Projects in the Black Community," Report, F.B.I., "Drum and Spear Bookstore," September 25, 1969, Bureau File 7-0000-264.
9. Jonathan J. Bean, "'Burn, Baby, Burn': Small Businesses in the Urban Riots of the 1960s," *Independent Review* 5, no. 2 (Fall 2000): 165-170.
10. In 1969 alone, over forty black-owned bookstores had been established in practically every major city in the United States. Some examples include Aquarian Spiritual Center Books in Los Angeles, House of Knowledge in Chicago, The More Books in San Francisco, Spirit House in Newark, and the United Education Center in Detroit. "List of Bookstores, 1969," Box 7, Folder 11, Hoyt Fuller Papers, Woodruff Library of the Atlanta University Center.
11. Kenneth Turan and Laton McCartney, "You Are What You Read: Sketches of Six Special Bookstores," *Washington Post*, 12 November 1972, 26.
12. Adrienne Manns, "Ghetto Book Shop Finds Untapped Literary Market," *Washington Post*, 27 August 1968: B1.
13. Stokely Carmichael (Kwame Ture) with Michael Thelwell, *Ready for Revolution: The Life and Struggles of Stokely Carmichael* (New York: Scribner, 2003), 654-658.
14. Bean, "Burn, Baby, Burn," 168-172.
15. See Nathan Wright Jr., *Black Power and Urban Unrest: Creative Possibilities* (New York: Hawthorn Books, 1967).
16. Ibid. Also see Tom Sherwood, *Dream City: Race, Power and the Decline of Washington, D.C.* (New York: Simon & Schuster, 1994).
17. Alyce C. Gullattee, "The April DC Riot in Washington DC," *Journal of the National Medical Association* 60, no. 3 (May 1968): 244-245; Ben W. Gilbert, *Ten Blocks from the White House: Anatomy of the Washington Riots of 1968* (New York: Praeger, 1968).
18. Bean, "Burn, Baby, Burn," 172-176.
19. Turan and McCartney, "You Are What You Read," 26.
20. Center for Black Education, *The Struggle for Black Education* (Washington, DC: Drum and Spear Press, 1972), 3; "City College Ends Black Study Unit," *Washington Post*, 20 September 1969, B1.
21. It is important to note that civil rights activism of the early 1960s was instrumental in the passing of the National Defense Act (1958), the Library Services Construction Act (1963), and the Elementary and Secondary School Act (1965). These acts signified major investments in education that would lead to the rise in literacy rates and enrollment in higher education among blacks.
22. Examples include Jihad Productions in Newark; Alkebu-lan Books, Edward W. Blyden Press, and The East in New York City; the Journal of Black Poetry Press, Third World Press, and Afro-American Publishing in Chicago; Broadside Press, Lotus Press, Agasha Productions, and Black Star Publishers in Detroit; Sapphire Publishing in San Francisco; and Energy Blacksouth Press in New Orleans.
23. Melba Joyce Boyd, *Wrestling with the Muse: Dudley Randall and the Broadside Press* (New York: Columbia University Press, 2003), 3-4; Donald F. Joyce, *Gatekeepers of Black Culture:*

Black-Owned Book Publishing in the United States, 1817-1981 (Westport, CT: Greenwood Press, 1983), 100-109; Bradford Chambers, "Book Publishing: A Racist Club?," *Publisher's Weekly*, 1 February 1971, 40-47; Bradford Chambers, "Why Minority Publishing? New Voices Heard." *Publisher's Weekly*, 15 March 1971, 35-50; Gerald Fraser, "Minorities Press Publishing Goals," *New York Times*, 23 March 1972, 44. Also see William L. Van Deburg, *New Day in Babylon: The Black Power Movement and American Culture, 1965-1975* (Chicago: University of Chicago Press, 1992), 253-259. White Left publishers who tended to publish black radical texts such as SWP were also targeted, although with much less hostility than toward mainstream white-owned presses.

24. Betty Medsger, "Episcopal Church Backs Grant to Black Separatist Groups," *Washington Post*, 19 February 1970, C9.

25. Letter from Locksley Edmondson to C.L.R. James, 29 May 1968, Box 2, Folder 40, CLR James Collection, Alma Jordan Library, University of the West Indies, St. Augustine, Trinidad and Tobago [hereafter cited as James Collection].

26. Drum and Spear members such as Charlie Cobb and Jimmy Garrett were hired by FCC to create a Black Studies program, only to have their efforts thwarted due to their radical politics. See "A College Beset by Black Revolutionaries," *U.S. News and World Report*, 12 May 1969, 38; "'Black Studies' at FCC," *Washington Post*, 9 March 1969, B6.

27. Box 2, Folder 307, James Collection.

28. C.L.R. James, *A History of Pan-African Revolt* (Washington, DC: Drum and Spear Press, 1969), 117.

29. Robin D. G. Kelley, "The World the Diaspora Made: CLR James and the Politics of History," in *Rethinking CLR James*, ed. Grant Farred (Cambridge, MA: Blackwell Publishers, 1996), 116-118. Also see Robin D. G. Kelley, "Introduction," in C.L.R. James, *A History of Pan-African Revolt* (Chicago: Charles H. Kerr, 1995), 1-33.

30. Marvin Holloway, "Introduction," in James, *A History of Pan-African Revolt* (1969), vii.

31. Angela Blackwell, "Review: A History of Pan African Revolt," *Black Scholar* 2, no. 7 (March 1971): 54-57.

32. Publishing *A History of Pan-African Revolt* in no way implied that the DSP ignored Third World liberation struggles outside of Africa. Its internationalist sensibilities were evident in the publication of *Enemy of the Sun: Poetry of Palestinian Resistance* (1969). This anthology, largely published through Forrester's efforts, boldly offered a pro-Palestinian perspective on the 1967 Israeli-Palestine conflict and its aftermath during a time when mainstream-media coverage unapologetically sided with Israel in its reckless treatment of Palestinians as uncivilized terrorists. Other publications by Drum and Spear Press include Center for Black Education, *The Struggle for Black Education* (Washington, DC: Drum and Spear Press, 1972); Drum and Spear Press, *The Book of African Names as told by Chief Osuntoki* (Washington, DC: Drum and Spear Press, 1970); Eloise Greenfield, *Bubbles* (Washington, DC: Drum and Spear Press, 1972); George Padmore, *The Life and Struggle of Negro Toilers* (Washington, DC: Drum and Spear Press, 1971); Edward Wilmot Blyden, *African Life and Customs* (Washington, DC: Drum and Spear Press, 1971); Dusé Muhammed Ali, *In the Land of the Pharaohs* (Washington, DC: Drum and Spear Press, 1971); Bernard Muganda, *Call Me Doctor* (Washington, DC: Drum and Spear Press, 1971); *Arusha and Beyond: Tanzania's Fight for Self-Reliance* (Washington, DC: Drum and Spear Press, 1971).

33. See Martha Biondi, *The Black Revolution on Campus* (Berkeley: University of California Press,

2012); Fabio Rojas, *From Black Power to Black Studies: How a Radical Social Movement Became an Academic Discipline* (Baltimore: Johns Hopkins University Press, 2007); Nowile M. Rooks, *White Money/Black Power: The Surprising History of African American Studies and the Crisis of Race and Higher Education* (Boston: Beacon Press, 2006); Peniel E. Joseph, ed., *The Black Power Movement: Rethinking the Civil Rights-Black Power Era* (New York: Routledge, 2006).

34. Colin A. Beckles, "Black Bookstores, Black Power, and the F.B.I.: The Case of Drum and Spear," *Western Journal of Black Studies* 20 (Summer 1996): 65-66; Markle, "Book Publishers for a Pan-African World," 19; Dera Tompkins interview with author.

35. "Drum and Spear Press," Box 8, Folder 11, Hoyt Fuller Papers, Schomburg Center for Research in Black Culture, New York, NY. DSP boasted about this expansive network to members of its advisory board. Notable advisory board members were the black poets Gwendolyn Brooks, Don L. Lee, and Sterling Brown, and black radical scholars C.L.R. James and John Henrik Clarke.

36. Markle, "Book Publishers for a Pan-African World," 19; See James Forman, *Sammy Younge, Jr.: The First Black Student to Die in the Black Liberation Movement* (Washington, DC: Open Hand Publishing, 1986), 214-216.

37. Markle, "Book Publishers for a Pan-African World," 19.

38. It should be noted, however, that black women in these cultural-nationalist organizations that openly structured their organizations along patriarchal lines fought internal sexism, particularly the practice of polygamy, and sought to push the issue of women's liberation by creating separate women's divisions. See Scott Brown, *Fighting for US: Maulana Karenga, the US Organization, and Black Cultural Nationalism* (New York: New York University Press, 2003), 62-65; Komozi Woodard, *A Nation within a Nation: Amiri Baraka (LeRoi Jones) and Black Power Politics* (Chapel Hill: University of North Carolina Press, 1999), 180-181; David Martin, "'Lift Up Yourself!' Reinterpreting Amiri Baraka (LeRoi Jones), Black Power, and the Uplift Tradition," *Journal of American History* 93, no. 1 (June 2006): 91-116.

39. Barbara Ransby, *Ella Baker and the Black Freedom Movement: A Radical Democratic Vision* (Chapel Hill: University of North Carolina Press, 2003), 291. Also see Kristen Anderson-Bricker, "'Triple Jeopardy': Black Women and the Growth of Feminist Consciousness in SNCC, 1964-1975," in *Still Lifting, Still Climbing: Contemporary African American Women's Activism*, ed. Kimberley Springer (New York: New York University Press, 1999), 70-90; Dennis L. Urban Jr., "The Women of SNCC: Struggle, Sexism and the Emergence of Feminist Consciousness, 1960-1966," *International Social Review* 77, nos. 3 & 4 (Fall 2002): 185-190.

40. Interestingly, aspects of the clothing style were influenced by Nyerere's cosmopolitan leftist fashion style of collarless safari suits and kitenge, which Nyerere had appropriated from Mao Tse-Tung of China and Nehru of India. See May Joseph, "Soul, Transnationalism, and Imaginings of Revolution: Tanzanian Ujamaa and the Politics of Enjoyment," in *Soul: Black Power, Politics, and Pleasure*, ed. Monique Guillory and Richard C. Green (New York: New York University Press, 1998), 126-133.

41. Van Deburg, *New Day in Babylon*, 197-198.

42. "Book Review: *The Book of African Names* as told by Chief Osuntoki," *Pan-African*, 2 November 1970, 3. Assata Shakur (JoAnne Chesimard), the famous Black Panther of the New York chapter who is currently in exile in Cuba, captures this sentiment of changing one's name in her popular autobiography. She writes: "The name JoAnne began to irk my nerves. I had changed a lot and moved to a different beat, felt like a different person . . . I didn't feel like no JoAnne,

or no Negro, or no amerikan. I felt like an African woman ... My life became an African life, my surroundings took on an African flavor, my spirit took on an African glow ... My mind, heart, and soul had gone back to Africa, but my name was still stranded in Europe somewhere. JoAnne was bad enough, but at least my mother had given it to me. As for Chesimard, well, I could only come to one conclusion. Somebody named Chesimard had been the slavemaster of my ex-husband's ancestors. Chesimard, like most other last names Black people use today, was derived from the massa ... I would stare up at the ceiling wondering how many black women Chesimard had raped, how many black babies he had fathered, and how many Black people he had been responsible for killing. So the name finally had to go ... My new name had to mean something really special to me ... I wanted a name that had something to do with struggle, something to do with the liberation of our people. I decided on Assata Olugbala Shakur. Assata means 'She who struggles,' Olugbala means 'Love for the people,' ... and Shakur means 'the thankful.'" Assata Shakur, *Assata: An Autobiography* (Chicago: Lawrence Hill Books, 1987), 185-186.

43. Drum and Spear Press, *The Book of African Names as Told by Chief Osuntoki* (Washington, DC: Drum and Spear Press, 1970).

44. Ibid.

45. "African Names: Beautiful," *Tri-State Defender*, 4 August 1973, 3; "African Names: Beautiful," *Chicago Defender*, 11 August 1973, 23.

46. Angela Terrell, "What's That New Thing up the Street?—It's a Black Cultural Center," *Washington Post*, 13 August 1972, M1.

47. James, *A History of Pan-African Revolt*, 131-143.

48. Charlie Cobb, "African Notebook—Black Americans in Africa: Views on Returning Home," *Black World* 21, no. 7 (May 1972): 24.

49. Lindsay Barnett, "Should Black Men Speak Kiswahili? Ask Afro Americans," *Ebony* 18, no. 18 (December 1968): 168; Adhama Oluwa Kijembe, "Swahili and Black Americans," *Negro Digest* 18, no. 9 (July 1969): 4-9.

50. Anthony Bogues, *Black Heretics, Black Prophets: Radical Political Intellectuals* (New York: Routledge, 2003), 102-105.

51. W. H. Whiteley, "Swahili: The Nationalist Language of Tanzania," in *Self-Reliant Tanzania*, ed. Knud Erik Svendsen and Merete Teisen (Dar es Salaam: Tanzania Publishing House, 1969), 111-118; C. K. Omari, "The Management of Tribal and Religious Diversity," in *Mwalimu: The Influence of Nyerere*, ed. Colin Legum and Geoffrey Nmari (Oxford: James Currey, 1995), 28-30.

52. In the late 1970s, Nyerere translated William Shakespeare's classic *Julius Caesar* in Kiswahili. The book was titled *Julius Kaizari*.

53. Bernard Muganda, *Speaking Swahili [Kusema Kiswahili]* (Washington, DC: Drum and Spear Press, 1970), vii-viii.

54. Ibid.

55. Ibid., 60-61; translation and subsequent translations by the author.

56. Ibid. Muganda used the following Kiswahili texts containing Nyerere's political writings: Julius Nyerere, *Uhuru na Maendelea* (Dar es Salaam: Government Printers, 1966); Julius Nyerere, *Elimu ya Kujitegemea* (Dar es Salaam: Government Printers, 1966); Julius Nyerere, *Ujamaa Vijini* (Dar es Salaam: Government Printers, 1967).

57. Markle, "Book Publishers for a Pan-African World," 20-21. Also see Walter Bgoya, "From

Tanzania to Kansas and Back Again," in *Claim No Easy Victories: African Liberation and American Activists over a Half Century, 1950-2000*, ed. William Minter, Gail Hovey, and Charles Cobb Jr. (Trenton, NJ: Africa World Press, 2008), 103-105.

58. Bgoya, "From Tanzania to Kansas and Back Again," 103-105.
59. Langston Hughes went on a grand tour of Africa under the auspices of the U.S. State Department. Biographer Arnold Rampersad only devotes a paragraph to Hughes's experience in Tanzania. Also see Arnold Rampersad, *The Life of Langston Hughes*, vol. 2, *1941-1967: I Dream a World* (Oxford: Oxford University Press, 2002), 406.
60. While working for Lowndes County Freedom Organization (LCFO), Lawson produced a comic book, *Mr. Black Man*. The objective of the comic book was to get people to vote. This civil rights superhero's motto was "Vote for the Black Panther and go home." She was the illustrator of the famous Black Panther image that would eventually be appropriated by the Black Panther Party founded in Oakland in 1966. Lawson also was interested in African American southern folklore and all the great stories she heard while organizing in the Deep South. Along with SNCC member Julius Lester, they published a book with illustrations done by Lawson titled *Our Folktales*. Jennifer Lawson interview with author.
61. Jennifer Lawson interview with author.
62. "Self-Reliance: Pivot of True Freedom," *Nationalist*, 2 April 1970, 6.
63. Jennifer Lawson interview with author; Charlie Cobb interview with author.
64. Charlie Cobb interview with author.
65. This is not to say that the social life was without challenges, especially for African American women expatriates who had to contend with Tanzanian cultural norms of social and sexual behavior. For example, polygamy proved to be a big issue of concern. See Ernest Dunbar, ed., *The Black Expatriates: A Study of American Negroes in Exile* (New York: Dutton, 1968), 25-38.
66. In a written document issued to all TANU government ministries and administrative bodies on January 7, 1964, Nyerere stated: "Two years ago we introduced a form of racism discrimination into the civil service. For both recruitment and promotion we gave Tanganyika citizens of African descent priority over other Tanganyika citizens. There were good reasons for this action then, which we fully explained. It was necessary to counteract the effects of past discrimination against citizens of African descent so that our civil service could develop a 'local look,' and there was also an unavoidable uncertainty about which people of non-African descent were really committed to Tanganyika. The time for this compromise with principles has now past. The reasons which were valid in 1961 are not valid in 1964." Julius Nyerere, *Freedom and Unity: A Collection of Writings and Speeches, 1952-1965* (Dar es Salaam: Oxford University Press, 1966), 258-260. Also see William R. Duggart and John R. Civille, *Tanzania and Nyerere: A Study of Nationhood* (Maryknoll, NY: Orbis Books, 1976), 81-82. Two years into independence, British expatriates occupied all officer positions above the rank of captain. See John Hatch, *Tanzania: A Profile* (New York: Praeger, 1972); William Tordoff, *Government and Politics in Tanzania: A Collection of Essays Covering the Period from September 1960-July 1966* (Nairobi: East African Publishing House, 1967), 89, 162-171. For a discussion of the interventionist role of British armed forces in the mutiny, see Tony Laurence and Christopher MacRae, *The Dar Mutiny of 1964, and the Armed Intervention That Ended It* (Sussex, England: Book Guild Publishing, 2007); "Africanize 'in Orderly Fashion,'" *Standard*, 9 August 1962, 5; "C.L.A. Warned on Africanization," *Standard*, 13 June 1963, 1; "Inducement Pay Must Not Be Stopped," *Standard*, 19 May 1960, 3.

67. "Renting Expatriate Skills until Trained Tanzanians Can Be Brought Forward," *Annual Manpower Report to President, 1969*, submitted by Manpower Planning Division of the Ministry of Economic Affairs (Dar es Salaam, 1969), East African Archives, University of Dar es Salaam Library, University of Dar es Salaam, Dar es Salaam, Tanzania.
68. "Our Black Brothers in 'Babylon,'" *Nationalist*, 18 January 1972, 5.
69. "Printed from *The Nationalist*, 1967—A Tanzania Newspaper," Box 1, Folder 4, Pan African Skills Project, 1970-1981, Schomburg Center for Research in Black Culture, New York, NY [hereafter cited as the PASP Collection].
70. They were also referred to as "WaAfro" in reference to the dominant hairstyles of African American expatriates, and the less popular "WaNegro."
71. "King's Assassination," *Nationalist*, 6 April 1968, 4. Also see "Dr. Martin Luther King Murdered," *Nationalist*, 6 April 1968, 1.
72. "World Mourns," *Nationalist*, 6 April 1968, 1.
73. Andrew M. Ivaska, "Of Students, 'Nizers,' and the Struggle over Youth: Tanzania's 1966 National Service Crisis," *Africa Today* 51, no. 3 (Spring 2005): 68-83.
74. "Soul Digging," *Nationalist*, 15 November 1969, 4.
75. "The Soulless Souls," *Nationalist*, 22 November 1969, 4.
76. For a discussion of soul music, see Monique Guillory and Richard C. Green, eds., *Soul: Black Power, Politics, and Pleasure* (New York: New York University Press, 1998); Gayle Wald, *It's Been Beautiful: Soul! and Black Power Television* (Durham, NC: Duke University Press Books, 2015); Tanisha Ford, *Liberated Threads: Black Women, Style, and the Global Politics of Soul* (Chapel Hill: University of North Carolina Press, 2015).
77. "Black Is Beautiful," *Nationalist*, 28 January 1969, 4. Also see Charlene Mitchell and Michael Myerson, "Africa's Impact on Black America," *African Communist* 43 (1970): 100-111.
78. J. K. Obatala, "U.S. 'Soul' Music in Africa," *African Communist* 41 (1970): 82; J. K. Obatala, "Soul Music in Africa: Has Charlie Got a Brand New Bag?," *Black Scholar* 2, no. 6 (February 1971): 8-12.
79. Charlie Cobb interview with author.
80. "Imperialist Intelligence Services," *Nationalist*, 15 January 1969, 4. Also see A. M. Babu, "Pressman's Commentary: 'Exposure' of CIA," *Nationalist*, 6 May 1966, 4.
81. "The C.I.A., Black Power and Africa," *Cheche*, no. 3 (September 1970): 8-9. This debate dated back to the immediate years of independence as critics took aim at the U.S. Peace Corps volunteer initiative sponsored by the U.S. State Department. See "C.I.A. Warned on Africanization," *Standard*, 13 June 1963, 1.
82. Idrian N. Resnick, *The Long Transition: Building Socialism in Tanzania* (New York: Monthly Review Press, 1981), 112.
83. John Nottingham, "Establishing an African Publishing Industry: A Study in Decolonization," *African Affairs* 68, no. 271 (April 1969): 139-140.
84. Nyerere, *Freedom and Socialism*, 108.
85. "Book Famine Hits Our Cause," *Daily News*, 30 April 1972, 9.
86. Walter Bgoya, *Books and Reading in Tanzania* (Paris: UNESCO, 1987), 39-41.
87. "Swahili Novel Competition," *Nationalist*, 3 January 1970, 8; "New Books in Dar Bookshops,"

Nationalist, 23 February 1970, 4; "Adult Education and Libraries in Tanzania," *Nationalist*, 12 April 1970, 4; "A History of African Literature," *Nationalist*, 5 May 1970, 4; "Tanganyika Library Services," *Nationalist*, 26 May 1970, 3; "Reading Habit," *Nationalist*, 8 August 1970, 4; "International Day of Literacy," *Nationalist*, 8 September 1970, 4; "Step Up Campaign against Illiteracy Plea," *Nationalist*, 8 September 1970, 8; "Dar to Have Government Bookshop," *Nationalist*, 26 September 1970, 8; "Library Service for Peasants," *Nationalist*, 28 September 1970, 4; "Tanzania Fighting Illiteracy," *Nationalist*, 4 December 1970, 4; "EAPH: The Institution That Preserves Our Culture," *Nationalist*, 7 December 1970, 3; "Libraries on Wheels Serve Villages," *Daily News*, 12 June 1972, 4; "Printpak: Quality in Trademark," *Daily News*, 15 June 1972, 12. Other institutions, such as the Institute of Swahili Research, the Inter-territorial Language Committee, and the Ministry of National Education, Community Development, and National Culture played key roles as well in promoting Kiswahili books education in the country.

88. Bgoya, *Books and Reading in Tanzania*, 39–41.
89. "Afro-American Resources, Minutes of Meeting, 1971," Courtland Cox Papers, in possession of author [hereafter cited as Cox Papers].
90. Nancy J. Schmidt, "Children's Literature about Africa: A Reassessment," *African Studies Review* 3, no. 3 (December 1970): 477.
91. Bgoya, *Books and Reading in Tanzania*, 16–22.
92. "What to Teach African Children," *Nationalist*, 1 March 1969, 3; "Your Children and the Library," *Nationalist*, 22 November 1969, 3.
93. "Nyerere Urges Tanzanians to Regain Pride in Heritage," *Muhammad Speaks*, 2 August 1968, 22.
94. Rochelle Cortez, "Books for the Young," *Black Books Bulletin* 1, no. 4 (1973): 36.
95. Drum and Spear Press, *Children of Africa: A Coloring Book* (Chicago: Third World Press, 1993), 17.
96. Ibid., ii.
97. Ibid., 8, 10, 12.
98. I have yet to find a copy of the Kiswahili version of *Children of Africa* for critical analysis.
99. Bgoya, who was working at the Tanzania embassy in Peking between 1970 and 1972, was among a number of leftist TANU members who were either sacked or demoted from positions in various ministries as a result of a series of government reshuffling initiatives. See William Tordoff and Ali A. Mazrui, "The Left and the Super-Left in Tanzania," *Journal of Modern African Studies* 10, no. 3 (October 1972): 427–445.
100. The other four were the Ministry of Education, Dar es Salaam University Press, Tanzania Library Services, and East African Publications.
101. "The Challenge Facing Publishers," *Daily News*, 28 May 1972, 9.
102. Walter Bgoya, "Walter Rodney," *UDSM Newsletter* 4, nos. 3 & 4 (September 2005): 4–5.
103. Robert Hutchinson, "Neo-colonial Tactics: Macmillans and the Tanzania Publishing House," in *African Socialism in Practice: The Tanzanian Experience*, ed. Andrew Cohen (Nottingham, UK: Spokesman, 1979), 228–236.
104. Shivji's *Class Struggles in Tanzania* was both an outgrowth and response to his critics over his first work, *Tanzania: The Silent Class Struggle*, which first appeared in the University of Dar es

Salaam's radical student journal, *Maji Maji*. This latter work in particular would spark a critical debate among African Marxists over the nature of imperialism and class struggle in Africa. For insight into this rich debate, see the following publications, some of which were published by Tanzania Publishing House: Lionel Cliffe and John S. Saul, eds., *Socialism in Tanzania: An Interdisciplinary Reader*, vol. 2, *Policies* (Nairobi: East Africa Publishing House, 1973), 331–358; Yash Tandon, ed., *University of Dar es Salaam Debate on Class, State and Imperialism* (Dar es Salaam: Tanzania Publishing House, 1982); Dan Nabudere, *The Political Economy of Imperialism: Its Theoretical and Polemical Treatment from Mercantilist to Multilateral Imperialism* (Dar es Salaam: Tanzania Publishing House, 1977); Abdulrahman Mohamed Babu's *African Socialism or Socialist Africa* (Dar es Salaam: Tanzania Publishing House, 1981).

105. "Bourgeois Books: A Major Contradiction," *Daily News*, 15 May 1974, 5. Freddy Macha had cause for concern. From 1971 to 1974, Tanzania imported an estimated 122,517 books from the United States. See Bgoya, "The Problems of Bourgeois Books," *Daily News*, 22 May 1974, 5; "Letter to the Editor: Library," *Daily News*, 15 May 1974, 5; "More Swahili Books Needed to Fill Vacuum, Says Mwinyi," *Daily News*, 11 July 1974, 3. Also see Edwina Oluwasanmi, Eva McLean, and Hans Zell, eds., *Publishing in Africa in the Seventies: Proceedings of an International Conference on Publishing and Book Development Held at the University of Ife, Ile-Ife, Nigeria, 16–20 December 1973* (Ile-Ife, Nigeria: University of Ife Press, 1975), 1–16.

106. Walter Bgoya, *Books and Reading in Tanzania* (Paris: UNESCO, 1985), 42.

107. Minutes of the Afro-American Resources, Inc. meeting, 1971–1972, Cox Papers.

108. Ibid.

109. Ibid.

110. Ibid.

111. Ibid.

112. Ibid. It is instructive to note that Cobb tempered his criticism of Nyerere, however, by claiming that Nyerere was "under a fantastic amount of pressure."

113. Ibid.

114. Ibid.

115. Joyce, *Gatekeepers of Black Culture*, 109; "Black Book Publishers," *Black Enterprise* 3, no. 2 (September 1972): 39–42; John A. Williams, "Black Publisher, Black Writer: An Impasse," *Black World* 26, no. 5 (March 1975): 28–31; Dudley Randall, "Black Publisher, Black Writer: An Answer," *Black World* 26, no. 5 (March 1975): 32–37; Sheila Smith-Hobson, "Black Book Publishing: Protest, Pride, and Little Profit," *Black Enterprise* 8, no. 10 (May 1978): 39–41.

116. Beckles, "Black Bookstores, Black Power, and the F.B.I," 67–70.

117. See Ben W. Gilbert, *Ten Blocks from the White House: Anatomy of the Washington Riots of 1968* (New York: Praeger, 1968).

CHAPTER 5. CONVERGENCE AND REJECTION AT THE SIXTH PAN-AFRICAN CONGRESS

1. Vincent B. Thompson, *Africa and Unity: The Evolution of Pan-Africanism* (London: Longmans, Green and Co., 1969), 119–221; George Padmore, *Pan-Africanism or Communism* (Garden City,

NY: Anchor Books, 1972), 130–267.

2. Ronald Walters, *Pan-Africanism in the African Diaspora: An Analysis of Modern Afrocentric Political Movements* (Detroit: Wayne State University Press, 1993), 81.

3. Walters, *Pan-Africanism in the African Diaspora*, 76. For a thorough historical analysis of Black Power politics in Bermuda, see Quito Swan, *Black Power in Bermuda: The Struggle for Decolonization* (New York: Palgrave, 2009).

4. Grace Lee Boggs, "C.L.R. James: Organizing in the USA, 1938–1953," in *C.LR. James: His Intellectual Legacies*, ed. Selwyn R. Cudjoe and William E. Cain (Amherst: University of Massachusetts Press, 1995), 163–172; Kent Worcester, *C.L.R. James: A Political Biography* (Albany: State University of New York Press, 1996), 55–116.

5. For analyses on James's views on the Black Power movement, also see "The Black Scholar Interviews CLR James," *Black Scholar* 2, no. 1 (September 1970): 35–43; Glen Richards, "C.L.R. James on Black Self-Determination in the United States and the Caribbean," in *C.L.R. James*, ed. Cudjoe and Cain, 317–327.

6. Patrick Griffith, "An Interview: C.L.R. James and Pan-Africanism," *Black World* 21, no. 1 (November 1971): 5.

7. The Black Power movement and its relationship to education activism is critically examined in Russell Rickford, *We Are an African People: Independent Education, Black Power, and the Radical Imagination* (Oxford: Oxford University Press, 2016).

8. "The Center for Black Education, 1971–72," Cox Papers.

9. "The Center For Black Education, 1971–1972: Structure: '71–'72," Cox Papers.

10. James Garrett, "A Historical Sketch: The Sixth Pan African Congress," *Black World* 26, no. 5 (March 1975): 15. Cox ultimately replaced his cousin Winston Wiltshire, who assumed an unofficial secretary general role after Roosevelt Browne faded into the background by 1970–1971. Garrett notes that very few wanted the responsibilities of being secretary general, and therefore it was a position that Cox reluctantly agreed to hold since nobody else wanted it.

11. For an insightful examination of Black Power organizing in Alabama from the mid to late 1960s, especially the formation of the Lowndes County Freedom Organization and role of Courtland Cox and other SNCC activists, see Hassan Jeffries, *Bloody Lowndes: Civil Rights and Black Power in Alabama's Black Belt* (New York: New York University Press, 2009).

12. "The Center for Black Education, 1971–1972: Structure '71–'72," Cox Papers.

13. Charlie Cobb was initially involved in planning, but later withdrew from helping to organize the congress.

14. "Official Draft: The Sixth Pan African Congress," p. 5, Cox Papers.

15. Barry Munslow, *Mozambique: The Revolution and Its Origins* (New York: Longman, 1983); Thomas H. Henriksen, *Revolution and Counterrevolution: Mozambique's War of Independence, 1964–1974* (Westport, CT: Greenwood Press, 1983).

16. Basil Davidson, *In the Eye of the Storm: Angola's People* (New York: Doubleday, 1973); John Marcum, *The Angolan Revolution*, vol. 2, *Exile Politics and Guerilla Warfare, 1962–1976* (Cambridge, MA: MIT Press, 1978); Stewart Lloyd-Jones and Antonio Costa Pinto, eds., *The Lasting Empire: Thirty Years of Portuguese Decolonization* (Portland, OR: Intellect Books, 2003); Norma Kriger, *Zimbabwe's Guerrilla War: Peasant Voices* (New York: Cambridge University Press, 1992); Eliakim M. Sibanda, *The Zimbabwe African People's Union, 1961–1987: A Political History of Insurgency in Rhodesia* (Trenton, NJ: Africa World Press, 2005); Terrence O.

Ranger, *Peasant Consciousness and Guerrilla War in Zimbabwe: A Comparative Study* (Berkeley: University of California Press, 1985).

17. Stephen Ellis, *Comrades against Apartheid: The ANC and the South African Communist Party in Exile* (Bloomington: Indiana University Press, 1992); Heidi Holland, *Struggle: The History of the African National Congress* (New York: G. Braziller, 1990); Gail Gerhart, *Black Power in South Africa: The Evolution of an Ideology* (Berkeley: University of California Press, 1992); Rocky Williams, "The Other Armies: A Brief Historical Overview of Umkhonto We Sizwe (MK), 1961-1994," *Military History Journal* 11, no. 5 (June 2000): 173-185; David Soggot, *Namibia: The Violent Heritage* (New York: St. Martin's Press, 1988); Colin Leys and John S. Saul, eds., *Namibia's Liberation Struggle: The Two-Edged Sword* (Athens: Ohio University Press, 1995).

18. William Bundy, *A Tangled Web: The Making of Foreign Policy in the Nixon Presidency* (New York: Hill and Wang, 1998); Seymour Hersh, *The Price of Power: Kissinger in the Nixon White House* (New York: Summit Books, 1983); Gerald Horne, *From the Barrel of a Gun: The United States and the War against Zimbabwe* (Chapel Hill: University of North Carolina Press, 2001); Anthony Lake, *The "Tar Baby" Option: American Policy toward Southern Rhodesia* (New York: Columbia University Press, 1976); René Lemarchand, ed., *American Policy in Southern Africa: The Stakes and the Stance* (Washington, DC: University Press of America, 1978).

19. "Official Draft: The Sixth Pan-African Congress," p. 4, Cox Papers.

20. "Background," 1972, Cox Papers.

21. "Official Draft: The Sixth Pan African Congress," p. 5, Cox Papers.

22. Ibid., 5-6.

23. Held March 10-12, 1972, close to seven thousand African Americans, representing a host of organizations across the political spectrum, converged on Gary, Indiana, for this historic conference. While three days of discussion did little to bridge the ideological gap between black liberals, moderates, and radicals, participants were able to craft an internationalist agenda that prioritized the support of liberation movements in Africa. For a substantive critique of some of the failures of this convention, see Cedric Johnson, *Revolutionaries to Race Leaders: Black Power and the Making of African American Politics* (Minneapolis: University of Minnesota Press, 2007), 85-130.

24. Komozi Woodard, *A Nation within a Nation: Amiri Baraka (LeRoi Jones) and Black Power Politics* (Chapel Hill: University of North Carolina Press, 1999), 162-172.

25. An estimated 30,000 people showed up for ALD in Washington, DC, which brought attention to the plight of Africans on the continent and in the diaspora. See Johnson, *Revolutionaries to Race Leaders*, 132-147.

26. Ibid., 132-172; Peniel E. Joseph, *Waiting Till the Midnight Hour: The Black Power Movement, 1955-1975* (New York: Henry Holt, 2006), 285-301.

27. "Official Draft: The Sixth Pan African Congress, 1971," p. 1, Cox Papers.

28. Ibid., 6.

29. "Internal Memorandum, 1971," Cox Papers.

30. "Official Draft: The Sixth Pan African Congress, 1971," Cox Papers.

31. "Appendix: The Call to the Sixth Pan African Congress," in *Resolutions and Selected Speeches from the Sixth Pan African Congress*, 219.

32. Ibid.

Notes

33. Ibid., 221–222.
34. "Internal Memorandum, 1971," Cox Papers.
35. In the minutes to this secretariat meeting, James went so far as to proclaim that 6PAC aimed at exposing African ruling elites, particularly "the internal relations that leads to rural people and resources being exploited in the interest of the urban areas." The Temporary Secretariat, therefore, wanted to "mobilize one section of African People and African States against others who are holding up progress of African People or moving backwards, e.g. those who are in dialogue with South Africa." See "Discussions," 1971, p. 1, Cox Papers.
36. Garrett, "A Historical Sketch," 11–12.
37. "The Sixth Pan African Congress," *Black World* 32, No. 3 (January 1974): 82; Letter from CLR James to Shirley Graham Dubois, Cox Papers.
38. Garrett, "A Historical Sketch," 11–12; "Internal Memorandum, 1971," Cox Papers.
39. After visiting Nyerere, Cox traveled to Guinea alone and met with President Touré, who agreed to support and attend the congress.
40. "Report of the Proceedings and Resolutions of the North American Region Planning Conference for the Sixth Pan African Congress Held May 11-13, 1973, Kent State University," Box 128-19, Folder 417, Dubu Gizenga Collection on Kwame Nkrumah, Moorland-Spingarn Research Center, Washington, DC [hereafter cited as Dubu Gizenga Collection].
41. "Summary of Address Delivered by Courtland Cox—Secretary General to the Sixth Pan African Congress, at the North American Region Planning Conference—May 12, 1973: Why the Sixth Pan African Congress?," 12 May 1973, Cox Papers.
42. Ibid.
43. "Report of the Proceedings and Resolutions of the North American Region Planning Conference for the Sixth Pan African Congress Held May 11-13, 1973, Kent State University," Box 128-19, Folder 417, Dubu Gizenga Collection.
44. Courtland Cox, "Monthly Report—August 1973—Secretary-General's Report," August 1973, p. 2, Cox Papers.
45. Ibid., 3.
46. Ibid.
47. "Memo to TANU: Structural and Programmatic Clarifications, etc.," 15 December 1971, Cox Papers.
48. Garrett, "A Historical Sketch," 16–17. In describing Tanzania's motivations for involvement in the congress, Garrett wrote: "We also learned that Tanzania not only wanted the Congress for historic reasons but that the Government seemed to feel that Tanzania was isolated as a progressive state in East Africa and believed that the Congress would provide enough international visibility to help break that isolation."
49. Garrett, "A Historical Sketch," 4–6. Sykes attended numerous meetings in 1971 and 1972, most notably the first meeting with black political groups in Europe in January 1972; Paul Bomani interview with author, 27 July 2004, Dar es Salaam, Tanzania.
50. Paul Bomani interview with author, 27 July 2004, Dar es Salaam, Tanzania.
51. Laura Kurtz, *Historical Dictionary of Tanzania* (London: Scarecrow Press, 1978), 24–25.
52. Voters of the Mwanza East, the local constituency Bomani represented, had grown tired of Bomani and his family's dominance in the Victoria Federation of Cooperative Unions

and thus elected a local farmer and TANU member to replace Bomani, much to Nyerere's disappointment. However, President Nyerere's intervention was a lawful act since the 1965 Interim Constitution gave him the executive power to nominate ten Tanzanian citizens to the National Assembly, regardless of whether they were elected by the majority or not. See William Tordoff, *Government and Politics in Tanzania: A Collection of Essays Covering the Period from September 1960 to July 1966* (Nairobi: East African Publishing House, 1967), 34-47.

53. *TANU Guidelines* (Dar es Salaam: Government Printer, 1971), 6.
54. "Tanzanian Envoy Asks Black Unity," Box 50, Folder 7, Vincent Harding Papers.
55. Letter from Amiri Baraka to Paul Bomani, 18 January 1973, Tanzanian Embassy Folder, Amiri Baraka Papers; Paul Bomani interview with author.
56. "On African Unity: An Interview with President Nyerere of Tanzania, The Sixth Pan African Congress, 1973," p. 2, Box 128-19, Folder 417, Dubu Gizenga Collection. This interview was reprinted and published in other black independent journals.
57. Ibid., 5.
58. Ibid., 6.
59. "Addendum: Visitation Delegation Agenda, Part I" [no date], pp. 7-8, Cox Papers. The Tanzanian state-owned newspaper, the *Daily News* (a merger between the *Nationalist* and the *Standard*, taking place in the early 1970s) also began to promote the congress as early as 1972, often giving Tanzania its due credit in making possible such a historic event.
60. "Memorandum to the Tanzanian African National Union," dated 15 December 1971, pp. 1-3, Cox Papers.
61. Garrett, "A Historical Sketch," 19.
62. It is interesting to note that both houses were located in the more affluent neighborhood in Tanzania where the white expatriates, diplomats, and government officials lived. The location of the housing did little to annoy Cox, who remembered having a daily view of sensational sunsets.
63. Edie Wilson interview with author.
64. Edie Wilson interview with author. Wilson also took part in a number of delegation visits to African countries. Most notable was her visit to Ghana and Nigeria in April 1973 to secure funding from the Ghanaian and Nigerian heads of state, Colonel Ignatius Kutu Acheamong and General Yakubu Gowan, respectively, who both happened to be African military leaders who assumed positions of state power via military coup d'état.
65. Gerri Augusto phone interview with author. *Sauti* was later censored by the Jewish owners of the radio station for their pro-Palestinian coverage.
66. Gerri Augusto phone interview with author.
67. Ibid.
68. "CLR James in a Tangle," *Nationalist* [date not provided], Cox Papers.
69. Ibid.
70. Garrett, "A Historical Sketch," 15-16.
71. Bill Sutherland and Matt Meyer, *Guns and Gandhi in Africa: Pan-African Insights on Non-Violence, Armed Liberation Struggle, and Liberation in Africa* (Trenton, NJ: Africa World Press, 2000), 216-217.

72. Brenda Gayle Plummer, *In Search of Power: African Americans in the Era of Decolonization, 1956-1974* (Cambridge: Cambridge University Press, 2013), 325.
73. Ibid.
74. Garrett, "A Historical Sketch," 19.
75. Ibid.
76. Bereket Habte Selassie, "The OAU and Regional Conflicts: Focus on the Eritrean War," *Africa Today* 35, no. 3/4 (1988): 61-67.
77. Garrett, "A Historical Sketch," 19-20.
78. Plummer, *In Search of Power*, 330.
79. Courtland Cox interview with author; Gerri Augusto interview with author.
80. Examples include the Biafran secession movement in Nigeria from 1967 to 1970, the border dispute between Ethiopia and Somalia, the intervention in gross human rights violations in Uganda during Idi Amin's rule, and communist rule in Ethiopia after Selassie was overthrown in a military coup.
81. Garrett, "A Historical Sketch," 20.
82. Also see Sylvia Hill, "Progress Report on Congress Organizing," *Black Scholar* 5, no. 7 (April 1974): 35-39.
83. Garrett, "A Historical Sketch," 20-21. In a series of correspondences, Baraka was displeased with the fact that the Temporary Secretariat was making "all the decisions" and that Cox, in particular, was not communicating effectively with CAP. See 6PAC Folder 2, Amiri Baraka Papers, Moorland-Spingarn Research Center, Howard University, Washington, DC.
84. Courtland Cox interview with author; Edie Wilson interview with author; Gerri Augusto interview with author.
85. Courtland Cox interview with author; Plummer, *In Search of Power*, 330-331.
86. "Comment," *Daily News* [no date], Cox Papers.
87. "President Mwalimu Julius K. Nyerere's Opening Speech," in *Resolutions and Selected Speeches from the Sixth Pan African Congress*, 3.
88. Ibid., 6.
89. Ibid., 7.
90. Ibid., 8.
91. Sékou Touré, "Message of President Sekou Touré," in *Resolutions and Selected Speeches from the Sixth Pan African Congress*, 15.
92. Ibid., 15-16.
93. "Sixth PAC: The Voice of Freedom Fighters," *Daily News*, 24 June 1974, 4.
94. "Africa and the Unity of African Peoples," in *Resolutions and Selected Speeches from the Sixth Pan African Congress*, 35-40.
95. "Pan Africanism Should Fight Imperialism and Racism," in *Resolutions and Selected Speeches from the Sixth Pan African Congress*, 43.
96. FRELIMO, "On the Liberation of Mozambique," in *Resolutions and Selected Speeches from the Sixth Pan African Congress*, 103.
97. ZAPU, "On the Liberation of Zimbabwe," in *Resolutions and Selected Speeches from the Sixth Pan*

African Congress, 117-118.

98. Imamu Amiri Baraka, "Revolutionary Culture and the Future of Pan African Culture," in *Resolutions and Selected Speeches from the Sixth Pan African Congress*, 175.
99. Ibid., 176.
100. Ibid., 177.
101. Owusu Saduakai, "Political and Material Support for the Liberation Movements," in *Resolutions and Selected Speeches from the Sixth Pan African Congress*, 140-141.
102. Ibid.
103. Ibid., 142-143.
104. Both Baraka and Saduakai cite Cabral's writings on revolutionary culture to support their positions on pan-Africanism, particularly from his speeches and writings that would later make up his book *Return to the Source: Selected Speeches* (New York: Monthly Review Press, 1974).
105. Lerone Bennett Jr., "Opening Remarks to Sixth Pan African Congress in Response to President's Nyerere's Address," P. Bai Akridge personal papers, in possession of author [cited hereafter as PBA Papers].
106. Plummer, *In Search of Power*, 324.
107. P. Bai Akridge interview with author; Ronald Walters interview with author; Sylvia Hill interview with author.
108. "Afros Ready to Help Probe Infiltration," *Daily News*, 17 June 1974, 1.
109. For example, the North American delegation came up against some difficulties with securing flights to Dar es Salaam due to U.S. government meddling. It was not until Nyerere intervened that those flights were secured. Sylvia Hill interview with author.
110. Walter Rodney, "Towards the 6th Pan African Congress: Aspects of the International Class Struggle in Africa, the Caribbean and America," *Maji Maji*, no. 16 (July 1974): 1.
111. Ibid., 8-12.
112. Ibid., 9.
113. "Communiqué: From the Caribbean Steering Committee Which Has Been Excluded from This Congress," PBA Papers.
114. Ibid.
115. P. Bai Akridge interview with author. In January 1974, a few months before 6PAC commenced, Akridge enrolled at the University of Wisconsin to pursue graduate degrees in political science and public administration.
116. P. Bai Akridge, "The Sixth Pan African Congress: Chaos or Community?," June 1974, 2, PBA Papers.
117. Ibid., 5.
118. P. Bai Akridge interview with author.
119. Ibid.
120. "Sixth PAC: North American Women," *Daily News*, 26 June 1974, 4.
121. Leading up to the congress, many African Americans published articles that supported the PACST initiative. See Benjamin F. Scott, "The Technology of Liberation," *Black World* 21, no. 9 (March 1972): 29-39; David Graham Du Bois, "Toward Pan-African Media Workers Unity,"

Notes

Black Scholar 5, no. 1 (September 1973): 11–14; J. Fletcher Robinson, "Self-Development in the Black World: On Science and Technology," *Black World* 23, no. 5 (March 1974): 26–31.

122. Committee on Science and Technology, "A Proposal for a Pan-African Center of Science and Technology (PACST)," PBA Papers. Other position papers that discuss science and technology include A. William Douglass, "Technology and Development of Natural Resources: An Overview"; J. D. Buliro, "An Assessment of African Scientific and Technical Skills"; Paulu Kamarakafego, "Fish Farming"; Stadi Taut, "Notes on the Air Computer"; Clarence J. Harris, "Cleaner Energy"—all in PBA Papers.

123. The committee later learned that Egypt also had its own aspirations to create and administer a science and technology center of its own; Neville Parker interview with author; Walters, *Pan-Africanism in the African Diaspora*, 80.

124. Walters, *Pan-Africanism in the African Diaspora*, 80; Ronald Walters interview with author.

125. David Lawrence Horne, "The Pan-African Congress: A Positive Assessment," *Black Scholar* 5, no. 10 (July–August 1974): 9.

126. "General Declaration of the Sixth Pan African Congress," in *Resolutions and Selected Speeches from the Sixth Pan African Congress* (Dar es Salaam: Tanzania Publishing House, 1976), 87.

127. Ibid., 88.

128. Ibid., 89.

129. Ibid.

130. Walters, *Pan-Africanism in the African Diaspora*, 80.

131. Courtland Cox, "Closing Remarks by the Secretary General," in *Resolutions and Selected Speeches from the Sixth Pan African Congress*, 217.

132. Ibid., 218.

133. Aboud Jumbe, "Closing Address by the Chairman, First Vice-President of Tanzania," in *Resolutions and Selected Speeches from the Sixth Pan African Congress*, 215–216.

134. Lawrence Still, "Falls Short in Action Policy," *Chicago Defender*, 18 July 1974, 12.

135. Earl Ofari, "Pan-African Congress Failed to Fulfill Promise of Earlier Session," *Los Angeles Times*, 26 July 1974, B7. Also see Earl Ofari, "A Critical Review of the Pan African Congress," *Black Scholar* 5, no. 10 (July–August 1974): 12–15.

136. "PAC: Towards New Heights," *Daily News*, 25 July 1974, 4.

137. Anthony Monteiro, "The Sixth Pan-African Congress: Agenda for African–Afro-American Solidarity," *Freedomways* 14 (1974): 298.

138. Ibid., 300.

139. Lerone Bennett Jr., "Pan Africanism at a Crossroads," *Ebony* 29, no. 11 (September 1974): 156. Also see Ladun Anise, "Africa: Challenge of Unfinished Revolution," *Black Scholar* 5, no. 7 (April 1975): 2–10.

140. Abdulkahir N. Said, "The Sixth Pan African Congress: Black Unity: Coming of Age in Dar-es-Salaam" [Howard University Publication], p. 11, 6PAC Folder 2, Amiri Baraka Papers.

141. Bai Kisogie, "Report from Dar: State Exhibitionists and Ideological Glamour," *Transition* 9 (October/December 1974): 9. Nigerian novelist and playwright Wole Soyinka, a stern critic of the Nigerian government, made the same comments at the congress in an interview with the Tanzanian press: "I came to see a people's gathering but observed that it was in fact nothing

but a junior league and an extension of the OAU"; "No Alternative to Socialism," *Daily News*, 14 July 1974, 5.
142. Ibid., 6.
143. Ibid., 7.
144. Haki R. Madhubuti, "The Latest Purge: The Attack on Black Nationalism and Pan-Afrikanism by the New Left, the Sons and Daughters of the Old Left," *Black Scholar* 6, no. 1 (September 1974): 46. Also see Haki Madhubuti, "Sixth Pan-Afrikan Congress: What Is Being Done to Save the Black Race," *Black Books Bulletin* 2, no. 4 (Fall 1974): 43–56.
145. Ibid., 50.
146. Ibid., 47–49. To support his arguments, Madhubuti used the works of black vindicationist scholars such as Chancellor Williams, Cheikh A. Diop, John Henrik Clarke, Yosef ben-Jochannan, and Leo Hansberry, whose works on ancient Africa had gained currency during this period.
147. Ibid., 54.
148. Imamu Amiri Baraka, "Some Questions about the Sixth Pan-African Congress," *Black Scholar* 6, no. 2 (October 1974): 46. Also see Amiri Baraka, "Toward Ideological Clarity," *Black World* 24, no. 1 (November 1974): 24–40.
149. Ibid., 43. Ron Walters, a Howard University professor who played an organizing role in the North American delegation, found little fault with Madhubuti's arguments, but refused to go as far as to claim that black activists' turn to Marxism was a reflection of their desires to be white. See Ronald Walters, "A Response to Haki Madhubuti," *Black Scholar* 6, no. 4 (October 1974): 47–53. Coming to the defense of Madhubuti was cultural-nationalist and Black Arts advocate Kalamu Ya Salaam, who took issue with President Touré's opening remarks about narrow skin-color politics. He wrote: "Blackness for us means more than skin color. Blackness means color, culture and consciousness. By color we mean the race, not a shade or specific hue." See Kalamu Ya Salaam, "A Response to Haki Madhubuti," *Black Scholar* 6, no. 5 (January–February 1975): 41–42. Mark Smith, an ALD organizer and member of the ALSC came to Baraka's defense, arguing that the "class struggle is the fundamental element in the world today," that not all whites are innately racist, and that embracing Marxism-Leninism does not mean one has become a victim of European brainwashing; Mark Smith, "A Response to Haki Madhubuti," *Black Scholar* 6, no. 5 (January–February 1975): 44–52. Also see Ron Maulana Karenga, "Which Road: Nationalism, Pan-Africanism, Socialism?," *Black Scholar* 6, no. 2 (October 1974): 21–29.
150. Garrett, "A Historical Sketch," 20.
151. Sutherland and Meyer, *Guns and Gandhi in Africa*, 220–221.
152. David L. Horne, "The Pan-African Congress: A Positive Assessment," *Black Scholar* 5, no. 10 (July–August 1974): 10. During the organizing phase, Black Power activists clearly hoped a Permanent Secretariat would be institutionalized at the conference. It would be based somewhere in Africa and assigned the task of carrying out congress resolutions.
153. "Sixth PAC: North American Women," *Daily News*, 26 June 1974, 4.
154. P. Bai Akridge interview with author.
155. See Winston Grady-Willis, *Challenging US Apartheid: Atlanta and Black Struggles for Human Rights* (Durham, NC: Duke University Press, 2005); David Hostetter, *Movement Matters: American Antiapartheid Activism and the Rise of Multicultural Politics* (New York: Routledge, 2005); William Minter, Gail Hovey, and Charles Cobb Jr., eds., *No Easy Victories: African*

Liberation and American Activists over a Half Century, 1950-2000 (Trenton, NJ: Africa World Press, 2008), 113-216.

156. Alma Robinson, "A Meeting with Nyerere," pp. 18-19, Box 128-19, Folder 217, Dubu Gizenga Collection.
157. Neville Parker interview with author.
158. Gerri Augusto phone interview with author.
159. Edie Wilson interview with author.
160. Courtland Cox interview with author.
161. Joseph, *Waiting Till the Midnight Hour*, 296-304.

CONCLUSION

1. Just as Drum and Spear Press tended to act beyond its own financial means, PASP leaders' expansive vision reflected the sense of urgency that made Black Power activists ignore such limitations. With expansion, limited operational funds, and Davis devoting more time to other PASP-related projects in other African nations and the newly formed Patrice Lumumba Coalition based in Harlem, PASP in Tanzania fell into stagnation after 1974. Another contributing factor to PASP's decline was Davis's declining health, for he never fully recovered from his car accident in Dar es Salaam. The injuries sustained in the accident are said to have contributed to his death in 1980, which marked the end of the Pan-African Skills Project. See "Financial Chart for PASP," July 1, 1973-July 1, 1974, Box 1, Folder 6, PASP Collection.
2. For example, see Göran Hydén, *Beyond Ujamaa in Tanzania: Underdevelopment and an Uncaptured Peasantry* (Berkeley: University of California Press, 1980); Yash Tandon, ed., *University of Dar es Salaam Debate on Class, State and Imperialism* (Dar es Salaam: Tanzania Publishing House, 1982); Horace Campbell, *Tanzania and the IMF: The Dynamics of Liberalization* (Boulder, CO: Westview Press, 1992); Bonny Ibhawoh and J. I. Dibua, "Deconstructing Ujamaa: The Legacy of Julius Nyerere in the Quest for Social and Economic Development in Africa," *African Journal of Political Science* 8, no. 1 (2003): 64-70; Michael Jennings, *Surrogates of the State: NGOs, Development and Ujamaa in Tanzania* (Bloomfield, CT: Kumarian Press, 2008); Ralph Ibbott, *Ujamaa—The Hidden Story of Tanzania's Socialist Villages* (Watsonville, CA: Crossroads Books, 2014); Priya Lal, *African Socialism in Postcolonial Tanzania: Between the Village and the World* (Cambridge: Cambridge University Press, 2015).
3. After the Sixth Pan-African Congress, Sutherland remained in Tanzania for the next twenty plus years. In 1974, he joined the international staff of the American Friends Service Committee (AFSC), a Quaker-based nonviolent organization.
4. Quoted in Bill Sutherland and Matt Meyer, *Guns and Gandhi in Africa: Pan-African Insights on Non-Violence, Armed Liberation Struggle, and Liberation in Africa* (Trenton, NJ: Africa World Press, 2000), 74-75.
5. Ibid., 76-77.
6. After his presidency, Nyerere embraced the role of elder statesman. He remained the chair of the party—Chama Cha Mapinduzi (CCM), formerly TANU, and chairman of both the Intergovernmental South Center and the independent International South Commission. By the mid-1990s, he gradually withdrew from politics and retired to his ancestral village in Butiama.

In 1996, in one of his last diplomatic activities, Nyerere served as the chief mediator in the Burundi conflict.

7. International Committee of the Black Radical Congress, "Condolence Message of the International Committee of the Black Radical Congress to the Family, the Government and People of Tanzania on the Passing of Mwalimu Julius Nyerere, 19 October 1999," *World History Archives*, http://www.hartford-hwp.com/archives/30/082.html.

8. The Pan-African Skills Project continued to send skilled technicians to Tanzania and other African nations until Irving Davis's death in 1980. By the late 1970s and early 1980s, Black Power politics had given way to mainstream electoral politics and diplomacy. This era witnessed two diplomatic encounters between African Americans and Tanzania: African American activist Jesse Jackson attempted to rebuild bridges with Africa through his organization PUSH, and Andrew Young, the first African American to serve as the U.S. ambassador to the United Nations, worked with Nyerere to end white minority rule in Rhodesia. See D. Michael Cheers, "Jesse Jackson: Rebuilding Bridges to Africa," *Ebony* (December 1986): 132-140; Andrew J. DeRoche, *Andrew Young: Civil Rights Ambassador* (Lanham, MD: S. R. Books, 2003), 83-85, 97.

9. For more information on the work of UAACC, go to http://www.uaacc.habari.co.tz. Two documentary films have been produced about the O'Neals and their experience in Tanzania. See *A Panther in Africa*, DVD, directed by Aaron Matthews (New York: PBS/POV, 2004); *Mama C: Urban Warrior in the African Bush*, directed by Joanne Hershfield (Blooming Grove, NY: New Day Films, 2013). Also, for an excellent study of the experiences of Black Panther exiles in Tanzania, see Gaidi Faraj, "Unearthing the Underground: A Study of Radical Activism in the Black Panther Party and the Black Liberation Army" (PhD diss., University of California, Berkeley, 2007).

10. Seth M. Markle and Mejah Mbuya, "Death of a Panther: Remembering G," *Pambazuka News*, no. 534, 9 June 2011, http://www.pambazuka.org/resources/death-panther.

11. JCB, Fid Q, Dunga, Lavotsi, and Mama C, "Rest in Uhuru," YouTube video, 20 July 2011, https://youtu.be/6UWUbK2nmS0.

12. Nikki Mbishi, "Outro," *Malcolm XI*, recorded 2011; Tamaduni Muzik, 2012.

13. "Dar Tours," Afriroots Adventures, Inc., http://afriroots.co.tz/dar-tours/.

14. Agence-France Presse, "A Revolutionary Trip down Tanzania's Memory Lane," NDTV.com, 2 May 2014, http://www.ndtv.com/world-news/a-revolutionary-trip-down-tanzanias-memory-lane-559792.

15. Walter Bgoya, "From Tanzania to Kansas and Back Again," in *Claim No Easy Victories: African Liberation, and American Activists over a Half Century, 1950-2000*, ed. William Minter, Gail Hovey, and Charles Cobb Jr. (Trenton, NJ: Africa World Press, 2008), 105.

Bibliography

MANUSCRIPT SOURCES

Atlanta, Georgia

Atlanta University Center, Robert W. Woodruff Library

    Walter Rodney Collection, 1960-1987

    Hoyt Fuller Papers

Robert W. Woodruff Library, Emory University

    Vincent Harding Papers

    John O. Killens Papers

Boston, Massachusetts

Northeastern University Archives, Snell Library, Northeastern University

    Muriel S. & Otto P. Snowden Papers

Schlesinger Library, Radcliffe College

    Shirley Graham Du Bois Papers

    Maida Springer Kemp Papers

    Pauli Murray Papers

John F. Kennedy Library

    William K. Leonhart Personal Papers

Bibliography

Hartford, Connecticut

In possession of Seth M. Markle

    Courtland Cox Personal Papers

    P. Bai Akridge Personal Papers

    Oscar Kambona Personal Papers

    Jennifer Lawson Personal Papers

Trinity College

    Struggles for Freedom in Southern Africa Collection

New York, New York

Schomburg Center for Research in Black Culture

    Irving Davis/Pan-African Skills Project Collection

    St. Clair Drake Papers

    F.B.I. Files, Student Nonviolent Coordinating Committee (microfilm)

    F.B.I. Files, Organization of Afro-American Unity (microfilm)

    C.L.R. James Papers

    Julian Mayfield Papers

    Larry Neal Papers

    Malcolm X Papers

    Student Nonviolent Coordinating Committee Papers (microfilm)

    Republic of New Africa Records

    Revolutionary Action Movement Papers (microfilm)

    The Black Power Movement: Part 1: The Papers of Amiri Baraka

    The Black Power Movement: Part 2: The Papers of Robert F. Williams

    The Black Power Movement: Part 3: The Papers of the Revolutionary Action Movement

Tamiment Institute Archives, Bobst Library, New York University

    Vertical files, Student Non-Violent Coordinating Committee

    May 2nd Movement

United Nations Documents, Bobst Library, New York University

    UN General Assembly. *Report of the Special Committee on the Policies of Apartheid of the Government of the Republic of South Africa, 18 October 1967.* (A/6864). New York: United Nations, 1968.

    UN General Assembly. *International on Seminar on Apartheid, Racial Discrimination and Colonialism in Southern Africa.* (A/AC.109/236). New York: United Nations, 1968.

    Official Records of the General Assembly, 19th Session, Plenary Meetings. Verbatim Records of Meeting. Vol. 1, *1 December 1964–15 December 1964.* (A/PV.1286–1302). New York: United Nations, 1966.

C.L.R. James Institute

    C.L.R. James Papers

St. Augustine, Trinidad and Tobago

The Alma Jordan Library, University of the West Indies

    C.L.R. James Collection

Washington, DC

Moorland-Spingarn Research Center, Howard University

    Amiri Baraka Papers

    Dubu Gizenga Collection on Kwame Nkrumah

GOVERNMENT PUBLICATIONS

Dar es Salaam, Tanzania

East African Archives, University of Dar es Salaam

Ministry of Manpower Development Annual Reports (1968-1974)

Ministry of Foreign Affairs Annual Reports (1968-1974)

United States Information Services Bulletin (1966-1971)

> *Address by the President Mwalimu Julius K. Nyerere at the Tanganyika African National Union National Conference, 16th October 1967*. Dar es Salaam: Ministry of Information, 1968.
>
> Ministry of Economic Affairs and Development Planning, Manpower Planning Division. *Government Policy on Employment of Non-Citizens in Tanzania: Guidelines and Procedures to Assist Employers of Non-Citizens in Handling Their Training Requirements under the Revised Immigration Regulations*. Dar es Salaam: Manpower Planning Division, 1966.
>
> Ministry of Economic Affairs and Development Planning, Manpower Planning Division. Annual Manpower Report to President. Calendar Year 1969.

Tanzania National Archives

> TNA Accession 482. Prime Minister's Office and Second Vice President (British and Tanzanian), 1957-1967.
>
> TNA Accession 590. Policy Statements—Minister of State, President's Office.
>
> South African Development Community Research Secretariat: Hashim Mbita Project. Hashim Mbita Papers.

United States of America

Central Intelligence Agency. "Special Report: Tanzania Taking the Left Turn." 21 May 1965. Central Intelligence Agency. Https://www.cia.gov/library/readingroom/docs/DOC_0000126865.pdf.

MISCELLANEOUS ORAL HISTORIES AND INTERVIEWS

Hartford, Connecticut (in possession of author)
Cobb, Charles. Transcribed interview by Afro-American Resources, Inc., 1971.

San Francisco, California
Robert F. Williams and the Freedom Archives, eds. *Robert Williams: Self-Respect, Self-Defense, and Self-Determination, as told by Mabel Williams.* AK Press, 2005. CD.

SECONDARY SOURCES

Abrahams, R. G., ed. *Villages and the State in Modern Tanzania.* Cambridge: Center for African Studies, 1985.

Abu-Jamal, Mumia. *We Want Freedom: A Life in the Black Panther Party.* Boston: South End Press, 2004.

Adeleke, Tunde. *UnAfrican Americans: Nineteenth-Century Black Nationalists and the Civilizing Mission.* Lexington: University of Kentucky Press, 1998.

African Information Service, ed. *Return to the Source: Selected Speeches (Amilcar Cabral).* New York: Monthly Review Press, 1974.

"African Leaders Quiz." *Negro Digest* 11, no. 3 (January 1962): 82-83.

Agyeman, Opoku. *Nkrumah's Ghana and East Africa: Pan-Africanism and Interstate Relations.* London: Associated University Press, 1992.

Ahmad, Muhammad, and Max Stanford. *We Will Return in the Whirlwind: Black Radical Organizations, 1960-1975.* Chicago: Charles H. Kerr, 2007.

Akaraogun, Olu. "Is Africa Ripe for Revolution?" *Black World* 21, no. 10 (August 1972): 76-84.

———. "An Overview: The Eleventh Summit Meeting of African Heads of State." *Black World* 24, no. 1 (November 1974): 34-39.

Akoto, Kwame A. *Nationbuilding: Theory and Practice in Afrikan Centered Education.* Washington, DC: Pan Afrikan World Institute, 1992.

Alonso, Ana Maria. "The Politics of Space, Time and Substance: State Formation, Nationalism, and Ethnicity." *Annual Review of Anthropology* 23 (1994): 379-405.

Alpers, Edward, and Pierre-Michel Fontaine, eds. *Walter Rodney—Revolutionary Scholar: A Tribute.* Los Angeles: Center for Afro-American Studies and African Studies Center, University of California Press, 1982.

Aminzade, Ronald. "The Politics of Race and Nation: Citizenship and Africanization in Tanganyika." *Political Power and Social Theory* 14 (2000): 53-90.

———. *Race, Nation, and Citizenship in Post-Colonial Africa: The Case of Tanzania.* Cambridge: Cambridge University Press, 2013.

Anderson, Benedict. *Imagined Communities: Reflections on the Origin and Spread of Nationalism.*

London: Verso, 1991.

Anderson, Carol. *Eyes off the Prize: The United Nations and the African American Struggle for Human Rights, 1944-1955*. Cambridge: Cambridge University Press, 2003.

Anderson-Bricker, Kristen. "'Triple Jeopardy': Black Women and the Growth of Feminist Consciousness in SNCC, 1964-1975." In *Still Lifting, Still Climbing: Contemporary African American Women's Activism*, ed. Kimberley Springer, 70-90. New York: New York University Press, 1999.

Angelou, Maya. *All God's Children Need Traveling Shoes*. New York: Vintage, 1991.

Anise, Ladun. "Africa: Challenge of Unfinished Revolution." *Black Scholar* 5, no. 7 (April 1975): 2-10.

Amate, C. O. C. *Inside the OAU: Pan-Africanism in Practice*. London: Macmillan, 1986.

Anthony, Earl. *The Time of Furnaces: A Case Study of Black Student Revolt*. New York: Dial Press, 1971.

Appiah, Kwame Anthony. *In My Father's House: Africa in the Philosophy of Culture*. New York: Oxford University Press, 1992.

Arend, Orissa. *Showdown in Desire: The Black Panthers Take a Stand in New Orleans*. Fayetteville: University of Arkansas Press, 2009.

Arsenault, Raymond. *Freedom Riders: 1961 and the Struggle for Racial Justice*. Oxford: Oxford University Press, 2007.

Askew, Kelly. *Performing the Nation: Swahili Music and Cultural Politics in Tanzania*. Chicago: University of Chicago Press, 2002.

Atkins, Lenton. "Pan-Africanism: Self-Determination and Nation Building." *Black World* 11, no. 1 (November 1971): 23-29.

Austin, Curtis. *Up against the Wall: Violence in the Making and Unmaking of the Black Panther Party*. Fayetteville: University of Arkansas Press, 2006.

Austin, David. "Introduction to Walter Rodney." *Small Axe* 5, no. 2 (September 2001): 60-65.

———, ed. *You Don't Play with Revolution: The Montreal Lectures of C.L.R. James*. Oakland, CA: AK Press, 2009.

Babu, Abdulrahman Mohamed. *African Socialism or Socialist Africa?* Dar es Salaam: Tanzania Publishing House, 1981.

———. "Memoirs: An Outline." In *Babu: I Saw the Future and It Works*, ed. Haroub Othman. Dar es Salaam: E&D Limited, 2001.

Babu, Salma, and Amrit Wilson, eds. *The Future That Works: Selected Writings of A.M. Babu*. Trenton, NJ: Africa World Press, 2002.

Baldwin, James. *The Fire Next Time*. New York: Vintage Books, 1963.

Bambara, Toni Cade. *The Black Woman: An Anthology*. New York: Signet, 1970.

Baraka, Amiri. *The Autobiography of LeRoi Jones*. Chicago: Lawrence Hill Books, 1997.

———. "Black 'Revolutionary' Poets Should Also Be Playwrights." *Black World* 21, no. 6 (April 1972): 4-6.

———. "Some Questions about the Sixth Pan-African Congress." *Black Scholar* 6, no. 2 (October 1974): 42-46.

———. "Tanzania Independence Celebration." *Black World* 11, no. 5 (March 1972): 65-67.

———. "Toward Ideological Clarity." *Black World* 24, no. 1 (November 1974): 24-40.

Barbour, Floyd, ed. *The Black Power Revolt*. Boston: Extending Horizons Books, 1968.

Barkan, Joel. *An African Dilemma: University Students, Development and Politics in Ghana, Tanzania and Uganda*. Nairobi: Oxford University Press, 1975.

Barrett, Lindsay. "Should Black Americans Be Involved in African Affairs?" *Negro Digest* 18, no. 10 (August 1969): 10-17.

Bayart, Jean-François. *The State in Africa: The Politics of the Belly*. London: Longman, 1993.

Bean, Jonathan J. "'Burn, Baby, Burn': Small Businesses in the Urban Riots of the 1960s." *Independent Review* 5, no. 2 (Fall 2000): 165-170.

Beckles, Colin A. "Black Bookstores, Black Power, and the F.B.I.: The Case of Drum and Spear." *Western Journal of Black Studies* 20 (Summer 1996): 63-70.

Bedasse, Monique. "To Set up Jah Kingdom: Joshua Mkhululi, Rastafarian Repatriation, and the Black Radical Network in Tanzania." *Journal of African Religions* 1, no. 3 (2013): 293-323.

Behnken, Brian D. *Civil Rights and Beyond: African American and Latino/a Activism in the Twentieth-Century United States*. Athens: University of Georgia Press, 2016.

Bennett, Lerone, Jr. *Before the Mayflower: A History of the Negro in America, 1619-1964*. Penguin Books, 1984.

———. "Black Power." *Ebony* 21, no. 6 (November 1965): 28-29.

———. "Report by Lerone Bennett: Pan-Africanism at a Crossroads." *Ebony* 29, no. 11 (September 1974): 148-160.

———. "Seeks to End Racial Movements." *Jet* (August 1974): 45-48.

Beole van Hensbroek, Pieter. *Political Discourses in African Thought, 1860 to the Present*. Westport, CT: Praeger, 1999.

Bertz, Ned. *Diaspora and Nation in the Indian Ocean: Transnational Histories of Race and Urban Space in Tanzania*. Honolulu: University of Hawaii Press, 2015.

Bgoya, Walter. *Books and Reading in Tanzania*. Paris: UNESCO, 1987.

———. "From Tanzania to Kansas and Back Again." In *Claim No Easy Victories: African Liberation and American Activists over a Half Century, 1950-2000*, ed. William Minter, Gail Hovey, and Charles Cobb Jr. Trenton, NJ: Africa World Press, 2008.

———. "Walter Rodney." *UDSM Newsletter* 4, no. 3/4 (September 2005): 4-5.

Bienen, Henry. *Tanzania Policy: Party Transformation and Economic Development*. Princeton, NJ: Princeton University Press, 1970.

Biondi, Martha. *The Black Revolution on Campus*. Berkeley: University of California Press, 2012.

"Black Book Publishers." *Black Enterprise* 3, no. 2 (September 1972): 39-42.

"Black Books Bulletin Interviews Imamu Amiri Baraka." *Black Books Bulletin* 2 (Fall 1974): 33-43.

"The Black Scholar Interviews: C.L.R James." *Black Scholar* 2, no. 1 (September 1970): 35-43.

"The Black Scholar Interviews: Queen Mother Moore." *Black Scholar* 4, no. 6/7 (March-April 1973): 47-55.

"The Black Scholar Interviews: Robert F. Williams." *Black Scholar* 1, no. 7 (May 1970): 2-14.

"The Black Scholar Interviews: Walter Rodney." *Black Scholar* 6, no. 3 (November 1974): 38-47.

Blackwell, Angela. "Review: A History of Pan African Revolt." *Black Scholar* 2, no. 7 (March 1971): 54-57.

Blommaert, Jan. *State Ideology and Language in Tanzania*. Edinburgh: Edinburgh University Press, 2014.

Bloom, Alexander, and Wini Breines, eds. *"Takin' It to the Streets": A Sixties Reader*. Oxford: Oxford University Press, 2015.

Bloom, Joshua, and Waldo E. Martin Jr. *Black against Empire: The History and Politics of the Black Panther Party*. Berkeley: University of California Press, 2013.

Blum, William. *The C.I.A: A Forgotten History: U.S. Global Interventions since World War 2*. London: Zed Books, 1986.

Bogart, Leo. *Premises for Propaganda: The United States Information Agency's Operating Assumptions in the Cold War*. New York: Free Press, 1976.

Bogues, Anthony. *Black Heretics, Black Prophets: Radical Political Intellectuals*. New York: Routledge, 2003.

Boone, Catherine. "The Making of a Rentier Class: Wealth Accumulation and Political Control in Senegal." *Journal of Development Studies* 26, no. 3 (1990): 425-449.

Boyd, Melba Joyce. *Wrestling with the Muse: Dudley Randall and the Broadside Press*. New York: Columbia University Press, 2003.

Bracey, John, August Meier, and Elliot Rudwick, eds. *Black Nationalism in America*. New York: Bobbs-Merrill, 1970.

———. *Black Protest from the Sixties: Articles from the New York Times*. New York: Markus Wiener, 1991.

Branch, Taylor. *At Canaan's Edge: America in the King Years, 1965-1968*. New York: Simon and Schuster, 2006.

Breitman, George, ed. *The Assassination of Malcolm X*. New York: Pathfinder Press, 1991.

———. *Malcolm X Speaks: Selected Speeches and Statements*. New York: Grove Weidenfeld, 1965.

———. *The Last Year of Malcolm X: The Evolution of a Revolutionary*. New York: Schocken Books, 1967.

Brennan, James R. "Blood Enemies: Exploitation and Urban Citizenship in the Nationalist Political Thought of Tanzania, 1958-1975." *Journal of African History* 47, no. 3 (November 2006): 389-424.

———. "Nation, Race and Urbanization in Dar es Salaam, Tanzania, 1916-1976. PhD diss., Northwestern University, 2002.

———. *Taifa: Making Nation and Race in Urban Tanzania*. Athens: Ohio University Press, 2012.

Brimmer, Andrew. "Economic Situation of Blacks in the United States." *Review of Black Political Economy* 2, no. 4 (1972): 34-54.

Brock, Lisa, Robin D. G. Kelly, and Karen Sotiropoulos, eds. "Introduction: Transnational Black Studies." *Radical History Review* 87 (Fall 2003): 1-4.

Brown, Elaine. *A Taste of Power: A Black Woman's Story*. New York: Anchor Books, 1994.

Brown, H. Rap. *Die Nigger Die! A Political Autobiography*. New York: Lawrence Hill Books, 2002.

Brown, Irene, and Roland Brown. "Approach to Rural Mass Poverty." In *Mwalimu: The Influence of Nyerere*, ed. Colin Legum and Geoffrey Mmari, 10-13. London: James Currey, 1995.

Brown, Scott. *Fighting for US: Maulana Karenga, the US Organization and Black Cultural Nationalism*. New York: New York University Press, 2003.

Buhle, Paul, ed. *C.L.R. James: His Life and Work*. London: Allison & Busby, 1986.

———. *C.L.R. James: The Artist as Revolutionary*. London: Verso, 1988.

Bundy, William. *A Tangled Web: The Making of Foreign Policy in the Nixon Presidency*. New York: Hill and Wang, 1998.

Burgess, G. Thomas. "Cinema, Bell Bottoms, and Miniskirts: Struggles over Youth and Citizenship in Revolutionary Zanzibar." *International Journal of African Historical Studies* 35, no. 2 (2002): 287–313.

———. "An Imagined Generation: Umma Youth in Nationalist Zanzibar." In *In Search of a Nation: Histories of Authority and Dissidence in Tanzania*, ed. Gregory Maddox and James L. Giblin. Oxford: James Currey, 2005.

———. *Race, Revolution, and the Struggle for Human Rights in Zanzibar: The Memoirs of Ali Sultan Issa and Seif Sharif Hamad*. Athens: Ohio University Press, 2009.

———. "Youth and the Revolution: Mobility and Discipline in Zanzibar, 1960–1980." PhD diss., Indiana University, 2001.

Burton, Andrew, and Michael Jennings, eds. *African Underclass: Urbanization, Crime, and Colonial Disorder in Dar es Salaam, 1919-1961*. Athens: Ohio University Press, 2005.

———. *The Emperor's New Clothes: Continuity and Change in East Africa, 1950–2000*. London: James Currey, 2004.

Burton, Antoinette, Augusto Espiritu, and Fanon Che Wilkins. "Introduction: The Fate of Nationalisms in the Age of Bandung." *Radical History Review* 95, no. 5 (Spring 2006): 145–148.

Bush, Roderick. "Black Internationalism and the Decline of White World Supremacy." *Sage* 30, no. 3 (2005): 5–29.

———. *We Are Not What We Seem: Black Nationalism and Class Struggle in the American Century*. New York: New York University Press, 2000.

Cabral, Amilcar. *Return to the Source: Selected Speeches*. New York: Monthly Review Press, 1974.

Cajee, Amin, and Terry Bell. *Fordsburg Fighter: The Journey of an MK Volunteer*. Muizenberg, South Africa: Cover2Cover Books, 2016.

Campbell, Horace, ed. *Pan-Africanism—The Struggle against Imperialism and Neo-colonialism: Documents of the Sixth Pan-African Congress*. Toronto: Afro-Carib Publications, 1975.

Campbell, Horace, and Howard Stein, eds. *Tanzania and the IMF: The Dynamics of Liberalization*. Boulder: CO: Westview Press, 1992.

Campbell, James T. *Middle Passages: African American Journeys to Africa, 1787-2005*. New York: Penguin Books, 2006.

Carew, Jan. *Ghosts in Our Blood: With Malcolm X in Africa, England, and the Caribbean*. Chicago: Lawrence Hill Books, 1994.

Carmichael, Stokely. *Stokely Speaks: From Black Power to Pan-Africanism*. New York: Random House, 1969.

Carmichael, Stokely, and Charles V. Hamilton. *Black Power: The Politics of Liberation*. New York: Vintage Books, 1967.

Carmichael, Stokely, (Kwame Ture), with Ekwueme Michael Thelwell. *Ready for Revolution: The Life and Struggles of Stokely Carmichael*. New York: Scribner, 2003.

Carson, Clayborne. *In Struggle: SNCC and the Black Awakening of the 1960s*. Cambridge, MA: Harvard University Press, 1995.

———. ed. *Malcolm X: The FBI File*. New York: Carroll & Graf Publishers, 1991.

Center for Black Education. *The Struggle for Black Education*. Washington, DC: Drum and Spear Press, 1972.

Chabal, Patrick. *Amilcar Cabral: Revolutionary Leadership and People's War*. Trenton, NJ: Africa World Press, 2003.

Chachage, Chachage S. L. "Socialist Ideology and the Reality of Tanzania." PhD diss., Glasgow University, 2002.

Cha-Jua, Sundiata, and Clarence Lang. "The 'Long Movement' as Vampire: Temporal and Spatial Fallacies in Recent Black Freedom Studies." *Journal of African American History* 92, no. 1 (Spring 2007): 265-288.

Chachage, Chachage, and Annar Cassam. *Africa's Liberation: The Legacy of Nyerere*. Nairobi: Pambazuka Press, 2010.

Chappel, Anne M. *Zanzibar Uhuru: Revolution, Two Women and the Challenge of Survival*. N.p.: Anne M. Chappel, 2014.

Chazan, Naomi, Robert Mortimer, John Ravenhill, and Donald Rothchild, eds. *Politics and Society in Contemporary Africa*. Boulder, CO: Lynne Rienner Publishers, 1999.

Chilcoat, George W., and Jerry A. Ligon. "'We Talk Here: This Is a School for Talking': Participatory Democracy from the Classroom out into the Community: How Discussion Was Used in the Mississippi Freedom Schools." *Curriculum Inquiry* 28, no. 2 (Summer 1968): 165-193.

Chimerah, Rocha. *Kiswahili: Past, Present, and Future Horizons*. Nairobi: Nairobi University Press, 1992.

Churchill, Ward, and Jim Vander Wall. *Agents of Repression: The FBI's Secret Wars against the Black Panther Party and the American Indian Movement*. Boston: South End Press, 1990.

Clark, Steve. *Malcolm X: February 1965; The Final Speeches*. New York: Pathfinder, 1992.

Clarke, John Henrik. "The Afro-American Image of Africa." *Black World* 23, no. 4 (February 1974): 4-21.

———, ed. *Malcolm X: The Man and His Times*. New York: Macmillan, 1969.

Cleaver, Kathleen, and George Katsiaficas, eds. *Liberation, Imagination, and the Black Panther Party: A New Look at the Panthers and Their Legacy*. New York: Routledge, 2001.

Clegg III, Claude. *An Original Man: The Life and Times of Elijah Muhammad*. New York: St. Martin's Press, 2000.

Cliffe, Lionel, and John Saul, eds. *Socialism in Tanzania: An Interdisciplinary Reader*. Vol. 2. Nairobi: East African Publishing House, 1973.

Clifford, James. *Routes: Travel and Translation in the Late Twentieth Century*. Cambridge, MA: Harvard University Press, 1997.

Cobb, Charlie. "African Notebook—Black Americans in Africa: Views on Returning Home." *Black World* 21, no. 7 (May 1972): 22-37.

———. "Containing Communism." African American Involvement in the Vietnam War. Http://www.aavw.org/special_features/pofidr_poetry_cobb.html.

———. *Furrows*. Tougaloo, MS: N.p., 1967.

———. "Nation." African American Involvement in the Vietnam War. Http://www.aavw.org/special_features/pofidr_poetry_cobb.html.

———. "Negro Rights and the American Future." *Negro Digest* 15, no. 12 (October 1966): 22, 77-79.

———. "Prospectus for a Summer Freedom School Program." *Radical Teacher*, no. 40 (Fall 1991): 37-40.

Cohen, Robert. *Black Crusader: A Biography of Robert F. Williams*. Secaucus, NJ: Lyle Stuart, 1972.

Collier, Paul, Samir Radwan, Samuel Wangwe, and Albert Wagner, eds. *Labor and Poverty in Rural Tanzania: Ujamaa and Rural Development in the United Republic of Tanzania*. Broadbridge, UK: Clarendon Press, 1986.

Collier-Thomas, Bettye, and V. P. Franklin, eds. *Sisters in Struggle: African American Women in the Civil Rights-Black Power Movement*. New York: New York University Press, 2001.

Collins, Lisa Gail, and Margo Natalie Crawford, eds. *New Thoughts on the Black Arts Movement*. New Brunswick, NJ: Rutgers University Press, 2006.

Collins, Patricia Hill. *From Black Power to Hip Hop: Racism, Nationalism, and Feminism*. Philadelphia: Temple University Press, 2006.

Condon, John C. "Nation Building and Image Building in the Tanzanian Press." *Journal of Modern African Studies* 5, no. 3 (November 1967): 335-354.

Cone, James H. *Black Theology and Black Power*. Maryknoll, NY: Orbis Books, 1997.

Cooper, Frederick. "Africa and the World Economy." *African Studies Review* 24, no. 2/3 (June-September, 1981): 1-86.

———. *Africa since 1940: The Past of the Present*. Cambridge: Cambridge University Press, 2002.

———. *Decolonization and African Society: The Labor Question in French and British Africa*. Cambridge: Cambridge University Press, 1996.

———. "Possibility and Constraint: African Independence in Historical Perspective." *Journal of African History* 49, no. 2 (July 2008): 167-197.

Cortez, Rochelle. "Books for the Young." *Black Books Bulletin* 1, no. 4 (1973).

Coulson, Andrew. *African Socialism in Practice—The Tanzanian Experience*. Nottingham, UK: Spokesman Books, 1978.

———. *Tanzania: A Political Economy*. Oxford: Clarendon Press, 1982.

Countryman, Matthew J. *Up South: Civil Rights and Black Power in Philly*. Philadelphia: University of Pennsylvania Press, 2005.

Cox, Courtland, and Gerri Stark. "An Interview with President Nyerere." *Black World* 22, no. 12 (October 1973): 4-8.

———. "Sixth Pan African Congress." *Black Scholar* 5, no. 7 (April 1974): 32-34.

Cox, Richard. "Julius Nyerere: East African Moderate." *Negro Digest* 11, no. 5 (March 1962): 31-36.

Crouch, Susan C. *Western Responses to Tanzanian Socialism, 1967-1983*. Avebury, UK: Aldershot, 1987.

Cruse, Harold. "'Black Politics' Series: The Methodology of Pan-Africanism." *Black World* 24, no. 3 (January 1975): 4-21.

———. *Rebellion or Revolution*. New York: William Morrow, 1968.

Cudjoe, Selwyn R., and William E. Cain, eds. *C.L.R. James: His Intellectual Legacies*. Amherst: University of Massachusetts Press, 1995.

Davidson, Basil. *In the Eye of the Storm: Angola's People*. New York: Doubleday, 1973.

Davies, Carole Boyce. *Left of Karl Marx: The Political Life of Black Communist Claudia Jones*. Durham,

NC: Duke University Press, 2007.

Davis, John A. "Do American Negroes Have What Africa Needs? (A Reply)" *Negro Digest* 12, no. 1 (November 1962): 75-77.

Dawson, Michael C. *Black Visions: The Roots of Contemporary African American Political Ideologies.* Chicago: University of Chicago Press, 2001.

Death of a Prophet: The Last Days of Malcolm X. DVD. Directed by Woodie King Jr. 1981. La Crosse, WI: Echo Bridge Home Entertainment, 2006.

D'Emilio, John. *Lost Prophet: The Life and Times of Bayard Rustin*. New York: Free Press, 2003.

Denoon, Donald, and Adam Kuper. "Nationalist Historians in Search of a Nation: The 'New Historiography' in Dar es Salaam." In *African Nationalism and Revolution: Colonialism and Nationalism in Africa*, ed. Gregory Maddox and Timothy Welliver, 4:329-349. New York: Garland, 1993.

DeRoche, Andrew J. *Andrew Young: Civil Rights Ambassador*. Lanham, MD: S. R. Books, 2003.

De Witte, Ludo. *The Assassination of Lumumba*. London: Verso, 2001.

Diawara, Manthia. *In Search of Africa*. Cambridge, MA: Harvard University Press, 1998.

Downs, Donald Alexander. *Cornell '69: Liberalism and the Crisis of the American University*. Ithaca, NY: Cornell University Press, 1999.

Drachler, Jacob, ed. *Black Homeland/Black Diaspora: Cross-Currents of African Relationships*. New York: Kennikat Press, 1975.

Drum and Spear Bookstore. *Catalogue 3, 1971/Drum and Spear Bookstore*. Washington, DC: Drum and Spear Press, 1971.

Drum and Spear Press. *The Book of African Names as Told by Chief Osuntoki*. Washington, DC: Drum and Spear Press, 1970.

———. *Children of Africa: A Coloring Book*. Chicago: Third World Press, 1993.

Du Bois, David Graham. "Afro-American Militants in Africa: Problems and Responsibilities." *Black World* 11, no. 4 (February 1972): 4-11.

———. "Toward Pan-African Media Workers Unity." *Black Scholar* 5, no. 1 (September 1973): 11-14.

Du Bois, Shirley Graham. "What Happened in Ghana? The Inside Story." In *Freedomways Reader: Prophets in Their Own Country*, ed. Esther Cooper Jackson, 131. Boulder, CO: Westview Press, 2000.

Dudziak, Mary L. *Cold War Civil Rights: Race and the Image of American Democracy*. Princeton, NJ: Princeton University Press, 2000.

Due, Jean M. *Costs, Returns, Repayments: Experiences of Ujamaa Villages in Tanzania, 1973-1976*. Washington, DC: University Press of America, 1980.

Dugan, William, and John R. Civille. *Tanzania and Nyerere*. Maryknoll, NY: Orbis Books, 1976.

Dunbar, Ernest, ed. *The Black Expatriates: A Study of American Negroes in Exile*. New York: Dutton, 1968.

Edmondson, Laura. *Performance and Politics in Tanzania: The Nation on Stage*. Bloomington: Indiana University Press, 2007.

Edwards, Brent Hayes. *The Practice of Diaspora: Literature, Translation, and the Rise of Black Internationalism*. Cambridge, MA: Harvard University Press, 2003.

———. "The Uses of Diaspora." *Social Text* 19, no. 1 (Spring 2001): 45-73.

Edwards, Sebastian. *Toxic Aid: Economic Collapse and Recovery in Tanzania*. Oxford: Oxford University Press, 2014.

Ellis, Stephen. *Comrades against Apartheid: The ANC and the South African Communist Party in Exile*. Bloomington: Indiana University Press, 1992.

Ellison, Julian. "Afro-American Expertise in Africa." *Africa* 52 (December 1975): 128–135.

Epps, Archie, ed. *Malcolm X: Speeches at Harvard*. New York: Paragon House, 1991.

Esedebe, P. Olisanwuche. *Pan-Africanism: The Idea and Movement, 1776–1991*. Washington, DC: Howard University Press, 1994.

Essack, Karim. *The Road to Liberation: The Pan African Path*. Dar es Salaam: Thackers, 1993.

Estes, Steve. *I Am a Man: Race, Manhood, and the Civil Rights Movement*. Chapel Hill: University of North Carolina Press, 2005.

Evanzz, Karl. *The Judas Factor: The Plot to Kill Malcolm X*. New York: Thunder's Mouth Press, 1992.

Exum, William H. *Paradoxes of Protest: Black Student Activism in a White University*. Philadelphia: Temple University Press, 1985.

Eynon, Bret. "Cast upon the Shore: Oral History and the New Scholarship on the Movement of the 1960s." *Journal of American History* 83, no. 2 (September 1996): 560–570.

Falola, Toyin, and Kwame Essien. *Pan-Africanism, and the Politics of African Citizenship and Identity*. New York: Routledge, 2013.

Falzon, Mark-Anthony. "Introduction." In *Multi-sited Ethnography: Theory, Praxis and Locality in Contemporary Research*, ed. Mark-Anthony Falzon, 1–24. London: Ashgate, 2009.

Faraj, Gaidi. "Unearthing the Underground: A Study of Radical Activism in the Black Panther Party and the Black Liberation Army." PhD diss., University of California, Berkeley, 2007.

Farred, Grant, ed. *Rethinking C.L.R. James*. Cambridge: Blackwell Publishers, 1996.

Fatton, Robert, Jr. "Clientism and Patronage in Senegal." *African Studies Review* 29, no. 4 (December 1986): 61–78.

Feirce, Milfred C. *The Pan-African Idea in the United States: African-American Interest and Interaction in West Africa*. New York: Garland Publishing, 1993.

Finney, Ron. "'We Are All Babylonians': Afro-Americans in Africa." *Black Scholar* 4, no. 5 (February 1971): 45–48.

Fleming, Tyler. "A Marriage of Inconvenience: Miriam Makeba's Relationship with Stokely Carmichael and Her Music Career in the United States." *Journal of South African and American Studies* 17, no. 3 (2016): 312–338.

Foner, Philip S., ed. *The Black Panthers Speak*. New York: De Capo Press, 1995.

Ford, Tanisha. *Liberated Threads: Black Women, Style, and the Global Politics of Soul*. Chapel Hill: University of North Carolina Press, 2015.

Forman, James. *High Tide of Black Resistance*. Seattle: Open Hand Publishing, 1994.

———. *The Making of Black Revolutionaries*. Seattle: University of Washington Press, 1985.

———. *The Political Thought of James Forman*. Detroit: Black Star Publishing, 1970.

———. *Sammy Younge, Jr.: The First Black Student to Die in the Black Liberation Movement*. Washington, DC: Open Hand Publishing, 1986.

Fouéré, Marie-Aude. *Remembering Julius Nyerere in Tanzania: History, Memory, Legacy*. Dar es Salaam:

Mkuki na Nyota Publishers, 2015.

Frazier, E. Franklin. "Do American Negroes Have What Africa Needs?" *Negro Digest* 12, no. 1 (November 1962): 62-74.

Frazier, Robeson Taj P. "The Congress of African People: Baraka, Brother Mao, and the Year 1974." *Souls* 8, no. 3 (Summer 2006): 142-159.

Freud, William M. "Class Conflict, Political Economy and the Struggle for Socialism in Tanzania." *African Affairs* 80, no. 321 (October 1981): 483-499.

Gaines, Kevin. "The African American Expatriate Community in Nkrumah's Ghana." In *Cold War Constructions: The Political Culture of United States Imperialism, 1945-1966*, ed. Christian G. Appey, 257-269. Amherst: University of Massachusetts Press, 2000.

———. "African Americans in Ghana and the Black Radical Tradition." *Souls* 1, no. 4 (Fall 1999): 64-71.

———. *American Africans in Ghana: Black Expatriates and the Civil Rights Era*. Chapel Hill: University of North Carolina Press, 2006.

———. "The Cold War and the African American Expatriate Community in Nkrumah's Ghana." In *Universities and Empires: Money and Politics in the Social Sciences during the Cold War*, ed. Christopher Simpson, 135-158. New York: New Press, 1998.

———. "Revisiting Richard Wright in Ghana: Black Radicalism and the Dialectics of Diaspora." *Social Text* 67, no. 2 (Summer 2001): 75-101.

Gallicchio, Marc. *Black Internationalism in Asia, 1885-1945: The African American Encounter with Japan and China*. Chapel Hill: University of North Carolina Press, 2000.

Garrett, James. "A Historical Sketch: The Sixth Pan African Congress." *Black World* 26, no. 5 (March 1975): 4-21.

Geiger, Susan. "Tanganyikan Nationalism as 'Women's Work': Life Histories, Collective Biography and Changing Historiography." *Journal of African History* 37, no. 3 (1996): 464-478.

———. *TANU Women: Gender and Culture in the Making of Tanganyikan Nationalism, 1955-1965*. Portsmouth, NH: Heinemann, 1997.

Gerhart, Gail. *Black Power in South Africa: The Evolution of an Ideology*. Berkeley: University of California Press, 1992.

Geshwerder, James. *Class, Race, and Worker Insurgency: The League of Revolutionary Black Workers*. Boston: South End Press, 1998.

Gibbons, R. Arnold. "Problems of Educational Technology in Africa." *Black Scholar* 5, no. 1 (September 1973): 15-19.

Giblin, James L. *A History of the Excluded: Making Family a Refuge from State in Twentieth-Century Tanzania*. Oxford: James Currey, 2005.

Gibson, Richard. "Richard Wright's 'Island of Hallucination' and the 'Gibson Affair.'" *MFS Modern Fiction Studies* 51, no. 4 (2005): 896-920.

Gilbert, Ben W. *Ten Blocks from the White House: Anatomy of the Washington Riots of 1968*. New York: Praeger, 1968.

Gilroy, Paul. *The Black Atlantic: Modernity and Double Consciousness*. Cambridge, MA: Harvard University Press, 1993.

Glasker, Wayne. *Black Students in the Ivory Tower: African American Student Activism at the University of Pennsylvania, 1967-1990*. Amherst: University of Massachusetts Press, 2002.

Glaude, Eddie S., Jr., ed. *Is It Nation Time? Contemporary Essays on Black Power and Black Nationalism*. Chicago: University of Chicago Press, 2002.

Gleijeses, Piero. *Conflicting Missions: Havana, Washington, and Africa, 1959-1976*. Chapel Hill: University of North Carolina Press, 2002.

Goldman, Peter. *The Death and Life of Malcolm X*. Urbana: University of Illinois Press, 1979.

Gomez, Michael A. *Black Crescent: The Experience and Legacy of African Muslims in the Americas*. Cambridge: Cambridge University Press, 2005.

———, ed. *Diasporic Africans: A Reader*. New York: New York University Press, 2006.

Goodwin, Everett E. "Africans and Afro-American Identity: Problems and Possibilities." *Black World* 12, no. 7 (May 1973): 37-39, 73-78.

Gore, Dayo. "From Communist Politics to Black Power: The Visionary Politics and Transnational Solidarities of Victoria 'Vicki' Ama Garvin." In *Want to Start a Revolution? Radical Women in the Black Freedom Struggle*, ed. Dayo F. Gore, Jeanne Theoharis, and Komozi Woodard, 72-94. New York: New York University Press, 2009.

———. *Radicalism at the Crossroads: African American Women Activists in the Cold War*. New York: New York University Press, 2012.

———"To Light a Candle in a Gale Wind: Three Black Women Radicals and Post World War II United States Politics." PhD diss., New York University, 2003.

Grady-Willis, Winston. *Challenging US Apartheid: Atlanta and Black Struggles for Human Rights*. Durham, NC: Duke University Press, 2005.

Graham, Herman, III. *The Brothers' Vietnam War: Black Power, Manhood, and the Military Experience*. Gainesville: University Press of Florida, 2003.

Green, Maia. *The Development State: Aid, Culture and Civil Society in Tanzania*. Oxford: James Currey, 2014.

Green, Reginald. "Four African Development Plans: Ghana, Kenya, Nigeria and Tanzania." *Journal of Modern African Studies* 3, no. 2 (1965): 249-279.

———. "'A Time of Struggle': Exogenous Shocks, Structural Transformation and Crisis in Tanzania." *Millennium: Journal of International Studies* 10, no. 1 (1981): 29-41.

———. *Toward Socialism and Self-Reliance: Tanzania's Striving for Sustained Transition Projected*. Uppsala, Sweden: Scandinavian Institute of African Studies, 1977.

———. "The Treaty for East African Cooperation: A Summary and Interpretation." *Journal of Modern African Studies* 5, no. 1 (1967): 414-419.

Green, Reginald, and Hasa M. Mlawa, eds. *Through Structural Adjustment to Transformation in Sub-Saharan Africa*. Dar es Salaam: Dar es Salaam University Press, 2002.

Greenberg, Cheryl. *A Circle of Trust: Remembering SNCC*. New Brunswick, NJ: Rutgers University Press, 1998.

Grele, Ronald J. *Envelopes of Sound: Six Practitioners Discuss the Method, Theory, and Practice of Oral History and Oral Testimony*. Chicago: Precedent Publishing, 1975.

Griffith, Patrick. "C.L.R. James and Pan-Africanism: An Interview." *Black World* 21, no. 1 (November 1971): 4-13.

Grimshaw, Anna, ed. *The C.L.R. James Reader*. Oxford: Blackwell, 1992.

Guevara, Ernesto "Che." *The African Dream: The Diaries of the Revolutionary War in the Congo.* New York: Grove Press, 1999.

Guillory, Monique, and Richard C. Green, eds. *Soul: Black Power, Politics, and Pleasure.* New York: New York University Press, 1998.

Gullattee, Alyce C. "The April DC Riot in Washington DC." *Journal of the National Medical Association* 60, no. 3 (May 1968): 220-245.

Haas, Jeffrey. *The Assassination of Fred Hampton: How the F.B.I. and the Chicago Police Murdered a Black Panther.* New York: Lawrence Hill Books, 2009.

Haines, Herbert. *Black Radicals and the Civil Rights Mainstream, 1954-1970.* Knoxville: University of Tennessee Press, 1988.

Hajivayanis, George G. "Night-Shift Comrades." In *Cheche: Reminiscences of a Radical Magazine,* ed. Karim F. Hirji. Dar es Salaam: Mkuki Na Nyota, 2010.

Hall, Raymond. *Black Separatism in the United States.* Dartmouth, NH: University Press of New England, 1978.

Hall, Stuart. "Cultural Identity and Diaspora." In *Identity: Community, Culture, Difference,* ed. Jonathan Rutherford, 223-237. London: Lawrence & Wishart, 1990.

Hanchard, Michael. "Afro-Modernity: Temporality, Politics, and the African Diaspora." *Public Culture* 11, no. 1 (1999): 245-268.

——. "Black Memory versus State Memory: Notes toward a Method." *Small Axe* 12, no. 2 (June 2008): 45-62.

——. *Party/Politics: Horizons in Black Political Thought.* New York: Oxford University Press, 2006.

——. "Translation, Political Community, and Black Internationalism: Some Comments on Brent Hayes Edwards's *The Practice of Diaspora*." *Small Axe* 9, no. 1 (March 2005): 112-119.

Harris, Donald. "The Black Ghetto as Colony: A Theoretical Critique and Alternative Formulation." *Review of Black Political Economy* 2, no. 4 (Summer 1972): 3-33.

Harris, Joseph, ed. *African American Reactions to War in Ethiopia, 1936-1941.* Baton Rouge: Louisiana State University Press, 1994.

——. *Global Dimensions of the African Diaspora.* Washington, DC: Howard University Press, 1993.

Hartman, Douglass. *Race, Culture, and the Revolt of the Black Athlete: The 1968 Olympic Protests and Their Aftermath.* Chicago: University of Chicago Press, 2007.

Hatch, John. *Tanzania: A Profile.* New York: Praeger, 1972.

Henriksen, Thomas. *Revolution and Counterrevolution: Mozambique's War of Independence, 1964-1974.* Westport, CT: Greenwood Press, 1983.

Hersh, Seymour. *The Price of Power: Kissinger in the Nixon White House.* New York: Summit Books, 1983.

Hill, Lance. *The Deacons for Defense: Armed Resistance and the Civil Rights Movement.* Chapel Hill: University of North Carolina Press, 2004.

Hill, Sylvia. "Progress Report on Congress Organizing." *Black Scholar* 5, no. 7 (April 1974): 35-40.

Hilliard, David, and Lewis Cole. *This Side of Glory.* Boston: Little, Brown & Co., 1993.

Hilliard, David, and Donald Weise, eds. *The Huey P. Newton Reader.* New York: Seven Stories, 2002.

Hirji, Karim F. *Cheche,* ed. *Reminiscences of a Radical Magazine.* Dar es Salaam: Mkuki Na Nyota, 2010.

———. *Growing Up with Tanzania: Memories, Musings and Maths*. Dar es Salaam: Mkuki na Nyota Publishers, 2014.

Hogan, Wesley C. *Many Minds, One Heart: SNCC's Dream for a New America*. Chapel Hill: University of North Carolina Press, 2007.

Holland, Heidi. *Struggle: The History of the African National Congress*. New York: G. Braziller, 1990.

Horbst, Jeffrey. *States and Power in Africa: Comparative Lessons in Authority and Control*. Princeton, NJ: Princeton University Press, 2000.

Horne, David L. "The Pan-African Congress: A Positive Assessment." *Black Scholar* 5, no. 10 (July-August 1974): 2–11.

Horne, Gerald. *Black and Red: W.E.B. Du Bois and the Afro-American Response to the Cold War, 1944-1963*. Herndon, VA: State University of New York Press, 1986.

———. *Black Liberation/Red Scare: Ben Davis and the Communist Party*. Newark: University of Delaware Press, 1994.

———. *Communist Front? The Civil Rights Congress, 1946-1956*. Madison, NJ: Fairleigh Dickenson University Press, 1988.

———. *From the Barrel of a Gun: The United States and the War against Zimbabwe*. Chapel Hill: University of North Carolina Press, 2001.

———. *Race Woman: The Lives of Shirley Graham Du Bois*. New York: New York University Press, 2000.

———. "Toward a Transnational Research Agenda for African American History in the 21st Century." *Journal of African American History* 91, no. 3 (Spring 2006): 288–304.

Hostetter, David. *Movement Matters: American Antiapartheid Activism and the Rise of Multicultural Politics*. New York: Routledge, 2005.

Hunter, Emma. *Political Thought and the Public Sphere in Tanzania: Freedom, Democracy and Citizenship in the Era of Decolonization*. Cambridge: Cambridge University Press, 2015.

Hunton, Dorothy. *Alphaeus Hunton: The Unsung Valiant*. New York: Dorothy Hunton, 1986.

Hutchinson, Robert. "Neo-colonial Tactics: Macmillans and the Tanzania Publishing House." In *African Socialism in Practice: The Tanzanian Experience*, ed. Andrew Cohen, 228–236. Nottingham, UK: Spokesman, 1979.

Hydén, Göran. *Beyond Ujamaa in Tanzania: Underdevelopment and an Uncaptured Peasantry*. Berkeley: University of California Press, 1980.

Hydén, Göran, and R. S. Mukandala, eds. *Agencies in Foreign Aid: Comparing China, Sweden and the United States in Tanzania*. New York: St. Martin's Press, 1999.

Ibbott, Ralph. *Ujamaa—The Hidden Story of Tanzania's Socialist Villages*. Watsonville, CA: Crossroads Books, 2014.

Ibhawoh, Bonny, and J. I. Dibua. "Deconstructing Ujamaa: The Legacy of Julius Nyerere in the Quest for Social and Economic Development in Africa." *African Journal of Political Science* 8, no. 1 (2003): 59–83.

Iliffe, John. *A Modern History of Tanganyika*. Cambridge: Cambridge University Press, 1979.

International Committee of the Black Radical Congress. "Condolence Message of the International Committee of the Black Radical Congress to the Family, the Government and People of Tanzania on the Passing of Mwalimu Julius Nyerere, 19 October 1999." World History Archives. Http://hartford-hwp.com/archives/30/082.html.

"Interview: Nyerere and African Unity." *Africa*, no. 32 (April 1974): 64–65.

"Interview with Gerri Stark of the Temporary Secretariat." *Ufahamu*, no. 3 (Winter 1974): 3–10.

Institute of the Black World. *Education and Black Struggle—Notes from the Colonized World.* Cambridge, MA: Harvard Educational Review, 1974.

Isserman, Maurice. *If I Had a Hammer: The Death of the Old Left and the Birth of the New Left.* New York: Basic Books, 1987.

Ivaska, Andrew M. *Cultured States: Youth, Gender, and Modern Style in 1960s Dar es Salaam.* Durham, NC: Duke University Press, 2011.

———. "Of Students, 'Nizers,' and the Struggle over Youth: Tanzania's 1966 National Service Crisis." *Africa Today* 51, no. 3 (Spring 2005): 83–107.

Jackson, Esther Cooper, ed. *Freedomways Reader: Prophets in Their Own Country.* Boulder, CO: Westview Press, 2000.

Jackson, George. *Soledad Brother: The Prison Letters of George Jackson.* New York: Bantam Books, 1970.

James, C.L.R. *A History of Pan-African Revolt.* Chicago: Charles H. Kerr, 1995.

———. "Historical Developments of 6 PAC by CLR James." *Black Books Bulletin* 2, no. 2 (Fall 1974): 4–9.

———. *Nkrumah and the Ghana Revolution.* Westport, CT: Lawrence Hill, 1977.

James, Leslie. *George Padmore and Decolonization from Below: Pan-Africanism, the Cold War and the End of Empire.* London: Palgrave Macmillan, 2015.

Janken, Kenneth Robert. *The Wilmington Ten: Violence, Injustice, and the Rise of Black Politics in the 1970s.* Chapel Hill: University of North Carolina Press, 2015.

JCB, Fid Q, Dunga, Lavotsi, and Mama C. "Rest in Uhuru." YouTube video, July 20, 2011. Https://youtu.be/6UWUbK2nmS0.

Jeffries, Hassan. *Bloody Lowndes: Civil Rights and Black Power in Alabama's Black Belt.* New York: New York University Press, 2009.

Jeffries, Judson L., and Tiyi M. Morris, eds. *Black Power in the Belly of the Beast.* Urbana: University of Illinois, 2006.

Jenkins, David. *Black Zion: Africa, Imagined and Real, as Seen by Today's Blacks.* New York: Harcourt Brace Jovanovich, 1975.

Jennings, Michael. *Surrogates of the State: NGOs, Development and Ujamaa in Tanzania.* Bloomfield, CT: Kumarian Press, 2008.

Johnson, Brooks. "New Dilemma for the West: The Red Chinese in Africa." *Negro Digest* 13, no. 2 (December 1963): 27–35.

Johnson, Cedric. "From Popular Anti-Imperialism to Sectarianism: The African Liberation Support Committee and Black Power Radicals." *New Political Science* 25, no. 4 (December 2003): 477–507.

———. *Revolutionaries to Race Leaders: Black Power and the Making of African American Politics.* Minneapolis: University of Minnesota Press, 2007.

Johnson, Robert. *Why Blacks Left America for Africa: Interviews with Repatriates, 1971–1999.* Westport, CT: Praeger, 1999.

Jones, Charles E., ed. *The Black Panther Party Reconsidered.* Baltimore, MD: Baltimore Classic Press, 1998.

Joseph, May. *Nomadic Identities: The Performance of Citizenship*. Minneapolis: University of Minnesota Press, 1999.

———. "Soul, Transnationalism, and Imaginings of Revolution: Tanzanian Ujamaa and the Politics of Enjoyment." In *Soul: Black Power, Politics, and Pleasure*, ed. Monique Guillory and Richard C. Green, 126–138. New York: New York University Press, 1998.

Joseph, Peniel E. "Black Liberation without Apology: Reconceptualizing the Black Power Movement." *Black Scholar* 31, no. 3/4 (Fall/Winter 2001): 2–19.

———, ed. *The Black Power Movement: Rethinking the Civil Rights–Black Power Era*. New York: Routledge, 2006.

———. "Dashikis and Democracy: Black Studies, Student Activism, and the Black Power Movement." *Journal of African American History* 88, no. 2 (Spring 2003): 182–201.

———. *Stokely: A Life*. New York: Basic Civitas Books, 2014.

———. "Waiting 'Til the Midnight Hour: Reconceptualizing the Heroic Period of the Civil Rights Movement, 1954–1965." *Souls* 2, no. 2 (Spring 2000): 6–17.

———. *Waiting Till the Midnight Hour: The Black Power Movement, 1955–1975*. New York: Henry Holt, 2006.

———. "Where Blackness Is Bright? Cuba, Africa, and Black Liberation during the Age of Civil Rights." *New Formations: Journal of Culture/Theory/Politics* 45 (Winter 2001/2002): 111–124.

Jordon, Jennifer. "Cultural Nationalism in the 1960s: Politics and Poetry." In *Race, Politics, and Culture: Critical Essays on the Radicalism of the 1960s*, ed. Adolph Reed Jr., 29–60. Westport, CT: Greenwood Press, 1986.

Joyce, Donald F. *Gatekeepers of Black Culture: Black-Owned Book Publishing in the United States, 1817–1981*. Westport, CT: Greenwood Press, 1983.

Kairoki, James N. "Tanzania and the Resurrection of Pan-Africanism." *Review of Black Political Economy* 4, no. 4 (Summer 1974): 1–26.

Karagueuzian, Dikran. *Blow It Up! The Black Student Revolt at San Francisco State and the Emergence of Dr. Hayakawa*. Boston: Gambit, 1971.

Karenga, Maulana Ron. "Which Road: Nationalism, Pan-Africanism, Socialism?" *Black Scholar* 6, no. 2 (October 1974): 21–29.

Karim, Benjamin. *The End of White Supremacy: Four Speeches by Malcolm X*. New York: Arcade Publishing, 1971.

Kassum, Al Noor. *Africa's Winds of Change: Memoirs of an International Tanzanian*. London: I. B. Touris & Co., 2007.

Katsiaficas, George. *The Imagination of the New Left: A Global Analysis of 1968*. Boston: South End Press, 1987.

Kaufman, Stuart J. *Nationalist Passions*. Ithaca, NY: Cornell University Press, 2015.

Kee, Alistair. *The Rise and Demise of Black Theology*. Trenton, NJ: Africa World Press, 2006.

Kelley, Robin D. G. *Africa Speaks, America Answers: Modern Jazz Revolutionary Times*. Cambridge, MA: Harvard University Press, 2012.

———. *Freedom Dreams: The Black Radical Imagination*. Boston: Beacon Press, 2002.

———. *Race Rebels: Culture, Politics, and the Black Working Class*. New York: Free Press, 1994.

———. "Stormy Weather: Reconstructing Black (Inter)Nationalism in the Cold War Era." In *It's*

Nation Time: Contemporary Essays on Black Power and Black Nationalism, ed. Eddie Glaude Jr. Chicago: University of Chicago Press, 2002.

———. "The World the Diaspora Made: CLR James and the Politics of History." In *Rethinking CLR James*, ed. Grant Farred, 116-118. Cambridge, MA: Blackwell Publishers, 1996.

———. *Yo' Mama's Disfunktional! Fighting the Culture Wars in Urban America*. Boston: Beacon Press, 1997.

Kelley, Robin D. G., and Betsy Esch. "Black Like Mao: Red China and Black Revolution." *Souls* 1, no. 4 (Fall 1999): 6-41.

Kgositsile, Keopapeste. "Africans and African Americans: Towards Our Freedom." *Negro Digest* 17, no. 7 (May 1968): 25-30.

Khamisi, Lucas. *Imperialism Today*. Dar es Salaam: Tanzania Publishing House, 1983.

Kijembe, Adhama Oluwa. "Swahili and Black Americans." *Negro Digest* 18, no. 9 (July 1969): 4-9.

Kimambo, I. N., and A. J. Temu, eds. *A History of Tanzania*. Nairobi: East African Publishing House for the Historical Association of Tanzania, 1969.

Kinchen, Shirletta. *Black Power in the Bluff City: African American Youth and Student Activism in Memphis, 1965-1975*. Knoxville: University of Tennessee Press, 2015.

King, Martin Luther, Jr. *Where Do We Go from Here: Chaos or Community?* Boston: Beacon Press, 1967.

King, Robert Hillary, and Terry Kupers. *From the Bottom of the Heap: The Autobiography of Black Panther Robert Hillary King*. Oakland, CA: PM Press, 2010.

Konde, Hadji. *Freedom of the Press in Tanzania*. Arusha, Tanzania: East African Publications, 1984.

Kriger, Norma. *Zimbabwe's Guerrilla War: Peasant Voices*. New York: Cambridge University Press, 1992.

Kurtz, Laura. *Historical Dictionary of Tanzania*. London: Scarecrow Press, 1978.

Lacy, Leslie A. *The Rise and Fall of a Proper Negro*. New York: Macmillan, 1970.

Ladner, Joyce. "Tanzanian Women and Nation Building." *Black Scholar*, no. 4 (December 1971): 22-28.

Lake, Anthony. *The "Tar Baby" Option: American Policy toward Southern Rhodesia*. New York: Columbia University Press, 1976.

Lal, Priya. *African Socialism in Postcolonial Tanzania: Between the Village and the World*. Cambridge: Cambridge University Press, 2015.

Larkin, Bruce D. *China and Africa, 1949-1970: The Foreign Policy of the People's Republic of China*. Berkeley: University of California Press, 1971.

Laurence, Tony, and Christopher MacRae. *The Dar Mutiny of 1964, and the Armed Intervention That Ended It*. Sussex, England: Book Guild Publishing, 2007.

Lazerow, Jama, and Yohuru Williams, eds. *In Search of the Black Panther Party: New Perspectives on a Revolutionary Movement*. Durham, NC: Duke University Press, 2006.

Lee, Christopher J. *Making a World after Empire: The Bandung Moment and Its Political Afterlives*. Athens: Ohio University Press, 2010.

Lee, Don L. *From Plan to Planet: Life Studies: The Need for Afrikan Minds and Institutions*. Detroit: Broadside Press, 1973.

Legum, Colin. *Africa—The Year of the Students: A Survey of Student Politics in Universities and Schools*. London: Rex Collings, 1972.

Legum, Colin, and Geoffrey Mmari, ed. *Mwalimu: The Influence of Nyerere*. London: James Currey, 1995.

Lemarchand, René, ed. *American Policy in Southern Africa: The Stakes and the Stance*. Washington, DC: University Press of America, 1978.

Lemelle, Sidney, and Robin D. G. Kelley, eds. *Imagining Home: Class, Culture, and Nationalism in the African Diaspora*. New York: Verso, 1994.

Leslie, J.A.K. *A Survey of Dar es Salaam*. London: Oxford University Press, 1963.

Lester, Julius. *Search for the New Land: History as Subjective Experience*. New York: Dial Press, 1969.

Le Sueur, James, ed. *The Decolonization Reader*. New York: Routledge, 2003.

Lewis, David Levering. *W.E.B. Du Bois: The Fight for Equality and the American Century, 1919–1963*. New York: Henry Holt & Co., 2000.

Lewis, Earl. "To Turn as on a Pivot: Writing African Americans into a History of Overlapping Diasporas." *American Historical Review* 100, no. 3 (June 1995).

Lewis, John. *Walking with the Wind: A Memoir of the Movement*. New York: Harcourt Brace & Co., 1998.

Lewis, Rupert C. *Walter Rodney's Intellectual and Political Thought*. Detroit: Wayne State University Press, 1998.

Leys, Colin, and John S. Saul, eds. *Namibia's Liberation Struggle: The Two-Edged Sword*. Athens: Ohio University Press, 1995.

Lincoln, C. Eric. *The Black Muslims in America*. Boston: Beacon Press, 1961.

Lindsay, Lisa A., and Stephan F. Miescher, eds. *Men and Masculinities in Modern Africa*. Portsmouth, NH: Heinemann, 2003.

Ling, Peter J., and Sharon Monteith, eds. *Gender and the Civil Rights Movement*. Chapel Hill, NC: Longleaf, 2004.

Lloyd-Jones, Stewart, and Antonio Costa Pinto, eds. *The Lasting Empire: Thirty Years of Portuguese Decolonization*. Portland, OR: Intellect Books, 2003.

Lofchie, Michael F. *Zanzibar: Background to Revolution*. Princeton, NJ: Princeton University Press, 1965.

Maddox, Gregory, and Ernest M. Kongola. *Practicing History in Central Tanzania: Writing, Memory, and Performance*. Portsmouth, NH: Heinemann, 2005.

Maddox, Gregory, and James L. Giblin, eds. *In Search of a Nation: Histories of Authority and Dissidence in Tanzania*. Athens: Ohio University Press, 2006.

Madhubuti, Haki R. "Enemy: From the White Left, White Right and In-Between." *Black World* 23, no. 12 (October 1974): 36–55.

———. "The Latest Purge: The Attack on Black Nationalism and Pan-Afrikanism by the New Left, the Sons and Daughters of the Old Left." *Black Scholar* 6, no. 1 (September 1974): 43–56.

———. "Sixth Pan-Afrikan Congress: What Is Being Done to Save the Black Race." *Black Books Bulletin* 2, no. 4 (Fall 1974): 43–56.

Magubane, Bernard. *The Ties That Bind: African-American Consciousness of Africa*. Trenton, NJ: Africa World Press, 1987.

Mahoney, Richard. *JFK: Ordeal in Africa*. New York: Oxford University Press, 1983.

Makeba, Miriam, and James Hall. *Makeba: My Story*. New York: Dutton Adult, 1988.

Malcolm X and Alex Haley. *The Autobiography of Malcolm X as Told to Alex Haley.* New York: Ballantine Books, 1965.

Malson, Robert A. "The Black Power Rebellion at Howard University." *Negro Digest* 17, no. 2 (December 1967): 20-30.

Mamdani, Mahmood. *Citizen and Subject.* Princeton, NJ: Princeton University Press, 1996.

Marcus, George E. "Ethnography in/of the World System: The Emergence of Multi-Sited Ethnography." *Annual Review of Anthropology* 24 (1995): 95-117.

Markle, Seth. "'Book Publishers for a Pan-African World': Drum and Spear Press and Tanzania's Ujamaa Ideology." *Black Scholar* 37, no. 4 (Winter 2008): 16-25.

Markle, Seth M., and Mejah Mbuya. "Death of a Panther: Remembering G." *Pambazuka News*, no. 534 (9 June 2011). Http://www.pambazuka.org/resources/death-panther.

Marable, Manning. *Malcolm X: A Life of Reinvention.* New York: Penguin Books, 2011.

———. *Race, Reform, and Rebellion: The Second Reconstruction in Black America, 1945-1982.* London: Macmillan, 1984.

Marcum, John. *The Angolan Revolution.* Vol. 2, *Exile Politics and Guerrilla Warfare, 1962-1976.* Cambridge, MA: MIT Press, 1978.

Martin, David. "'Lift Up Yourself!' Reinterpreting Amiri Baraka (LeRoi Jones), Black Power, and the Uplift Tradition." *Journal of American History* 93, no. 1 (June 2006): 91-116.

Matthews, K., and S. S. Mushi, eds. *Foreign Policy in Tanzania, 1961-1981: A Reader.* Dar es Salaam: Tanzania Publishing House, 1981.

Mazrui, Ali. "Tanzaphilia: A Diagnosis." *Transition* 31, no. 6 (June/July 1967): 8.

Mazrui, Ali, and Lindah L. Mhando. *Julius Nyerere, Africa's Titan on a Global Stage: Perspectives from Arusha to Obama.* Durham, NC: Carolina Academic Press, 2012.

Mbilinyi, Marjorie, ed. *Gender Profile of Tanzania.* Dar es Salaam: Tanzania Gender Networking Project, 1993.

Mbishi, Nikki. *Malcolm XI.* Tamaduni Muzik, 2012. CD.

Mbogoni, Lawrence E. Y. *Aspects of Colonial Tanzania History.* Dar es Salaam: Mkuki na Nyota Publishers, 2013.

Mboya, Tom. *The Challenge of Nationhood.* New York: Praeger, 1970.

———. *Freedom and After.* London: Andre Deutsch, 1963.

Mbughuni, L. A. *The Cultural Policy of the United Republic of Tanzania.* Paris: UNESCO, 1974.

McCartney, John T. *Black Power Ideologies: An Essay in African-American Political Thought.* Philadelphia: Temple University, 1992.

McCormick, Richard P. *The Black Student Protest Movement at Rutgers.* New Brunswick, NJ: Rutgers University Press, 1990.

McDuffie, Erik. *Sojourning for Freedom: Black Women, American Communism, and the Making of Black Left Feminism.* Durham, NC: Duke University Press, 2011.

McEvoy, James, and Abraham Miller, eds. *Black Power and Student Rebellion.* Belmont, CA: Wadsworth Publishing, 1969.

McHenry, Dean, Jr. *Ujamaa Villages: The Implementation of a Rural Development Strategy.* Berkeley: Institute of International Studies, University of California Press, 1979.

McLaughlin, Malcolm. "Ghetto Formation and Armed Resistance in East St. Louis, Illinois." *Journal of American Studies* 41 (2007): 435–467.

Meriwether, James H. *Proudly We Can Be Africans: Black Americans and Africa, 1935–1961*. Chapel Hill: University of North Carolina Press, 2002.

Mhunzi, Burham H. "The Press in Tanzania: A Study of Ownership, and the Role under British Colonial Time and Post-Independence Period from 1954 to 1993." MA thesis, University of Dar es Salaam, 1995.

Milne, June, ed. *Kwame Nkrumah: The Conakry Years: His Life and Letters*. London: Panaf, 1990.

Minter, William, Gail Hovey, and Charles Cobb Jr., eds. *No Easy Victories: African Liberation and American Activists over a Half Century, 1950–2000*. Trenton, NJ: Africa World Press, 2008.

Mitchell, Charlene, and Michael Myerson. "Africa's Impact on Black America." *African Communist* 43 (1970).

Molony, Thomas, ed. *Julius Kambarage Nyerere: Life, Times, Legacy*. London: FIRST, 2009.

———. *Nyerere: The Early Years*. Oxford: James Currey, 2014.

Monson, Ingrid. *Freedom Sounds: Civil Rights Call Out to Jazz and Africa*. Oxford: Oxford University Press, 2007.

Monteiro, Anthony. "The Sixth Pan-African Congress: Agenda for African–African American Solidarity." *Freedomways* 14 (4th Quarter 1974): 295–302.

Moses, Wilson J. *Afrotopia: The Roots of African American Popular Literature and Culture*. Cambridge: Cambridge University Press, 1998.

———. *The Golden Age of Black Nationalism, 1850–1925: The History of an Idea in America from Alexander Crummell to Marcus Garvey*. Rumford, RI: Black Smith Shop, 1978.

———, ed. *Liberian Dreams: Back-to-Africa Narratives from the 1850s*. University Park, PA: Penn State University Press, 1998.

Msweka, Pius. *Towards Party Supremacy*. Arusha, Tanzania: East African Publications, 1977.

Muganda, Bernard. *Speaking Swahili [Kusema Kiswahili]*. Washington, DC: Drum and Spear Press, 1970.

Mullen, Bill. *Afro-Orientalism*. Minneapolis: University of Minnesota Press, 2004.

Munslow, Barry. *Mozambique: The Revolution and Its Origins*. New York: Longman, 1983.

Murray, Pauli. *The Autobiography of a Black Activist, Feminist, Lawyer, Priest, and Poet*. Knoxville: University of Tennessee Press, 1987.

Murray, Rolland. *Our Living Manhood: Literature, Black Power, and Masculine Ideology*. Philadelphia: University of Pennsylvania Press, 2006.

Mushi, Philemon A. K. *History and Development of Education in Tanzania*. Dar es Salaam: Dar es Salaam University Press, 2009.

Mwakikagile, Godfrey. *Nyerere and Africa: An End of an Era: Biography of Julius Kambarage Nyerere*. London: Protea Publishing Co., 2002.

———. *Relations between Africans and African Americans: Misconceptions, Myths, and Realities*. Morrisville, NC: Lulu, 2004.

Mwansasu, Bismarck, and Cranford Pratt, eds. *Toward Socialism in Tanzania*. Toronto: University of Toronto Press, 1979.

Nabudere, Dan. *The Political Economy of Imperialism: Its Theoretical and Polemical Treatment from*

Mercantilist to Multilateral Imperialism. Dar es Salaam: Tanzania Publishing House, 1997.

Naison, Mark. *Communists in Harlem during the Great Depression.* Chicago: University of Illinois Press, 1983.

Nesbitt, Francis N. *Race for Sanctions: African Americans against Apartheid, 1946-1994.* Bloomington: Indiana University Press, 2004.

Njoroge, Njoroge. *Chocolate Surrealism: Music, Movement, Memory, and History in the Circum-Caribbean.* Jackson: University Press of Mississippi, 2007.

Nkrumah, Kwame. *Africa Must Unite.* London: Panaf, 1963.

———. *Class Struggle in Africa.* New York: International Publishers, 1970.

———. *Dark Days in Ghana.* London: Panaf, 1968.

———. *Neo-Colonialism: The Last Stage of Imperialism.* London: Panaf, 1965.

———. *Revolutionary Path.* New York: International Publishers, 1973.

Nnoli, Okwudiba. *Self-Reliance and Foreign Policy in Tanzania: The Dynamics of Diplomacy of a New State, 1961-1971.* New York: NOK Publishers, 1978.

Noer, Thomas J. *Cold War and Black Liberation: The United States and White Rule in Africa, 1948-1968.* Columbia: University of Missouri Press, 1985.

Nottingham, John. "Establishing an African Publishing Industry: A Study in Decolonization." *African Affairs* 68, no. 271 (April 1969): 139-144.

Nye, Joseph S. *Pan-Africanism and East African Integration.* Cambridge, MA: Harvard University Press, 1965.

Nyerere, Julius K. "Capitalism or Socialism? The Rational Choice." *Black World* 23, no. 5 (March 1974): 38-48.

———. *Education for Self-Reliance.* Dar es Salaam: Government Printer, 1967.

———. *Freedom and Socialism.* London: Oxford University Press, 1968.

———. *Freedom and Unity: A Collection of Writings and Speeches, 1952-1965.* Dar es Salaam: Oxford University Press, 1966.

———. *Man and Development.* Dar es Salaam: Oxford University Press, 1974.

———. *Stability and Change in Africa: Address by President Julius K. Nyerere of the United Republic of Tanzania at University of Toronto, Canada, 2nd October 1969.* Dar es Salaam: Dar es Salaam Business Machine Services, 1980.

———. *This Is the Way Forward: Republic Day Broadcast by President Nyerere, 9th December 1963.* Dar es Salaam: Ministry of Information, 1964.

———. *Ujamaa: Essays on Socialism.* Dar es Salaam: Oxford University Press, 1968.

Obadele, Imari Abubakari. "Republic of New Africa: The Struggle for Land in Mississippi." *Black World* 22, no. 4 (February 1973): 37, 66-73.

Obatala, J. K. "Soul Music in Africa: Has Charlie Got a Brand New Bag?" *Black Scholar* 2, no. 6 (February 1971): 8-12.

———. "U.S. 'Soul' Music in Africa." *African Communist*, no. 41 (1970): 80-89.

Odei, Ernest L. "Towards Pan-Africanism: The O.A.U. Liberation Committee Meeting at Accra." *Black World* 22, no. 7 (May 1973): 34-37.

Ofari, Earl. "A Critical Review of the Pan-African Congress." *Black Scholar* 5, no. 10 (July-August

1974): 12–15.

Ogbar, Jeffrey O. G. *Black Power: Radical Politics and African American Identity*. Baltimore: Johns Hopkins University Press, 2004.

Ogletree, Charles J., Jr. *All Deliberate Speed: Reflections on the First Half of the Century of Brown v. Board of Education*. New York: W.W. Norton and Co., 2004.

Okoko, Kimse. *Socialism and Self-Reliance*. London: Routledge and Kegan Paul, 1987.

Olsen, Jack. *Last Man Standing: The Tragedy and Triumph of Geronimo Pratt*. New York: Doubleday, 2000.

Oluwasanmi, Edwina, Eva McLean, and Hans Zell, eds. *Publishing in Africa in the Seventies: Proceedings of an International Conference on Publishing and Book Development Held at the University of Ife, Ile-Ife, Nigeria, 16–20 December 1973*. Ile-Ife, Nigeria: University of Ife Press, 1975.

Omari. C. K. "The Management of Tribal and Religious Diversity." In *Mwalimu: The Influence of Nyerere*, ed. Colin Legum and Geoffrey Nmari, 28–30. Oxford: James Currey, 1995.

O'Neil, Norman, and Kmeal Mustafa, eds. *Capitalism, Socialism and the Development Crisis in Tanzania*. Surrey, UK: Aldershot, 1990.

Othman, Haroub, ed. *Babu: I Saw the Future and It Works*. Dar es Salaam: E&D, 2001.

———. *The State in Tanzania: Who Controls It and Whose Interest Does It Serve?* Dar es Salaam: University of Dar es Salaam, 1980.

Ouzgane, Lahoucine, and Robert Morrell, eds. *African Masculinities: Men in Africa from the Late 19th Century to the Present*. New York: Palgrave Macmillan, 2005.

Padmore, George. *Pan-Africanism or Communism*. Garden City, NY: Anchor Books, 1972.

Parks, Carole A. "African Liberation Day—May 26, 1973: 'Africa Is at War.'" *Black World* 22, no. 7 (May 1973): 78–79.

———. "African Liberation Month—Now More Than Ever." *Black World* 23, no. 7 (May 1974): 45–48.

Patterson, Tiffany Ruby, and Robin D. G. Kelley. "Unfinished Migrations: Reflections on the African Diaspora and the Making of the Modern World." *African Studies Review* 43, no. 1 (April 2000): 11–45.

Payne, Charles M. *I've Got the Light of Freedom: The Organizing Tradition and the Mississippi Freedom Struggle*. Los Angeles: University of California Press, 1995.

Perlstein, Daniel. "Teaching Freedom: SNCC and the Creation of the Mississippi Freedom Schools." *History of Education Quarterly* 3, no. 3 (Fall 1990): 297–394.

Perry, Bruce, ed. *Malcolm X: The Last Speeches*. New York: Pathfinder, 1989.

Petterson, Don. *Revolution in Zanzibar: An American's Cold War Tale*. Boulder, CO: Westview Press, 2002.

Pierre, Jemima. *The Predicament of Blackness: Postcolonial Ghana and the Politics of Race*. Chicago: University of Chicago Press, 2012.

Pinkney, Alphonso. *Red, Black and Green: Black Nationalism in the United States*. Cambridge: Cambridge University Press, 1976.

Plummer, Brenda Gayle. *In Search of Power: African Americans in the Era of Decolonization, 1956–1974*. Cambridge: Cambridge University Press, 2013.

———. *Rising Wind: Black Americans and U.S. Foreign Affairs, 1935–1960*. Chapel Hill: University of

North Carolina Press, 1996.

———, ed. *Window on Freedom: Race, Civil Rights, and Foreign Affairs, 1945-1988*. Chapel Hill: University of North Carolina Press, 2003.

Poinsett, Alex. "Should Black Men Speak Swahili? Ask Afro-Americans." *Ebony* 24, no. 2 (December 1968): 163-165.

Polome, Edgar, and C. P. Hill. *Language in Tanzania*. London: Oxford University Press, 1980.

Prashad, Vijay. *Everybody Was Kung Fu Fighting: Afro-Asian Connections and the Myth of Cultural Purity*. Boston: Beacon Press, 2001.

Pratt, Cranford. *The Critical Phase in Tanzania, 1945-1968: Nyerere and the Emergence of a Socialist Strategy*. New York: Cambridge University Press, 1976.

Presse, Agence-France. "A Revolutionary Trip down Tanzania's Memory Lane." NDTV.com, 2 May 2014. Http://www.ndtv.com/world-news/a-revolutionary-trip-down-tanzanias-memory-lane-559792.

Pulido, Laura. *Black, Brown, Yellow, and Left: Radical Activism in Los Angeles*. Berkeley: University of California Press, 2006.

Quinn, Kate, ed. *Black Power in the Caribbean*. Gainesville: University Press of Florida, 2015.

Rabe, Stephen G. *U.S. Intervention in British Guiana: A Cold War Story*. Chapel Hill: University of North Carolina Press, 2005.

Rachal, John R. "We'll Never Turn Back: Adult Education and the Struggle for Citizenship in Mississippi's Freedom Summer." *American Educational Research Journal* 35, no. 2 (Summer 1998): 167-198.

Radcliffe, Kendahl, Jennifer Scott, and Anja Werner, eds. *Anywhere but Here: Black Intellectuals in the Atlantic World and Beyond*. Jackson: University Press of Mississippi, 2014.

Rake, Alan. "Jomo Kenyatta: The Man and the Myth." *Negro Digest* 10, no. 10 (August 1961): 33-37.

Rampersad, Arnold. *The Life of Langston Hughes*. Vol. 2, *1941-1967: I Dream a World*. Oxford: Oxford University Press, 2002.

Randall, Dudley. "Black Publisher, Black Writer: An Answer." *Black World* 26, no. 5 (March 1975): 32-37.

Ranger, Terrence O. *Peasant Consciousness and Guerrilla War in Zimbabwe: A Comparative Study*. Berkeley: University of California Press, 1985.

Ransby, Barbara. *Ella Baker and the Black Freedom Movement: A Radical Democratic Vision*. Chapel Hill: University of North Carolina Press, 2003.

Raphael-Hernandez, Heike, and Shannon Steen, eds. *AfroAsian Encounters: Culture, History, Politics*. New York: New York University Press, 2006.

Ratcliff, Anthony. "Liberation at the End of a Pen: Writing Pan-African Politics of Cultural Struggle." PhD diss., University of Massachusetts, Amherst, 2009.

Redding, Saunders. "Home to Africa." *Negro Digest* 12, no. 7 (May 1963): 80-87.

Redkey, Edward S. *Black Exodus: Black Nationalist and Back-to-Africa Movements, 1890-1910*. New Haven, CT: Yale University Press, 1969.

Redmond, Shana L. *Anthem: Social Movements and the Sound of Solidarity in the African Diaspora*. New York: New York University Press, 2013.

Resnick, Idrian N., ed. *The Long Transition: Building Socialism in Tanzania*. New York: Monthly

Review Press, 1981.

———. *Tanzania—Revolution by Education*. Arusha, Tanzania: Longmans of Tanzania, 1968.

Resolutions and Selected Speeches from the Sixth Pan-African Congress. Dar es Salaam: Tanzania Publishing House, 1976.

Richards, Yevette. "African and African-American Labor Leaders in the Struggle over International Affiliations." *International Journal of African Historical Studies* 31, no. 2 (1998): 301-334.

———. *Conversations with Maida Springer: A Personal History of Labor, Race, and International Relations*. Pittsburgh, PA: University of Pittsburgh Press, 2004.

———. *Maida Springer: Pan-Africanist and International Labor Leader*. Pittsburgh, PA: University of Pittsburgh Press, 2000.

Rickford, Russell. *We Are an African People: Independent Education, Black Power, and the Radical Imagination*. Oxford: Oxford University Press, 2016.

Roberts, Glyn. *Volunteers and Neocolonialism: An Inquiry into the Role of Foreign Volunteers in the Third World*. Manchester: A.J. Wright & Sons, 1969.

Robinson, Cedric. *Black Marxism: The Making of the Black Radical Tradition*. Chapel Hill: University of North Carolina Press, 1983.

Robinson, J. Fletcher. ""Self-Development in the Black World: On Science and Technology." *Black World* 23, no. 5 (March 1974): 26-31.

Robinson, Randall. *Defending the Spirit: A Black Life in America*. New York: Dutton, 1998.

Rodney, Walter. "Education and Tanzanian Socialism." In *Tanzania: Revolution by Education*, ed. Idrian Resnick. Arusha, Tanzania: Longmans, 1968.

———. *The Groundings with My Brothers*. London: Bogle-L'Ouverture Publications, 1975.

———. *How Europe Underdeveloped Africa*. Washington, DC: Howard University Press, 1982.

———. "Problems of Third World Development: A Discussion of Imperialism and Underdevelopment." *Ufahamu* 3, no. 2 (Fall 1972): 27-47.

———. "Tanzania Ujamaa and Scientific Socialism." *African Review* 1, no. 4 (1971): 61-76.

———. *Walter Rodney Speaks: The Making of an African Intellectual*. Trenton, NJ: Africa World Press, 1990.

Rogers, Ibram. "Remembering the Black Campus Movement: An Oral History Interview with James P. Garrett." *Journal of Pan African Studies* 2, no. 10 (June 2009): 30-41.

Rogers, Kim Lacy. "Oral History and the History of the Civil Rights Movement." *Journal of American History* 75, no. 2 (September 1998): 567-576.

Rojas, Fabio. *From Black Power to Black Studies: How a Radical Social Movement Became an Academic Discipline*. Baltimore: Johns Hopkins University Press, 2007.

Rooks, Nowile M. *White Money/Black Power: The Surprising History of African American Studies and the Crisis of Race and Higher Education*. Boston: Beacon Press, 2006.

Rothschild, Mary Aikin. "The Volunteers and the Freedom Schools: Education for Social Change in Mississippi." *History of Education Quarterly* 22, no. 4 (Winter 1982): 401-420.

Rugumamu, Severine M. *Lethal Aid: The Illusion of Socialism and Self-Reliance in Tanzania*. Trenton, NJ: Africa World Press, 1997.

Sabot, R. H. *Economic Development and Urban Migration: Tanzania, 1900-1971*. Oxford: Oxford University Press, 1979.

Salaam, Kalamu Ya. "African Liberation Day: An Assessment—Tell No Lies, Claim No Easy Victories." *Black World* 23, no. 12 (October 1974): 18-34.

———. "A Response to Haki Madhubuti." *Black Scholar* 6, no. 5 (January-February 1975): 40-43.

Sales, William, Jr. *From Civil Rights to Black Liberation: Malcolm X and the Organization of African Unity*. Boston: South End Press, 1994.

Sandbrook, Richard. *The Politics of Africa's Economic Stagnation*. Cambridge: Cambridge University Press, 1985.

Sapire, Hilary, and Chris Saunders, eds. *Southern African Liberation Struggles: New Local, Regional and Global Perspectives*. Cape Town: University of Cape Town Press, 2012.

Saul, John S. *The Next Liberation Struggle: Capitalism, Socialism and Democracy in Southern Africa*. Toronto: Between the Lines, 2005.

———. "Radicalism and the Hill." *East African Journal* 7, no. 12 (December 1970): 289-290.

———. *The State and Revolution in Eastern Africa*. New York: Monthly Review Press, 1979.

Sayres, Sohnya, ed. *The Sixties without Apologies*. Minneapolis: University of Minnesota Press, 1984.

Scheer, Robert, ed. *Eldridge Cleaver: Post-Prison Writings and Speeches*. New York: Ramparts, 1969.

Schmidt, Nancy J. "Children's Literature about Africa: A Reassessment." *African Studies Review* 13, no. 3 (December 1970): 469-488.

Schneider, Leander. "Colonial Legacies and Postcolonial Authoritarianism in Tanzania: Connects and Disconnects." *African Studies Review* 49, no. 1 (April 2006): 93-118.

———. "Developmentalism and Its Failings: Why Rural Development Went Wrong in 1960s and 1970s Tanzania." PhD diss., Columbia University, 2003.

Schroeder, Richard A. *Africa after Apartheid: South Africa, Race, and Nation in Tanzania*. Bloomington: Indiana University Press, 2012.

Scott, Benjamin F. "The Technology of Liberation." *Black World* 21, no. 9 (March 1972): 29-39.

Scott, David. "The Archaeology of Black Memory: An Interview with Robert A. Hill." *Small Axe*, no. 5 (March 1999): 80-150.

———. "Introduction: On the Archaeologies of Black Memory." *Small Axe* 12, no. 2 (June 2008): v-xvi.

Scott, James C. *Domination and the Arts of Resistance: Hidden Transcripts*. New Haven, CT: Yale University Press, 1990.

———. *Seeing Like a State: How Certain Schemes to Improve the Human Condition Have Failed*. New Haven, CT: Yale University Press, 1998.

———. *Weapons of the Weak: Everyday Forms of Peasant Resistance*. New Haven, CT: Yale University Press, 1985.

Scott, William R. *Suns of Sheba's Race: African Americans and the Italo-Ethiopian Crisis, 1935-1941*. Bloomington: Indiana University Press, 1993.

Seale, Bobby. *Seize the Time: The Story of the Black Panther Party and Huey P. Newton*. Baltimore: Black Classic Press, 1991.

Selassie, Bereket Habte. "The OAU and Regional Conflicts: Focus on the Eritrean War." *Africa Today* 35, no. 3/4 (1988): 61-67.

Sellars, Cleveland. *The River of No Return: The Autobiography of a Black Militant and the Life and Death of SNCC*. Jackson: University Press of Mississippi, 1990.

Shabazz, Betty, ed. *Malcolm X by Any Means Necessary*. New York: Pathfinder Press, 1970.

Shakur, Assata. *Assata: An Autobiography*. Chicago: Lawrence Hill Books, 1987.

Sherwood, Tom. *Dream City: Race, Power, and the Decline of Washington, D.C.* New York: Simon & Schuster, 1994.

Shivji, Issa G. *Class Struggles in Tanzania*. Dar es Salaam: Tanzania Publishing House, 1975.

———. *Intellectuals at the Hill: Essays and Talks, 1969-1993*. Dar es Salaam: Dar es Salaam University Press, 1993.

———. "The Life and Times of Babu: The Age of Liberation and Revolution." *Review of African Political Economy* 30, no. 95 (October 2001): 10-16.

———. "Nationalism and Pan-Africanism: Decisive Moments in Nyerere's Intellectual and Political Thought: Preliminary Notes." Dar es Salaam: (Unpublished paper, n.d.).

———. *Pan Africanism or Pragmatism: Lessons from the Tanganyika-Zanzibar Union*. Dar es Salaam: Mkuki na Nyota Publishers, 2008.

Sibanda, Eliakim M. *The Zimbabwe African People's Union, 1961-1987: A Political History of Insurgency in Rhodesia*. Trenton, NJ: Africa World Press, 2005.

Sixth Pan-African Congress. "A Briefing Paper." *Black World* 23, no. 5 (March 1974): 5-10.

Slate, Nico. *Black Power beyond Borders: The Global Dimensions of the Black Power Movement*. London: Palgrave Macmillan, 2012.

Smith, Marcia. *Black America: A Photographic Journey: Past and Present*. San Diego: Thunder Bay Press, 2002.

Smith, Mark. "A Response to Haki Madhubuti." *Black Scholar* 6, no. 5 (January-February 1975): 44-52.

Smith, Suzanne E. *Dancing in the Streets: Motown and the Cultural Politics of Detroit*. Cambridge, MA: Harvard University Press, 1999.

Smith, William E. *We Must Run, While They Walk: A Portrait of Africa's Julius Nyerere*. New York: Random House, 1972.

Smith-Hobson, Sheila. "Black Book Publishing: Protest, Pride, and Little Profit." *Black Enterprise* 8, no. 10 (May 1978): 39-41.

Snow, Nancy. *Propaganda, Inc.: Selling America's Culture to the World*. New York: Seven Stories Press, 2002.

Soggot, David. *Namibia: The Violent Heritage*. New York: St. Martin's Press, 1988.

Southerland, Ellease. "Seventeen Days in Nigeria: A Diary." *Black World* 11, no. 3 (January 1972): 29-40.

"Special Interview with Julius K. Nyerere." *Africa Now* (December 1983): 98-104.

Springer, Kimberly, ed. *Living for the Revolution: Black Feminist Organizations, 1968-1980*. Durham, NC: Duke University Press, 2005.

———. *Still Lifting, Still Climbing: Contemporary African American Women's Activism*. New York: New York University Press, 1999.

Stephens, Michelle. "Disarticulating Black Internationalisms: West Indian Radicals and the Practice of Diaspora." *Small Axe* 9, no. 1 (March 2005): 100-111.

———. "Re-Imagining the Shape and Borders of Black Political Space." *Radical History Review* 87 (2003): 169-182.

Stoger-Eising, Victoria. "Ujamaa Revisited: Indigenous and European Influences in Nyerere's Social and Political Thought." *Africa* 70 (2000): 118-143.

Sturner, Martin. *The Media History of Tanzania*. Ndanda, Tanzania: Ndanda Mission Press, 1998.

Sundiata, Ibrahim. *Brothers and Strangers: Black Zion, Black Slavery, 1914-1940*. Durham, NC: Duke University Press, 2004.

Sutherland, Bill, and Matt Meyer. *Guns and Gandhi in Africa: Pan-African Insights on Non-Violence, Armed Liberation Struggle, and Liberation in Africa*. Trenton, NJ: Africa World Press, 2000.

Swai, Bonaventure. "Rodney on Scholarship and Activism: Parts 1 and 2." *Journal of African Marxists* 1 (November 1981) and 2 (August 1982).

Swan, Quito. *Black Power in Bermuda: The Struggle for Decolonization*. New York: Palgrave, 2009.

Swift, Charles R. *Dar Days: The Early Years in Tanzania*. Lanham, MD: University Press of America, 2002.

Tambo, Adelaide, ed. *Preparing for Power: Oliver Tambo Speaks*. New York: George Braziller, 1988.

Tandon, Yash, ed. *University of Dar es Salaam Debate on Class, State and Imperialism*. Dar es Salaam: Tanzania Publishing House, 1982.

Tanganyika African National Union. *The Arusha Declaration and TANU's Policy on Socialism and Self-Reliance*. Dar es Salaam: Publicity Section, TANU, 1967.

"Tanzania Government Invites Black Americans to Join in Nation Building." *Jet* 41, no. 22 (February 1972): 21.

Tate, Leslie B. "The Power of Pan Africanism: Tanzania/African American Linkages, 1947-1997." PhD diss., University of Illinois at Urbana-Champaign, 2015.

Taylor, J. Clagget. *The Political Development of Tanganyika*. Stanford, CA: Stanford University Press, 1963.

Technical Assistance Information Clearing House. *Development of Assistance Programs of U.S. Nonprofit Organizations in Tanzania, December 1974*. New York: American Council of Voluntary Agencies for Foreign Service, 1974.

Temu, A. J. "Problems of Creating the African University: The Case of the University of Dar es Salaam." *Social Praxis* 1, no. 2 (1972): 141-151.

Temu, A. J., and Bonaventure, Swai. "The Intellectual and the State in Postcolonial Africa: The Tanzania Case." *Social Praxis* 8, no. 3/4 (1981).

Tordoff, William. *Government and Politics in Tanzania: A Collection of Essays Covering the Period from September 1960 to July 1966*. Nairobi: East African Publishing House, 1967.

Tordoff, William, and Ali Mazrui. "The Left and the Super-Left in Tanzania." *Journal of Modern African Studies* 10, no. 3 (1972): 427-455.

Thompson, Era Bell. *Africa—Land of My Fathers*. New York: Doubleday, 1954.

———. "Are Black Americans Welcome in Africa?" *Ebony* 24, no. 3 (January 1969): 44-51.

Thompson, Julius E. *Dudley Randall, Broadside Press, and the Black Arts Movement*. Jefferson, NC: McFarland & Co., 1999.

Thompson, Vincent B. *Africa and Unity: The Evolution of Pan-Africanism*. London: Longmans, Green & Co., 1969.

Trouillot, Michel-Rolph. *Silencing the Past: Power and the Production of History*. Boston: Beacon Press, 1995.

Turner, James. "Historical Perspectives." *Black World* 23, no. 5 (March 1974): 11-19.

Turuka, Urban Elias. "The Role Played by Tanzania in the African Liberation Struggle." Dar es Salaam: South African Development Community Research Secretariat: Hashim Mbita Project, 2006. (Unpublished paper).

Tyson, Timothy. *Radio Free Dixie: Robert F. Williams and the Roots of Black Power*. Chapel Hill: University of North Carolina Press, 1998.

Umoja, Akinyele O. "1964: The Beginning and End of Nonviolence in the Mississippi Freedom Movement." *Radical History Review* 85 (2003): 201-226.

———. "The Ballot and the Bullet: A Comparative Analysis of Armed Resistance in the Civil Rights Movement." *Journal of African American History* 29, no. 4 (1999): 558-578.

Urban, Dennis L., Jr. "The Women of SNCC: Struggle, Sexism and the Emergence of Feminist Consciousness, 1960-1966." *International Social Review* 77, nos. 3 & 4 (Fall 2002): 185-190.

Valk, Anne. "Separatism and Sisterhood: Race, Sex, and Women's Activism in Washington, DC, 1963-1980." PhD diss., Duke University, 1996.

Van Deburg, William L. *New Day in Babylon: The Black Power Movement and American Culture, 1965-1975*. Chicago: University of Chicago Press, 1992.

———, ed. *Modern Black Nationalism: From Marcus Garvey to Louis Farrakhan*. New York: New York University Press, 1997.

Von Eschen, Penny M. *Race against Empire: Black Americans and Anti-colonialism, 1937-1957*. Ithaca, NY: Cornell University Press, 1998.

———. *Satchmo Blows Up the World: Jazz Ambassadors Play the Cold War*. Cambridge, MA: Harvard University Press, 2004.

Vinokurov, Y. N., ed. *Julius Nyerere: Humanist, Politician, Thinker*. Dar es Salaam: Mkuki na Nyota Publishers, 2005.

Vitalis, Robert. *White World Order, Black Power Politics: The Birth of American International Relations*. Ithaca, NY: Cornell University Press, 2015.

Von Freyhold, Michaela. *Ujamaa in Tanzania: Analysis of a Social Experiment*. London: Heinemann, 1979.

Wald, Gayle. *It's Been Beautiful: Soul! and Black Power Television*. Durham, NC: Duke University Press, 2015.

Walters, Ronald. "In World Relations: The Future of Pan-Africanism." *Black World* 24, no. 12 (October 1975): 4-19.

———. *Pan-Africanism in the African Diaspora: An Analysis of Modern Afrocentric Political Movements*. Detroit: Wayne State University Press, 1993.

———. "A Response to Haki Madhubuti." *Black Scholar* 6, no. 4 (October 1974): 47-53.

Wamba, Philippe E. *Kinship: A Family's Journey in Africa and America*. New York: Dutton, 1999.

Watts, Jerry Gafo. *Amiri Baraka: The Politics of a Black Intellectual*. New York: New York University Press, 2001.

Weisbord, Robert G. *Ebony Kinship: Africa, Africans, and the Afro-American*. London: Greenwood Press, 1973.

West, Cornel. "Marxist Theory and the Specificity of Afro-American Oppression." In *Marxism and the Interpretation of Culture*, ed. Cary Nelson and Lawrence Grossberg, 17-30. Urbana:

University of Illinois Press, 1988.

———. *Prophesy Deliverance! An Afro-American Revolutionary Christianity*. Philadelphia: Westminster Press, 1982.

West, Michael O. "Seeing Darkly: Guyana, Black Power, and Walter Rodney's Expulsion from Jamaica." *Small Axe* 1, no. 2 (February 2008): 93-104.

———. "Walter Rodney and Black Power: Jamaican Intelligence and US Diplomacy." *African Journal of Criminology & Justice Studies* 1, no. 2 (2005): 1-50.

West, Michael O., William G. Martin, and Fanon Che Wilkins, eds. *From Toussaint to Tupac: The Black International since the Age of Revolution*. Chapel Hill: University of North Carolina Press, 2009.

Weston, Randy. *Uhuru Afrika*. Roulette Records, 1960. CD.

Weston, Randy, and Willard Jenkins. *African Rhythms: The Autobiography of Randy Weston*. Durham, NC: Duke University Press, 2015.

White, E. Frances. "Africa on My Mind: Gender, Counter Discourse and African American Nationalism." *Journal of Women's History* 2, no. 1 (Spring 1990): 73-97.

Whiteley, W. H. "Swahili: The Nationalist Language of Tanzania." In *Self-Reliant Tanzania*, ed. Knud Erik Svendsen and Merete Teisen, 111-118. Dar es Salaam: Tanzania Publishing House, 1969.

Whitely, Wilfred. *Swahili: The Rise of a National Language*. New York: Barnes and Noble, 1969.

Widell, Robert W., Jr. *Birmingham and the Long Black Freedom Struggle*. London: Palgrave Macmillan, 2013.

Wilkins, Fanon Che. "In the Belly of the Beast: Anti-Imperialism, and the African Liberation Solidarity Movement, 1968-1975." PhD diss., New York University, 2000.

Williams, John A. "Black Publisher, Black Writer: An Impasse." *Black World* 26, no. 5 (March 1975).

Williams, Rocky. "The Other Armies: A Brief Historical Overview of Umkhonto We Sizwe (MK), 1961-1994." *Military History Journal* 11, no. 5 (June 2000): 173-185.

Williams, Yohuru. *Black Politics/White Power: Civil Rights, Black Power, and the Black Panthers in New Haven*. Boston: Blackwell Press, 2008.

———. *Rethinking the Black Freedom Movement*. New York: Routledge, 2015.

Williams, Yohuru, and Jama Lazerow, eds. *Liberated Territory: Toward a Local History of the Black Panther Party*. Durham, NC: Duke University Press, 2009.

Williamson, Joy Ann. *Black Power on Campus: University of Illinois, 1965-1975*. Urbana: University of Illinois Press, 2003.

Wilson, Amrit. *The Threat of Liberation: Imperialism and Revolution in Zanzibar*. London: Pluto Press, 2013.

———. *U.S. Foreign Policy and Revolution: The Creation of Tanzania*. London: Pluto Press, 1989.

Wilkins, Fanon Che. "Beyond Bandung: The Critical Nationalism of Lorraine Hansberry, 1950-1965." *Radical History Review* 95 (Spring 2006): 191-210.

———. "The Making of Black Internationalists: SNCC and Africa before the Launching of Black Power." *Journal of African American History* 92, no. 3 (Summer 2007): 467-488.

Woodard, Komozi. "Amiri Baraka, the Congress of African People, and Black Power Politics from the 1961 United Nations Protest to the 1972 Gary Convention." In *The Black Power Movement: Rethinking the Civil Rights-Black Power Era*, ed. Peniel E. Joseph, 55-60. New York: Routledge, 2006.

———. *A Nation within a Nation: Amiri Baraka (LeRoi Jones) and Black Power Politics*. Chapel Hill: University of North Carolina Press, 1999.

Worcester, Kent. *C.L.R. James: A Political Biography*. Albany: State University of New York Press, 1996.

Woronoff, Jon. *Organizing African Unity*. Metuchen, NJ: Scarecrow Press, 1970.

Wright, Nathan, Jr. *Black Power and Urban Unrest: Creative Possibilities*. New York: Hawthorn Books, 1967.

Wright, Richard. *Black Power: A Record of Reactions in a Land of Pathos*. Westport, CT: Greenwood Press, 1954.

Yeager, Rodger. *Tanzania: An African Experiment*. Boulder, CO: Westview Press, 1989.

Young, Crawford. *The African Colonial State in a Comparative Perspective*. New Haven, CT: Yale University Press, 1994.

Young, Cynthia. *Soul Power: Culture, Radicalism, and the Making of a U.S. Third World Left*. Durham, NC: Duke University Press, 2006.

Zinn, Howard. *SNCC: The New Abolitionists*. Boston: South End Press, 2002.

Index

A

Africa Today, 6

African Americans, 6, 19; African decolonization and, 29; anticommunism among, 23, 24; black nationalism and, 59, 108; communism and, 68; diaspora consciousness of, 124; expatriates, 126, 127, 133, 135, 165, 178; inferiority complex of, 40–41; Kiswahili and, 118; labor leaders, 6, 7, 19–20; pan-Africanism and, 10, 27, 42, 167; Sixth Pan-African Congress and, 157, 158–159, 161, 162, 163–165, 175; Tanzanian views of, 123–124

African Liberation Day (ALD), 146, 213 (n.25), 219 (n.149)

African Liberation Day Coordinating Committee (ALDCC), 146

African Liberation Support Committee (ALSC), 98, 146, 159, 163, 171, 172, 219 (n.149)

African National Congress (ANC), 47, 62, 183; in exile in Tanzania, 55; on Malcolm X's assassination, 41–42; rift with Carmichael, 66–67

African Outlook, 21

African Party for Independence of Guinea-Bissau and Cape Verde (PAIGC), 58, 160, 164

"African Safari" (Robert F. Williams), 1, 2

African socialism, 2, 32, 49, 119, 132, 170. *See also* Ujamaa socialism

African Society for Cultural Relations with Independent Africa (ASCRIA), 158, 167

African unity, 5, 9, 23, 46; SNCC support for, 52; as "United States of Africa," 47–48

Africanization, 22, 50, 54, 123, 208 (n.66)

Afriroots, 183

Afro-American, 10

Afro-American Resources, Inc. (AAR), 108–111, 114, 116, 133, 134, 135, 144; CBE created by, 143; postcolonial nationalism and, 136

Afro-American Skills Bank, 54, 56–57, 70, 124

Afro-Shirazi Party (ASP), 20, 22

Akridge, P. Bai, 167–168, 174, 217 (n.115)

Algeria, 5, 21, 26–27, 40; Ben Bella overthrown in, 48; Carmichael in, 58; Pan-African Cultural Festival in, 120; Sixth Pan-African Congress and, 156, 158, 172

All-African People's Conference, 21, 33, 178

American Committee on Africa (ACOA), 6, 9, 11

American Friends Service Committee (AFSC), 33, 220 (n.2)

Amin, Idi, 134, 167, 172, 173, 216 (n.80)

Angola, 28, 47, 122, 131, 184; FNLA, 145; independence of, 176; liberated zones in, 92; Sixth Pan-African Congress and, 160; UNITA, 145. *See also* People's Movement for the Liberation of Angola (MPLA)

anticommunism, 6, 9, 20

apartheid, 10, 11, 30, 44; UN Special Commission on, 51; U.S. government support of, 67–68. *See also* South Africa

"Appeal to the Heads of State" (Malcolm X), 30, 35

Arusha Declaration (1967), 42, 48–49, 53, 69, 80, 103, 177; "TANU Creed," 50; USARF and, 82, 84

Asia, 45, 122

B

Babu, Abdulrahman Mohamed, 20–23, 24, 82, 185; on Black Power, 43, 69; Carmichael defended by, 68–69; editorials, 59, 60; Malcolm X and, 29–30, 32, 34, 37, 39, 60, 192 (n.50); in New York City, 37–39, 194 (n.83); popularity in Tanzania, 59–60

Backlash, 39

"Ballot or the Bullet, The" (Malcolm X), 182

Bandung Revolution, 21, 23

Baraka, Amiri (LeRoi Jones), 39, 146, 163, 166, 172, 179, 216 (n.83), 217 (n.104)

Barasa, Wasilwa, 68

Belgium, 37

Ben Bella, Ahmed, 5, 40, 48

Bennett, Lerone, 163, 164, 171

Bgoya, Walter, 120, 122, 131, 174, 185

"Big Bust," 165

Birmingham church bombing (1963), 12, 124

black nationalism, 1, 25, 34, 169; Sixth Pan-African Congress critics of, 162, 163, 168, 169, 170, 171. *See also* cultural nationalism

Black Panther Party (BPP), 57, 98, 100, 179, 197 (n.47); Lawson illustration and, 208 (n.60)

Black Power, 2, 13, 42, 43, 98, 183, 195 (n.4); African Diaspora consciousness and, 185; as African liberation, 63; Babu's editorials about, 68–69; CBE and, 143–144; civil rights taken over by, 124; decline of, 127, 176; international dimensions of, 141; Marxism and, 164; self-determination and, 184; shift from rural South to urban North, 95; Sixth Pan-African Congress and, 143, 146, 156, 159, 174–176, 219 (n.152); struggle over meaning of, 45; TANU and, 44, 57, 70, 153; Tanzanian press coverage of, 59; tension within, 99; Third World struggles and, 58; in Washington, DC, 109–110

Black Power Conference (1969), 142, 157

Black Radical Congress (BRC), 179

Black Studies programs, 111, 114, 143, 205 (n.26)

Bogues, Anthony, 117

Bomani, Paul, 152–153, 157, 185, 214 (n.52)

Book of African Names, The (Chief Osuntoki), 115–117, 119

bookstores and publishers, black-owned, 109, 204 (n.10), 204 (n.22)

Britain, 4, 6, 10, 47–48

British Commonwealth, 2, 11, 151

Brown, H. Rap, 55, 98

Brown, James, 125, 126

Browne, Roosevelt, 143, 212 (n.10)

Burgess, Thomas, 21

Burnham, Forbes, 101, 102, 151, 157, 166

Burns, Jon, 85

Byrd Amendment (1971), 145

C

Cabral, Amilcar, 58, 82, 132, 164, 217 (n.104)

Cape Verde Islands, 184

capitalism, 27, 49, 87; African American culture and, 126; Black Power and, 99; black resistance to, 95; history of, 96; publishing and, 112

Caribbean region, 41, 76, 86, 94, 122, 148, 183; economic dependency in, 186; Francophone, 106; nationalists in, 2; Sixth Pan-African Congress and, 151–152, 157, 158, 159, 165–167, 168. *See also* West Indies

Caribbean Regional Meeting (1973), 157

Carmichael, Stokely, 44–45, 71, 76, 106, 144, 183; African leaders criticized by, 62, 65–66, 184; on class and race, 63–65; as critic of U.S. imperialism, 57–58; elected as SNCC chairman, 45; international travels of, 58, 61, 197 (n.53); in Tanzania (1967), 57, 58–59, 61–70, 75, 98, 102, 122; USARF and, 99; Washington, DC, uprising (1968) and, 109

Carter, W. Beverly, 157

Center for Black Education (CBE), 111-112, 113, 143-144, 149, 154, 155
Chama Cha Mapinduzi (CCM), 220 (n.6)
Cheche, 88-89, 92, 93, 99. See also *Maji Maji*
Chicago Defender, 10, 23, 46, 171
Children of Africa (Drum and Spear Press), 129, 130-131, 132, 138, 210 (n.98)
China, 59
Chinese revolution, 21, 22, 23, 36, 39, 85, 185; Nyerere on, 49
Chou en Lai, 21
CIA (Central Intelligence Agency), 22-23, 54, 67, 99, 127, 165
civil rights, 6, 13, 25, 57, 63; education and, 204 (n.21); integrationist strategy of, 25; momentum of, 57; multiracial character of, 59; nonviolence philosophy of, 20, 25; Nyerere's support for, 11, 12, 19, 35; SNCC and, 43; Tanzanian press coverage of, 98
Civil Rights Act (1964), 29, 30, 31, 44
class oppression, 64, 65
class struggle, 69, 86, 92, 95; Sixth Pan-African Congress and, 172, 219 (n.149)
Class Struggles in Tanzania (Shivji), 131, 210 (n.104)
Cobb, Charlie, 106-108, 121, 122, 123, 144, 183; Kiswahili and, 128; on Nyerere and Ujamaa, 134-135, 211 (n.112); on romantic views of Africa, 133; soul music and, 126; on Tanzania, 134
Cohen, Robert, 201 (n.34)
Cold War, 11, 23, 24, 122; African dictatorships and, 178; American policy in Africa and, 37; ANC criticism of Carmichael and, 66-67; anti-imperialism and, 141; cultural imperialism and, 127; military coups and, 48
colonialism, 4, 9, 10, 75, 171; dismantling of, 19; Kiswahili and, 117, 129; legacy of, 80, 81; United Nations and, 44; in Zanzibar, 39. See also apartheid; neocolonialism; Portuguese colonies
Committee to Fund a NewArk (CFUN), 114
communism, 5, 7, 67, 117; Chinese revolution and, 21; European models of, 119; South African Communist Party, 126; Soviet and Chinese influence in Africa, 23, 145; Ujamaa socialism and, 84

Comoro Islands, 42
Conflicting Missions (Gleijeses), 58
Congo (Kinshasa), 5, 10, 19, 38, 122, 193 (n.77); nationalism in, 6; U.S. and Western military intervention in, 37, 39
Congress of African People (CAP), 98, 114, 146, 159, 163, 216 (n.83)
CORE (Congress of Racial Equality), 6, 25, 33, 51, 57, 98
Cox, Courtland, 107, 108, 111, 134, 212 (n.10); as general secretary of Temporary Secretariat, 144; Sixth Pan-African Congress and, 149-151, 155, 158, 170-171
Cuba, 20, 21, 83, 206 (n.42); Carmichael in, 58, 61; Rodney and, 76, 85, 90; Sixth Pan-African Congress and, 172; Zanzibar revolution and, 22, 23
cultural nationalism, 99, 163, 164, 171; Drum and Spear Press and, 114, 115; sexism and, 114, 206 (n.38)

D

Dar es Salaam, 1, 5, 7, 53, 108; African novelists in, 123; Calito barracks in, 22; Carmichael in, 61-62, 68; "Dar Liberation Tour," 182-183; history of, 121-122; "Information Village" idea for, 121, 133; Kilimanjaro Hotel, 122; Kongo Ujamaa Village in, 87; National Stadium, 2; New African Hotel, 35; Paradise Hotel, 35, 122; radical politics and culture in, 2; soul music in, 125; University College, 71; U.S. embassy in, 12. See also University College of Dar es Salaam (UCD); University of Dar es Salaam (UDSM)
Davis, Angela, 98, 99, 100, 101, 179
Davis, Irving, 56, 221 (n.8)
dead prez, 180
decolonization, 1, 6, 13, 20, 29, 118; first wave of, 48; Sixth Pan-African Congress and, 152; SNCC support for, 52, 56; U.S. Cold War and, 145
democracy, 13, 22, 50, 182; in the United States, 57
Detroit, 41, 55, 61
Diaspora, African, 1, 6, 31, 39, 98, 136-137, 183; African Americans as part of, 8; black nationalism in, 59; Ghana and, 77;

nation-building in Africa and, 184; Sixth Pan-African Congress and, 161, 162, 164; Tanzania as political homeland for, 53
Diggs, Charles, 157
"Dr. Rodney Clarifies" (Rodney), 91–92
Drum and Spear Bookstore, 111, 121
"Drum and Spear Complex," 111, 121, 149, 155
Drum and Spear Press (DSP), 111, 112, 113, 121, 132, 220 (n.1); demise of, 137; Kiswahili and, 117–119, 129; networks of, 114, 136, 137, 206 (n.35); Tanzanian nation-building and, 133; Third World struggles and, 205 (n.32)
Du Bois, W.E.B., 161
Dunga, 180

E

"Education and Tanzanian Socialism" (Rodney), 81
"Education for Self-Reliance" (Nyerere), 80, 81, 103
Egypt, 5, 31, 40; Nyerere in, 27; Sixth Pan-African Congress and, 156, 158, 169, 172
Engels, Frederick, 82, 87
Epton, William, 39
Eritrea, 157–158
Eritrean Liberation Front (ELF), 157
Ethiopia, 83, 93, 148; communism in, 216 (n.80); Eritrean conflict with, 157–158

F

Fanon, Frantz, 46, 82, 87, 101, 106; USARF symposium on, 86; *The Wretched of the Earth*, 90, 105, 167
FBI (Federal Bureau of Investigation), 38, 55, 137, 180
Federal City College (FCC), 111, 112, 143, 205 (n.26)
Fellowship of Reconciliation (FOR), 6
Fid Q, 180, 181–182
Forman, James, 44, 45–46, 53, 71, 183; Afro-American Skills Bank and, 54, 124; on colonialism and apartheid, 52–53; Nyerere's meeting with, 54
Forrester, Anne, 114, 115–116, 118, 119–120, 183, 205 (n.32)
Freedom and Socialism (Nyerere), 117
Freedom Rides, 57

G

Garrett, Jimmy, 144, 155, 158, 173, 214 (n.48)
Garvey, Marcus, 25, 148
"George Jackson" (Rodney), 100
Ghana, 4, 6, 9, 26–27, 88, 122; independence of, 12, 106; Malcolm X in, 27, 32, 33, 192 (n.52); military coup (1966), 42, 77, 134, 183
Gibson, Kenneth, 173
Gibson, Richard, 57, 66
Gleijeses, Piero, 58
Gold Coast, 4, 6, 21
guerrilla war, 58, 65, 66, 194 (n.83); in Congo, 37; Nyerere's support for, 36; in Portuguese and settler colonies, 33; training in Cuba, 20
Guevara, Ernesto "Che," 38, 132, 183, 194 (n.83)
Guinea, 5, 40, 61, 107; Carmichael in, 71; French colonialism in, 77; Nkrumah in exile in, 58; Sixth Pan-African Congress and, 150, 158, 160, 169, 172, 214 (n.39)
Guinea-Bissau, 29, 58, 145, 160, 176, 184
Guyana, 76, 101–102, 151, 157

H

Hajivayanis, George, 83, 85, 90
Harlem, 29, 37, 41, 44
hip-hop, 180
Hirji, Karim, 83, 87–88, 90, 185, 202 (n.75), 203 (n.77); as *Cheche* editor, 89; "Militancy at the Hill," 93; on role of intellectuals at UDSM, 86
History of Negro Revolt, A (James). See *History of Pan-African Revolt, A*
History of Pan-African Revolt, A (James), 112, 113, 117, 144, 149, 205 (n.32)
"History of the Upper Guinea Coast, 1554–1800, A," (Rodney), 76
Holloway, Marvin, 108, 113, 115, 116, 144
How Europe Underdeveloped Africa (Rodney), 97–98, 105–106, 131
Howard University, 57, 112, 144, 168, 219 (n.149); Black Power and, 109; Black Studies program at, 114, 120; Cobb at, 106
Hughes, Langston, 8, 120, 208 (n.59)
human rights, 30, 32, 38; United States as violator of, 28, 30
Hutchinson, Earl Ofari, 171

Hutchison, Robert, 131

I

"Ideology of the African Revolution, The" (Rodney), 90
imperialism, 10, 23, 30, 31, 79, 171; African leaders and, 90; cultural, 127, 163; economic aid and, 135; racial character of, 146; Rodney's lectures on, 87; Sixth Pan-African Congress and, 150; Third World struggles against, 45; U.S. foreign policy and, 52-53, 58, 125; U.S. intervention in Congo as, 37; white supremacy and, 173
In Search of Power (Plummer), 56-57
"Indivisible Struggle against Racism, Colonialism and Apartheid, The" (Forman), 52
Ingalls, Leonard, 9
International Affairs Commission (IAC), 45, 56
International Monetary Fund (IMF), 178
International War Crimes Tribunal, 107
"Introduction: Uhuru Kwanza (Part One)" (Weston), 8-9
Israeli-Palestinian conflict, 205 (n.32)

J

Jackson, George, 99, 100
Jackson, Jesse, 221 (n.8)
Jamaica, 78, 151, 157
James, C. L. R., 76, 156, 183; Sixth Pan-African Congress and, 143-144, 148-151, 156, 159, 214 (n.35); in Washington, DC, 112-113, 155. See also *History of Pan-African Revolt, A*
JCB, 180-181
Ji Gaga, Geronimo, 180
Johnson administration, 110
Jones, LeRoi. *See* Baraka, Amiri (LeRoi Jones)
Jumbe, Aboud, 170

K

Kabila, Laurent, 194 (n.83)
Kamenju, Grant, 80, 86, 123
Karume, Abeid, 20, 24
Kawawa, Rashidi, 7, 79, 165
Kelley, Robin D. G., 8, 113
Kennedy, John F., 11, 12, 26, 189 (n.38), 193 (n.70)

Kenya, 5, 9, 40, 83, 93, 122; Mau Mau in, 6, 106; nationalism in, 6; soldiers' mutiny in, 22, 23
Kenyatta, Jomo, 5, 6, 7, 9, 19, 40
King, Martin Luther, Jr., 12, 59, 98, 109; assassination of, 124-125; *Where Do We Go from Here*, 167
Kiswahili, 2, 8, 41, 210 (n.87); Drum and Spear Press and, 117-119; English books translated into, 128-129, 207 (n.52); literature in, 129, 132; newspapers in, 49; Nyerere's writings in, 118-119, 207 (n.56)
Kusema Kiswahili (Muganda), 118, 119, 138

L

Latin America, 45, 86, 96
Lavotsi, 180
Lawson, Jennifer, 114, 115, 121, 123, 128, 183, 208 (n.60)
Lenin, Vladimir, 4, 46, 87, 164
Liberation Committee on Africa (LCA), 23-24
Liberia, 107, 156
Libya, 150, 156
Liundi, Chris, 62
Lowndes County Freedom Organization (LCFO), 57, 208 (n.60)
Lumumba, Patrice, 5, 6, 19, 37, 48, 62

M

Macha, Freddy, 132
Madhubuti, Haki, 172-173, 219 (n.149)
Maji Maji, 100-101, 102, 166, 210 (n.104). See also *Cheche*
Makeba, Miriam, 61, 62, 198 (nn.65-66)
Malawi, 83, 93, 156
Malcolm X, 25-26, 38, 58, 60, 70, 76, 100; on African identity, 40-41; "Appeal to the Heads of State," 30, 35; assassination of, 41-42, 43, 194 (n.98); *The Autobiography of Malcolm X*, 105; "The Ballot or the Bullet" speech, 182; FBI surveillance of, 38; on Kennedy assassination, 193 (n.70); Nation of Islam and, 25-26, 36, 39, 41; Nyerere's meeting with, 34-37; OAAU and, 19, 27-28, 34, 37, 44, 56, 183; OAU and, 29-33; pilgrimage to Mecca, 28; Sutherland and, 33-34; travels in Africa, 27, 29, 32; visit to Tanzania (1964), 32-37, 58, 75, 122, 192 (n.50)

Malcolm X Grassroots Movement (MXGM), 180
Malcolm XI (Mbishi), 182
Malecela, John, 51, 52, 53, 55, 149, 185
Manley, Michael, 151
Mao Tse-Tung, 21, 46, 67; clothing style of, 206 (n.40); *Quotations of Mao Tse Tung*, 105; writings of, 132
Mapolu, Henry, 83, 89, 97, 185
Mapunda, Geslier, 157
March on Washington for Jobs and Freedom (1963), 12, 59, 144
Marx, Karl, 4, 82, 86
Marxism, 20, 21, 23, 60, 219 (n.149); African Americans and, 68-69; Black Power and, 13, 63; of CAP, 163; pan-Africanism and, 76, 89; in Rodney's teaching, 94, 97; Sixth Pan-African Congress and, 163, 164, 169, 172; TPH and, 131; USARF and, 84, 87
Mau Mau movement, 6, 106
Mbishi, Nikki, 182
Mbuya, Mejah, 183
Meghji, Ramadhan, 83, 85
Meghji, Zakia Hamdani, 83, 84, 88, 89, 96-97, 185
Meredith March Against Fear (1966), 44-45
"Militancy at the Hill" (Hirji), 93
Minwyi (chairman), 132
Mississippi Freedom Democratic Party (MFDP), 57
Mkapa, Benjamin, 59, 60, 89, 120, 123
Mobutu Sese Seko (Joseph Mobutu), 62, 173
Mohammed, Bibi Titi, 7, 34
Monteiro, Anthony, 171
Moore, Audley, 174
Moore, Harold, 52
Morocco, 26-27, 156
Movement for Colonial Freedom (MCF), 21
Mozambique, 29, 85, 122, 131, 184; independence of, 176; liberated zones in, 92; liberation movements in, 47, 145; Sixth Pan-African Congress and, 160
Mozambique Liberation Front (FRELIMO), 47, 85-86, 162, 172, 183
Mpaganla, Maynard, 7
Mpugunzi Ujamaa Village, Dodoma, 87, 88
"Mr. Politician" (Nakaaya), 180
Muganda, Bernard, 118, 149
Muhammad, Elijah, 25, 26, 27, 194 (n.90)

Muhammad Speaks, 24, 155
Museveni, Yoweri, 82-83, 84
Muslim Mosque, Inc., 27
Mwakawago, D., 128
Myth of Black Capitalism, The (Hutchinson), 171

N

NAACP (National Association for the Advancement of Colored People), 25, 51, 52
National Anti-Imperialist Movement in Solidarity with African Liberation (NAIMSAL), 171
National Liberation Front of Angola (FNLA), 145
Nair, Vinad, 67, 68
Nakaaya, 180
Namano, A. S., 90
Namibia, 47, 122, 160
Nasser, Gamal Abdel, 5, 31, 40
Nation of Islam (NOI), 24, 25-26, 39, 41; *Muhammad Speaks* newspaper, 24, 155
National Black Political Convention (1972), 146, 213 (n.23)
National Development Corporation (NDC), 127, 131
National Front for the Liberation of Cayenne, 167
National Joint Action Committee, 167
National Service crisis (1965), 79-80, 82, 92
National Swahili Council, 132
National Union for the Total Independence of Angola (UNITA), 145
nationalism, 1, 4, 9, 48, 60, 163; Black Power and, 13; Drum and Spear Press and, 136. *See also* black nationalism; cultural nationalism
Nationalist, 32, 59-61, 89; African American recruitment advocated by, 123-124; "Black Is Beautiful" editorial, 126; Carmichael and, 61, 63, 65, 69; coverage of African Americans in, 98; Drum and Spear Press and, 120, 121; "Revolutionary Hot Air" editorial, 91; Sixth Pan-African Congress and, 156, 215 (n.59)
nation-building, 6, 48, 53, 70, 75-76, 102; Africanization and, 54; book publishing and, 127; "Drum and Spear Complex" and, 121, 149; Nyerere on challenges of,

178; Sixth Pan-African Congress and, 165, 167-168, 174, 175
NATO (North Atlantic Treaty Organization), 145, 152
"Nature and Requirements of African Unity, The" (Nyerere), 47
Négritude, 106, 161, 170
Negro Digest, 10
neocolonialism, 88, 91, 133, 166
New York City, 37-39, 56, 57, 194 (n.83)
Newton, Huey P., 98
Nigeria, 26-27, 122, 218 (n.141); civil war in, 72, 216 (n.80); Sixth Pan-African Congress and, 150, 158
Nixon, Richard, 110, 127, 145
Nkrumah, Kwame, 4, 5, 6, 19, 33, 87, 112; on African unity, 32; Carmichael and, 58, 197 (n.53); Malcolm X and, 40; Nyerere compared with, 10; overthrown in coup, 42, 48, 58, 77
nonalignment, 23, 46
Nonviolent Action Group (NAG), 57, 106, 144
Nyerere Burite, 3
Nyerere, Julius, 3-5, 40, 58, 92, 112, 174; on African history, 75; Africanization policy and, 54, 123, 208 (n.66); American media views of, 9-10, 36; anti-apartheid views of, 10, 11-12; army mutiny in Tanganyika and, 22, 24; on books and literacy, 105; Carmichael and, 58, 62, 197 (n.55); Chinese revolution and, 49; constitution of 1965 and, 46; critics of, 23-24; death of, 178-179; on effects of colonialism, 129; at independence ceremony (1961), 2-3; Kiswahili and, 118, 119; Malcolm X's meeting with, 34-37; National Service crisis and, 79-80; in New York City, 6; Nkrumah compared with, 10; pan-Africanism and, 6, 11, 19, 22, 149, 161, 179; on the postcolonial state, 178; post-presidential activities of, 178, 220 (n.6); pragmatism of, 24, 47-48; on relations with Britain, 47-48; Rodney and, 91, 94; Sixth Pan-African Congress and, 149, 152, 153-158, 160-161, 171; socialism and, 7, 36; Vietnam War opposed by, 69, 199 (n.97)
WRITINGS AND SPEECHES: 118-119, 207 (n.56); "Education for Self-Reliance," 80, 81, 103;

Freedom and Socialism, 117; "The Nature and Requirements of African Unity," 47; "Ujamaa—The Basis of African Socialism," 32-33, 49
Nyerere, Mugaya, 3

O

Obatala, J. K., 126
Obote, Milton, 134
O'Neal, Pete and Charlotte, 179-180
Operation Crossroads Africa, 115
"Operation Vijana," 125
Organization for Black Cultural Awareness, 166
Organization of African Unity (OAU), 10, 22, 134, 147; Cairo summit, 27-31, 33; Eritrean independence issue and, 157-158; Liberation Committee (LC), 47, 48, 122, 145, 155; principle of territorial integrity and, 158; Sixth Pan-African Congress and, 151, 157, 166, 173; Tanzania's role in, 59, 62
Organization of Afro-American Unity (OAAU), 19, 27-28, 34, 37, 42, 183; *Backlash* journal, 39; internationalist agenda, 36, 56; SNCC activists and, 44
Osuntoki, Chief, 115, 116

P

pacifism, 33
Pan African Center of Science and Technology (PACST), 168
Pan African Freedom Movement of South and Central Africa (PAFMESCA), 10, 21, 33
Pan-African Congress (PAC), 42, 47, 58, 62, 172
Pan-African Congress, Fifth (1945), 6, 148, 150
Pan-African Congress, Sixth (6PAC, 1974), 101, 138, 142, 146-147, 149-150, 164; African American delegates, 163-165, 167-169, 217 (n.109); alienation of Diaspora activists and, 184; assessments of, 171-176; "The Call," 147-148, 153, 167; Cox's closing speech, 170-171; Dar es Salaam Coordinating Committee ("Dar Committee"), 154, 156; General Declaration of, 141, 169-170, 173; opening of, 160-162; organizing phase of, 142-160, 173; position papers at, 165-166; "secret communiqué" of Caribbean nongovernmental delegation, 165-167,

168. *See also* Temporary Secretariat (Sixth Pan-African Congress)
Pan-African Skills Project (PASP), 56, 127, 152, 153, 177, 220 (n.1), 221 (n.8)
pan-Africanism, 1, 4, 21, 60, 76, 136, 159; African Diaspora and, 37, 98; African names and, 116; CBE and, 144; changing character of, 143; critiques of, 162-163, 169-170; decline of, 177; effects of coups in African states, 48; emergence of independent states and, 40; "frontline fighters," 58; Malcolm X and, 31, 44; nation-state and, 163, 164, 184; Nyerere's credibility with, 22; OAU and, 138, 142; in Paris, 106; political differences over meaning of, 175; radical and gradualist, 10-11; Rodney's teaching and, 95; role of the state and, 24, 160; in Tanzania foreign policy, 33; Tanzania in leadership role, 47, 48
"Pan-Africanism and Democracy" (Sutherland), 33-34
Paris, Brenda, 171
Parker, Neville, 168, 174
Peace Corps, 11, 34-35, 209 (n.81)
peasantry, 20, 21, 84, 86, 87, 93; Arusha Declaration and, 84; Black Power and, 43; policies favoring interests of, 50; as producer class, 96; Sixth Pan-African Congress and, 148; "true socialism" and, 49; Ujamaa Villages and, 88-89, 177
People's Movement for the Liberation of Angola (MPLA), 47
Plummer, Brenda Gayle, 56-57
Portuguese colonies, 11, 33, 46, 64, 89; armed liberation struggles in, 145, 184; end of, 176. *See also* Angola; Guinea-Bissau; Mozambique
Présence Africaine, 106, 108

R

"Racial Discrimination in the United States," 30-31
racial justice, 13, 19, 28, 57
"racialism," 9, 11, 35-36, 43, 69, 161
racism, 13, 26, 31, 33, 59, 70, 169; black inferiority complex and, 40-41; in Britain, 76; colonialism and, 54; elimination of, 170; global dimensions of, 63-64; as human right issue, 11; Nyerere's remarks about, 161; in U.S. cities, 25
Ranger, Terrence, 78
"Rest in Uhuru [Rest in Freedom]" (Fid Q and JCB), 180-182
"Revolution Culture and the Future of Pan African Culture" (Baraka), 163
Revolutionary Action Movement (RAM), 23, 39
Rhodesia, Southern, 10, 28, 29, 47; liberation movements in, 47; white-minority independence in, 46-47, 145, 176. *See also* Zimbabwe
Richardson, Judy, 114, 115, 183
River of No Return, The (Sellars), 44
Robinson, J. Fletcher, 151, 159, 168
Rodney, Walter, 71, 86, 87, 98, 103, 123, 183; on African socialism, 90-91; "The Arusha Declaration—Problem of Implication," 81; "Black People in the Americas" course taught by, 94-95; Caribbean community of Dar es Salaam and, 122; *Cheche* and, 89; death of, 102; decision to go to Tanzania, 77, 81-82; "Dr. Rodney Clarifies," 91-92; early life and education, 76; "Education and Tanzanian Socialism," 81, 82; "George Jackson," 100; "Historians and Revolutions" course taught by, 94; "A History of the Upper Guinea Coast, 1554-1800," 76; *How Europe Underdeveloped Africa*, 97-98, 105-106, 131; "The Ideology of the African Revolution," 90; Marxist politics of, 83, 96; pan-Africanism and, 149; position paper at Sixth Pan-African Congress, 165, 166, 168; return to Guyana, 101-102; Second Seminar of East and Central African Youth and, 90; teaching, 94-98; "Towards the 6th Pan African Congress," 165, 166
Ruhinda, Ferdinand, 120, 123
Russian Revolution, 88, 94
Rwanda-Burundi, 10

S

Saduakai, Owusu, 98, 146, 151, 163-164, 217 (n.104)
Sales, William, 42
Sanga, Tuntemeke, 8, 9
Saul, John, 86, 89, 202 (n.57)

Sauti radio show, 155, 215 (n.65)
Schleifler, Mark, 39
Schuyler, George, 23
Second Seminar of East and Central African Youth, 90
segregation, 11, 43, 95
Selassie, Emperor Haile, 157-158, 216 (n.80)
Sellars, Cleveland, 44
Senegal, 5, 107
Senghor, Léopold, 5, 106
sexism, 114, 206 (n.38)
Shakur, Assata (JoAnne Chesimard), 206-207 (n.42)
shamba (farm) work, 88
Sharp, Monroe, 120
Shearer, Hugh, 78
Shepherd, George, 7
Shija, Andrew, 83
Shivji, Issa, 83, 84, 87, 101, 131
sit-in movement, 43
"slave names," 117, 206-207 (n.42)
slave trade, transatlantic, 13, 30, 40, 64; African Diaspora and aftermath of, 130; Rodney's analysis of, 94-95, 97
Slavery and Capitalism (E. Williams), 95
SNCC (Student Nonviolent Coordinating Committee), 13, 25, 42, 52, 60, 98, 183; anti-imperialism of, 63, 70; Black Panther Party and, 197 (n.47); Black Power and, 57; decline of, 71; Drum and Spear Press and, 114, 115, 121; FBI campaign against, 55; fieldwork in the Deep South, 106-107, 121; founding and early history of, 43-44, 144; Malcolm X and, 43-44; OAU and, 46; TANU Party and, 58; United Nations and, 44, 46, 54-55
socialism, 42, 143; education and, 81-82; European models of, 4, 119; nationalist identity and, 3; "scientific," 163; traditional African societies and, 32, 49. *See also* African socialism; Ujamaa socialism
Socialist Club, 82, 99
Soledad Brother (Jackson), 100
Somalia, 162, 172, 216 (n.80)
soul music, 125, 126-127
South Africa, 28, 55, 122; anti-apartheid struggle in, 174, 178, 183-184; black worker strikes in, 160; Communist Party, 126; liberation movements in, 47; pan-Africanism in, 10; Sharpeville Massacre, 53. *See also* African National Congress (ANC); apartheid
South West African People's Organization (SWAPO), 42, 47, 172
Southern Christian Leadership Conference (SCLC), 25, 51, 52
Soviet Union, 22, 76
Soyinka, Wole, 172, 218 (n.141)
Stanford, Max, 23
Stark, Gerri, 114, 144, 153, 154, 174
Sutherland, Bill, 33-34, 120, 154, 156, 173-174, 178, 220 (n.2)
Sventes, Tama, 86, 87
Sweden, 89, 107
Sykes, Abbas, 152

T

Tambo, Oliver, 55
Tanganyika, 3-4, 6, 20; German colonialism in, 93; independence of, 9, 10, 78, 177; soldiers' mutiny in, 22, 23; Zanzibar unified with, 24, 26-27, 32, 39. *See also* Tanzania
Tanganyika African Association (TAA), 4, 5
Tanganyika African National Union (TANU), 2, 12, 32, 34, 46, 66, 103; African Americans viewed by, 136; Afro-American Skills Bank and, 124; anticolonial nationalist struggle of, 7; Arusha Declaration and, 183; "Big Bust" and, 165; black nationalism and, 123; Black Power activism and, 44, 57, 70, 153, 156, 157, 184; book publishing and, 132; CCM as successor of, 220 (n.6); conservative members of, 94, 127; Kiswahili and, 118-119; members' aims and objectives, 50-51; National Conference, 61; National Executive Committee, 48, 62; *Nationalist*, 32, 59, 63; Nyerere elected president of, 5; Operation Vijana, 126; Rodney and, 102; Sixth Pan-African Congress and, 142, 152, 155, 156, 167, 172, 175; SNCC and, 58; USARF and, 92; UWT, 101
Tanganyika African National Union Youth League (TYL), 59, 62, 80, 83, 193 (n.77); Drum and Spear Press and, 120; lack of presence on UCD campus, 82; Operation

Index

Vijana, 125; Second Seminar of East and Central African Youth, 90
Tanganyika African Welfare Association (TAWA), 4
Tanganyika Federation of Labor (TFL), 6, 7
Tanganyika Standard, 59, 61, 63, 65–66; African American freedom struggle reported in, 98; criticism of Carmichael in, 67; nationalization of, 92
Tanzania, 40, 58, 70, 102; African Americans in, 33–35; African Diaspora and, 1, 12–13; hip-hop exchange and, 180; U.S. economic aid and, 135; diplomatic break with Britain, 47–48; elections (1985), 177, 178; as epicenter of African liberation, 160; as frontline state, 47; independence of, 2; literacy rate in, 128; National Service crisis (1965), 79–80, 82, 92; pan-Africanism in, 29, 42; Second Five-Year Plan (1969–1974), 127; Sixth Pan-African Congress and, 142, 150, 158, 159–160, 172, 214 (n.48); SNCC activists and, 44. *See also* Tanganyika
Tanzania (Shivji), 210 (n.104)
Tanzania Publishing House (TPH), 103, 131, 133, 174
Tanzania Youth League–University College of Dar es Salaam (TYL-UCD), 82, 83, 85, 90; "FRELIMO Day" and, 86; membership requirements, 93; pan-Africanism and, 98; tension within Black Power movement and, 99
Tanzania Youth League–University of Dar es Salaam (TYL-UDSM), 94
Temporary Secretariat (Sixth Pan-African Congress), 144, 145, 147, 159, 173; office in Dar es Salaam, 154, 160; organization of, 148–149; TANU and, 152, 155, 157. *See also* Pan-African Congress, Sixth (6PAC, 1974)
Third World, 2, 12, 13, 27, 37, 161, 183; African American ties with, 25, 69; China's role in, 36; internationalism and, 86; revolutionary struggles in, 23, 45; threat to imperialism from, 29–30; white working class and, 64
Touré, Ahmed Sékou, 5, 40, 214 (n.39); Carmichael and, 58, 197 (n.53); pan-Africanism and, 150; at Sixth Pan-African Congress, 160, 161–162, 171, 219 (n.149)

Transition Magazine, 172
Trinidad-Tobago, 157, 158
Tri-State Defender, 24
Tshombe, Moïse, 37, 39, 40, 193 (n.77)
Turner, James, 159

U

Uganda, 4, 10, 83, 93, 115, 122; Idi Amin regime, 134, 167, 172, 173, 216 (n.80); OAU meeting in, 157; soldiers' mutiny in, 22, 23
Uhuru Africa (Weston), 8
"Ujamaa na Kujitegemea," 49, 61, 71, 87, 117; critique of, 177; shamba (farm) work and, 88
Ujamaa socialism, 89, 113, 117, 119, 137; African Americans views of, 125; economic failure of, 177–178; education and, 81; Kiswahili and, 118; as model of human development, 130; Ujamaa Villages, 87, 88, 92, 177–178; USARF and, 84
"Ujamaa—The Basis of African Socialism" (Nyerere), 32–33, 49
Umma (People's) Party, 20, 21–22
Umoja wa Wanawake (UWT), 101
Unilateral Declaration of Independence (UDI), 46
United African Alliance Community Center (UAACC), 179, 183
United Church Commission for Racial Justice, 108
United Nations, 6, 7, 28, 30, 55, 70, 221 (n.8); Africa and Asia Missions to, 54; conference on colonialism and apartheid, 44; Economic and Security Council, 45; General Assembly, 37, 51, 120, 194 (n.83); "International Book Year" (1972), 131; Resolution 390, 157; Special Committee on Apartheid, 51, 52; Tanzania and, 59; Trusteeship Council, 6, 8; UNESCO, 132
United Nations Jazz Society, 7
United States, 6, 7, 40, 94, 186; apartheid South Africa and, 10; as an empire, 57; imperialism, 52; mainstream media in, 9–10; Nyerere viewed by, press and government, 23, 24; prison movement in, 100; racial violence in, 61; segregation in Southern states, 11; Tanzanian views of racial violence in, 124–125; Zanzibar

revolution and, 22-23
United States Information Services (USIS), 34-35
Universal Negro Improvement Association (UNIA), 25, 148
University College of Dar es Salaam (UCD), 71, 78, 79, 81, 202 (n.57); International Congress of African History, 77
University College of the West Indies (UWI), 76, 78, 81
University of Dar es Salaam (UDSM), 94, 97, 112, 122, 127; Engineering Department, 174; Institute of Adult Education, 128; Sixth Pan-African Congress (1974) at, 138, 142
University Students African Revolutionary Front (USARF), 61, 82, 83-90, 184, 185; African American political leaders invited to campus by, 98-99; banning of, 93, 94; *Cheche*, 88-89; "FRELIMO Day" organized by, 85-86; "Ideological Classes" and, 87; Nyerere and, 92; "Rag Day" and, 84; Second Seminar of East and Central African Youth and, 90; Socialist Club and, 82, 99; women in, 96

V

Vietnam, 21, 58, 61, 185
Vietnam War, 52, 58, 63, 107; Nyerere's opposition to, 69, 199 (n.97); Tanzanians against, 85
Voting Rights Act (1965), 44

W

Walters, Ronald, 142, 170, 219 (n.149)
Walz, Jay, 9
Washington, DC, 143, 144, 155; Drum and Spear Bookstore, 108, 121; violence of 1968 in, 109-110, 111
Watoto wa Afrika (Drum and Spear Press). See *Children of Africa* (Drum and Spear Press)
West Indian Student Union, 76

West Indies, 142, 161, 164. *See also* Caribbean region
Weston, Randy, 7-9
Where Do We Go from Here (King), 167
white liberals, 45, 55, 115, 197 (n.47)
white minority rule, 75, 85, 145, 176, 221 (n.8)
white supremacy, 13, 55, 64, 96, 173
Wiley, Jean, 134
Williams, G. Mennen, 10, 12
Williams, Robert F., 1, 85, 98, 201 (n.34)
Wilson, Edie, 144, 151, 154-155, 174-175, 215 (n.64)
women, 4, 65; CBE and, 114-116; Sixth Pan-African Congress and, 154-155
working class, 76, 84, 96, 148; Sixth Pan-African Congress and, 162, 169-170
Working People's Alliance (WPA), 102
World Bank, 178
Wretched of the Earth, The (Fanon), 90, 105, 167

Y

Young, Andrew, 221 (n.8)

Z

Zaire, 62
Zambia, 70, 122, 154. *See also* Rhodesia, Northern
Zanzibar, 12, 22, 37, 122, 165; Malcolm X in, 35; postcolonial history of, 20; racial tensions between Arabs and Africans, 21; slavery and colonialism in, 39; Tanganyika unified with, 24, 26-27, 32, 39
Zanzibar Nationalist Party (ZNP), 20, 21, 23
Zimbabwe, 65, 83, 122; independence of, 174; Sixth Pan-African Congress and, 160. *See also* Rhodesia, Southern
Zimbabwe African National Union (ZANU), 47, 145, 172
Zimbabwe African People's Union (ZAPU), 47, 145, 162-163